MY LIFE

Golda Meir

My Life

Futura Publications Limited
A Futura Book

A Futura Book

First published in Great Britain in 1975
by Weidenfeld & Nicolson

First Futura Publications edition 1976

ISBN 0 8600 7394 7

Printed in Great Britain by
Hazell Watson & Viney Ltd
Aylesbury, Bucks

Futura Publications Limited
110 Warner Road
Camberwell, London SE5

To my sisters, Sheyna and Clara,
To our children,
And to our children's children.

CONTENTS

I have never kept diaries, nor have I ever been a writer of letters, and I certainly never expected to write the story of my life. But today, in the hope that perhaps those who read this book will learn and understand a little more about Israel, Zionism and the Jewish people, I have told of some of the men and women whom I have known, some of the places I have seen and, above all, some of the incredible events in which I have participated.

G.M.

Ramat Aviv
June 1975

1   My childhood

In a way, I suppose that the little I recall of my early childhood in Russia, my first eight years, sums up my beginnings, what now are called the formative years. If so, it is sad that I have very few happy or even pleasant memories of this time. The isolated episodes that have stayed with me throughout the past seventy years have to do mostly with the terrible hardships my family suffered, with poverty, cold, hunger and fear, and I suppose my recollection of being frightened is the clearest of all my memories. I must have been very young, maybe only three and a half or four. We lived then on the first floor of a small house in Kiev, and I can still recall quite distinctly hearing about a pogrom that was to descend upon us. I didn't know then, of course, what a pogrom was, but I knew it had something to do with being Jewish and with the rabble that used to surge through town, brandishing knives and huge sticks, screaming 'Christ-killers' as they looked for the Jews and who were now going to do terrible things to me and to my family.

I can remember how I stood on the stairs that led to the second floor, where another Jewish family lived, holding hands with their little daughter and watching our fathers trying to barricade the entrance with wooden boards. That pogrom never materialized, but to this day I remember how scared I was and how angry that all my father could do to protect me was to nail a few planks together while he waited for the hooligans to come. And, above all, I remember being aware that this was happening to me because I was Jewish, which made me different from most of the other children in the yard. It was a feeling that I was to know again many times during my life – the fear, the frustration, the consciousness of being different and the profound instinctive belief that if one wanted to survive, one had to take effective action about it personally.

Also, I remember all too clearly how poor we were. There was never enough of anything, not food, nor warm clothing, nor heat at home. I was always a little too cold outside and a little too empty inside. Even now, from that very distant past, I can summon up with no effort at all, almost intact, the picture of myself sitting in the kitchen in tears, watching my mother feed to my younger sister, Zipke, some of the gruel that rightfully belonged to me. Gruel was a great luxury in our home in those days, and I bitterly resented having to share any of it even with the baby. Years later I was to experience the dread of my own children's hunger and to learn for myself what it is like to have to decide which child is to receive more food. But, of course, in that kitchen in Kiev, I knew only that life was hard and that there was no justice anywhere. I am glad that no one told me then that my older sister, Sheyna, often fainted from hunger in school.

My parents were newcomers in Kiev. They had met and married in Pinsk, where my mother's family lived, and it was to Pinsk that we all returned within a few years – in 1903, when I was five. My mother was very proud of her romance with my father and often told us about it, but though I came to know the story by heart, I never tired of hearing it. My parents had married very unconventionally, without the benefit of a *shadchan*, the traditional matchmaker.

I don't know exactly how it happened that my father, who was born in the Ukraine, had to report for military duty in Pinsk, but it was there that my mother once saw him in the street. He was a tall handsome young man with whom she instantly fell in love and about whom she even dared tell her parents. A matchmaker was called in eventually, but only for what might be termed the 'technical arrangements'. What was even more impressive – in her eyes and ours – was the fact that she managed to persuade her parents that love at first sight was enough, even though my father, who had been orphaned of his father, had no money at all and his family could claim very little distinction. There was one saving fact, however. He was not an ignoramus. In his very early teens, he had studied for a while in a *yeshivah*, a Jewish religious seminary, and he knew the *Torah*. My grandfather duly took this fact into account, though I have always suspected that he was also influenced by the fact that my mother had never been known to change her mind about anything substantive.

My parents were very different from each other. My father, Moshe Yitzhak Mabovitch, was a slender, delicately featured, fundamentally optimistic man, much given to believing in people – unless and until proven wrong; a trait that, on the whole, was to make his life a failure in worldly terms. In short, he was what you might call an innocent, the kind of man who would probably have been more successful if circumstances had ever been just slightly easier. Blume, my copper-haired mother, was pretty, energetic, bright and far more sophisticated and enterprising than my father, but like him a born optimist and very sociable. Despite everything, on Friday nights our house was always full of people, mostly members of the family. I remember swarms of cousins, second cousins, aunts and uncles. None of them were to survive the Holocaust, but they live on in my mind's eye, sitting around our kitchen table, drinking tea out of glasses and, on the Sabbath and holidays, singing for hours – and I remember my parents' sweet voices ringing out above the others.

It was not a particularly religious household. My parents, of course, observed Jewish tradition. They kept a kosher kitchen and celebrated all the Jewish holidays and festivals. But religion as such – to the extent that it can be separated from tradition for Jews – played a very small role in our lives. I can't remember as a child ever having thought very much about God or praying to a personal deity, though when I was older – we were in America already – I sometimes argued about religion with my mother. I remember that once she wanted to prove to me that God existed. She said, 'Why does it rain or snow, for instance?' So I explained what I had learned in school about rain, and then she said to me, '*Nu, Goldele, du bist aza chachome, mach du zol gein a reigen!*' (So, Goldele, if you're so clever, *you* make it rain!). Since no one had heard of cloud-seeding in those days, I couldn't think of an answer. As for the Jews being a chosen people, I never quite accepted that. It seemed – and still seems to me – more reasonable to believe not that God chose the Jews but that the Jews were the first people that chose God, the first people in history to have done something truly revolutionary, and it was this choice that made them unique.

At any rate, we lived in this – as in other respects – in the way most Jews lived in the towns and villages of Eastern Europe. We went to *shul* (synagogue) on festivals and fast days, we blessed the Sabbath and we kept two calendars: one Russian, the other relating to that far-off land from which we had been exiled 2,000 years before and whose seasons and ancient customs we still marked in Kiev and Pinsk.

My parents had moved to Kiev when Sheyna (who was nine years my senior) was still very small. My father wanted to better his situation, and although Kiev was beyond the Pale of Settlement and in that part of Russia in which Jews were normally forbidden to live, he was an artisan and, as such, if he could prove that he was a skilled carpenter by passing the necessary examination, he might receive the precious permit to move to Kiev. So he made a perfect chess table, passed the test, and we packed our bags and left Pinsk, filled with hope. In Kiev, Father found work for the government, making furniture for school libraries, and even got an advance. With this money, plus money my parents borrowed, he built a little carpentry shop of his own, and it seemed as though all would be well. But in the end, the job fell through. Perhaps, as he said, it was because he was Jewish, and Kiev was noted for its anti-Semitism. At all events, very soon there was no job, no money and debts that had to be paid somehow. It was a crisis that was to recur throughout my childhood.

My father began desperately to look for work everywhere; he would be out all day – and much of the night – and when he came home in the bitter dark of a Russian winter, there was rarely enough food in the house to make him a meal. Bread and salt herring had to do.

But my mother had other troubles too. Four little boys and a girl all fell ill: two of them died before they were a year old; another two of them went within one month. My mother mourned each one of her babies with a broken heart, but like most Jewish mothers of that generation, she accepted the will of God and drew no conclusions about child-rearing from the row of little graves. Then, right after the last of the babies had died, a well-to-do family who lived near us offered my mother a job as wetnurse to their new baby. They made one condition: my parents and Sheyna were to move from their miserable, damp little room to a larger, lighter, airier one, and a nurse was to come and teach my poor young mother the rudiments of child-care. So it was thanks to this 'foster child' that Sheyna's life improved and that I was born into relative order, cleanliness and health. Our benefactors saw to it that my mother always had enough to eat, and soon my parents had three children, Sheyna, Zipke and I.

In 1903, when I was about five, we went back to Pinsk. Father, never one to give up, now had a new dream. Never mind the failure of Kiev, he said. He would go to America, to the *Goldene Medineh* – the 'Golden

Land', as the Jews called it – and make his fortune there. Mother, Sheyna, Zipke (the new daughter), and I would wait for him in Pinsk. So he gathered up his few belongings again and left for the unknown continent, and we moved to my grandparents' house.

I don't know to what extent any of my grandparents influenced me – though in Pinsk I lived with my mother's parents for a long time. Certainly it is hard for me to believe that my father's father played any role at all in my life, as he died before my parents met. But somehow or other he became one of the personalities that peopled my childhood, and now, going back into the past, I feel he belongs to this story. He had been one of the thousands of 'kidnapped' Jewish children of Russia, shanghaied into the czar's army to serve for twenty-five years. Ill-clothed, ill-fed, terrified children, more often than not they were under constant pressure- to convert to Christianity. My Mabovitch grandfather had been snatched by the army when he was all of thirteen, the son of a highly religious family, brought up to observe the finest points of orthodox Jewish tradition. He served in the Russian army for another thirteen years, and never once, despite threats, derision and often punishment, did he touch *treife* (non-kosher) food. All these years he kept himself alive on uncooked vegetables and bread. Though pressed hard to change his religion and often made to pay for his refusal by being forced to kneel for hours on a stone floor, he never gave in. When he was released and came back home, he was nonetheless haunted by the fear that inadvertently he might somehow have broken the Law. So to atone for the sin he might have committed, he slept for years on a bench in an unheated synagogue with only a stone at his head for a pillow. Little wonder that he died young.

Grandfather Mabovitch was not my only tenacious – or, to use a more fashionable word applied frequently to me by people who are not great admirers of mine, 'intransigent' – relative. There was also my maternal great-grandmother, whom I never knew and after whom I was named. She was known for her will of iron and for her bossiness. No one in the family, so we were told, ever dared to take a step without consulting her. For instance, it was my Bobbe Golde who was really responsible for the fact that my parents were allowed to marry each other. When my father came to Grandfather Naiditch to ask for my mother's hand in marriage, my grandfather shook his head unhappily and heaved great sighs at the idea that his darling Blume was to marry a mere carpenter, even if that carpenter could be described as a cabinet-maker. But my great-grandmother came to the rescue at once: 'What matters most of all,' she said firmly, 'is whether or not he is a *mensch*. If he is, then a carpenter too can become a merchant one day.' My father was to remain a carpenter all his life, but thanks to Bobbe Golde's ruling, my grandfather gave his blessing to the marriage. Bobbe Golde lived to be ninety-four and one of the stories I remember most distinctly about her is that she always took salt instead of sugar in her tea because, she said, 'I want to take the taste of the *Goless* [Diaspora] with me into the other world.' Interestingly enough, so my parents told me, we bore a striking resemblance to each other.

They are all gone now, of course; they and their children and their children's children; they and their way of life. The *shtetl* of Eastern Europe has gone too, destroyed in flames, its memory preserved accurately only in the Yiddish literature to which it gave birth and through which it expressed itself. That *shtetl*, reconstructed in novels and films, which has become known today in places my grandparents never even heard of; that gay, heart-warming, charming *shtetl* on whose roofs fiddlers eternally play sentimental music has almost nothing to do with anything I remember, with the poverty-stricken, wretched little communities in which Jews eked out a living, comforting themselves with the hope that things would somehow be better one day and with their belief that there was a point to their misery.

They were God-fearing and brave people, most of them, but their lives, like my Mabovitch grandfather's, were essentially tragic. And I myself have never felt – not even for a minute – any nostalgia for the past into which I was born, though it deeply coloured and affected my life and my convictions, both about the way in which all men, women and children everywhere, and whoever they are, are entitled to spend their lives – productively and free of humiliation – and, even more, about the way in which Jews, in particular, should live. I have often told my own children, and more recently my grandchildren, about life in the *shtetl* as I myself dimly remember it, and there is nothing that makes me happier than the certain knowledge that for them it is only a history lesson: a very important lesson about a very important part of their heritage, but not something with which they can ever really identify themselves because their lives were so totally different from the start.

Anyhow, Father spent three difficult, lonely years in America. He had painfully scraped together the money to get there and, like many thousands of the Russian Jews who streamed into the *Goldene Medineh* at the turn of the century, he had thought of America as the one place where he would surely make the fortune that would allow him to return home, to Russia, and to a new life there. Of course, it didn't work out like that – not for him nor for the thousands like him – but the idea that he would come back to us made our three years without him easier to bear.

Although the Kiev of my birth is lost to me in the fog of time, I have retained some sort of inner image of Pinsk, perhaps because I have heard and read about it so much. Many of the people I was to meet in later life came originally from Pinsk or from the townlets that clustered around it, including the families of Chaim Weizmann and Moshe Sharett.

Many years later, I twice nearly went back to Pinsk. In 1939, when I was in Poland on a mission for the Labour movement, I fell ill on the very day I was to visit the town, and the trip was cancelled. Then, in the summer of 1948, when I was appointed Israel's minister to the Soviet Union, I was seized by a sudden desire to go back to Pinsk and see for myself if any of my relatives had survived the Nazis, but the Soviet government refused to permit me to go. I hoped that in the course of time I would be allowed to make the journey, but in the beginning of 1949 I had to return to Israel, and my visit to Pinsk was postponed indefinitely. Perhaps it was just as well; I learned later that only one very distant relative out of our whole large family was still alive.

The town that I remember was filled with Jews. Pinsk was one of the most celebrated centres of Russian-Jewish life and at one time even had had a Jewish majority. It was built on two great rivers, the Pina and the Pripet – both of which flow into the Dnieper – and it was these rivers that supplied most of the Jews of Pinsk with their livelihood. They fished, unloaded cargo, did porterage, broke the giant ice floes in winter and dragged the ice to huge storage cellars in the houses of the well-to-do, where they served to create cooling facilities all through the summer. At one time my grandfather, who was fairly well off compared to my parents, owned such a cellar to which neighbours brought their Sabbath and holiday dishes when it was very hot and from which they took ice for the sick. The richer Jews dealt in timber and in the salt trade; and Pinsk even had nail, plywood and match factories that were owned by Jews and, of course, gave employment to dozens of Jewish workers.

But I remember mostly the *Pinsker blotte*, as we called them at home, the swamps that seemed to me then like oceans of mud and which we were taught to avoid like the plague. In my memory, those swamps are forever linked to my persistent terror of the Cossacks, to a winter night when I played with other children in a narrow lane near the forbidden *blotte* and then suddenly, as though out of nowhere, or maybe out of the swamps themselves, came the Cossacks on their horses, literally galloping over our crouching, shivering bodies. 'Well,' said my mother later, shivering and crying herself, 'what did I tell you?'

Cossacks and the black bottomless swamps, however, were not the only terrors Pinsk held for me. I can remember a row of big buildings on a street that led to the river and the monastery that stood opposite the buildings on a hill. In front of it, all day, sat or lay numbers of wild-haired wild-eyed cripples who prayed aloud and begged for alms. I tried to avoid passing them, and when I had to I closed my eyes and ran. But if Mother really wanted to frighten me, she knew that all she had to do was mention the beggars and I would abandon all defiance.

Still, not everything could have been so fearful. I was a child, and like all children I played and sang and made up stories to tell the baby. With Sheyna's help, I learned to read and write and even do a little arithmetic, though I didn't start school in Pinsk, as I should have. 'A golden child, they called you,' my mother said. 'Always busy with something.' But what I was really busy doing in Pinsk, I suppose, was learning about life – again, chiefly from Sheyna.

Sheyna was fourteen when Father left for the States, a remarkable, intense, intelligent girl who became, and who remained, one of the great influences of my life – perhaps the greatest, apart from the man I married. By any standard, she was an unusual person, and for me she was a shining example, my dearest friend and my mentor. Even late in life when we were both grown women, grandmothers in fact, Sheyna was the one person whose praise and approval – when I won them, which was not easy – meant most to me. Sheyna, in fact, is part and parcel of the story of my life. She died in 1972, but I think of her constantly, and her children and grandchildren are as dear to me as my own.

In Pinsk, although we were so pitifully poor and Mother only barely managed (with my grandfather's help) to keep us going, Sheyna refused to go to work. The move back to Pinsk had been very hard on her. She had gone to a wonderful school in Kiev, and she was bent on studying, on acquiring knowledge and getting an education, not only so that she herself would have a fuller and better life but, even more, so that she could help to change and better the world. At fourteen,

Sheyna was a revolutionary, an earnest, dedicated member of the Socialist–Zionist movement, and as such doubly dangerous in the eyes of the police and liable to punishment. Not only were she and her friends 'conspiring' to overthrow the all-powerful czar, but they also proclaimed their dream to bring into existence a Jewish socialist state in Palestine. In the Russia of the early twentieth century, even a fourteen- or fifteen-year-old schoolgirl who held such views would be arrested for subversive activity, and I still remember hearing the screams of young men and women being brutally beaten in the police station around the corner from where we lived.

My mother heard those screams, too, and daily begged Sheyna to have nothing to do with the movement; she could endanger herself and us and even Father in America! But Sheyna was very stubborn. It was not enough for her to want changes; she herself had to participate in bringing them about. Night after night, my mother kept herself awake until Sheyna came home from her mysterious meetings, while I lay in bed taking it all in silently – Sheyna's devotion to the cause in which she believed so strongly, Mother's overwhelming anxiety, Father's (to me, inexplicable) absence and the periodic and fearful sound of the hooves of Cossack horses outside.

On Saturdays, when Mother went off to synagogue, Sheyna organized meetings at home. Even when Mother found out about them and pleaded with Sheyna not to imperil us, there was nothing she could do about these meetings except nervously walk up and down outside the house when she got back on Saturday morning, patrolling it like a sentry so that when a policeman approached she could at least warn the young conspirators. But it wasn't only the idea that an ordinary policeman might swoop down at any moment and arrest Sheyna that so worried my poor mother. What really gnawed at her heart throughout all those months was the fear (always rampant in the Russia of those days) that one or another of Sheyna's friends might turn out to be an *agent provocateur*.

Of course, I was much too small to understand the reason for the arguments and tears and door-slammings, but I used to squeeze myself on to the flat top of our big coal stove (which was built into the wall) and sit there for hours on those Saturday mornings, listening to Sheyna and her friends and trying to make out what it was that they were all so excited about and why it made my mother cry so. Sometimes when I pretended to be engrossed in drawing or in copying the strangely shaped letters in the *siddur* (the Hebrew prayer book), which was one of the few books in our house, I tried to follow what Sheyna was so fervently explaining to my mother, but all I gathered was that she was involved in a special kind of struggle that concerned not only the Russian people but also, and more especially, the Jews.

A great deal has already been written – and much more will certainly be written in the future – about the Zionist movement, and most people by now have at least some notion of what the word Zionism means and that it has to do with the return of the Jewish people to the land of their forefathers – the Land of Israel as it is called in Hebrew. But perhaps even today not everyone realizes that this remarkable move- ment sprang up spontaneously towards the end of the nineteenth cen- tury, and more or less simultaneously in various parts of Europe. It was like a drama that was being enacted in different ways on different stages in different languages but which dealt with the same theme everywhere: that the so-called Jewish problem (of course, it was really a Christian problem) was basically the result of Jewish homelessness, and that it could not, and would not, be solved unless and until the Jews had a land of their own again. Obviously, this land could only be Zion, the land from which the Jews had been exiled 2,000 years before but which had remained the spiritual centre of Jewry throughout the centuries and which when I was a little girl in Pinsk, and up to the end of the First World War, was a desolate and neglected province of the Ottoman Empire called Palestine.

The first Jews who made the modern return to Zion came there as early as 1878 to found a pioneering village which they named *Petach Tikvah* (the Gate of Hope). By 1882, small groups of Zionists from Russia who called themselves the *Hovevei Zion* (Lovers of Zion) had arrived in the country determined to reclaim the land, farm it and defend it. But in 1882 Theodor Herzl, who was to be the founder of the World Zionist Organization and thus, essentially, the father of the State of Israel, was still quite unaware of what was happening to the Jews in Eastern Europe and of the existence of the *Hovevei Zion*. The successful and sophisticated Paris correspondent of the important Vienna newspaper the *Neue Freie Presse*, Herzl became interested in the fate of the Jews only in 1894, when he was assigned to cover the trial of Captain Dreyfus. Shocked by the injustice done to this Jewish officer – and by the open anti-Semitism of the French army – Herzl, too, came to believe that there was only one possible permanent solution to the situation of the Jews. His subsequent achievements and failures – the whole amazing story of his attempt to create a Jewish state – are part of the history learned by all Israeli schoolchildren and should be studied by anyone who wants to understand what Zionism is really all about.

Although my mother and Sheyna knew about Herzl, the first time I can remember hearing his name was when an aunt of mine (who lived in the same house as the Weizmann family and who was therefore often the bearer of important tidings, both good and bad) came in one day, her eyes brimming with tears, to tell my mother that the unthinkable had happened: Herzl was dead. I have never forgotten the stunned silence that greeted her announcement. As for Sheyna, she decided – typically – to wear only black clothes in mourning for Herzl from that afternoon in the summer of 1904 until we reached Milwaukee two long years later.

Although the yearning of the Jews for their own land was not the direct result of pogroms (the idea of the Jewish resettlement of Palestine had been urged by Jews and even some non-Jews long before the word 'pogrom' became part of the vocabulary of European Jewry), the Russian pogroms of my childhood gave the idea immediacy, especially when it became clear to the Jews that the Russian government itself was using them as scapegoats in the struggle to put down the revolutionary movement.

Most of the young Jewish revolutionaries in Pinsk, though united in their determination to press for an end to the czarist regime and in their immense enthusiasm for education as a tool with which to liberate Russia's exploited and oppressed masses, were divided at that point into two main groups. There were the members of the *Bund* (Union), who believed that the solution to the plight of the Jews in Russia and elsewhere would be found when Socialism prevailed. Once the economic and social structure of the Jews was changed, said the Bundists, anti-Semitism would totally disappear. In that better, brighter, socialist world, the Jews could still, if they so desired, retain their cultural identity, go on speaking Yiddish, maintain whatever customs and traditions they chose, eat whatever food they wanted to eat. But there would be no reason at all for clinging to the obsolete idea of Jewish nationhood.

The *Poalei-Zion* (Labour-Zionists), like Sheyna, saw it all quite differently. They believed that the so-called Jewish problem had other roots, and its solution therefore had to be more far-reaching and radical than merely the righting of economic wrongs or social inequalities. In addition to the shared social ideal, they clung to a national ideal based on the concept of Jewish peoplehood and the re-establishment of Jewish independence. At the time, though both these movements were secret and illegal, ironically enough, the bitterest enemies of Zionism were the Bundists, and most of the debates that whirled about my head whenever Sheyna and her friends got together in our house had to do with the conflict between the two groups.

Sometimes, when Sheyna and I got into a fight and I lost my temper, I used to threaten to tell Maxim, the big, red-faced policeman in our neighbourhood, all about her political activities. Of course I never did, and of course Sheyna knew that my threats were empty, but they worried her all the same. 'What will you tell Maxim?' she asked. 'I'll tell him that you and all your friends want to do away with the czar.' I would shriek. 'Do you know what will happen to me then? I'll be sent away to Siberia, where I'll die of cold and never come back,' she'd say. 'That's what happens to people who are exiled.' Truth to tell, I was always very careful to keep out of Maxim's way. Whenever I saw him lumbering in my direction, I took to my heels and fled. Years later Sheyna told me that although Maxim had never arrested anyone himself, she was quite sure that he provided the authorities regularly with plenty of information about all of the youngsters with whom she associated.

On second thoughts, I must also have learned at least one very important non-political lesson on top of the stove: that nothing in life just happens. It isn't enough to believe in something; you have to have the stamina to meet obstacles and to struggle to overcome them. I must have begun, when I was about six or seven, to grasp the philosophy that underlay everything that Sheyna did. There is only one way to do anything; the right way. Sheyna at fifteen was already a perfectionist, a girl who lived according to the highest principles, whatever the price; a severe taskmaster and very austere.

Even after we had both been living for years in what was first Palestine, then Israel, and she could have afforded some of the things that make life a little easier, she did without them because she felt they represented a standard of living that was too high for the country. As late as the 1960s, when she was old and not well, her sole luxury was a refrigerator, nothing else. She did without an oven, cooked all her life on a gas burner and thought that an electric mixer was more than she could permit herself to own, considering where she was living. Had she been more flexible, less strict with herself and with others, she might have understood what those meetings of hers in Pinsk cost my mother in terms of dread and sorrow and perhaps have compromised a little. But she was relentless about the things that really mattered to her, and the political meetings in our house went on, despite the never-ending battles about them. Once Sheyna even left home and went to live for a while with an aunt of ours, but that household turned out to be even less tolerant than our own, and she reluctantly came back.

It was around this time that Sheyna met Shamai Korngold, her husband-to-be, a strong, clever, gifted boy who had given up the great joy of studying and his burning interest in mathematics in order to join the revolutionary movement. A close-to-wordless romance blossomed between them, and Shamai also became and stayed part of my life. He was one of the leaders of the young Socialist-Zionists, nicknamed 'Copernicus' in the movement. Shamai was the only grandson of a well-known Torah scholar, in whose house he and his parents lived and upon whom they were financially dependent. He visited us often, and I can remember his whispered conversations with Sheyna about the increased revolutionary ferment in town and the regiment of Cossacks who were on their way to subdue Pinsk with their flashing swords. It was from these conversations that I gathered that something frightful had happened to the Jews of Kishiniev, and that in Pinsk the Jews were planning to defend themselves with arms and home-made bombs.

In response to the worsening situation, Sheyna and Shamai did more than merely hold or attend conspiratorial meetings; they did their best to bring other young people into the movement, even, to his horror, the only daughter of our white-bearded *shochet*, the ultra-orthodox ritual slaughterer from whom we rented the room in which we lived. Eventually, Mother's anxiety – for Sheyna and Zipke and me – became intolerable, and she began to write frantic letters to my father. It was out of the question, she wrote, for us to stay in Pinsk any longer. We must join him in America.

But like many things in life, this was far easier said than done. My father, who had by now moved from New York to Milwaukee, was barely making a living. He wrote back that he hoped to get a job working on the railway, and soon he would have enough money for our tickets. We moved out of the *shochet*'s house to a room in a bagel-baker's flat. The bagels were baked at night, so the flat was always hot, and the baker gave my mother a job. Then, late in 1905, a letter came from Milwaukee. My father was working, so we could start getting ready to leave.

The preparations for our journey were long and complicated. It was not a simple matter then for a woman and three girls, two of them still very small, to travel all the way from Pinsk to Milwaukee by them-selves. For my mother, relief must have been combined with new anxieties, and for Sheyna leaving Russia meant leaving Shamai and everything for which they had worked so hard and risked so much. I can remember only the hustle and bustle of those last weeks in Pinsk, the farewells from the family, the embraces and the tears. Going to America then was almost like going to the moon. Perhaps had my mother or aunts known that one day I would be back in Russia as a representative of a Jewish state – or that, as prime minister of Israel, I would one day welcome to that country hundreds upon hundreds of Russian Jews with embraces and tears, they might have cried less bitterly, though God knows the intervening years were to bring more than tears to the family we left behind. And perhaps if we had known that throughout Europe thousands of families like ours were on the move, headed towards what they, too, firmly believed would be, and was indeed, a better life in the New World, we would have been less frightened. But we knew nothing about the many women and children who were travelling then under similar conditions from countries like Ireland, Italy and Poland to join husbands and fathers in America, and we were very scared.

Not many of the details of our voyage to Milwaukee in 1906 have re-mained in my memory, and most of what I think I remember is prob-ably made up of stories my mother and Sheyna told to me. What I do recall is that we had to cross the border into Galicia secretly, because three years earlier my father had helped a friend to reach America by taking that man's wife and daughters with him on his papers and pre-tending that they were members of his family. So when our turn came to leave, we also had to pretend to be other people. Although we obediently memorized false names and details about our make-believe identities and Sheyna sternly drilled us all until we were letter perfect – even Zipke – our actual crossing was effected by bribing the police with money Mother had somehow managed to raise. In the confusion, most of our 'luggage' got lost – or perhaps it was stolen. Anyhow, I remember that early one icy spring morning we finally entered Galicia and the shack in which we waited for the train that would take us to the port. We lived in that unheated shack for two days, sleeping on the unheated floor, and I remember that Zipke cried most of the time until the train finally arrived and distracted her. Then we moved on past a series of unremembered stops, first to Vienna and then to Antwerp, where we spent another forty-eight hours in an immigration centre, this time waiting for the ship that was to take us to America and to my father.

It was not a pleasure trip, that fourteen-day journey aboard ship. Crammed into a dark, stuffy cabin with four other people, we spent the nights on sheetless bunks and most of the days standing in line for food that was ladled out to us as though we were cattle. Mother, Sheyna and Zipke were sea-sick most of the time, but I felt well and can remember staring at the sea for hours, wondering what Milwaukee would be like. The ship was packed with immigrants from Russia – pale, exhausted and just as scared as we were. Sometimes I would play with some of the other children who, like us, were travelling steerage, and we would tell each other stories about the unimaginable riches that awaited us in the *Goldene Medineh*. But I suspect that they, too, knew that in fact we were all bound for places about which we knew nothing at all and for a country that was totally strange to us.

2

A political adolescence

My father met us in Milwaukee, and he seemed changed: beardless, American-looking, in fact a stranger. He hadn't managed to find an apartment for us yet, so we moved, temporarily and not comfortably, into his one room in a house that belonged to a family of recently arrived Polish Jews. Milwaukee – even the small part of it that I saw during those first few days – overwhelmed me: new food, the baffling sounds of an entirely unfamiliar language, the confusion of getting used to a parent I had almost forgotten. It all gave me a feeling of unreality so strong that I can still remember standing in the street and wondering who and where I was.

I suppose that being together with his family again after so long was not easy for my father either. At any rate, even before we really had time to rest up from the journey or get to know him again, he did a most extraordinary thing: refusing to listen to any arguments, on the morning after our arrival he determinedly marched all of us downtown on a shopping expedition. He was horrified, he said, by our appearance. We looked so dowdy and 'Old World', particularly Sheyna in her matronly black dress. He insisted on buying us all new clothes, as though by dressing us differently he could turn us, within twenty-four hours, into three American-looking girls. His first purchase was for Sheyna – a frilly blouse and a straw hat with a broad brim covered in poppies, daisies and cornflowers. 'Now you look like a human being,' he said. 'This is how we dress in America.' Sheyna immediately burst into tears of rage and shame. 'Maybe that's how you dress in America,' she shouted, 'but I am certainly not going to dress like that!' She absolutely refused to wear either the hat or the blouse, and I think perhaps that premature excursion downtown marked the actual start of what were to be years of tension between them.

Not only were their personalities very different, but for three long years Father had been receiving complaining letters from Mother about Sheyna and her selfish behaviour, and in his heart of hearts he must have blamed Sheyna for his not having been able to go back to Russia again and the family's having to come to the States. Not that he was unhappy in Milwaukee. On the contrary, by the time we came he was already part of the immigrant life there. He was a member of a synagogue, he had joined a trade union (he was employed, off and on, in the workshops of the Milwaukee railroad) and he had accumulated a number of cronies. In his own eyes, he was on the way to becoming a full-fledged American-Jew, and he liked it. The last thing in the world he wanted was a disobedient, sullen daughter who demanded the right to live and dress in Milwaukee as though it were Pinsk, and the argument that first morning in Schuster's Department Store was soon to develop into a far more serious conflict. But I was delighted by my pretty new clothes, by the soda pop and ice cream and by the excitement of being in a real skyscraper, the first five-storey building I had ever seen. In general, I thought Milwaukee was wonderful. Everything looked so colourful and fresh, as though it had just been created, and I stood for hours staring at the traffic and the people. The automobile in which my father had fetched us from the train was the first I had ever ridden in, and I was fascinated by what seemed like the endless procession of cars, trolleys and shiny bicycles on the street.

We went for a walk and I peered, unbelieving, into the interior of the pharmacy with its *papier mâché* fisherman advertising cod-liver oil, the barbershop with its weird chairs and the cigar store with its wooden Indian. I remember enviously watching a little girl of my own age dressed up in her Sunday best, with puffed sleeves and high-button shoes, proudly wheeling a doll that reclined grandly on a pillow of its own, and marvelling at the sight of the women in long white skirts and men in white shirts and neckties. It was all completely strange and unlike anything I had seen or known before, and I spent the first days in Milwaukee in a kind of trance.

Very soon we moved to a little apartment of our own on Walnut Street, in the city's poorer Jewish section. Today, that part of Milwaukee is inhabited by blacks who are, for the most part, as poor as we were then. But in 1906, the clapboard houses with their pretty porches and steps looked like palaces to me. I even thought that our flat (which had no electricity and no bathroom) was the height of luxury. The apartment had two rooms, a tiny kitchenette and a long corridor that led to what was its greatest attraction for my mother, though I must say not for anyone else: a vacant shop that she instantly decided to run. My father, whose feelings undoubtedly were hurt by her obvious lack of faith in his ability to support us and who was not about to give up his carpentry, announced at once that she could do whatever she wanted, but that he would have nothing to do with the shop. It became the bane of my life; it began as a dairy store and then developed into a grocery, but it never prospered, and it almost ruined the years I spent in Milwaukee.

Looking back at my mother's decision, I can only marvel at her determination. We hadn't been in Milwaukee for more than a week or two; she didn't know one word of English; she had no inkling at all of which products were likely to sell well; she had never run or even worked in a shop before. Nonetheless, probably because she was so terrified of our being as abjectly poor as we had been in Russia, she took this tremendous responsibility upon herself without stopping to think through the consequences. Running the shop meant that she not only had to buy stock on credit (because obviously we had no surplus cash), but also that she would have to get up at dawn every day to buy whatever was needed at the market and then drag her purchases back home. Fortunately, the women in the neighbourhood rallied round her. Many of them were new immigrants themselves, and their natural reaction was to assist another newcomer. They taught her a few English phrases, how to behave behind the counter, how to work the cash register and scales and to whom she could safely allow credit.

Like my father's ill-fated shopping trip, my mother's hasty decision about the shop was almost certainly part of my parents' reaction to finding themselves in such alien surroundings. But unfortunately both of these precipitous steps were to have a serious effect not only on Sheyna's life but also on mine, although in very differing degrees. As far as I was concerned, my mother's enforced absence every morning meant that somebody had to mind the store while she was gone. Sheyna, like my father, refused to help out in any way. Her socialist principles, she declared, made it impossible. 'I did not come to America to turn into a shopkeeper, into a social parasite,' she declared. My parents were very angry with her but, characteristically, she did what her principles dictated: she found herself a job – making button-holes by hand in a tailor shop. It was difficult work, which she did badly and hated, even though she was now entitled to consider herself a real member of the proletariat. After she had earned the grand total of 30 cents for three days' work, my father made her give up the job and help mother. Still, she managed to get away from the shop whenever she could, and for months I had to stand behind the counter every morning until mother returned from the market. For an eight- or nine-year-old girl, this was not an easy chore.

I started school in a huge, fortress-like building on Fourth Street near Milwaukee's famous Schlitz beer factory, and I loved it. I can't remember how long it took me to learn English (at home, of course, we spoke Yiddish and, luckily, so did almost everyone else on Walnut Street), but I have no recollection of the language ever being a real problem for me, so I must have picked it up quickly. I made friends quickly, too. Two of those early first- or second-grade friends remained friends all my life, and both live in Israel now. One was Regina Hamburger (today Medzini), who lived on our street and who was to leave America when I did; the other was Sarah Feder, who became one of the leaders of Labour-Zionism in the United States. Anyhow, coming late to class almost every day was awful, and I used to cry all the way to school. Once a policeman even came to the shop to explain to my mother about truancy. She listened attentively but barely understood anything he said, so I went on being late for school, and sometimes never got there at all – an even greater disgrace. My mother didn't seem to be moved by my bitter resentment of the shop – not that she had much alternative. 'We have to live, don't we?' she claimed, and if my father and Sheyna – each for his and her own reasons – would not help, that didn't mean that *I* was absolved of the task. 'So it will take you a little longer to become a *rebbetzin* (a blue-stocking),' she added. I never became a blue-stocking, of course, but I learned a lot at that school.

More than fifty years later – when I was seventy-one and a prime minister – I went back to the school for a few hours. It had not changed very much in all those years except that the vast majority of its pupils were now black, not Jewish as in 1906. They welcomed me as though I was a queen. Standing in rows on the creaky old stage I remembered so well, freshly scrubbed and neat as pins, they serenaded me with Yiddish and Hebrew songs and raised their voices to peal out the Israeli anthem '*Hatikvah*', which made my eyes fill with tears. Each one of the classrooms had been beautifully decorated with posters about Israel and signs reading '*Shalom*' (one of the children thought it was my family name), and when I entered the school two little girls wearing headbands with Stars of David on them solemnly presented me with an enormous white rose made of tissue paper and pipe cleaners, which I wore all day and carefully carried back to Israel with me.

Another of the gifts I got that day in 1971 from the Fourth Street School was a record of my grades for one of the years I had spent there: 95 in reading, 90 in spelling, 95 in arithmetic, 85 in music and a mysterious 90 in something called manual arts, which I cannot remember at all. But when the children asked me to talk to them for a few minutes, it was not about book-learning that I chose to speak. I had learned much more than fractions or how to spell at Fourth Street, and I decided to tell those eager attentive children – born, as I myself had been, into a minority and living, as I myself had lived, without much extravagance (to put it mildly) – what the gist of that learning had been. 'It isn't really important to decide when you are very young just exactly what you want to become when you grow up,' I told them. 'It is much more important to decide on the way you want to live. If you are going to be honest with yourself and honest with your friends, if you are going to get involved with causes which are good for others, not only for yourselves, then it seems to me that that is sufficient, and maybe what you will be is only a matter of chance.' I had a feeling that they understood me.

At all events, apart from the shop and being aware of Sheyna's evident misery about having to live at home – and having had to part from Shamai, who was still in Russia and whom she missed terribly – I think back on those five years in Milwaukee with great pleasure. There was so much to see and do and learn that the memory of Pinsk was almost erased. Almost but not entirely. In September, when we had been in America just over three months, my father told us to be sure and watch the famous Labor Day parade in which he, too, would be marching. Dressed up in our new clothes, Mother, Zipke and I took our places at the street corner he recommended and waited for the parade to begin, not knowing exactly what a parade was, but looking forward to it anyway. Suddenly Zipke saw the mounted police who led the parade. She was absolutely terrified. 'It's the Cossacks! The Cossacks are coming!' she screamed, and sobbed so hard that she had to be taken home and put to bed. But for me that parade – the crowds, the brass bands, the floats, the smell of popcorn and hotdogs – symbolized American freedom. Police on horseback were actually escorting the marchers instead of dispersing them and trampling them underfoot, as they were doing in Russia, and I felt the impact of a new way of life. I didn't know or care about it then – or for some time to come – but it occurs to me now that both Wisconsin in general and Milwaukee in particular were blessed by extremely liberal administrations. Milwaukee was a city of immigrants and had a strong socialist tradition, a socialist mayor for many years and America's first socialist congressman, Victor Berger. But, of course, we would have responded in much the same way to any kind of parade in any American city; or maybe there really was some special vitality about Labor Day then in Milwaukee, a city to which so many German liberals and intellectuals had fled after the unsuccessful revolution of 1848 and which was as well known for its vigorous trade unions as for its beer gardens. In any case, to see my father marching on that September day was like coming out of the dark into the light.

Of course, it would have been better if Mother hadn't had to work so hard, if Sheyna had gotten along with my parents more easily, if we had had just a little more money. But even as it was, even with my secret sorrow about and loathing for the store, those early years in Milwaukee were full and good years for me. But they were less so for Sheyna. Almost everything was going wrong for her: she found it extremely hard to adjust, to learn English, to make friends. She was inexplicably tired, even listless, much of the time, and the constant conflict at home didn't help – particularly my parents' rather clumsy attempts to find her a husband as though Shamai didn't exist. At eighteen, her life had suddenly narrowed itself down to almost nothing.

Then – it seemed like a miracle – she heard about an opening in a big men's clothing factory in Chicago and was taken on there. But for some reason that didn't work out either, and she started work as a seamstress in a smaller factory – a sweat shop really – for women's clothing, where she finally settled down. After a while, however, she was back in Milwaukee with a badly infected finger. Had she been less run down, it would have undoubtedly healed faster, but as it was she had to stay at home for several weeks. My parents were triumphant about her return, but I felt very sorry for her, and during those weeks when I helped to take care of her, comb her hair and dress her, we grew closer.

One day Sheyna told me that she had received a letter from our aunt in Pinsk about Shamai. He had been arrested but had escaped from jail and was now on his way to New York. Thoughtfully our aunt enclosed his address, and Sheyna wrote to him at once. By the time she heard from him, her finger was completely healed, she had found another job and was busily planning Shamai's arriving in Milwaukee.

Needless to say, I was delighted that her spirits had lifted at last. Perhaps now that Shamai was coming, Sheyna would always be happy and perhaps the atmosphere at home would change. I couldn't remember much about Shamai, but I looked forward to his arrival with a heart almost as full as Sheyna's. Unfortunately my parents, especially my mother, greeted the news very differently. 'Marry Shamai? But he has no prospects at all,' my mother said. 'He is a pauper, a greenhorn, a young man with no means and without a future.' And – never mind the logic – at the same time he was too good for Sheyna; he came from a well-to-do family which would never give its approval. The match would be a disaster however one looked at it.

As usual, Sheyna went ahead and did as she thought best. She rented a room for Shamai and summoned him to Milwaukee. He arrived depressed and unsure of himself, but Sheyna was confident that together they could overcome any and all obstacles. Eventually he got a job in a cigarette factory, and they set about learning English at night.

Then Sheyna fell ill, and this time it was serious: the diagnosis was TB. She would have to go to a sanatorium, and it was questionable whether she would ever be allowed to get married. Her entire world caved in. She gave up her job and her room and reluctantly came home again. My parents hid their worry for her under a storm of rebuke and nagging, and I did my childish and not very effective best to cheer up both Sheyna and Shamai and to intervene on their behalf with my mother and father whenever the tension seemed about to explode into a crisis.

Within a few weeks, everything had changed. Sheyna left for the Jewish Hospital for Consumptives in Denver, Shamai left for Chicago and began forlornly to look for a job there, and I started saving up my meagre 'lunch' money for stamps that I sent to Sheyna so she could write to me. Once or twice I even 'borrowed' the stamp money from Mother's till, but since there was no correspondence at all between Sheyna and my parents I was really her only link with the family – which I thought justified the crime.

In my letters to Sheyna, which to my surprise she kept for years, I told her about my life at home. 'I am very good in school,' I wrote in

1908. 'I am now in third high and in June I am going to pass in fourth low.' And, 'I can tell you Pa does not work yet and in the store it is not very busy and I am glad you are out of bed.'

The truth of the matter was that work of the kind my father could do was very scarce in Milwaukee then, and even when he did get a job it was usually only for 20 or 25 cents an hour. The shop was also doing very badly, and to make matters worse my mother suffered a miscarriage and the doctor made her stay in bed for several weeks, so I cooked and scrubbed, hung laundry and minded the store, choking back tears of rage all the time because I was forced to miss even more school. But I didn't want Sheyna to have to worry about us. She was having a hard enough time herself in Denver, and I saw to it that my letters remained rather terse, though I never deliberately misled her regarding the state of affairs at home.

I missed Sheyna terribly, but the years without her went by quickly. School absorbed me, and in the little time I had left over from the shop (and helping my mother at home and Zipke – who had now been renamed Clara by Mr Finn, the school principal – with her lessons) I read and read. Every now and then, Regina Hamburger and I got tickets (perhaps through the school) for a play or a movie. Those were very rare treats, and to this day I remember one of them distinctly – seeing *Uncle Tom's Cabin* and suffering through every moment of it with Uncle Tom and Eva. I can still recall jumping to my feet in the theatre, literally beside myself with hatred for Simon Legree. I think it must have been the first thing I ever saw on a stage, and I told my mother and Clara the story over and over again. It had a kind of special reality for all of us.

One important event (to me) took place when I was in the fourth grade. I got involved in my first 'public work'. Although school in Milwaukee was free, a nominal sum was charged for textbooks, which many of the children in my class could not afford. Obviously someone had to do something to solve the problem, so I decided to launch a fund. It was to be my very first experience as a fundraiser but hardly the last!

Regina and I collected a group of girls from the school, explained the purpose of the fund, and we all painted posters announcing that the American Young Sisters Society (we were particularly proud of the name we had made up for our non-existent organization) was to hold a public meeting on the subject of textbooks. Then, having appointed myself chairman of the society, I hired a hall and sent invitations out

to the entire district. Today it seems incredible to me that anyone
would agree to rent a hall to a child of eleven, but the meeting took
place as scheduled one Saturday evening and dozens of people came.
The programme was very simple: I spoke about the need for all children to have textbooks whether they had money or not, and Clara,
who was then about eight, recited a socialist poem in Yiddish. I can see
her now, a very small, red-headed child, standing in front of the audience in Packen Hall, gesturing dramatically as she declaimed. The
result of the meeting was two-fold: a considerable amount of money
(by our standards) was raised, and my parents showered praise on
Clara and me while walking home that evening. I only wished that
Sheyna had been there. But at least I could send her the clipping,
together with a picture of me from a Milwaukee paper that referred to
the meeting:

A score of little children who give their playtime and scant pennies to
charity, and charity organized on their own initiative, too . . . And it is worthy
of comment that this charity is itself a loud comment on the fact that little
children may go to the public schools without proper provision of books.
Think what that means . . .

The letter I wrote to Sheyna about the meeting was almost as
dramatic as Clara's poem. 'Dear Sister,' it read, 'Now I can tell you
that we had the greatest success that there ever was in Packen Hall.
And the entertainment was grand . . .'

My mother had begged me to write out my 'speech', but it made
more sense to me just to say what I wanted to say, what was in my
heart. And considering it was my first public address, I think I did
rather well. At any rate, with the exception of major policy statements at the United Nations or the Knesset, I never got into the habit
of using a written text, and I went on for the next half-century making
'speeches from my head', as I described it to Sheyna in that letter I
wrote her in the summer of 1909.

Eventually, during the summer vacation, Regina and I got our first
real jobs: very junior salesgirls at a department store downtown.
What we really did, for the most part, was wrap packages and run
errands, but we made a few dollars each week and I was released from
having to stand in our shop all day. My father, very much against his
will, took my place there, and it was with a sense of great independence
that I pressed my skirt and blouse each evening and set out at dawn
each day to walk to work. It was a long walk, but the carfare I saved

went towards a winter coat – the first thing I ever bought with my own earnings.

When I was fourteen, I finished elementary school. My marks were good and I was chosen to be class valedictorian. The future seemed very bright and clear to me; obviously I would go on to high school, and then, perhaps, even become a teacher, which is what I most wanted to be. I thought – and still think today – that teaching is the noblest and the most satisfying profession of all. A good teacher opens up the whole world for children, makes it possible for them to learn to use their minds and in many ways equips them for life. I *knew* I could teach well, once I was sufficiently educated myself, and I wanted that kind of responsibility. Regina, Sarah and I talked endlessly about what we would do when we grew up. I remember on those summer evenings how we sat for hours on the steps of my house and discussed our futures. Like teenage girls everywhere, we thought these were the most important decisions we would ever have to take – other than marriage, and that certainly seemed much too remote to be worth our talking about.

My parents however – as I ought to have understood but did not – had other plans for me. I think my father would have liked me to be educated, and at my Fourth Street graduation ceremony his eyes were moist. He understood, I believe, what was involved, but in a way his own life had defeated him and he was unable to be of much help to me. My mother, as usual and despite her disastrous relationship with Sheyna, knew exactly what I should do. Now that I had finished elementary school, spoke English well and without an accent and had developed into what the neighbours said was a *dervaksene shein meydl* (a fine, upstanding girl), I could work in the shop full time and sooner or later – but better sooner – start thinking seriously about getting married, which, she reminded me, was forbidden to women teachers by state law.

If I insisted on acquiring a profession, she said, I could go to secretarial school and learn to become a shorthand typist. At least I wouldn't remain an old maid that way. My father nodded his head, 'It doesn't pay to be too clever,' he warned. 'Men don't like smart girls.' As Sheyna had done before me, I tried in every way I knew to change my parents' mind. In tears, I explained that nowadays an education was important, even for a married woman, and argued that in any case I had no intention whatsoever of getting married for a very long time. Besides, I sobbed, I would rather die than spend my life – or even part of it – hunched over a typewriter in some dingy office.

But neither my arguments nor my tears were of any avail. My parents were convinced that high school, for me at least, was an un-warranted luxury – not only unnecessary but undesirable. From the distance of Denver, Sheyna (now convalescent and out of the sana-torium) encouraged me in my campaign, and so did Shamai, who had joined her there. As they wrote to me often, sending their letters to Regina's house so my parents wouldn't find out about the correspon-dence, I knew that Shamai had first washed dishes in the sanatorium and had then been taken on to work in a small dry-cleaning plant that served one of the big Denver hotels. In his spare time he was studying bookkeeping and, most important of all, in the face of repeated warn-ings from Sheyna's doctor, they were going to be married. 'Better we should live less,' Shamai had decided, 'but live together.' It was to be one of the happiest marriages I ever knew and, despite the doctor's grim prediction, it lasted forty-three years and resulted in three children.

My parents were very upset at first, especially my mother. 'Another lunatic with grand ideas and not a cent in his pocket,' she sniffed. That was a husband for Sheyna? That was a man who could support and take care of her? But Shamai not only loved Sheyna; he understood her. He never argued with her. When he was quite sure that he was right about something, he went ahead and did it, and Sheyna always knew when she was beaten. But when she wanted something and it was really important to her, Shamai never stood in her way. To me, the news of their marriage meant that Sheyna now had what she most needed and wanted – and that I, at last, had a brother.

In my secret letters to Denver, I wrote in detail about the con-tinuing fights over school that were making my life at home almost in-tolerable and were leading me to decide to become independent as soon as possible. That autumn, the autumn of 1912, I defiantly began my first term at Milwaukee's North Division High School and in the afternoons and on weekends worked at a variety of odd jobs, determined never again to ask my parents for money. But none of this helped; the disputes at home went on and on.

The last straw was my mother's attempt to find me a husband. She didn't want me to get married at once, of course, but she very much wanted to be sure not only that I would get married at what she con-sidered a reasonable age, but that, unlike Sheyna, *I* at least would marry somebody substantial. Not rich – that was out of the question –

but at least solid. In actual fact, she was already discreetly negotiating with a Mr Goodstein, a pleasant, friendly, relatively well-to-do man in his early thirties, whom I knew because he used to come into the store now and then to chat for a while. Mr Goodstein! But he was an old man! Twice my age! I sent a furious letter to poor Sheyna. The reply came from Denver by return mail: 'No, you shouldn't stop school. You are too young to work; you have good chances to become something,' Shamai wrote. And with perfect generosity: 'My advice is that you should get ready and come to us. We are not rich either, but you will have good chances here to study and we will do all we can for you.' At the bottom of his letter, Sheyna wrote her own warming invitation: 'You must come to us immediately.' There would be enough of every-thing for all of us, she assured me. All together, we would manage. 'First, you'll have all the opportunities to study; second you'll have plenty to eat; third, you'll have the necessary clothes that a person ought to have.'

I was very touched by their letter, but reading it today I am even more moved by the readiness of those two young people, still so far from being established themselves, to take me in and share whatever they had with me. That letter, written from Denver in November 1912, was a turning point in my life, because it was in Denver that my real education began and that I started to grow up. I suppose that if Sheyna and Shamai had not come to my rescue, I would have gone on fighting with my parents, crying at night and still somehow going to high school. I can't imagine that I would have agreed under any circumstances to stop studying and marry the probably much-maligned Mr Goodstein; but Sheyna and Shamai's offer was like a lifeline, and I grabbed at it.

In the years that have passed since that November, I have also often thought of Sheyna's last letter to me before I joined her in Denver. 'The main thing,' she wrote, 'is never to be excited. Always be calm and act coolly. This way of action will always bring you good results. Be brave.' That was advice about running away from home, but I never forgot it and it stood me in good stead within a few years when I came to what was to be my real home, the land in which I was prepared to fight to the death in order to stay.

Getting to Denver was not easy. I couldn't possibly expect my parents to agree to my leaving home and going to live with Sheyna. They would never have permitted it. The only solution was not to tell them anything at all; simply to leave. It might not be the bravest

course, but it would certainly be the most efficient. Sheyna and Shamai
sent me some money for a railway ticket, and Regina and I planned
my flight down to the last detail. The first problem to be solved was
how to get together enough money to pay for the rest of my ticket. I
borrowed some of it from Sarah (which was certainly a very 'cool'
action considering that I had no idea how I would ever pay it back),
and Regina and I persuaded a number of new immigrants on the
street into taking English lessons from us for 10 cents an hour. When we
had collected enough money, we set about plotting the details of my
departure.

Regina was a marvellously devoted ally. Not only was she absolutely
trustworthy and could be relied upon not to tell either my parents or
her own anything about my plans, but she was also very imaginative –
though now that I write about it, I have an idea that she must have
mixed my escape up with an elopement. What she proposed – and what
I very gladly accepted – was that since we lived above the store then,
I should make a bundle of my clothes (just as well that it wouldn't be
a very large bundle) and lower it the evening before my departure to
Regina, who would spirit it away to the baggage department of the railway station. Then, in the morning, instead of going to school, I could
go right to the train.

When the fateful evening arrived, I sat in the kitchen with my
parents as though it were just any ordinary night, but my heart was
very heavy. While they drank tea and talked, I scribbled a note for
them to read the next day. It was only a few words and not very well-
chosen ones at that. 'I am going to live with Sheyna, so that I can
study,' I wrote, adding that there was nothing for them to worry about
and that I would write from Denver. It must have hurt them terribly
to read that note the next morning, and if I were to write it today I
would do so only after much thought and with very great care. But I
was under extreme pressure then and only fifteen. Before I went to
sleep that night I went over to Clara's bed and looked at her for a
minute. I felt very guilty about leaving her without even saying good-
bye, and I wondered what would happen to her now that both Sheyna
and I were out of the house, as I thought, for good. Clara was growing
up to be the most 'American' of us all, a quiet, shy, undemanding little
girl whom everyone liked but to whom I had never paid much attention and whom I didn't know very well. Now that I was going to leave
her, I remember feeling a sudden sense of responsibility. It turned out,
though I couldn't have known it then, that being the only child at

home was actually to make her life easier. My parents were far more lenient with Clara than they had ever been with Sheyna or with me, and my mother even spoiled her sometimes. We weren't a demonstrative family, but that night I stroked her face and kissed her, though she slept through my farewell.

Very early the next morning, I left home as planned and went to the station to board the train for Denver. I had never travelled alone before, and the idea that trains run according to a timetable had never occurred either to me or to my fellow-conspirator, so I was still sitting nervously on a bench in the station with a pounding heart, when my parents opened and read the note I had written for them at home. But, as the Yiddish saying goes, I had considerably more luck than brains, and somehow or other, in the confusion, no one looked for me until the train had left and I was on my way to Sheyna, knowing that I had done something that deeply wounded my mother and father but that was truly essential for me. In the two years that I was to spend in Denver, my father, unforgiving, only wrote to me once. But from time to time my mother and I exchanged letters, and by the time I came back I no longer had to battle for the right to do as I wanted.

Regina and Clara both sent me vivid descriptions of the reactions at home to my leaving. Clara's letter was full of accusations. My mother had wept bitter tears, then dried her eyes and gone to see Regina's mother. By the time Regina came back from school feeling very pleased with herself, her mother had heard all about her 'disgraceful' assistance to me, and Regina was given a sound hiding. Good friend that she was, she avoided any recriminations in her own letter to me. On the contrary, it was rather apologetic. 'I hope I won't hurt your feelings, but everyone thought you had eloped with an Italian. How they got the idea, I can't get at . . . Now, dear Goldie, don't get angry at me for writing this, but I can't help it, you asked . . . I burned with anger and resentment, but what could I do?'

In Denver, life really opened up for me, although Sheyna and Shamai proved to be almost as strict as my parents and we all had to work very hard. Shamai was now employed as a part-time janitor at the local telephone company, as well as working in his own dry-cleaning shop, and the arrangement was that when I got through with school in the afternoons, I would take over for him in the shop so that he could go on to his second job. I could do my homework at the shop, and if a customer wanted something pressed, I could do that too.

In the evenings, after supper, Sheyna badgered me to go on with my school-work, but I was fascinated by the people who used to drop in to their home and sit around talking till late at night. I found the endless discussions about politics much more interesting than any of my lessons. Sheyna's small apartment had become a kind of centre in Denver for the Jewish immigrants from Russia who had come out West to receive treatment for TB at the hospital for consumptives in which Sheyna herself had spent so much time. Almost all of them were unmarried. Some of them were anarchists, some were socialists, and some were Socialist-Zionists. They had all either been ill or were still ill, they were all uprooted, they were all passionately and vitally concerned with the major issues of the day. They talked, argued and even quarrelled for hours about what was happening in the world, and what ought to happen. They talked about the anarchist philosophy of Emma Goldman and Peter Kropotkin, about President Wilson and the European situation, about pacifism, the role of women in society, the future of the Jewish people – and they drank cup after cup of tea with lemon. I blessed those rounds of tea because although Sheyna so strongly disapproved of the hours I was keeping, I managed to stay up most nights by volunteering to disinfect the cups afterwards – an offer which was rarely turned down.

Of course, I was always the youngest person in the room and my Yiddish wasn't as literary as that of many of the debaters, but I hung on their words as though they would change the fate of mankind and sometimes, after a while, even voiced opinions of my own. Much of that nightly conversation was way over my head. I didn't know what dialectical materialism was or who, exactly, Hegel, Kant or Schopenhauer were, but I knew that socialism meant democracy, the right of workers to a decent life, an eight-hour work day and no exploitation. And I understood that tyrants had to be overthrown, but dictatorship of any kind – including that of the proletariat – held no appeal for me at all.

I listened raptly to everyone holding forth, but it was to the Socialist-Zionists that I found myself listening most attentively and it was their political philosophy that made the most sense to me. I understood and responded fully to the idea of a national home for the Jews – one place on the face of the earth where Jews could be free and independent – and I took it for granted that in such a place no one would be in want, or exploited or live in fear of other men. I was much more interested in the kind of Jewish national home the Zionists wanted to create in

Palestine than I was in the political scene in Denver itself, or even in what was then going on in Russia.

The talk at Sheyna's – almost all of it in Yiddish, since very few of the talkers spoke English well enough to express themselves properly on these urgent ideological matters – was very free-ranging. There were evenings in which most of the discussion was about Yiddish literature – Sholom Aleichem, Peretz, Mendele Mocher Sforim – and other evenings that were devoted to specific questions such as women's suffrage or the future of trade unionism. I was interested in all of it, but when they talked about people like Aaron David Gordon, for instance, who had gone to Palestine in 1905 and helped found Degania (the kibbutz established three years later on the deserted edge of the Sea of Galilee), I was absolutely fascinated and found myself dreaming about joining the pioneers in Palestine.

I can't remember which of the young men it was who first spoke about Gordon at Sheyna's, but I do remember how fascinated I was by what he told us about that middle-aged man with a long white beard that made him look like Father Time, a man who had never done any physical work before and who came to Palestine with his family when he was almost fifty to till its soil with his own hands and write about the 'religion of labour', as his credo came to be known by his disciples. The building of Palestine, Gordon believed, was to be *the* great Jewish contribution to humanity. In the Land of Israel, the Jews would find their way to the making of a just society through their own physical labour – provided that each and every individual made a massive personal effort in this direction.

Gordon died in 1922 – one year after I myself came to Palestine – and I never met him. But I think that of all the world's great thinkers and revolutionaries about whom I heard so much at Sheyna's, he is perhaps the one I would most have wanted to know myself – and would most like my grandchildren to meet.

I was enthralled also by the romantic story of Rachel Bluwstein, a delicate girl from Russia who came to Palestine at about the same time as Gordon and was deeply influenced by him. A remarkably gifted poet, she went to work on the soil in a new settlement near the Sea of Galilee, where some of her most beautiful poems were written. Although she didn't know a word of Hebrew before she came to Palestine, she was to become one of the first modern Hebrew poets, and many of her poems have been set to music and are still sung in Israel. Eventually she became too ill (with the TB that killed her at forty) to work the land she loved so much, but she was still alive and young when I was in Denver and heard her name for the first time from someone who had known her in Russia.

Years later, when it became fashionable for young people to deride my generation for its rigidity, conventionality and loyalty to the 'Establishment', it was about intellectual rebels such as A. D. Gordon and Rachel and dozens of others like them that I used to think. No modern hippie, in my opinion, has ever revolted as effectively against the 'Establishment' of the day as those pioneers did at the beginning of the century. Many of them came from the homes of merchants and scholars, many even from prosperous assimilated families. If Zionism alone had fired them, they could have come to Palestine, bought orange groves there and hired Arabs to do all the work for them. It would have been easier. But they were radicals at heart and deeply believed that only self-labour could truly liberate the Jews from the ghetto and its mentality and make it possible for them to reclaim the land and earn a moral right to it, in addition to the historic right. Some of them were poets, some were cranks, some had stormy personal lives; but what they all had in common was a fervour to experiment, to build a good society in Palestine, or at least a society that would be better than what had been known in most parts of the world. The communes they founded – the kibbutzim of Israel – have endured, I am sure, only because of this genuinely revolutionary social ideal that underlay and still underlies them.

At all events, to the extent that my own future convictions were shaped and given form, and ideas were discarded or accepted by me while I was growing, those talk-filled nights in Denver played a considerable role. But my stay in Denver had other consequences, too. One of the less articulate young men who came to Sheyna's often was a gentle, soft-spoken friend of theirs, Morris Meyerson, whose sister had met Sheyna in the sanatorium. Morris's family had immigrated to America from Lithuania and, like ours, was very poor. His father had died when he was just a boy, and he had gone to work early in life in order to support his mother and three sisters. At the time we met, he was working sporadically as a sign painter.

Although he never raised his voice, even during the stormiest of the nightly sessions, I think I first noticed Morris because although he was almost entirely self-educated, he was so well versed in the kind of things that neither I nor most of Sheyna and Shamai's friends knew anything at all about. He loved poetry, art and music and knew and understood a great deal about them; and he was prepared to talk at length on the merits of a given sonnet or sonata to someone as interested (and as ignorant) as I was.

When Morris and I came to know each other better, we started to go to free concerts in the park together, and Morris patiently introduced me to the joys of classical music, read Byron, Shelley, Keats and the Rubiyyat of Omar Khayyam to me, and took me to lectures on literature, history and philosophy. To this day, I associate certain pieces of music with the clear, dry mountain air of Denver and the wonderful parks in which Morris and I walked every Sunday in the spring and summer of 1913.

One of those concerts left an indelible impression on me, not so much because of the music – which I barely heard – but because of the threateningly clouded sky. I had wanted to look my very best for Morris, so the day before I had gone off to a five-and-ten-cent store and bought myself a new straw hat. The only colour they had in stock was bright red, so I took it, a little reluctantly because it seemed rather too frivolous, but it was very becoming and I hoped that Morris would like it. I still remember with horror the first afternoon I wore it. It was a cloudy, dark day, and Morris didn't even notice my hat; but I was so terrified that it would rain and that the red would trickle all over me that I spent the entire time worrying about the weather.

I admired Morris enormously – more than I had ever admired anyone except Sheyna – not only for his encyclopaedic knowledge, but for his gentleness, his intelligence and his wonderful sense of humour. He was only five or six years my senior, but he seemed much older, much calmer and much steadier. Without at first being aware of what was happening to me, I fell in love with him and couldn't help realizing that he loved me, too, though for a long time we said nothing to each other about the way we felt.

Sheyna was very fond of Morris, too, and luckily approved of my seeing him so often. Still, that was not, she informed me sternly, why she had helped me to run away from home. I had come to Denver to study, she said, not to listen to music or learn poetry. She took her mission of being my guardian very seriously, which meant watching me like a hawk, and after several months I began to feel that I might just as well have stayed in Milwaukee. Shamai put much less pressure on me, but the reins had definitely tightened and I began to feel very restive. One day after Sheyna had been particularly bossy, ordering me about and scolding me as though I were still a child, I decided that the time had come for me to try to live alone, without a mother-hen and without being nagged all the time, and I marched out of the apartment in the black skirt and white blouse I had been wearing all day without taking anything else with me, not even a night-gown. If I was leaving Sheyna's home and authority, I was not entitled, I thought, to keep anything that Sheyna or Shamai had bought for me. I closed the door behind me, and that, I thought, was that: I was on my own at last.

It was something of a comedown to realize ten minutes later that now I had to find somewhere to live until I could support myself. A little crestfallen but very grateful, I accepted the invitation extended by two of Sheyna's friends who had always been especially nice to me and to whom I confided that 'for the moment' I was homeless. Unfortunately, it was not exactly the best choice of a haven. Both my hosts were in a fairly advanced stage of TB, and to this day I can offer no explanation other than what my mother used to call 'a na'ar's mazel' (the luck of a fool) for the fact that I remained free of the disease. They lived in rather cramped quarters that consisted of a room (with a niche at one end of it) and a kitchen. The niche was mine for as long as I wanted it, they told me, but since they were both so sick, I felt I had to let them go to bed early, and I didn't dare switch the light on over my couch when it grew dark. In fact, the only place I could read without bothering them – or be disturbed myself by their night-long coughing – was the bathroom, where, wrapped up in a blanket and armed with Morris's current reading list (which was always terrifyingly long) and a pile of books, I used to spend most of my nights.

At sixteen, of course, one can do without almost everything, including sleep, and I was delighted with my set-up – and even more, to be quite honest, with myself. Not only had I found myself somewhere to live, but I had also come to the conclusion that high school would have to wait after all. It was even more important for me to learn to cope with life alone, I told myself, than to acquire the schooling for which I had so longed. The first thing to do now that I had my niche was to find a job. My father used to say, fatalistically, 'when you chop wood, you get splinters', so I was now preparing myself for the splinters; a job might be hard to get. But within a day or two, I found work in a shop where my chief responsibility was to take measurements for custommade skirt linings. It wasn't exactly a stimulating or elevating job, but it kept me going and soon made it possible for me to rent a tiny, but at least germ-free, room of my own. Incidentally, one by-product of that job is that even today I find myself automatically giving a quick glance at the hems of skirts and can run one up with total confidence.

I may have felt, and looked, very grown-up for my age, but the truth was that there were many moments when I would have preferred to have been back living with Sheyna, Shamai and their new baby, Judith. I had Morris, of course, about whom I had by now even written to Regina ('He isn't very handsome, but he has a beautiful soul!'), and several other friends – in particular a most extraordinary young man from Chicago called Yossel Kopelov, who chose to be a barber because he was convinced that this was the only profession that would leave him enough time to read and with whom Morris and I spent a lot of time. But friends and family are very different things, and I was sometimes almost as lonely as I was independent, particularly when Morris wasn't around. However, since neither Sheyna nor I were very good at admitting to error or apologizing, it took several months before we finally made up.

Then, after I had been on my own for about a year, I got a letter from my father, the only one he wrote to me during this period. It was very short and to the point: if I valued my mother's life, he wrote, I should come back home at once. I understood that for him to write to me at all meant swallowing his pride and he would only have done so if I were really needed at home. So Morris and I talked it over and I decided that I should go back – to Milwaukee, to my parents and Clara and to high school. To be quite frank, I was not sorry to return, though it meant leaving Morris, who had to stay on in Denver for a while till his sister recovered. One night before I left, Morris told me shyly that he was in love with me and wanted to marry me. I explained happily and just as shyly that I loved him, too, but that I was still much too young for marriage, and we agreed that we would have to wait. In the meantime, we would keep our relationship a secret and write to each other all the time. So I left for Milwaukee in what I told Regina the next day was a 'blissful' state of mind.

3

I choose Palestine

I FOUND OUR HOME quite changed. My parents had mellowed a lot, their economic situation had improved and Clara was already a teen-ager. The family had moved to a new and nicer apartment on Tenth Street, and it bustled with people and activity. My mother and father now took it for granted that I would be going to high school, and even after I graduated from high school and registered in October 1916 at the Milwaukee Normal School (the Teachers' Training College, as it was then called), they made no protest at all. I don't think that they really ever believed I needed any more education, but they let me have my way, and our relationships improved beyond recognition – though my mother and I still fought sometimes. One of those rows was about Morris's letters to me. My mother felt that it was her duty to know all about my romance in Denver (about which someone, per-haps Sheyna, had written to her), and once she even made Clara read a bunch of them and translate them into Yiddish for her (Morris and I wrote to each other in English, which my mother found hard to read). Aware of the fact that she had done something dreadful, Clara told me about it later, swearing that she had left out what she tactfully called 'the more personal bits', and from then on Morris sent his letters to Regina's house.

As their life grew easier, my parents had become much more active in the community. My mother – who I think, was probably never aware of the need to express herself beyond the immediate family circle or the routine of family duties – had nonetheless developed what must have been a natural talent for good works, perhaps through the people she met in the shop and the problems they unfolded before her while she weighed rice and sugar for them. At all events, she was now busier than ever but much more relaxed, despite her habit (which annoyed me tremendously) of claiming that nothing in Milwaukee was as good as Pinsk. 'Take the fruit, for instance.' Who ate fruit in Pinsk? Certainly not my family! Still my mother went on praising the invented delights of 'home', and I eventually learned not to explode each time she did it.

Mother was forever cooking and baking, listening to some stranger's troubles or helping to run a neighbourhood bazaar or raffle. She was a very good cook and taught me how to make plain, nourishing Jewish food, the kind that I prepare and like to this day – though my son and one of my grandsons, who consider themselves to be gourmet cooks and make everything with wine, turn up their noses at my 'un-imaginative' food. (Not that they ever refuse it!) On Friday evenings, when we sat down for the Sabbath meal – chicken soup, *gefilte* fish, and meat braised with potatoes and onions, with a carrot-and-prune *tzimmes* on the side – in addition to Father, Clara and me, there would almost always be guests from out of town whose visits frequently lasted for several weeks.

During the First World War, my mother turned our house into a makeshift depot for the boys who had volunteered for the Jewish Legion and were going to fight under the Jewish flag within the frame-work of the British army to liberate Palestine from the Turks. Most of the young men from Milwaukee who joined the Legion (immigrants exempt from conscription) left our house equipped with little bags embroidered by my mother in which they kept their prayer shawls and phylacteries, and much larger bags full of cookies still warm from her oven. With an open heart, she ran an open house, and when I try to remember her at this period, I hear the sound of her laughter in the kitchen as she fried onions, peeled carrots and chopped fish for Friday night, talking to one of the guests who would be sleeping on our living room couch for the weekend.

My father, too, had become deeply involved with Jewish life in the city. Most of the people who slept on our famous couch during those years were socialists (Labour-Zionists) from the East, Yiddish writers on lecture tours or out-of-town members of the *B'nai B'rith* (the Jewish fraternal order to which my father belonged). My parents, in short, had become completely integrated, and their home had turned into a kind of institution, as far as the Jewish community in Milwaukee and its visitors were concerned. Of the many people whom I first met or first heard speak in public then, some were to become major influences not only on my life but, much more important, on the Zionist movement, particularly on Labour-Zionism. And some of them were later to be numbered among the founding fathers of the Jewish state.

If I pause now to recollect the men who made the strongest impression upon me as they passed through Milwaukee when I was in my late teens, I think first of all of such Jews as Nachman Syrkin, who was one of the most fiery ideologists of Labour-Zionism. A Russian Jew who had studied philosophy and psychology in Berlin, Syrkin returned to Russia after the 1905 Revolution and then emigrated to the United States, where he became the leader of the American *Poalei-Zion* (Labour-Zionists). Syrkin believed that the sole hope of the Jewish proletariat (which he labelled 'the slaves of slaves' or the 'proletariat of the proletariats') lay in mass immigration to Palestine, and he wrote and spoke brilliantly on this subject throughout Europe and the States. My favourite story about Syrkin (whose daughter Marie became my close friend and later my biographer) has to do with a debate that took place between him and Dr Chaim Zhitlovsky, a celebrated protagonist of Yiddish as the Jewish national language who believed primarily in the civil rights aspects of the Jewish problem, while Syrkin was a passionate Zionist and an advocate of the revival of the Hebrew language. In the course of the debate Syrkin said to Zhitlovsky: 'Alright, let's come to an agreement to divide it all up. You take everything that already exists and I'll take everything that doesn't exist yet. For example: *Eretz Yisroel* (the Land of Israel) as a Jewish state does *not* exist, so it's mine; the Diaspora exists, so it's yours. Yiddish exists so it's yours; but since Hebrew isn't spoken yet in everyday life, it'll be mine. Whatever is real and concrete will be yours and whatever you call empty dreams will be mine.'

Shmarya (his full name was Shmaryahu) Levin was another. He was without doubt one of the greatest Zionist orators of the day, a man whose wit and charm captivated thousands of Jews all over the world. Since those days, like Syrkin, he has somehow joined the company of the shadow figures of Zionism, known to most young Israelis, if at all, only because even the smallest town in Israel has a street named after him. But for my generation, he was one of the giants of the movement, and to the extent that my friends and I idolized anyone, it was the elegant, persuasive, deeply intellectual Shmarya. His humour was typically Yiddish, so much so that it is hard to translate any of its subtlety into English. For instance, he used to say sardonically of the

Jews: 'True, we are a very small people but remarkably hard to take.' Or, equally ironically, he described Palestine as a marvellous country where the winters can be spent in Egypt (where it rarely rains) and the summers in the mountains of Lebanon. Once, at a Zionist congress in Switzerland, he came up to me excitedly. 'Golda,' he said, 'I have a splendid moral for a fable. All I need now is the fable itself.' In 1924, Shmarya settled in Palestine and our paths crossed frequently, but my own vivid memory of him still has to do with the sheer dread that once seized me in Chicago in 1929 when I was asked to speak in public, for the first time at a very large meeting, and to my horror spotted Shmarya in one of the very first rows. My God, I thought, how can I open my mouth when Shmarya is sitting there? But I did and afterwards was overwhelmed with pleasure when he told me how well I had spoken.

The first Palestinians I ever encountered were Yitzhak Ben-Zvi, who was to become Israel's second president; Ya'akov Zerubavel, a well-known Labour-Zionist and writer, and David Ben-Gurion. Ben-Zvi and Ben-Gurion came to Milwaukee to recruit soldiers for the Jewish Legion in 1916, soon after they had been expelled from Palestine by the Turks and ordered never to return. Zerubavel, whom the Turks had sentenced to prison, had succeeded in escaping but was sentenced *in absentia* to fifteen years of penal servitude.

I had never met people like those Palestinians before nor heard stories like those they told about the *yishuv* (the small Jewish community of Palestine, which had by then been reduced from some 85,000 to only 56,000). This was my first clue about how terribly it was suffering from the brutality of the Turkish regime, which had already brought normal life in the country to a virtual standstill. They were in a fever of anxiety about the fate of the Jews of Palestine and convinced that an effective Jewish claim could be made to the Land of Israel after the war only if the Jewish people played a significant and visible military role, *as Jews*, in the fighting. In fact, they spoke about the Jewish Legion with such feeling that I immediately tried to volunteer for it – and was crushed when I learned that girls were not being accepted.

I knew much about Palestine by then, of course, but my knowledge was rather theoretical. These Palestinians, however, talked to us not about the vision or theory of Zionism, but about its reality. They told us in detail about the fifty-odd Jewish agricultural settlements that had already been established there and described Gordon's settlement,

Degania, in a way that made it seem real and populated by flesh-and-blood people, not mythical heroes and heroines. They told us also about Tel Aviv, which had just been founded on the sand dunes outside Jaffa, and about *Hashomer*, the *yishuv*'s Jewish self-defence organization, in which Ben-Zvi and Ben-Gurion were both active. But most of all, they talked about their hopes and dreams for an Allied victory over the Turks. They had all worked very closely together in Palestine, and Ben-Zvi often talked about a fourth member of their group, Rachel Yanait, who was later to become his wife. As I listened to him I began to think of her as typical of the women of the *yishuv*, who were proving that it was possible to function as wives, mothers and comrades-in-arms, enduring constant danger and hardship not only without complaining, but with a sense of enormous fulfilment; and it seemed to me that she, and women like her, were doing more to further the cause of our sex – without the benefit of publicity – than even the most militant of suffragettes in the United States or England.

I listened spellbound to the Palestinians, and I took every opportunity to hear them speak, though it was months before I actually dared to approach them myself. Ben-Zvi and Zerubavel were much easier to talk to than Ben-Gurion; they were far less dogmatic and warmer. Ben-Zvi came to Milwaukee – and to my parents' house – several times and would sit around, sing Yiddish folk songs with us and patiently answer all of our questions about Palestine. He was a tall, rather gawky young man with a sweet smile and a kindly hesitant manner that drew people to him at once.

As for Ben-Gurion, my first recollection is actually of *not* meeting him. He was due to visit Milwaukee, and it had been arranged for him to give a speech on Saturday night and to have lunch at our home on Sunday. But that Saturday night the Chicago Philharmonic was in town. Morris (who had come to Milwaukee by then) had invited me to the concert weeks earlier, and I felt duty-bound to go with him, though I can't say that I enjoyed the music much that night. The next morning the Labour-Zionists informed me that the lunch was off. It wasn't proper, they said, that a person who couldn't be bothered to hear Ben-Gurion speak – and of course, I was too embarrassed to explain the extremely personal reason for my absence – should have the privilege of entertaining him for lunch. I was heart-broken but thought that they were perfectly right, and I accepted their verdict stoically. Later, of course, I did meet Ben-Gurion, and I remember remaining in awe of him for a very long time. He was one of the least approachable men

I ever knew, and there was something about him even then that made it hard for one to get to know him. But more about Ben-Gurion later.

Slowly, Zionism was beginning to fill my mind – and my life. I believed absolutely that as a Jew I belonged in Palestine and that as a Labour-Zionist I could do my full share within the *yishuv* to help attain the goals of social and economic equality. The time hadn't quite come yet for me to decide to live there. But I knew that I was not going to be a parlour Zionist – advocating settlement in Palestine for others – and I refused to join the Labour-Zionist Party until I could make a binding decision.

In the meantime, there was school and Morris. While he was still in Denver we corresponded regularly and through those letters – read again after so many years – I see that there were also the small, private tragedies and doubts of every girl's life. Why didn't I have black hair and big lustrous eyes? Why wasn't I more attractive? How *could* Morris love me? *Did* he really love me? I must have peppered my letters to him with ill-concealed requests for assurance and the assurance always came – though it was not always phrased very gallantly. 'I have repeatedly asked you not to contradict me on the question of your beauty,' he wrote once. ' . . . You pop up every now and then with these same timid and self-deprecating remarks which I cannot bear.'

In other letters, we tried rather awkwardly to plan a joint future and inevitably ended up by writing to each other about Palestine. Morris was much less sure then about Zionism than I was, and he had a more romantic, more speculative nature. He dreamt of a world in which everyone would live in peace, and national self-determination held little attraction for him. He didn't really think that a sovereign state would help the Jews much. It would just be one more state with the usual burdens and penalties of statehood. One letter from him dated 1915 reads in part:

I don't know whether to be glad or sorry that you seem to be so enthusiastic a nationalist. I am altogether passive in this matter, though I give you full credit for your activity, as I do to all others engaged in doing something towards helping a distressed nation. The other day, I received a notice to attend one of the meetings . . . but since I do not care particularly as to whether the Jews are going to suffer in Russia or in the Holy Land, I didn't go . . .

By 1915, Jews were suffering in many places, and my father and I started to work together on a variety of relief activities, which were incidentally to bring us closer together. As was true in the Second

World War, most of the relief work for the Jews of Europe during the
First World War was handled by the newly formed Joint Distribution
Committee. But unlike the situation in the 1940s, this remarkable
organization was then being run badly from New York by a handful
of bureaucrats, and it had become the target of much sharp criticism.
One result of this situation was that the Jewish labour groups decided
to found their own organization, which they called the People's Relief
Committee, and that was the organization my father and I joined. We
worked very well together and today it fills me with joy to recall our
cooperation – though I think it came as somewhat of a shock to my
father that I was now on my way to becoming an adult. Father represented his trade union in the new organization, and I was the spokesman of a small Labour-Zionist literary group which I attended after
school. Although I no longer even remember its undoubtedly fancy
name, I was very active on its behalf. We had a lecture programme for
which we invited speakers from Chicago. They would come out to
Milwaukee every two weeks and we would hold what would now be
called seminars on various facets of Yiddish literature. We were chronically short of money to pay the speakers' expenses and rent a hall, so
we used to charge our members 25 cents per lecture – which was quite
a lot in those days. I remember one man who appeared at each lecture
but refused to pay anything. 'I'm not coming for the lecture,' he explained, 'I am coming to ask a question.'

Towards the end of the war, another major Jewish movement was
born: the American Jewish Congress, which was to play a leading role
in the formation of the World Jewish Congress in the 1930s. In those
days, although the *Bund* (which had been transplanted to the United
States) didn't object to the formation of the Congress, it violently
opposed its pro-Palestine orientation. In 1918, when elections to the
Congress were held in all of the large Jewish communities of the United
States (this was the first time that the Jews of America held elections
of their own) feelings ran high. The Zionists pulled one way, the Bundists pulled the other. My father and I were both actively involved in
that election campaign and felt strongly that the Congress must put
itself on record as favouring Zionism.

If you wanted to campaign among Jews, I decided, the logical place
to locate yourself was the neighbourhood synagogue, particularly
around the time of the Jewish High Holidays, when everyone went to
synagogue. But since only men were allowed to address the congregation, I put a box up just outside the synagogue, and people walking

out on their way home had no alternative other than to hear at least part of what I had to say about the Labour-Zionist platform. I suppose I had more than my fair share of self-confidence in this respect, if not in others, and when a great many people actually stopped to listen to me outside the synagogue I thought I ought to try it again in another place. But this time my father learned about my plans and we had a terrible row. Moshe Mabovitch's daughter, he stormed, was not going to stand on a box in the street and make a spectacle of herself. It was out of the question, a '*shandeh*' (a disgrace). I tried to explain that I had committed myself to going, that my friends were waiting for me in the street, that it was a perfectly acceptable thing to do. But my father was so angry that he didn't listen to a word I said. My mother stood between us like a referee at a fight, and we went on arguing at the top of our voices.

In the end, neither of us gave in: my father, red in the face with fury, said that if I insisted on going, he would come after me and publicly pull me home by my braid. I had no doubt that he would do so, because he generally kept his promises. But I went anyway. I warned my friends on the street corner that my father was on the war path, got up on my soap-box and made my speech – not without some panic. When I finally got home, I found my mother waiting up for me in the kitchen. Father was already asleep, she told me, but he had been at the street corner meeting, and had heard me speak. 'I don't know where she gets it from,' he said to her wonderingly. He had been so carried away listening to me perched on my soap-box that he had completely forgotten his threat! Neither of us ever referred to the incident again, but I consider that to have been the most successful speech I ever made.

Around this time, I began to do some real teaching. The Labour-Zionists had started a part-time *folk-schule*, a Yiddish school in the Jewish Centre of Milwaukee. Classes were held on Saturday afternoons, Sunday mornings and one other afternoon during the week. I taught Yiddish: reading, writing and some literature and history. Yiddish, it seemed to me, was one of the strongest links that existed between the Jews, and I loved teaching it. It *wasn't* what the Milwaukee Normal School was preparing me for, but I found it exceedingly satisfying to be able to introduce some of the Jewish children of the city to the great Yiddish writers I so admired. English was certainly a fine language, but Yiddish was the language of the Jewish street, the natural, warm, intimate language that united a scattered nation. In retrospect,

I can see that I was a bit of a prig then about Yiddish; there was no greater crime in my eyes at that stage than, for instance, for one of the children to mix Yiddish with English, and I even thought for a while that the Jews should have two languages in Palestine, Hebrew and Yiddish. How *could* one think of doing away with Yiddish there, of all places? When the Labour-Zionists wanted to start an English-speaking branch and asked me to take it over, I would have nothing to do with it. If people wanted to belong to the *Poalei-Zion*, they should at least know Yiddish! It turned out, of course, that I would have been better off applying myself to Hebrew, but who knew it then? Eventually, when we went to Palestine, I learned Hebrew, of course, but my Hebrew has never really been as good as my Yiddish.

I enjoyed teaching in the *folk-schule*. I liked the children, they liked me, and I felt useful. When the weather was good, on Sunday evenings after the *folk-schule* my family, some of my pupils and Morris (whenever he was in Milwaukee) used to go on picnics. My mother made mounds of food and we sat under a tree in a park and sang. I didn't smoke in those days, and I sang at the drop of a hat. Then my parents would fall asleep on the grass, their faces covered by the weekend edition of one of the Yiddish newspapers published in the East – which they read every weekend from start to finish – and the rest of us would talk about life, liberty and the pursuit of happiness until the sun set. Then we would go home and my mother would give the whole crowd of us supper.

Right after the war, when anti-Semitic pogroms broke out in the Ukraine and Poland (those in the Ukraine being largely the responsibility of the notorious commander of the Ukranian army, Simon Petlyura, whose units did away with whole Jewish communities), I helped to organize a protest march down one of Milwaukee's main streets. The Jewish owner of a big department store in town got wind of my plans and asked me to come and see him. 'I understand that you intend to lead a demonstration down Washington Avenue,' he said. 'If you do so, I want you to know that I shall leave town.' I told him that I had no objection at all to his leaving town and that I had every intention of going on with the plans for the march. However unwise he thought it might be, I wasn't at all worried about what people would think or say. There was nothing for the Jews to be ashamed of; on the contrary, I told him, I was sure that by showing how we felt about the murder and maiming of Jews overseas, we would earn the respect and sympathy of the rest of the city.

It turned out to be an extremely successful parade. Hundreds of people took part in it, though it seemed impossible that there were so many Jews in Milwaukee. Incidentally, it came as a surprise to me (despite my brave words to the store owner) that so many non-Jews participated in that demonstration, and I can remember looking into the eyes of the people who lined the street watching us and feeling how supportive they were. There weren't many protest marches in those days, and we got publicity all over America. Perhaps this is the place to mention that I myself never once encountered any anti-Semitism in Milwaukee. Although I lived in a Jewish district and mingled almost entirely with Jews, both in school and out of it, I had non-Jewish friends, of course – as I was to have all my life. But even though they were never quite as close to me as were the Jews, I felt entirely free and at home with them.

I think that it was while we were marching through town that day that I realized I could no longer postpone a final decision about Palestine. However hard it might be for those who were dearest to me, I could no longer put off making up my mind about where I was going to live. Palestine, I felt, not parades in Milwaukee, was the only real, meaningful answer to Petlyura's murderous mobs. The Jews must have a land of their own again – and I must help to build it, not by making speeches or raising funds, but by living and working there.

First I formally joined the Labour-Zionist (*Poalei-Zion*) Party, and thus took what for me was the first step on the road to Palestine. At that time, the Labour-Zionists didn't have a youth movement. According to the constitution of the party, only people over the age of eighteen were accepted. I was only seventeen, but I was already known to the membership and they let me enter the party ranks. Now I had to persuade Morris to come to Palestine with me, for it was unthinkable to me that we should not be together. I knew that even if he agreed to come we would still have to wait for a year or two – until we raised enough money for the fare, among other things – but it was imperative that before we got married, Morris should know that I was determined to live there. I didn't present the situation to him as an ultimatum, but I did make my position clear. I wanted very much to marry him *and* I was set on going to Palestine. 'I know that you don't feel as strongly about living in Palestine as I do,' I told him, 'but I beg you to come with me.' He loved me very much, Morris answered, but regarding Palestine he wanted to think things over and arrive at a decision himself. Today I understand that Morris, who was far more perceptive and far less impulsive than I, wanted time not only to weigh the matter of moving to Palestine but also perhaps to consider whether we were really suited to each other after all. In one of his letters to me from Denver, just before he came to Milwaukee, he had written: 'Have you ever stopped to think whether your Morris has the one attribute without which all other refinements are worthless, namely "the indomitable will'?" It was one of those questions that lovers ask each other without expecting or wanting an answer and I, for my part, had no doubt at all. But Morris was wiser and he must have sensed that in some ways we were very different and that, one day, those differences between us might be important.

So we parted for a while. I left school (how strange that it had lost its great importance for me) and went to Chicago, where, on the strength of my having worked briefly as a librarian in Milwaukee, I was taken on by the public library. Sheyna, Shamai and their two children had also moved to Chicago, and Shamai was working on a Jewish newspaper there. Regina came to Chicago, too, and I saw all of them quite often, although I stayed with another friend. But I wasn't at all happy. The idea that I might have to choose between Morris and Palestine made me miserable, and for the most part I kept to myself, working for the Labour-Zionists in my free time – making speeches, organizing meetings, raising funds. There was always something that took precedence over my private worries and therefore served to distract me from them – a situation that was not to change much in the course of the next six decades.

Fortunately, though he still had reservations about Palestine, Morris was sufficiently drawn to the idea of living there to agree to go with me. His decision was undoubtedly influenced to some extent by the fact that in November 1917 the British government announced that it favoured 'the establishment in Palestine of a National Home for the Jewish People' and that it would use 'its best endeavours to facilitate the achievement of this objective'. The Balfour Declaration – so named because it was signed by Arthur James Balfour, who was then Britain's foreign secretary – was couched in the form of a letter addressed by Lord Balfour to Lord Rothschild. It came just at the time that British forces, under General Allenby, had begun to conquer Palestine from the Turks, and although in years to come the ambiguous way in which it was worded was to be responsible for virtually endless bloodshed in the Middle East, in those days it was greeted by the Zionists as laying the foundations at last for a Jewish commonwealth in Palestine. It goes without saying that the announcement filled me with elation. The exile of the Jews had ended. Now, the ingathering would really begin, and Morris and I together would be among the millions of Jews who would surely stream to Palestine.

It was against the background of this historic event that we were married, on 24 December 1917, at my parents' home. Our marriage was preceded by a familiarly long and emotional argument with my mother. We wanted a civil ceremony, no guests and no fuss. We were socialists, tolerant of tradition, but in no way bound by ritual. We neither wanted nor needed a religious ceremony. But my mother informed me in no uncertain terms that a civil marriage would kill her, that she would have to leave Milwaukee at once and that I would be shaming the entire family, to say nothing of the Jewish people, if I didn't have a traditional wedding. Besides, would it harm us? So Morris and I gave in; indeed, what damage could fifteen minutes under the *chuppah* (bridal canopy) do to us, or to our principles? We invited a few people, my mother prepared refreshments and Rabbi Schonfeld, one of the true Jewish scholars of Milwaukee, officiated. To her dying day, my mother talked with pride about the fact that Rabbi Schonfeld had come to our house for my wedding, had made a short speech wishing us well and – even though he was known for his strictness in religious matters and as a rule refused to drink, let alone eat, anything outside his own home – had tasted a piece of her cake. I have often thought about how much that day meant to her and how I nearly ruined it for her by wanting to be married at City Hall.

Once again I was starting out on a new life; Pinsk, Milwaukee, Denver had all been stations of a sort. Now, I was nearly twenty, a married woman and on my way to the only place that had any real call on me. But since the war had not ended yet, it was still impossible for us to go. There wasn't any room in my parents' house for us, nor did we particularly want to live with anyone, so we moved to a place of our own for a couple of years. I travelled a lot for the Labour-Zionists during those years and seem to have been away from Milwaukee almost as much as I was there. I suppose that I was in demand because I was young, I could speak both English and Yiddish fluently and I was prepared to travel anywhere and to make speeches without much prior notice.

A few months after our marriage, for instance, the party decided to publish a national newspaper and asked me to help sell shares. My father was furious. 'Who leaves a new husband and goes on the road?' he shouted, outraged at the idea that I had agreed to be away from Milwaukee for more than a day or two. But Morris understood that I couldn't say no to the movement and I went. I was away for several weeks. The arrangement was that I was paid 15 dollars a week and all my expenses, which meant my meals – except for dessert. I paid for ice cream myself. No one in the party stayed in a hotel then. I slept over at the homes of other party members, sometimes even in the same bed with my hostess.

I went as far as Canada and then it turned out that I didn't have a passport. Morris wasn't an American citizen yet, and married women couldn't take out their own citizenship then. My father's passport would have helped, but he was still very angry with me for going and refused to send it to me. So I tried to cross into Canada without a passport. Of course, when we reached Montreal, I was taken off the train, marched to the immigration office and politely but firmly questioned as to what I thought I was doing. Not only did I come from Milwaukee – a socialist town – but I was Russian born! I suppose the Canadian authorities thought for a minute that they had caught a Bolshevik agent, but in the end a prominent Labour-Zionist came to my rescue and I was finally allowed into Canada. I sold a lot of shares for that paper; it was called *Die Zeit* (The Times), and when we moved to New York, I sold it on the streets in the evenings. But for all my efforts, it didn't survive long.

For Morris my frequent absences must have been very difficult, but he was immensely patient and understanding, and I can see now that, in a way, I took advantage of his forbearance. Whenever I was out of town, I wrote long letters to him, but they tended to be more about the meeting I had just addressed or the one I was about to address, the situation in Palestine or the movement than about us or our relationship. Morris consoled himself for my being away so much by turning our tiny apartment into the real home that awaited me whenever I was in Milwaukee. He cut out pictures from magazines and framed them to brighten the walls. And although we had no money and he was often without a job (he worked as a sign-painter whenever he could), there were always a few flowers in the house when I came back. He spent his free time when I was on the road reading, listening to music and helping Clara weather out some of the storms and stresses of adolescence. They went for long walks together, and Morris took her to concerts and the theatre. He was really the only member of the family to spend any time with her, and she adored him and told him all her secrets.

In the winter of 1918, the American Jewish Congress held its first convention in Philadelphia. The main purpose was the formulation of a programme (to be presented at the Peace Conference in Versailles) for the safeguarding of the civil rights of the Jews in Europe. To my astonishment and delight, I was chosen to be one of the delegates from Milwaukee. It was a marvellously stimulating experience for me; I can still remember how proud I was to have been chosen to represent my own community and what it was like sitting with the rest of the delegation in the overheated train on our way to Philadelphia. I was (as always in that period) the youngest in the group and, in a way, everyone pampered me – except when it came to giving me assignments. Today when journalists ask me when my political career actually began, my mind always flashes back to that convention, to the smoke-filled hall in a Philadelphia hotel where I sat for hours listening, completely absorbed, to the details of the programme being thrashed out; to the excitement of the debates and of being able to cast my own vote. 'I tell you that some moments reached such heights that after them one could have died happy,' I scribbled ecstatically to Morris.

From Chicago, Sheyna wrote less ecstatic letters warning me that I was becoming much too involved in matters of public – rather than private – concern. 'As far as personal happiness is concerned, grasp it, Goldie, and hold it tight,' she wrote in one troubled letter. 'The only thing I heartily wish you is that you should not try to be what you *ought* to be but what you are. If everybody would only be what they are, we would have a much finer world . . .' I was quite sure, however, that I could cope with everything and assured Morris that when we got to Palestine at last, I would no longer be constantly on the move.

By the winter of 1920, it began to look as though we might soon really be able to depart. We rented a flat in Morningside Heights in New York and started to prepare for the trip. Regina and a Canadian couple called Manson (who didn't go to Palestine in the end) and Yossel Kopelov joined us in the flat. In the early spring, we bought tickets for the S.S. *Pocahontas* and began to rid ourselves of those of our meagre possessions that seemed unsuitable for the life we were now going to lead as pioneers. Despite everything we had heard and read about Palestine, our ideas of life there were somewhat primitive; we expected to live in tents, so I cheerfully sold all of our furniture, our curtains, the iron, even the fur collar of my old winter coat (because we rather unrealistically believed that there was no need for winter clothes in Palestine). The only thing we agreed to take with us, in fact, was our gramophone and our records. The gramophone was the kind you wound by hand – so it could be played even in a tent – and we would at least have music in the wilderness for which we were headed. For the same reason, I stocked up on blankets, of all things. If we were going to sleep on the ground, better we should be prepared for it.

Then we began a round of farewells. On our way to Milwaukee to say good-bye to my parents and Clara, we stopped off in Chicago to part from Sheyna and Shamai. I felt a little anxious about the visit, since I knew that Sheyna didn't really approve of our going to Palestine ('Goldie, don't you think there is a middle road for idealism, right here on the spot?' she had asked in one of her recent letters). I remember how we sat in their tiny living-room with their children – ten-year-old Judith and three-year-old Chaim – and told them all about the ship, what we were taking with us and so forth. Sheyna listened so attentively to all the details that at one point Shamai said with a smile: 'Maybe *you'd* like to go, too?' To my utter astonishment – and probably hers also – Sheyna suddenly replied: 'Yes, I would.' For a moment, we thought she was joking, but she was absolutely serious. If we were going because we felt that it was necessary for us to go, then by the same token, it was no less necessary for her to go, too. What's more, she said, if Shamai was willing to stay behind in order to earn the money without which she wouldn't be able to keep them in Palestine, she would take the children with her.

In one sense, it cannot be said that Sheyna's abrupt announcement that day was entirely unexpected. She had been a Zionist since she was a young girl, and although she was much more cautious than I in certain respects, she was fundamentally and profoundly committed to the same cause. Of course, I don't really know just what it was that triggered her actual decision, but I would like to make the point that neither Morris nor Sheyna went to Palestine as my escorts. Both of them went because both of them had come to the conclusion that Palestine was where they should be.

I can think of no greater compliment to Sheyna or to the quality of her marriage than Shamai's loving acceptance of that decision. Not that he didn't try hard to get her to change her mind. He pleaded with her to wait until they could all go together and said that she had chosen the worst possible time for her to take the two children, because on 1 May 1921, following a series of attacks on the Jewish settlements in the north of the country, full-scale Arab riots against the Jews had broken out in Palestine. Over forty people, many of them new immigrants, had been murdered and mutilated. Only a year earlier, Jews had been murdered and raped by Arab gangs in the Old City of Jerusalem, and although it was hoped that the British civil administration (which had just taken over from the military) would deal sternly with those responsible for the riots and thus restore calm, violence had just erupted again. Within a few years, Shamai argued, Palestine might be at peace; the Arab nationalists might no longer be able to incite Arab villagers to bloodshed; it might become a reasonably safe country in which to live! But, having made her decision, Sheyna was adamant, and even after we learned that a Jew from Milwaukee had been killed in those riots, she serenely continued to pack.

In Milwaukee, we parted from my parents and Clara. It wasn't an easy parting, although we took it for granted that eventually, when Clara finished her studies at the University of Wisconsin, they would all follow us to Palestine. Still, I felt terribly sorry for my parents – especially for my father – when I kissed them good-bye at the station. My father was a strong man and able to bear pain, but that morning he just stood there, tears rolling down his cheeks. And my mother – perhaps remembering her own voyage across the ocean – looked so small and withdrawn.

The American chapter of my life was closing. I was to return to the United States often, in good times and bad, and even to remain there for many months at a time. But it was never to be my home again. I took a great deal with me from America to Palestine, more perhaps than I can express: an understanding of the meaning of freedom, an awareness of the opportunities offered to the individual in a true democracy and a permanent nostalgia for the great beauty of the American countryside. I loved America and was always glad to come back to it. But never in all the years that followed have I known one moment of homesickness or ever once regretted leaving it for Palestine. Nor, I am sure, did Sheyna. Of course, at the station that morning I thought I would never be back, and I parted from the friends of my youth very sorrowfully, promising to write and keep in touch.

About our voyage to Palestine aboard the wretched S.S. *Pocahontas*, one could write a whole book. It was doomed from the outset; whatever could possibly go wrong did, and the miracle was that we managed to live through it all. Because the vessel was known to be absolutely unseaworthy, the crew went on strike even before we embarked. The next day, 23 May 1921, we got under way – but not for long. The moment we put out to sea, supposedly repaired, the crew mutinied, expressing its resentment of the shipping company by tormenting the poor passengers. Not only did the sailors mix sea water with our drinking water and sprinkle salt on our food, but they managed to damage the engines severely, and the ship listed alarmingly, so that it even had to stop altogether now and then. It took a full week to get from New York to Boston, and then we had to wait for another nine days before we could continue the uneasy journey. In Boston, a delegation of Labour-Zionists came to visit us aboard ship; they brought refreshments, made speeches and cheered us up by referring to us as their heroic comrades. Three of our group (it numbered twenty-two at the start) proved, understandably enough, not to be so heroic; one old couple and a young bride left the ship in Boston. Sheyna received a pathetic cable from Shamai, begging her to disembark too, but of course she refused to budge.

At last we set off again. The voyage across the Atlantic was a nightmare. The mutiny had only subsided somewhat, not ended, and every day there were power cuts, salty water to drink and indescribably bad food. At Porto Delgato in the Azores, the *Pocahontas* was discovered to be in such bad shape that she required another week for repairs. Four crew members went ashore boasting that they would sink the ship before she got to Naples, and when the captain found out about their talk he clapped them into irons. In the meantime, we spent the week trying to relax, which was not easy. I remember touring the pretty port town, enjoying the mild climate and the lovely unfamiliar scenery. One curious aspect of our enforced stopover was that we discovered a tiny Sephardi Jewish community (some thirty people in all) which was extremely observant. The rabbi had died several years earlier and the community – like my grandfather – was so worried about the possibility of violating the Jewish dietary laws that it decided to forgo eating meat permanently. By the time we left the Azores we had been en route for one month already, but we still had to face the horror of the rest of the voyage. During the last lap of our trip – the semi-mutiny still in force – the ship's refrigerator was smashed, so we had to make do with rice and salty tea three times a day; but we were kept from being bored by a succession of incredible dramas. First of all, one of the passengers died, and since the *Pocahontas*'s cooling facilities no longer functioned, the body was simply thrown overboard. Then the captain's brother, who was also on board, went stark raving mad and had to be chained and locked up in his cabin. Finally, in a state of justified depression, just before we reached Naples the captain killed himself, though some people said he was murdered.

The state of affairs aboard the *Pocahontas* had not escaped attention abroad, and a rumour spread among our friends in New York and Boston that we had all gone down with the ship. But in Naples we were able to write home that we were more or less alright. We stayed in Naples for five days, ironing out the inevitable complications over our passports, buying oil lamps and some food and looking for our baggage which had disappeared. Finally, we boarded a train for Brindisi.

There we met up with a group of Labour-Zionists from Lithuania who had actually reached Palestine twice before but had been turned away. Now, they were going to try to enter the country again. We had never met 'real' pioneers of our own age before, and we were very impressed by them. They reminded me of people like Ben-Zvi and Ben-Gurion, though they were much younger. Compared to us they were so experienced and hardy and they seemed so sure of themselves. In Europe they had worked on training farms established by the Zionist movement and they obviously regarded themselves, not without reason, as being infinitely superior to us. They made it quite clear that we were 'soft', spoilt immigrants from the United States, members of the bourgeoisie, in fact, who would probably run away from Palestine after a few weeks. Although we were all bound for the same destination on the same ship, they were going to travel as deck passengers and wanted nothing to do with us. I could hardly take my eyes off them; they were everything I wanted and hoped to be myself – dedicated, austere and determined. I admired and envied them enormously and wanted them to accept us as comrades, but they were very aloof.

In a letter written to Shamai from Brindisi, Yossel described the Lithuanians as they appeared to us. 'Real Hercules,' he wrote, 'who are ready to build a land on just foundations with their backs. And not only a land but a new language ... splendid human material which would be the pride of any people.'

When we boarded the ship that was to take us to Alexandria, I suggested to my companions that we give up our 'luxurious' cabins and join the young Lithuanians on deck. No one was very keen about the idea, particularly since deck passengers were not entitled to any hot meals and by now we were all looking forward to some decent food. But I pressed the point; I argued that, in fact, it was our duty as potential pioneers ourselves to start sharing the life of our fellow-Zionists as soon as possible and that our behaviour, even on board ship, would be indicative of our sincerity and ability to take hardships in our stride. 'Let's organize our own "kitchen" on deck,' I proposed, adding that we could probably make some sort of arrangements so that the children in the group wouldn't have to sleep in the open. Gradually, despite their reluctance, I succeeded in wearing my friends down, and the Lithuanians thawed out a bit. For a few dollars we got the head waiter in the dining-room to agree to let the children eat there – after everyone else was through – and we found them empty cabins for the night (except for Sheyna's daughter; I persuaded the chief steward to let her sleep on a couch in the lounge, but she had to vacate it at 5 a.m.!). On deck, the barriers between the two groups finally collapsed. We told the Lithuanians about life in America, they told us how they had lived in Eastern Europe and as the stars came out we sang Hebrew and Yiddish songs together and danced the *hora*.

But bad luck still dogged us. In Alexandria, Egyptian police boarded the ship looking for a couple called Rapaport – 'miserable Communists' they called them. There were a pair of Rapaports travelling in our group, but, of course, they were the wrong ones. Nonetheless, they were hauled off the ship and questioned for hours. The incident frightened and depressed us all. When the Rapaports finally came back to the ship, we decided to continue by rail, so we said good-bye to our Lithuanian friends and set off for the station to take the train to Kantara. On the way to the station, we got our first taste of the Middle East at its very worst: crowds of beggars – men, women and children wrapped in filthy rags and covered with flies. They made me think of the beggars who had so terrified me in Pinsk, and I knew that if one of them actually touched me I would scream – pioneer or not. Somehow we pushed and shoved our way through them and got to the train. By now we were so resigned to minor disasters that we weren't really surprised to find it unspeakably dirty. The heat was close to unbearable, and there was no water to be had anywhere; but at least we knew that we were nearly at our journey's end. At last, the train moved out of Alexandria and we were on our way again, a bit more travel-stained and a bit tired, but still able to sing, quite rousingly, about our 'Return to Zion'.

In Kantara, covered with dust, we changed trains in the middle of the night. The procedure took hours; the immigration officials, when we finally found them, were in no hurry at all to attend to the necessary formalities and seemed unable to understand why we were all so despondent. I remember standing on that dark platform and losing my temper with one of them, to very little avail. But before dawn, we climbed wearily on to our last train, the one that was to bring us, jolting and jogging, through a blinding sandstorm, across the Sinai Peninsula to Palestine. Sitting there, on a hard, dirt-encrusted bench, with one of Sheyna's children asleep in my arms, I wondered for the first time since we left Milwaukee whether we would ever really reach Tel Aviv.

4

The start of a new life

ALTHOUGH TEL AVIV LOOKED TO ME like a large and not very attractive village on that scorching July morning when I first saw it through the filthy windows of the train from Kantara, it was, in fact, already well on its way to becoming the world's youngest city and the pride of the *yishuv*. I don't know what I had expected it to look like, but I certainly was not at all prepared for what I saw.

Actually all that I (or any of us, for that matter) knew about Tel Aviv at that point was that it had been founded in 1909 by sixty optimistic Jewish families. Some of them had even dared to predict that one day their new garden suburb (built on the outskirts of Arab Jaffa) might achieve a population of 25,000. But none of them dreamt in their wildest dreams that within only fifty years Tel Aviv would be a major metropolis with barely enough housing for its more than 400,000 inhabitants, or that in 1948 it would be the first provisional capital of a Jewish state.

During the war, Tel Aviv's entire population had been expelled by the Turks. But by the time we arrived in Tel Aviv, 15,000 people were living there again, and a real building boom was on. Some parts of the town, as I was to discover later, were really very pretty; row upon row of neat little houses, each with its own garden, was set out on paved streets lined with casuarina and pepper trees, through which caravans of donkeys and camels passed, laden with bags of coarse sand that was taken from the seashore for building. But other sections looked – and were – unplanned, unfinished and frightfully untidy. The May Day riots of 1921 had flooded Tel Aviv with Jewish refugees from Jaffa, and when we came, only a few weeks afterwards, several hundred of these refugees were still living in ramshackle huts and even in tents.

The population of Tel Aviv in 1921 was made up in part of Jews who had come to Palestine (mostly from Lithuania, Poland and Russia) in what was known as the third *Aliyah* (or wave) of Zionist immigration, and in part of 'oldtimers', who had been there from the beginning. Although some of the new immigrants were self-defined 'capitalists' – merchants and tradesmen who set up small factories and shops – the vast majority were labourers. Just a year earlier, a General Federation of Jewish Labour (the *Histadrut*) had been established, and within twelve months it already had a membership of over 4,000.

Although it was only twelve years old, Tel Aviv was rapidly becoming self-governing. It had just been permitted by the British mandatory government to levy its own taxes on buildings and workshops and to run its own water system. Also, though it had no prison – and was not to have one for many years – it had its own twenty-five-man, all-Jewish police force, of which everyone was very proud. The main street (named for Theodor Herzl) was adorned at one end by the Herzlia High School, which was the town's first and most imposing building. There were a few other streets, a small 'business district' and a water tower that served as a gathering place for the young people. Public transportation was either by small buses or horse-drawn carriages, while Tel Aviv's mayor, Meir Dizengoff, periodically rode through town on a splendid white horse.

By 1921 Tel Aviv already had a thriving cultural life; a number of writers were settling there, among them the great Jewish philosopher and writer, Ahad Ha-Am, and the poet Chaim Nachman Bialik. A workers' theatrical group called the *Ohel* (Tent) was already functioning, and so were a few cafés where lively debates on political and cultural problems went on every afternoon and evening. But none of this activity, or any of Tel Aviv's remarkable potential, was at all apparent to us as we pulled into the town's tiny railway station. We could hardly have arrived at a worse time; everything – the air, the sand, the white stucco houses – blazed in the midday sun, and as we stood wilting on the empty platform, we realized with sinking hearts that no one was coming to meet us, although we had carefully written to tell friends of ours in Tel Aviv (who had immigrated to Palestine two years before) when we were due. Later on, we learned that on that very day they had gone to Jerusalem to complete arrangements for *leaving* the country, news that added to our mood of confusion and uncertainty.

Anyhow, there we were – after that terrible journey – in Tel Aviv at last. Our dream had come true. The railway station, the houses we could see in the distance, even the deep sand that surrounded us were all part of the Jewish national home. But as we waited there in the glaring sun, not knowing where to go or even where to turn, it was hard to remember just why we had come. Someone in our group (it may have been Yossel) even put our feeling of anti-climax into words. He turned to me and said, only half-jokingly, 'Well, Goldie, you wanted to come to *Eretz Yisroel*. Here we are. Now we can all go back – it's enough.' I don't remember who said it, but I do remember that I didn't smile.

Suddenly a man came up to us and introduced himself, in Yiddish, as Mr Barash, the owner of a nearby hotel. Perhaps he could help us. He hailed a carriage for us and we gratefully piled our luggage into it. Then, as it led the way, we trudged wearily behind it, wondering how far we could manage to walk in the dreadful heat. Just outside the station, I caught sight of a tree. It wasn't a very large tree, by American standards, but it was the first one I had seen that day, and I thought that it was like a symbol of the young town itself, growing miraculously out of the sand.

In the hotel, we ate, drank and bathed. The rooms were large and light, and Mr and Mrs Barash were very hospitable. We cheered up considerably and decided not to unpack or make any plans until we had rested. Then, to our horror, we discovered that the beds bore traces of bed bugs. Mr Barash denied the accusation very indignantly; maybe there were fleas, he said, but bed bugs? Never! By the time the linen had been changed, Sheyna, Regina and I had lost any desire to sleep, and we spent the remainder of our first day in Tel Aviv assuring each other that problems more serious than bed bugs probably lay ahead of us.

Early the next morning, Sheyna volunteered to go to the market to buy some fruit for the children. In a little while she was back, filled with gloom. Everything was covered with flies, she said; no wrapping paper or paper bags were available; it was all so primitive and the sun was so strong that she could hardly stand it. I don't think I had ever heard Sheyna complain about anything before, and now I began to wonder how she and I would ever get used to our new life. It was all very well to talk in Milwaukee about pioneering, but was it, after all, possible that we weren't up to facing these minor inconveniences and that those Lithuanians on the trip were right when they thought we were too soft for the country? My sense of uneasiness and guilt about my own failings – to say nothing of my nervousness about Morris's reaction to these unfortunate experiences – lasted throughout our first week in Tel Aviv. Perhaps if we had arrived in the autumn, rather than in the middle of the summer, or stayed closer to the sea and its breezes, it would have been easier. But as it was, we were hot, tired and dispirited most of the time.

On top of everything else, our friends came back from Jerusalem and invited us for Saturday dinner. Not only did they go on at great length about all the difficulties we would encounter, but they fed us hamburgers that tasted of soap, and we couldn't make ourselves swallow them. After some embarrassment all around – and telling the children that they must stop choking and crying – it turned out that a piece of soap had fallen into the precious ground meat. But the explanation didn't make the meat more palatable, and we went back to Mr Barash's hotel feeling sick as well as dejected.

After a few days, there seemed no point in staying at Mr Barash's hotel any longer. Like that tree near the station, we had to strike roots sooner or later and, besides, our money was running out. True, we had come from America, but we nonetheless had only very limited funds – though no one seemed to believe this. That summer I met a woman in Tel Aviv who threw her arms around me, kissed me and said with tears in her eyes: 'Thank God you millionaires have come to us from America. *Now* everything will be alright here!'

Our original plan had been to stay in Tel Aviv for a week or two and then to join a kibbutz. In Milwaukee, we had even picked out the kibbutz to which we would apply for membership. But when we made enquiries in Tel Aviv, we were told to wait until the summer was over and then submit formal applications. So instead of starting our conquest of the land at once, we embarked on a far less heroic mission: the conquest of landlords. That wasn't a simple matter either. Housing was very scarce, prices were sky high and we needed room for at least seven beds. We split up into teams and began to house-hunt feverishly. Within a few days, we found a two-room apartment at the end of a still unpaved street in the oldest part of Tel Aviv, Neveh Zedek, a quarter that was actually founded even before Tel Aviv itself. The apartment had no electricity and no bathroom or toilets; these amenities, shared with some forty other people, were located in the yard. But there was a little kitchen and we were only asked to pay three months' rent in advance, despite the fact that we were from the States.

We moved in – without much enthusiasm but with great relief – and began to get organized. We borrowed sheets, pots and pans and some cutlery, and Sheyna undertook to housekeep for all of us, cooking on a primus stove (fuelled by kerosene), which periodically and noisily exploded. Regina got a job as a typist in an office; Yossel went to work in a barber shop: Morris was taken on as a sort of book-keeper in a British public works installation at Lydda and I began to give private English lessons. Actually, I was asked to teach at the high school, but since we were going to join a kibbutz as soon as possible, I thought it would be better not to commit myself to a steady job. Teaching, however, was regarded by most of the people we met in Tel Aviv then as being too intellectual an occupation for a would-be pioneer, and I had to keep explaining that it was only temporary and that I had not come to Palestine in order to spread American culture.

On the whole, we managed pretty well, though it took a long time for our neighbours to accept the strange American way in which we did things, like putting screens on our windows against flies. Everybody else had big mesh screens to protect them against the stray cats that roamed the city, but against flies? What was wrong with flies? Surely they were inevitable in this part of the world? Nonetheless, we persisted in trying to make the apartment livable, and on the whole we succeeded. When our trunks came from Naples, we turned them into sofas and tables. Morris decorated the bare walls for us, and we improvised bed-spreads and curtains. Our most cherished possessions, needless to say, were our record player and records, and slowly people began to drop by in the evenings to drink tea and listen to music with us.

I have often been tempted to explain to new immigrants to Israel just how well I understand the difficulties of adjustment and to tell them something of what it was like when I myself first came to Palestine; but I have learned, through bitter experience, that people tend to regard such stories as propaganda or, even worse, as preaching and generally would much rather not listen to them. Still, the fact remains that we had to make our way alone in the land in which we had chosen to live. There was no State of Israel then, no Ministry of Absorption, no Jewish Agency. No one helped us to settle or to learn Hebrew or to find a place to live. We had to do everything for ourselves, by ourselves, and it never occurred to us that anyone else was morally obligated to assist us. Not that we were in any way superior to the immigrants who come to Israel today, nor am I in the least sentimental about the greater discomforts (many of them quite unnecessary) that we faced sixty years ago and for which we were so woefully unprepared. But I am quite convinced, in retrospect, that having always to bear in mind the purpose for which we had come to Palestine and knowing that nobody had asked us to come or had promised us anything did, in the end, make our acclimatization fairly rapid. We knew that it was up to each one of us personally to make our life in Palestine easier or better or more meaningful and that we had no alternative other than to settle in and settle down as quickly as we possibly could.

At all events, though admittedly that first summer was no treat – to add to everything else, Sheyna's son, Chaim, developed badly infected eyes and Judith came down with an attack of boils that persisted for weeks – as far as I know, none of us ever seriously contemplated leaving the country, and gradually as the weeks went by we began to feel ourselves part of it. Of course, we wrote very cautious letters to our parents and friends, glossing over the more unpleasant aspects of the way we lived. But one letter which I wrote to Shamai after we had been in Palestine for about six weeks expresses something of our feelings about the great adventure:

Those who talk about returning are the recent arrivals. An old worker is full of inspiration and faith. I say that as long as those who created the little that is here are still here, I cannot leave and you must come. I would not say this if I did not know that you are ready to work hard. True, even hard work is hard to find, but I have no doubt you will find something. Of course this is no America, and one may have to suffer a lot economically. There may even be riots again. But if one wants one's own land and if one wants it with one's whole heart, one must be ready for this. When you come I am sure we will be able to plan . . . There is nothing to wait for.

It was, I suppose, natural that I should feel that way; after all, I was in my very early twenties, doing exactly what I wanted to do, physically fit, full of energy and together with the people who meant most to me – my husband, my sister, my best friend. I had no children to worry about and I didn't really care whether we had an ice-box or not, or if the butcher wrapped our meat in pieces of newspaper he picked up off the floor. There were all kinds of compensations for these small hardships, like walking down the street on our first Friday evening in Tel Aviv and feeling that life could hold no greater joy for me than to be where I was – in the only all-Jewish town in the world, where everyone from the bus driver to our landlady shared, in the deepest sense, not only a common past but also common goals for the future. These people hurrying home for the Sabbath, each one carrying a few flowers for the table, were really brothers and sisters of mine, and I knew we would remain bound to each other for all our lives. Although we had come to Palestine from different countries and from different cultures and often spoke different languages, we were alike in our belief that only here could Jews live as of right, rather than on sufferance, and only here could Jews be masters, not victims, of their fate. So it was not surprising that for all the petty irritations and problems, I was profoundly happy.

But when I remember how Sheyna managed to cope with everything and everybody without ever once suggesting that perhaps it was all too much for her – despite the fact that both her small children were sick and Shamai so far away and the postal service so inefficient that she only got letters from him months after they were written; or how determined Morris was to stick it out – despite his hesitations about coming to Palestine at all or the fact, for instance, that the books which meant so much to him arrived in Palestine torn and waterlogged – I am filled again with admiration for them and can only wonder whether in their place I myself would have been as adamant about staying. Of course, like those friends who were supposed to meet us when we first arrived, there were newcomers in Palestine even then who couldn't take it and who left – just as there are some who can't take it today and leave. I have always felt sorry for those people because, to my mind, the loss has always been theirs.

In September, we applied for membership to Kibbutz Merhavia in the Valley of Jezreel, which we call the Emek. We had chosen this particular kibbutz (as so often happens) for a not very important reason; a friend of Morris's and mine who had come to Palestine with the Jewish Legion was already there. We knew very little about Merhavia itself; in fact we knew very little about kibbutzim in general, other than that they were communal farming settlements in which there was no personal property, no hired labour and no private trading, and that the group as such was responsible for all production, all services and the supplying of all individual needs. But we both believed – I with complete faith, Morris less so – that the kibbutz way of life was more likely than any other to offer us a channel for expressing ourselves as Zionists, as Jews and as human beings

Perhaps at this point I should say something briefly about the Emek, because the story of the struggle to develop it is so integral a part of the story of the whole Zionist effort. When the First World War ended and the Mandate over Palestine was awarded by the League of Nations to Great Britain, the new hopes raised by the Balfour Declaration for the establishment of a full-fledged Jewish national home seemed to be on the way towards fulfilment. Years earlier, however, in 1901, the Jewish National Fund had already been formed by the Zionist movement for the exclusive purpose of buying and developing land in Palestine in the name of the entire Jewish people. And a great deal of the Jewish-owned land in Palestine was bought by 'the people' – the bakers, tailors and carpenters of Pinsk, Berlin and Milwaukee. As a matter of fact, ever since I was a little girl I can remember the small blue tin collection box that stood next to the Sabbath candles in our living-room and into which not only we, but our guests, dropped coins every week – and this 'blue box' was likewise a feature in every Jewish home we visited. The truth is, from 1904 on it was with these coins that the Jewish people began to buy extensive tracts of land in Palestine.

Come to think of it, I am more than a little tired of hearing about how the Jews 'stole' land from Arabs in Palestine. The facts are quite different. A lot of good money changed hands, and a lot of Arabs became very rich indeed. Of course, there were other organizations and countless individuals who also bought tracts. But by 1947 the JNF alone – millions of filled 'blue boxes' – owned over half of all the Jewish holdings in the country. So let that libel, at least, be done with.

Around the time that we came to Palestine, a number of such purchases were carried out in the Emek – despite the fact that much of the area consisted of the kind of deadly black swamps that inevitably brought malaria and blackwater fever in their wake. Still, what mattered most was that this pestilential land could be bought, though not cheaply; much of it, incidentally, was sold to the Jewish National Fund by a single well-to-do Arab family that lived in Beirut.

The next step was to make this land arable. In the nature of things, private farmers did not and could not interest themselves in a back-breaking and dangerous project which would obviously take years before it showed any profit. The only people who could possibly undertake the job of draining the Emek swamps were the highly motivated pioneers of the Labour-Zionist movement, who were prepared to reclaim the land, however difficult the circumstances and regardless of the human cost. What's more, they were prepared to do it themselves, rather than have the work done by hired Arab labourers under the supervision of Jewish farm managers. The early settlers of Merhavia were such people, and many of them lived to see the Emek become Israel's most fertile and loveliest valley, dotted by flourishing villages and collective settlements.

Merhavia (its name means God's wide spaces) was one of the first kibbutzim to be founded in the Emek. In 1911 a group of young people from Europe had set up a farm there, but they barely managed to keep it going. When war broke out in 1914, the combination of malaria, the hostility of their Arab neighbours and the attempts of the Turkish authorities to dissuade them from staying finally proved too strong, and the original group pulled up stakes and dispersed. After the war, another group of European pioneers founded a settlement in the same place, joined by British and American veterans of the Jewish Legion (and eventually by Morris and me), but later on it, too, dispersed. A third and final group of Labour-Zionist settlers took over the site in 1929, and this time the group made it – and remained there.

Since we were so anxious to join Merhavia and had applied for membership so quickly, we were very much taken aback when our application was turned down flat, for reasons that seemed to me to be quite inadequate. As a matter of fact, at first no one even wanted to explain to us why we had been rejected; but I insisted on being told the truth and, rather reluctantly, we were informed that there were two basic objections to us. One was that the kibbutz didn't want any married people yet; babies were a luxury that the young settlement couldn't afford. The other reason – and this was really unacceptable to me – was that the group, which was made up at that time of about seven women and thirty men, couldn't imagine that an 'American' girl either could or would do the extremely tough physical work that was required. Since many of the members had come from the States, they regarded themselves, understandably I suppose, as experts on everything American, including the character and capabilities of an 'American' girl like myself. And some of the single girls at Merhavia, who were already 'veterans' in Palestine and who had heard a lot about American girls from these expert males, objected even more strenuously to us. I felt as though I were back with the Lithuanians again, having to prove that even though I had lived in the States, I was still perfectly capable of doing a hard day's work. I argued fiercely that no one had the right to make such assumptions and that it was only fair to give us a chance to show what we could do. One of the specific points against me, I remember, was that in Tel Aviv I had chosen to give English lessons rather than do physical work, a decision that apparently indicated how 'spoilt' I was.

We won the battle. We were invited to come to Merhavia for a few days so that the members could look us over and make their minds up about us on the spot. I was quite sure that, in the end, they would let us stay – which was, in fact, what happened. Our Tel Aviv 'commune' began to disintegrate; Regina left for a new job, and Yossel also moved. Only Sheyna and the children remained in the apartment. I remember happily packing for Merhavia one hot evening in late September and suddenly realizing that in a way Morris and I were walking out on Sheyna, leaving her alone with a flat she couldn't afford to maintain by herself, with Shamai still thousands of miles away and both the children still ill. I asked her if she thought we should stay in Tel Aviv a little longer, but she wouldn't hear of any change in our plans. 'I am going to rent one of the two rooms,' she said crisply, 'and look for work. Don't worry about me.' She would try, she said, to get taken on as a volunteer nurse at the Hadassah Hospital that had just opened in Tel Aviv, and perhaps eventually she would be put on the payroll. As for Shamai, she was sure that he would be able to come to Palestine soon. In the interim, she could manage. Human nature being what it is, I pretended to believe her, though in my heart of hearts I knew that however hard life in Merhavia might be for us, it would be easier than whatever faced Sheyna on her own in Tel Aviv.

Today, Merhavia is a big, bustling settlement with a regional high school to which children come from all over the Emek. Like many other great kibbutzim, it has successfully combined industry with agriculture and now houses a factory for plastic pipes and a printing press. The men and women of modern Merhavia live well, though they still work hard. Their rooms are attractive and comfortable, the collective dining-room is spacious and air conditioned and the kitchen is fully mechanized, all without having to sacrifice or even change radically any of the principles upon which life in kibbutzim was based back in 1921. Today kibbutz members still work an eight-hour day at whatever jobs are assigned to them by the work committee, though nowadays they are usually able to do the work they do best, have been trained to do and enjoy. Everyone still takes turns with chores – serving in the dining-room, working in the kitchen, doing guard duty and so on – and everyone participates in all major decisions affecting the settlement, which are discussed and voted upon at the weekly general meeting. As was true in 1921, the kibbutz children are still brought up together; they eat together, sleep in dormitories and study together – though, of course, their parents' room is still home to them, the place reserved for the family, and in some kibbutzim children even sleep in an adjoining room.

I myself have always believed that the kibbutz is the one place in the world where people are judged, accepted and given a chance to participate fully in the community to which they belong not in accordance with the kind of work they do or how well they do it, but for their intrinsic value as human beings. Not that kibbutz life is never flawed by envy, dishonesty or laziness. Kibbutz members are not angels, but they are the only people, as far as I know, who truly share almost everything – problems, rewards, responsibilities, and satisfactions. And because of the way in which they live, they have certainly been able to contribute to Israel's development far in excess of their numbers. Today there are only some 230 kibbutzim in Israel, but it is impossible (at least for me) to imagine what the country would be like without them. My daughter Sarah has been a member of Kibbutz Revivim in the Negev for the past thirty years, and whenever I visit her and her family there – which in the past was only as often as circumstances permitted and therefore never often enough – I always recall with what mingled hopes and fears her father and I set out for Merhavia so long ago, fully expecting to remain there all our lives – if they would only have us.

For many years I hoped that one day I would be able to return to life on a kibbutz, and one of my great disappointments in myself has been that I never did so. Of course, there were always reasons why this seemed impossible, mostly the accumulating obligations of public life and my involvement with it. But to this day I deeply regret that I failed to find the strength within myself to ignore those pressures and persuasions, and when the time finally came I was too old to make the change. There are a great many things about which I am unsure, but of this I am certain: had I spent my life as a member of a kibbutz – a real member of a kibbutz, not just a weekend visitor – the inner rewards and satisfactions would have been at least as great as those I derived from public office.

The kibbutz to which we came in the autumn of 1921 consisted of a few houses and a cluster of trees left over from the original settlement. There were no orchards, no meadows, no flowers, nothing, in fact, except wind, rocks and some sun-scorched fields. In the spring, the entire Emek would bloom. The mountains that framed the valley, even the black swamps, would be covered with wild flowers, and for a few weeks Merhavia would turn into the most beautiful place I had ever seen. But my first sight of it was before the reviving winter rains fell, and it looked not at all as I had imagined it. The first and most important obstacle to be overcome, however, had nothing to do with scenery. I was determined to prove that I was at least as rugged as any of the other women in the settlement and that I could carry out whatever mission was assigned to me. I can't remember all of the jobs that I was given during that crucial 'trial period', but I know that I picked almonds for days on end in a grove near the kibbutz and that I helped to plant a little forest in the rocks on the road leading to Merhavia. Today it is quite an impressive forest, and whenever I pass it I remember how we dug endless holes in the soil between the rocks and then carefully planted each sapling, wondering whether it would ever grow to maturity there and thinking how lovely the roadside, the whole country in fact, would be if only those trees of ours managed to survive. I will never forget the first days I worked at that job. When I returned to my room in the evening, I couldn't as much as move a finger, but I knew that if I didn't show up for supper everyone would jeer: 'What did we tell you? That's American girls for you!' I would gladly have forgone my supper, for the chickpea mush we ate wasn't worth the effort of lifting the fork to my mouth; but I went. In the end, the trees survived, and so did I. After a few months, Morris and I were accepted as members, and Merhavia became our home.

Life on a kibbutz in the twenties was very far from luxurious. To begin with, there was very little to eat, and what was available tasted dreadful. The staples of our diet were sour cereals, unrefined oil (which we bought from the Arabs in goatskin bags, making it as bitter as death), a few vegetables from the kibbutz's own precious vegetable patch, tinned bully beef that came from British military supplies left over from the war and an incredible dish made up of herring preserved in tomato sauce, which, ironically enough, was known as 'fresh' (I suppose from the misleading 'fresh herring' printed on the label). We ate 'fresh' every morning for breakfast! When my turn came to work in the kitchen, to everyone's astonishment I was delighted. Now I could really do something about the frightful food.

Let me explain that in those days kibbutz women hated kitchen duty not because it was hard (compared to other work on the settlement, it was rather easy) but because they felt it to be demeaning. Their struggle wasn't for equal 'civic' rights, which they had in abundance, but for equal burdens. They wanted to be given whatever work their male comrades were given – paving roads, hoeing fields, building houses, or standing guard duty – not to be treated as though they were different and automatically relegated to the kitchen. All this was at least half a century before anyone invented the unfortunate term 'Women's Lib', but the fact is that kibbutz women were among the world's first and most successful fighters for true equality. But I didn't feel that way about working in the kitchen. I couldn't for the life of me understand what all the fuss was about and said so. 'Why is it so much better,' I asked the girls who were moping (or storming) about kitchen duty, 'to work in the barn and feed the cows, rather than in the kitchen and feed your comrades?' No one ever answered this question convincingly, and I remained more concerned with the quality of our diet than with 'feminine emancipation'.

I began energetically to reorganize the kitchen. First of all, I did away with the dreadful oil. Then I eliminated 'fresh' from the break-fast menu and substituted oatmeal, so that when people came in from work on cold, damp winter mornings they could at least have some-thing hot and nutritious to eat with their compulsory dose of quinine. No one objected to the disappearance of the oil, but there was an im-mediate outcry about the oatmeal. 'It's food for babies,' everyone said. 'One of her American ideas.' But I persisted, and gradually Merhavia became accustomed to the novelty. Next I decided that something had to be done about the way we ate; our enamel tea mugs – which looked so white and clean when they were brand new – became chipped and rusted after just a few weeks, and it depressed me even to look at them. So before my turn came again to work in the kitchen, encouraged by the success of the oatmeal I went off and bought glasses for everyone. They were much prettier and much more pleasant to drink from, though I must confess that almost all of them broke within a week and the whole kibbutz was reduced to drinking in shifts from the two or three glasses that were still intact.

The herring – eliminated for breakfast but now served in the middle of the day – also presented a problem. Not everyone had a knife, fork *and* spoon; mostly each person had one utensil – either a knife, a fork or a spoon. The girls who worked in the kitchen used to wash the herring and cut it into small pieces but they didn't peel off the skin, so that when the herring was brought to the table, everyone had to peel his own. And since there was nothing on which one could wipe one's hands, they were wiped on our work clothes. When I came to work in the kitchen, I decided to peel the herring. The other girls complained. 'You'll see, she'll get them used to that, too.' But I had an answer for this as well. 'What would you have done in your own home? How would you have served herring at your own family table? This is your home! They are your family!'

Saturday mornings we used to make coffee. Because we couldn't ship our milk to Haifa on the Sabbath, our Saturday menu was based on milk. We had coffee, and we made *leben* (cultured milk similar to yogurt) and *lebeniya* (a slightly enriched version of *leben*). The girl in charge of the cookies, who was on the Saturday morning kitchen shift, guarded them as if her life depended on it, because breakfast consisted of coffee and cookies. Friday nights, after supper, some of the young men used to start hunting for the cookies and sometimes managed to lay their hands on them, so that on Saturday mornings there would be a tragedy. When my turn came to work on Saturday morning, I figured as follows: we have no more oil, sugar, or eggs (we started off with a few scrawny chickens that laid a solitary egg now and again), so let's add more water and a little flour and make a lot of cookies, enough for Friday night and Saturday breakfast too. At first this was regarded as being 'counter-revolutionary' but after a while everyone quite liked the idea of cookies twice a week – for the same money.

My most celebrated 'bourgeois' contribution, however – about which settlers all over the Emek talked disparagingly for months – was the 'tablecloth' (made from a sheet) that I spread on the table for Friday night suppers – with a centrepiece of wild flowers, yet! The members of Merhavia sighed, grumbled and warned me that I was giving the kibbutz a bad name, but they let me have my way.

We had much the same arguments about other things – clothes, for instance. The girls all wore the same kind of dresses then, made of a rough material woven by the Arabs into which we cut three holes, one for the head and two for the arms. Then we tied a piece of rope around the waist, and that was that. On Friday evenings, it was customary for the kibbutzniks to change: the men put on clean shirts and the girls wore skirts and blouses instead of work dresses or bloomers. But I couldn't see the logic of once-a-week neatness. I didn't care what I wore every day, but it *had* to be ironed. Every night, using a heavy iron heated by coal, I religiously pressed my 'sack', knowing that the kibbutzniks not only thought I was mad, but also suspected me of not being a true pioneer at heart. There was similar disapproval about the flower designs that Morris painted on the walls of our room so that it would look nicer, to say nothing of the fuss about the crates he painted and turned into cupboards for us. It took quite a while, in fact, for the kibbutz to accept our strange 'American' ways and us. It is more than probable that the one most important factor in this acceptance was our famous record player. I had left it behind in Tel Aviv for Sheyna, but after a few months I felt that the kibbutz needed it more than she did and I ruthlessly hauled it off to the Emek, where it drew almost as many people to the kibbutz as it had done in Tel Aviv. I even wonder sometimes whether it might not have been a relief for Merhavia to accept the dowry without the bride!

That winter I was assigned to work in the kibbutz poultry yard and was sent to an agricultural school for a few weeks to study the finer points of poultry breeding. Years later, when I told my parents about this period of my life, they were very amused at my having become such an expert on poultry, since until we came to Merhavia I was known in the family for my marked lack of affection for any animals, including birds. I can't say that I ever grew really fond of the inhabitants of the poultry yard, but I did become very involved with them, and I was very proud when poultrymen throughout the Emek came to see Merhavia's chicken coops in order to learn how we succeeded in running them so efficiently. For a while, I talked poultry, poultry breeding and poultry feeding morning, noon and night, and when a jackal once raided the coops, I dreamt of the hen-house slaughter for weeks afterwards. There was also one significant by-product of the energy and time I invested in the poultry yard. Although God knows we could never afford to be lavish with them, eventually eggs and even chickens and geese appeared on the dining-room table. Sometimes when Sheyna came to visit us with Judith and Chaim, we made a Merhavia 'speciality': fried onions and bits of our own hard-boiled eggs washed down with tepid tea. It doesn't sound so good nowadays, but we thought it was marvellous then.

The months passed very quickly. We were always short of working hands and sometimes it seemed as if all the people who weren't down with malaria had dysentery or were sick with *papatache*, a very unpleasant local form of sandfly fever. All winter the kibbutz swam in a sea of mud, through which we waded for meals, to the outhouse and to work. The summers were no easier; they were very long and terribly hot. From spring to autumn, we were tormented by clouds of gnats, sandflies and mosquitoes. By 4 a.m. we were usually at work, since one had to come in from the fields by the time the merciless sun was up. Our only defences against the insects were vaseline (when it was available) – which we smeared on the exposed parts of our bodies and on to which the gnats and flies resolutely stuck – and the high collars, long skirts, sleeves and kerchiefs – which we wore miserably throughout the summer, despite the great heat. Once or twice, I fell ill myself, and to this day I remember how grateful I was when one of the boys brought me a lump of ice and a tiny lemon from a nearby village so I could make myself lemonade. Perhaps if we had been able to boil a cup of hot tea when it was cold or make a cold drink when we were exhausted by the summer heat, it wouldn't have been so physically gruelling. But kibbutz discipline included not taking anything unless it was shared by everyone.

I understood and approved of the underlying reason for this seemingly exaggerated attitude, but Morris, for whom kibbutz life was holding less and less charm as time passed, thought it was absurd for the group to be so rigid and for a difficult life to be made more difficult for doctrinaire reasons. He suffered greatly from the lack of privacy and from what he felt to be the intellectual limitations of our way of life. No one in Merhavia at that time was interested in talking about the kind of things that mattered to Morris – books and music and paintings. Not that the kibbutzniks were uneducated. Far from it. But their priorities were different. They were as concerned with whether the kibbutz could afford to buy a 'giant' 500-egg incubator or with thrashing out the ideological implications of something that someone had said at last Tuesday's general meeting as they were with books, music or painting. Nonetheless Morris felt that the people in Merhavia had one-track minds – and even that track was too narrow. Also, he said, they were much too earnest about everything and seemed to think that a sense of humour was somehow out of place.

He was not entirely wrong, of course. Now I can see that if the kibbutzim of that time had had the means and the ideological flexibility, for instance, to accept two things which today are commonplace – private showers and toilets and private tea-making facilities in members' rooms – thousands of people like Morris who later left the kibbutzim might have stayed. But these were the kind of things which no kibbutz could possibly afford in the 1920s – and I wasn't especially bothered by their absence.

I enjoyed being with people who were my kind of people, who shared my political and social views, who debated everything so thoroughly and with such intensity and who took social problems so seriously. I enjoyed everything about the kibbutz – whether it was working in the chicken coops, learning the mysteries of kneading dough for bread in the little shack we used as a bakery or sharing a midnight snack with the boys coming back from guard duty and staying on in the kitchen for hours to hear their stories. After a very short time, I felt completely at home, as though I had never lived anywhere else, and it was just those aspects of communal life which Morris regarded as impossible barriers to happiness that pleased me most. Of course, there were people in Merhavia to whom I found it difficult to adjust, particularly some of the 'veteran' women who regarded themselves as entitled to lay down the law as to how one should or should not behave on the kibbutz. But in the main, I felt absolutely fulfilled.

Naturally there were penalties to be paid for the hard work out of doors all year round and in all kinds of weather, and for the primitive conditions in which we lived. The wind and sun battered and burnt my skin, and in those days there were no beauty parlours or cosmeticians on kibbutzim, as there are now, so kibbutz women aged much more rapidly than women in the towns. But they weren't any the less feminine, despite their wrinkles. I remember a friend from Merhavia, a girl from New York who had come to the kibbutz about half a year before we did, telling me that she once went to say good-bye to a young poet who had served in Palestine with the Jewish Legion but was going back to the States. When she held her work-worn hand out to shake his, he said: 'In America, it was a pleasure to hold your hand. Now, it is an honour.' She was very impressed with this gallantry, but I thought it was nonsense. Men enjoyed holding women's hands on the kibbutz then – and still do – just as much as anywhere else. In those days – and now too – kibbutz romances and marriages were like romances and marriages everywhere, some better, some worse. Of course, young people then were much more discreet about their love lives and talked about them less openly than they do now; but that was because people were universally more puritanical in 1921, not because people didn't fall in love in Merhavia or Degania.

For all the hardship, though, I was very happy in those years. I liked the kibbutz and the kibbutz liked me and showed it. To begin with, I was elected to the settlement's 'steering committee' – the committee that was responsible for setting overall policy – which was a great honour for a relative newcomer. Then I was elected to be Merhavia's delegate to a convention of the kibbutz movement that took place in 1922, and this was really an accolade. Even now, writing about it, I have a sense of pride in the fact that the kibbutz trusted me enough to let me represent it at such an important gathering and even gave me special permission to make my remarks in Yiddish, since my Hebrew was still so halting.

The convention was held in Degania, 'mother of the kibbutzim', the settlement which Gordon had helped to build and where, within that year, he would be buried. The sessions I attended dealt mostly with issues that directly concerned the future of the kibbutz as such. To an outsider, I suppose, it might have seemed strange – even unrealistic, considering the times – for a group of intelligent adults to be spending several days in such intense discussion of the optimum size a kibbutz should attain, or how often during the day mothers should visit their infants in the communal baby house, or how applicants for membership could best be screened. After all, there were only a handful of kibbutzim in Palestine then, and their total membership was only a few hundred. The country had just suffered serious anti-Jewish riots, and in any case, the status of its by now 83,000-odd Jews (they made up about 11 per cent of the population in 1922) was very unclear. One might well have asked what was the point of those long, detailed debates that went on and on, far into the night, all that week. I can see us now, sitting around a smoky kerosene lamp, our entire beings concentrated on some still theoretical aspect of kibbutz life, trying to solve knotty problems – many of which had not even arisen yet.

On the other hand, in the final analysis, what is realistic and what is not realistic depends very much on who makes the definition. The fact is that none of the people at that meeting – who worked all day in what now would be considered intolerable conditions and divided the nights between standing guard duty and constructing complicated ideological arguments – had any doubt at all that they were laying the foundations for an ideal society in the very dawn of a great experiment in Jewish history. And, of course, they were right.

At Degania that week, I met many of the major personalities of the *yishuv*'s Labour movement – not only Ben-Gurion and Ben-Zvi, whom I had already met in Milwaukee, but also other remarkable people who were later to become close friends and colleagues of mine; men like Avraham Hartzfeld, Yitzhak Tabenkin, Levi Eshkol, Berl Katznelson, Zalman Rubashov (Shazar) and David Remez, to name just a few. I was to be intimately associated with all of them in the stormy years that lay ahead, but then, in Degania, I just listened to their speeches and drank in their words, hardly daring to talk to any of them. I came back to Merhavia stimulated, inspired and barely able to wait to tell Morris about everything that had been said and done.

I also started to see some of the country in those years. When Mrs Philip Snowden – married to one of the foremost leaders in the British

Labour Party and a prominent political figure in her own right – visited Palestine, she needed an English-speaking guide to accompany her, and the Labour movement called me to Tel Aviv and asked me to volunteer. 'I should waste my time travelling around the country with someone?' I asked furiously. But in the end party discipline won out, and I agreed, though not meekly. Afterwards I was glad I had gone. I saw a Bedouin encampment for the first time on that trip, and Mrs Snowden and I, sitting on the floor, consumed an immense meal of lamb, rice and *pitta* (flat bread), for which our Arab hosts thoughtfully provided us with spoons because I looked so aghast at the idea of eating with my hands, as everyone else was doing. Mrs Snowden must also have enjoyed herself because I was often to be asked to show VIPs around – though I never got used to doing it during work hours!

But life has a way of becoming complicated just when it seems to be at its smoothest. Morris was not only ill at ease in Merhavia, he was now actually physically ill. The climate, recurrent bouts of malaria, the food, the back-breaking work in the fields were all too hard for him. Although he was making an enormous effort for my sake, it was becoming increasingly clear now that one day we would have to leave the kibbutz, at least until he recovered his strength. That day came much sooner than I expected. We had been at Merhavia for about two and a half years then and Morris had been sick for several weeks in a row. One afternoon the doctor informed me gravely that it was absolutely out of the question for us to remain there any longer unless I wanted Morris to be chronically ill. We should leave Merhavia as soon as we could.

I have often wondered in the many years that have passed whether Morris would have made a better adjustment to the kibbutz, physically and emotionally, had I been more attentive, spent more time with him and generally been less involved with the group as a whole. But it had never occurred to me that by sitting up in the kitchen until all hours making snacks for the boys when they came off guard duty, or taking that poultry course, or spending so much time talking to and singing with other people I was depriving Morris of anything. If I had ever thought deeply enough about our marriage or worried enough about it, I would have realized, of course, that Morris was struggling all alone to get used to a way of life that was really immensely hard for him.

There was also one important and specific on-going disagreement between us. I wanted very much to have a baby, but Morris was tremendously opposed to the collective child-rearing methods of the kibbutz. Just as he wanted his wife for himself, so he wanted us to bring up our own children as he and I saw fit, not to subject each and every detail of their lives to the scrutiny and approval (or disapproval) of a committee and eventually of the entire kibbutz. And he refused to have children at all unless we left Merhavia. He might have changed his mind about this in time, but his health was so poor that we obviously had to leave in any case.

So we packed up again – for the third time in three years – and made our farewells. It was a great wrench for me to leave the kibbutz, but I consoled myself tearfully by hoping that we would both be back soon, that Morris would regain his health quickly, that we would have a baby and that the relationship between us – which had so deteriorated in Merhavia – would improve. If all this happened, I told myself, then leaving the kibbutz for a while was a very small price to pay. Unfortunately, it didn't work out that way.

For a few weeks, we stayed in Tel Aviv. Shamai had arrived in Palestine by then, and the family had moved to a new house (with a bathroom). Sheyna was earning a fairly good salary and Shamai eventually joined a not very successful shoe-manufacturing cooperative as its 'business manager'. Still, they had a home and were making enough money to live on. All in all, their situation was enviable compared to ours. Somehow or other, we couldn't find a place for ourselves in Tel Aviv. I got a job as a cashier in the *Histadrut*'s Public Works and Building Office (later to be renamed *Solel Boneh*), which had recently been established, and Morris tried to regain his health. But we couldn't settle down properly. I missed the kibbutz even more than I thought I would, and Morris was being bombarded by letters from his mother and sisters imploring him to return to the States and offering to pay for his fare. I knew he wouldn't leave me or the country, but we were both very restless and depressed.

Compared with 'God's wide spaces' in the Emek, Tel Aviv seemed unbearably small, noisy and crowded. It took Morris a long time to get back on his feet and to shake off the after-effects of months of sickness, and I felt lost and directionless away from Merhavia and as though we were now doomed to being transients forever. I missed the warmth of the friendships I had made on the kibbutz and the sense of accomplishment that my work there had given me. I couldn't help wondering whether my usual drive and optimism had gone for good, and if so what would happen to us. Also, though neither of us ever said anything aloud, I think we probably blamed each other for the situation we were

in now. After all, it was because of me that Morris had gone to Merhavia in the first place, and now it was because of Morris's 'failure'
there that I had to tear myself away from it. Maybe if we had reproached
each other openly, it would have been much better for us, but we
didn't. Instead, we both felt very much at loose ends and were irritable
most of the time.

Under the circumstances it was natural that when I bumped one day
into David Remez, whom I had met at Degania, and he asked me if
Morris and I would be willing to work in the Jerusalem office of
Solel Boneh, we both jumped at the opportunity to leave Tel Aviv.
Perhaps, we thought, in the crisp mountain air of Jerusalem we would
come alive again and everything would be alright. It seemed like a
spectacularly good omen to me when, on the very eve of our departure
from Tel Aviv, I learned that I was pregnant.

That autumn, in Jerusalem, on 23 November, our son, Menachem,
was born. He was a lovely, healthy baby, and Morris and I were overcome by being parents. We spent hours looking at the baby we had
produced and talking about his future. But I still had not gotten over
my hankering for Merhavia, and when Menachem was six months old
I returned to the kibbutz with him for a while. I thought that if I went
back, I could find myself again, but of course things are never so
simple. I couldn't settle down there without Morris, and by now I had
no illusions; it was clear that he neither could nor would ever go back
to Merhavia. A binding decision one way or the other had to be made,
and it was up to me to make it. To put it very bluntly, I had to decide
which came first: my duty to my husband, my home and my child or
the kind of life I myself really wanted. Not for the first time – and
certainly not for the last – I realized that in a conflict between my duty
and my innermost desires, it was my duty that had the prior claim.
There was really no alternative other than to stop pining for a way of
life that couldn't be mine, so I returned to Jerusalem – not without some
forebodings, but determined to make a fresh start. After all, I was a
very lucky woman indeed. I was married to a man I loved. True, he
was not a man who was cut out for communal life or manual work, but
I wanted to remain his wife and to make him happy, if only I possibly
could. And I thought that if I tried very hard I would succeed – particularly now that we shared a son.

5   Pioneers and problems

ALL OF THESE HOPES and good intentions notwithstanding, instead of the placid domestic life that I now told myself I was ready to accept, the four years that we lived in Jerusalem were the most miserable I ever experienced – and when you have lived as long as I have, that's saying a lot! Almost everything went wrong; sometimes I even felt that I was reliving the worst part of my mother's life, and I used to remember – with a heart like a stone – the stories she told us about the years when she and Father were so terribly poor in Russia. It wasn't that money, as such, really mattered to me then, or has ever mattered since, or that physical comfort was particularly important. To begin with, I had never had much of either, and anyhow we had not come to Palestine to improve our material circumstances. Both Morris and I had known poverty before only too well, and we were both used to a very modest standard of living, to say the least. We were also committed to a way of life that was based on wanting and having very little. Enough to eat, a clean place to sleep, a new book or record now and again were all that either of us hoped for, in material terms. The so-called better things of life not only were beyond our reach but, for the most part, unknown to us, and if times had been a little easier, we would have managed perfectly well on Morris's small salary.

But times were not easier and there were basic needs that had to be filled: our own needs and, above all, those of our children. They had to be decently fed and housed somehow. Freedom from the fear that you may not be able to give even these essentials to your children, however hard you try, is, I believe, the fundamental human right of all parents. I knew this in theory long before I experienced such anxiety myself, but having once experienced it, I never forgot it. One of the great built-in strengths of kibbutz life, of course, is that no one ever has to cope with this kind of anxiety alone. Even if a kibbutz is still very young or has had a poor year and the adults have to tighten their belts, kibbutz children always have enough to eat. I thought often and unhappily about Merhavia during that difficult time in Jerusalem, and twenty years later, in the early stages of the Second World War, remembering how I had felt then, I once suggested publicly that the entire *yishuv* turn itself into a kind of kibbutz for the duration of the emergency by establishing a network of cooperative kitchens, so that among other things, whatever else happened, the children would at least be guaranteed sufficient food. The suggestion was turned down, or anyhow never taken up, though I still think it made a lot of sense.

But it wasn't only our actual poverty – or even my constant fear that my children would be hungry – that made me so wretched. There was also my loneliness, the sense of isolation to which I was so unaccustomed and the constant feeling that I was being deprived of just those things for which I had come to Palestine in the first place. Instead of actively helping to build the Jewish national home and working hard and productively for it, I found myself cooped-up in a tiny flat in Jerusalem, all my thoughts and energy concentrated on making do with Morris's wages. To make things worse, his salary was more often than not paid by *Solel Boneh* in credit slips that no one – neither the landlord, milkman nor Menachem's nursery-school teacher – wanted to accept in lieu of cash.

On 'pay day' I used to dash to the little grocery store on the corner to try and talk the grocer into taking a chit worth one pound (100 piastres) for 80 piastres, which I knew was all he would give me for it. But even those 80 piastres were given not, God forbid, in cash but in a handful of more credit slips. With these I would then run to the woman who sold chickens, argue with her for twenty minutes or so and finally, on a good day, persuade her to take my slips (after she had deducted 10 or 15 per cent of their value) in exchange for a small piece of chicken with which I could make soup for the children.

Sometimes Shamai came up to Jerusalem for a day or two with some cheese or a box of fruit and vegetables that Sheyna sent with him. We would have a real 'banquet', and I would feel less tense about the family diet for a while. But most of the time I was eaten up with worry.

Until Sarah was born, in the spring of 1926, we made a little extra money by renting out one of our two rooms, though they lacked gas and electricity. But when Sarah arrived, we decided that we would have to forgo the rent, regardless of how difficult it would be to manage without it, so that the children might have a small room of their own. The only way we could possibly make up the difference would be for me to get some sort of work that I could do without leaving the baby alone. So I suggested to Menachem's nursery-school teacher that I do the laundry for the entire nursery-school in exchange for the school fees. So, standing in the yard for hours, I grimly scrubbed piles of little towels, aprons and bibs, heating pail after pail of water on the primus stove and wondering what I would do if the wash board broke.

It wasn't the work I minded. In Merhavia I had worked much harder – and liked it. But in Merhavia I had been part of a group, a member of a dynamic society whose success mattered to me more than almost anything else in the world. In Jerusalem I was a sort of prisoner, sentenced – as are millions of women by circumstances beyond their control – to battling over bills that I couldn't pay, trying to keep shoes from falling apart because it was impossible to buy another pair, worrying whenever a child coughed or ran a fever that our inadequate diet and inability to keep the flat warm in winter might be permanently damaging their health.

Of course, some days were better than others. When the sun shone and the sky was blue (and in Jerusalem the summer sky is bluer, I think, than anywhere else), I sat on the steps watching the children play and counted my blessings. But when it was windy and cold, and the children weren't well (particularly Sarah, who seemed to be sick much of the time), I was filled if not with despair then with a bitter resentment against my lot in life. Was this what it was all about – poverty, drudgery and worry? The worst of it was that I couldn't even tell Morris how I felt. He desperately needed rest, proper food and peace of mind, but none of these were available, and I couldn't see how anything would change in the immediate future.

Solel Boneh was doing very badly, too, and we were terrified that it might close down altogether. It was one thing to set out enthusiastically to create an unofficial Public Works Department and undertake to train and employ Jewish workers in the building trades, but an altogether different thing to acquire the necessary capital and the experience needed for building roads and houses. The only way *Solel Boneh* could pay anyone in those days was in promissory notes for 100 or 200 pounds, which were covered by larger promissory notes that *Solel Boneh* received as payment for work completed. One of the many stories people used to tell then about building in Palestine had to do with the Jew who said that if he only had a good feather pillow to start off with, he could build himself a house. How? Very simple, he said:

Look, you can sell a good pillow for a pound. With this pound you can pay the membership fee of a loan society, which will entitle you to borrow up to ten pounds. With ten pounds in hand you can begin looking around for a nice little plot of land. Once you've found a plot, you can approach the owner with your ten pounds *in cash*, and naturally he will agree to take the rest in promissory notes. Now you are a land owner and you can look for a contractor. To him you say: 'I have the land – now you build a house on it. All I want is a flat for myself and the family.'

But there was nothing funny about the way I felt. Sometimes Regina, who was working in the office of the Zionist Executive in Jerusalem then, came to see me and while I glumly cleaned house she listened to all my grievances and tried to cheer me up. Of course, when I wrote to my parents I painted a very different picture of our life, and I even tried to keep Sheyna from knowing how bad it really was – though I don't think I fooled her at all.

Strangely enough, when I look back to that time, I realize that I wasn't really aware of any but my most immediate surroundings, even though Jerusalem was the seat of the mandatory government then, the place from which the British High Commissioners – Sir Herbert Samuel, who was replaced in 1925 by Lord Plumer – governed the country. As it has always been throughout history, Jerusalem was a fascinating city. In part it was then, as it still is, a mosaic of shrines and holy places; in part it was the headquarters of a colonial administration. But above all it was the living symbol of the continuity of Jewish history and the tie that bound, and binds, the Jewish people to this land. Its population was unlike that of any other place in Palestine. Even our neighbourhood was exotic, located on the 'frontier' of Mea Shearim, the section of Jerusalem that is inhabited till today by ultra-orthodox Jews whose bearing, dress and religious practices have been carried over, almost intact, from sixteenth-century Eastern Europe and who thought that Jews like Morris and myself were only a step away from being pagan. But somehow the city's landmarks and landscapes, the colourful procession of people of all faiths and races who walked Jerusalem's streets even on the most ordinary days, didn't make much of an impression on me. I was too tired, too dispirited and too concerned with myself and my family to look about me as I should have.

One evening, however, I went to the Western Wall – not for the first time. Morris and I had gone there a week or two after our arrival in Palestine. I had grown up in a Jewish home, a good traditional Jewish home, but I wasn't at all pious myself, and the truth is that I went to the Wall without much emotion, just as something that I knew I ought to do. Then, all of a sudden, at the end of those narrow, winding alleys in the Old City, I saw it. The Wall itself looked much smaller than it does today, after all the excavations. But for the first time I saw the Jews, men and women, praying and weeping before it and putting *kvitlach* – their scribbled petitions to the Almighty – into its crannies. So this was what was left of a past glory, I thought, all that has remained of Solomon's Temple. But at least it was still there. And in those orthodox Jews with their *kvitlach*, I saw a nation's refusal to accept that only these stones were left to it and an expression of confidence in what was to come in the future. I left the Wall changed in feeling – uplifted is perhaps the word.

In 1971, some fifty years later, I was awarded the Freedom of Jerusalem – probably the greatest tribute ever paid me – and at that ceremony I told of yet another memorable visit I had made to the Wall, this time in 1967, after the Six Day War. For nineteen years, from 1948 to 1967, we were banned by the Arabs from going to the Old City or praying at the Wall. But on the third day of the Six Day War – Wednesday, 7 June – all Israel was electrified by the news that our soldiers had liberated the Old City and that it was open to us again. I had to fly to the United States three days later, but I couldn't bring myself to leave Israel without going to the Wall again. So that Friday morning – although civilians were not yet allowed to enter the Old City because shooting was still going on there – I received permission to go to the Wall, despite the fact that I wasn't in the government then but just an ordinary citizen, like any other.

I went to the Wall together with some soldiers. There in front of it stood a plain wooden table with some sub-machine guns on it. Uniformed paratroopers wrapped in prayer shawls clung so tightly to the Wall that it seemed impossible to separate them from it. They and the Wall were one. Only a few hours earlier they had fought furiously for the liberation of Jerusalem and had seen their comrades fall for its sake. Now, standing before the Wall, they wrapped themselves in prayer shawls and wept, and I, too, took a sheet of paper, wrote the

word 'shalom' on it and pushed it into a cranny of the Wall, as I had
seen the Jews do so long ago. As I stood there, one of the soldiers (I
doubt that he knew who I was) suddenly put his arms around me, laid
his head on my shoulder and we cried together. I suppose he needed
the release and the comfort of an old woman's warmth, and for me it
was one of the most moving moments of my life. But all that, of course,
belongs to a much later era.

The late 1920s were depressing years throughout Jewish Palestine,
not just for me. By 1927 7,000 men and women were without work in
the *yishuv* – a sobering 5 per cent of Palestine's total Jewish population.
It was almost as though Zionism, in its great zeal, had over-reached
itself. Many more immigrants were entering the country than the
yishuv could possibly employ. Of the 13,000 Jews who arrived in
Palestine in 1926, for instance, more than half left, and in 1927, for the
first time, emigration was ominously higher than immigration. Some
of the emigrants went to the United States, others to various parts of
the British Empire. There was also a group that included members of
the 'Labour Battalion' (which had been founded in 1920 to employ
immigrants in cooperative road-building and quarrying projects
financed by the mandatory government) – who returned to Russia for
ideological reasons, where many of them subsequently were sent to
Siberia or executed – also for 'ideological' reasons.

There were various reasons for the severe crisis. The *yishuv*'s economy
was still almost totally undeveloped. Other than in the building trades
(which employed almost half of all the Jewish workers in Palestine) and
the orange groves, there simply weren't enough job opportunities or
capital to go around. You could count the Jewish industrial enterprises
on the fingers of one hand. There were the Dead Sea Works, a salt
factory and quarries at Athlit, the Palestine Electric Corporation
(which had built a power station on the banks of the Jordan River), the
Shemen soap and edible oils factory, and the Nesher cement factory in
Haifa. There were also a few other smaller enterprises including printing plants and wine cellars, but that was all.

There was also another very serious problem. The wages of Jewish
workers were very low then but Arab labourers were willing to work
for even less, and many Jewish orange growers yielded to the temptation
of hiring the cheaper Arab labour. As for the mandatory government,
other than the network of roads it constructed, it did virtually nothing
to develop the economy of the country and had already begun to give
way to the anti-Jewish pressure of Arab extremists, such as the mufti of

Jerusalem, Haj Amin el-Husseini, and others. Although only a few years had passed since the Mandate over Palestine was granted to Britain, the government was already displaying considerable hostility to the Jews. Even worse, it had moved to curb the rate of Jewish immigration into Palestine, and in 1930 threatened to stop it altogether for a while. In short, the Jewish national home was not flourishing.

I hardly went to Tel Aviv during the years I lived in Jerusalem, and when I did go it was usually only to see Sheyna and her family or to visit my parents, who had come to Palestine in 1926. But in between the family visits, I did my best to see old friends, catch up on what was happening in the Labour movement, hear some gossip from or about Merhavia and feel myself again – if only for a few hours – part of what was going on in the country. My father, now that I come to think of it, was in a way typical of the immigrants of 1926 and 1927, even though he had come from the States and not from Europe. In Milwaukee he had managed to save up a little money, with which he proudly bought two plots of land in Palestine – partly because as a Zionist he wanted to live there, partly because he wanted to re-unite the family. Both of his plots were in places that were little more than sand. One was in Herzlia, a few miles north of Tel Aviv. The other was in Afula (not far from Merhavia), where he intended to build a house. When I asked him why he wanted to live in Afula, of all places, which was near neither to Sheyna nor to me, he told me that Afula was to be the site of Palestine's first opera house and that he would be living in a great centre of music. I knew Afula very well and had gone there often on errands when we lived in the kibbutz. It was a dusty little village, and I was pretty sure that an opera house wouldn't be built there – at least not in the foreseeable future. But my father was adamant. For a long time he refused to listen to any argument and accused Sheyna and me of having little faith. 'Tel Aviv was built on sand dunes, wasn't it?' he said reproachfully. In the end, my mother joined forces with us and, with a sigh, my father gave up the idea of living in the Emek and agreed to make his home in Herzlia – without arias.

He built that home largely with his own hands, as befitted a good carpenter. It was one of the first real houses in the area, and my parents settled down there as quickly as they had once settled in Milwaukee. My father joined the local synagogue, discovered that it had no cantor and promptly volunteered for the position himself. He also joined a carpenter's cooperative, but since work was scarce that didn't help much. But my enterprising mother had an idea. She would cook and serve mid-day meals and he would help her. There were very few restaurants anywhere in Palestine and none at all in Herzlia, so my mother's idea was very successful. For a few piastres, she provided the labourers in the vicinity with cheap, nourishing food.

But even so, for all of their determination to make a life for themselves in Palestine – though by now they were both well past their prime – my parents suffered greatly from the economic situation. I remember, for example, that once I took the children to Herzlia a week before Passover so I could help my mother prepare for the holiday. Morris was to join us on the eve of the holiday, and Sheyna and her family were also coming. But we were all so poor that there wasn't anything to prepare. My father walked around looking as though someone had beaten him over the head. Imagine, here he was in Palestine with almost his entire family (Clara was still in college then at Wisconsin University but planned to come to Palestine as soon as she got her degree) and there wasn't even a package of *matzah* or a bottle of wine in the house, let alone food for the *seder*. I couldn't bear to see him look so miserable, and I even thought that he might be driven to do something desperate. He was so humiliated, though poverty had never crushed him before.

Then a wonderful thing happened. I was bitten by a dog! For someone else it would have been terrible, but for me it was a miracle. I had to go to Tel Aviv for anti-rabies injections, and while I was there I could scour the town for someone who would lend me money. I managed to find a bank that was willing to lend me 10 pounds (which was a lot of money in those days) provided I had guarantors. So I ran around town again, but no one I found was good enough for the bank, and whenever the bank suggested a name to me, it was someone who wasn't about to run any risks. At last I found a man who had the necessary capital, a fine reputation and a good Jewish heart, and I came back to Herzlia with 10 whole pounds in my pocket for my father – and a warmer feeling for dogs than I had ever had in my life.

On those rare visits to Tel Aviv, I was always depressed and shocked by the sight of unemployed men on the street corners and the desolate look of half-finished buildings all over town. It was as though a huge burst of energy had worn itself out. Of course, outsiders might have seen it all differently. Despite the economic crisis, thousands of Jews were living in Palestine, raising their children there, developing their own leadership, creating agricultural and urban settlements and doing all this aided – in the final analysis – only by a Zionist movement abroad, which was in itself a remarkable achievement. Seen as historians would one day see it, even that bleak period would take on a brighter hue. But I wasn't an outsider or a historian, and I longed to take an active part in helping to improve the situation, to do something about it myself.

My great good fortune was that the *Histadrut*, the General Federation of Jewish Labour, that organization in which and for which I was to work for so many years, was interested in the services of someone like myself. I had already worked in Tel Aviv for *Solel Boneh* and had gone on working for it – though only briefly – in Jerusalem, and I knew many of the people in the Labour movement. They were the kind of men and women I most admired and liked. I wanted to learn from them and work with them, and I felt completely at home with them. They saw the basic aims of the *Histadrut* as I did – not so much the protection of the immediate bread-and-butter interests of the workers as the creation of a labour community committed to the future of the Jews of Palestine, those who were already there and those who were still to come.

In many ways, the *Histadrut* was entirely unique. It could model itself on no other existing labour organization because the position of the Jewish worker in Palestine then was totally unlike that of the worker in Britain, France, or America. As elsewhere, the economic rights of the Jewish worker, as well as the Arab worker, in Palestine had to be guarded, including the right to strike, the right to a decent wage, the right to paid annual holidays, to sick leave, and so forth. But even though its official title was the General Federation of Jewish Labour, it would be an over-simplification to describe the *Histadrut* only as a trade union, because it was much more than that, in concept as well as practice. First of all, the *Histadrut* based itself on the unity of *all* the workers in the *yishuv* – whether they were wage earners, members of kibbutzim, blue- or white-collar workers, manual labourers or intellectuals – and from the start it was in the forefront of the struggle to bring Jews to Palestine, even though the burden of increased immigration inevitably fell on its own shoulders.

Secondly, Palestine didn't have a 'ready-made' economy that could absorb the steady flow of Jewish immigrants into the country. There was the smattering of small industry, of course, and the agricultural settlements. But these enterprises couldn't sustain a country with a growing population; and we who had come to Palestine to build the Jewish national home knew that we had to create what today is so casually referred to as a 'national economy'! If you stop to think about what this involves – industry, transport, construction, finance, not to speak of tools for dealing with welfare, unemployment, and so forth – the job ahead of us was actually the creation of something almost out of nothing. Even at the time of which I .write, when the workers of Palestine were still few in number and very isolated, through the *Histadrut* they unhesitatingly undertook the responsibility of being the vanguard of a state-in-the-making, though certainly no one imposed this mission upon them.

Because it was so highly motivated from the very beginning by the Zionist ideal, the *Histadrut* regarded each and every facet of life in the Jewish national home as being of equal importance. There were (and there still are) two standards by which all *Histadrut* projects were judged: did they answer an urgent national need and were they acceptable (or necessary) from the socialist point of view.?

One good example is the *Histadrut*'s determination to develop its own economic enterprises, control of which would be vested ·in the labour community *as a whole*. As early as 1924, a legal body called *Hevrat Ha-Ovdim* (its clumsy English name was the General Cooperative Association of Jewish Labour in Palestine), representing each and every member of the *Histadrut*, became the 'owner' of all the *Histadrut*'s 'assets', of which there were not very many then. *Solel Boneh* was one of these 'assets', and when it over-expanded and collapsed in 1927 nobody outside the Labour movement imagined that it could ever be re-established. But the *Histadrut* knew that there was, and would always be, a great need for a building and public works company that could serve the national requirement in a way that no private company ever could or would. So, eventually, *Solel Boneh* was reborn. Today – having undergone various processes of reorganization, including its 1958 reconstruction on the basis of three companies (a building company, an overseas and harbour works company and an industrial holding company with its subsidiaries), it is one of the largest and most successful firms in the entire Middle East. When I recall the gloom and tension that existed in *Solel Boneh*'s dingy little office in Jerusalem in 1927, when there wasn't enough cash to pay the book-keeper even once a month, and then think of the 50,000 men and women employed last year by these three components of the original *Solel Boneh*, with their combined turnover of about $2\frac{1}{2}$ billion Israeli pounds, I defy anyone to argue that Zionism is not utterly incompatible with pessimism – or that socialism is, of necessity, inefficient unless combined with ruthlessness.

To those critics of the Jewish Labour movement who said fifty years ago that the *Histadrut*'s concept of its role was romantic, grandiose and doomed to failure, let me point out that *Solel Boneh* not only weathered five remarkably difficult decades but lived to play a most decisive role in the building of thousands of homes, roads, schools and hospitals in Israel as well as to pioneer in extensive Israeli projects carried out in Africa, parts of Asia and the Middle East itself. But *Solel Boneh* was only one of the *Histadrut*'s creations. There are dozens of others – agricultural, industrial, educational, cultural, and even medical – and all of them are rooted in the enduring conviction that the real strength of the workers in Israel expresses itself in the priority given to the upbuilding of what is now the Jewish state.

At all events, I was delighted (and very flattered) when one rainy day, as I stood talking to someone outside the *Histadrut* offices in Tel Aviv, David Remez (who had suggested four years earlier that Morris and I work for *Solel Boneh* in Jerusalem) asked me if I was interested in returning to work and whether I would like to become the secretary of the *Moetzet Hapoalot* (the Women's Labour Council) of the *Histadrut*. On the way back to Jerusalem, I made up my mind. It wasn't an easy decision to take. I knew that if I took the job, it would involve considerable travelling both in Palestine and abroad and that we would have to find a place to live in Tel Aviv – which was difficult. But, hardest and most serious of all, I had to face up to the fact that going back to work would spell the end to my attempts to devote myself entirely to the family. Although I wasn't yet prepared to concede total defeat, even to myself, I had already realized in the course of those four years in Jerusalem that my marriage was a failure. Taking on a full-time job, under the circumstances, meant reconciling myself to this, and the thought frightened me. On the other hand, I told myself that perhaps if I were happier and more fulfilled, it would be better for everyone – for Morris, for the children and for me. Perhaps I would be able to cope with everything: save what was left of my marriage from going further downhill, be a good mother to Sarah and Menachem and even have the kind of purposeful, interesting life for which I so yearned.

It didn't work out quite that way, of course. Nothing ever works out exactly as one expects it to. But I can't honestly say that I have ever regretted that decision or that in retrospect I think I was wrong to have made it. What I do regret – and bitterly so – is that although Morris and I remained married to each other and loving each other until the day he died in my house in 1951 (when, symbolically enough, I was away), I was not able to make a success of our marriage after all. That decision I took in 1928 actually marked the start of our separation, though it didn't become final for almost ten years.

The tragedy was not that Morris didn't understand me but, on the contrary, that he understood me only too well and felt that he couldn't make me over or change me. I had to be what I was – and what I was made it impossible for him to have the sort of wife he wanted and needed. So he didn't discourage me from going back to work, though he knew what it really meant.

He remained part of my life always, and, of course, of the children's. The bond between Sarah, Menachem and Morris never weakened. They adored him and saw him very often. He had a great deal to give them, just as he had given a great deal to me, and he was a wonderful father to them even after we began to live apart. He read to them, bought them books and talked to them for hours about music, always with the tenderness and warmth that characterized him. He had always been quiet and reserved. To the outside world he may have appeared ineffectual or unsuccessful, but the truth is that his inner life was very rich – richer than mine, for all of my activity and drive – and he shared it generously with his close friends, his family and, particularly, his children.

So in 1928 I left Jerusalem with Sarah and Menachem and returned to Tel Aviv; Morris came home to us only for weekends. The children went to a school – one of several that were run by the Labour movement – and I went back to work.

The Women's Labour Council and its sister-organization abroad, the Pioneer Women, were the first and last women's organizations for which I ever worked. I was attracted to them not so much because they concerned women, as such, but because I was very interested in the work they were doing, particularly in the agricultural training farms they set up for immigrant girls. Today the Labour Council (which is part of the *Histadrut*) is occupied mainly with social services and with labour legislation for women (maternity benefits, retirement, etc.), but in the 1930s its emphasis was almost entirely on vocational training for the hundreds of young girls who came to Palestine to work on the land but who had no farming background at all or any trade. The council's training farms gave those girls a lot more than just vocational know-how. They helped to speed up the girls' integration into the country, to teach them Hebrew and to give them a sense of stability in a new land, to which most of them came without families and some even without the consent of their parents. These 'working women's farms' were set up at a time when the idea that women should be trained for anything, let alone agriculture, was still considered absurd by most people.

I am not a great admirer of the kind of feminism that gives rise to bra-burning, hatred of men or a campaign against motherhood, but I had very great regard for those energetic hard-working women within the ranks of the Labour movement – Ada Maimon, Beba Idelson, Rachel Yanait-Ben-Zvi, to name just a few – who succeeded in equipping dozens of city-bred girls with the sort of theoretical knowledge and sound practical training that made it possible for them to do their share (and often much more than their share) of the work going on in agricultural settlements throughout Palestine. That to me is constructive feminism and matters much more than who sweeps the house or who sets the table.

About the position of women generally, of course, there is very much to say (and much, perhaps too much, has already been said), but I can put my own thoughts on the subject into a nutshell. Naturally women should be treated as the equals of men in all respects. But, as is true also of the Jewish people, they shouldn't have to be better than everyone else in order to live like human beings or feel that they must accomplish wonders all the time to be accepted at all. On the other hand, a story – which, as far as I know, is all it was – once went the rounds of Israel to the effect that Ben-Gurion described me as 'the only man' in his cabinet. What amused me about it was that obviously he (or whoever invented the story) thought that this was the greatest possible compliment that could be paid to a woman. I very much doubt that any man would have been flattered if I had said about him that he was the only woman in the government!

The fact is that I have lived and worked with men all my life, but being a woman has never hindered me in any way at all. It has never caused me unease or given me an inferiority complex or made me think that men are better off than women – or that it is a disaster to give birth to children. Not at all. Nor have men ever given me preferential treatment. But what is true, I think, is that women who want and need a life outside as well as inside the home have a much, much harder time than men because they carry such a heavy double burden (with the notable exception of women who live in kibbutzim, where life is organized to enable them to work and raise children at the same time).

And the life of a working mother who lives without the constant presence and support of the father of her children is three times harder than that of any man I have ever met.

To some extent my own life in Tel Aviv after we moved from Jerusalem is itself an illustration of those dilemmas and difficulties. I was always rushing from one place to another – to work, home, to a meeting, to take Menáchem to a music lesson, to keep a doctor's appointment with Sarah, to shop, to cook, to work and back home again. And still, to this day, I am not sure that I didn't harm the children or neglect them, despite the efforts I made not to be away from them even an hour more than was strictly necessary. They grew up to be healthy, productive, talented and good people, and they are both wonderful parents to their own children and wonderful companions to me. But when they were growing up, I know that they deeply resented my activities outside of our home.

I stayed up at night to cook for them. I mended their clothes. I went to concerts and films with them. We always talked and laughed a lot together. But were Sheyna and my mother right when they charged me for years with depriving the children of their due? I suppose that I shall never be able to answer this question to my own satisfaction – and that I will never stop asking it. Were they proud of me, then or later? I like to think so, of course, but I am not really sure that being proud of one's mother makes up for her frequent absences. I remember that once when I was the chairwoman of a public meeting and asked 'all those in favour' of whatever the issue was to raise their hands, to my utter astonishment I saw Sarah and Menachem (who had stolen into the hall to fetch me) loyally raise their hands to indicate their approval. It was the most reassuring vote of confidence I ever got, but it didn't keep me from feeling that being able to vote for your mother is not nearly as good or as important as having her at home when you get back from school.

And, of course, later on I was abroad often. When I travelled, my guilt was overwhelming. I wrote to them all the time, even made records for them, which seemed more intimate, and I never came back without presents. But I was also never free of the feeling that I was injuring them in some way. Years later I put some of these feelings into an article written anonymously for a collection of memoirs (it was called *The Ploughwoman*) by some of the women who were active in the *yishuv* in those days. A few paragraphs from that article written in 1930 may possibly be of interest to many women even today, because the problems that so preoccupied me then are not affected very much by today's washing machines, dishwashers or driers – though they all would certainly have been a great help to me:

Taken as a whole, the inner struggles and despairs of a mother who goes to work have few parallels. But within that whole there are many shades and variations. There are mothers who work only when they are forced to, when the husband is sick or unemployed or when the family has, in some other way, gone off the track of a normal life. In such cases the mother feels her course of action justified by necessity – her children would not be fed otherwise. But there is a type of woman who cannot remain home for other reasons. In spite of the place which her children and her family take up in her life, her nature and being demand something more; she cannot divorce herself from a larger social life. She cannot let her children narrow her horizon. And for such a woman, there is no rest.

Theoretically it looks straightforward enough. The woman who takes her place with the children is devoted, loves the children, is reliable and suited to the work; the children are fully looked after. But there are even pedagogic theorists who claim that it is actually better for the children not to have their mother hovering over them constantly; and a mother who is occupied outside the house of course has the great advantage of being able to develop . . . she can bring more to her children than if she were to remain at home . . . Is it not often true that a woman who has given up all the external world for her husband and her children has done it not out of a sense of duty, out of devotion and love, but out of incapacity, because her soul is not able to take into itself the many-sidedness of life, with its sufferings but also with its joys. And if a woman does remain with her children and gives herself to nothing else, does that really prove that she is more devoted than the other kind of mother? And if a wife has no intimate friends, does that prove that she has a greater love for her husband?

But the working mother also suffers in the very work she has taken up. Always she has the feeling that her work is not as productive as that of a man or even of an unmarried woman. The children, too, always demand her, in health and even more in sickness. And this eternal inner division, this double pull, this alternating feeling of unfulfilled duty – today toward her family, the next day toward her work – this is the burden of the working mother.

It wasn't a very elegantly written article and read today it seems a bit stiff to me, but I wrote it then in real anguish.

Apart from everything else, for several years Sarah wasn't at all well. We had been told that the trouble was with her kidneys, and there was hardly a month without an anxious visit to the doctor. She was a pretty, gay, very alert little girl and very good about the strict diet she had to keep, the medicines she had to swallow and having to be in bed for weeks at a time. On the days when she had to stay in bed, leaving her with someone else was not simple, and when she was up and around she had to be watched all the time. Sheyna and my mother were of great assistance, but I always felt I had to apologize to them for going to work in the morning and not coming back till the afternoon.

Not long ago I came across one of the letters I wrote to Sheyna around this time. I had been sent to the States for several weeks on a mission to the Pioneer Women. It was the first time I had been back in the States in seven years, and on my way I attended the Socialist International, which was then taking place in Brussels. Brussels overwhelmed me. I had completely forgotten what the world was like outside Palestine, and I could hardly believe the trees, the trams, the flower and fruit stalls, the cool, grey weather. It was all so unlike Tel Aviv. I was entranced by everything. Since I was the most junior member of our delegation (which included Ben-Gurion and Ben-Zvi), I had time to sightsee and to listen for hours to the speeches of famous socialists whom I had, of course, never seen before – men like Arthur Henderson, the British Labour Party leader, who was the president of the Socialist International; or Léon Blum, who became France's first socialist and first Jewish premier. Henderson had just agreed to organize a League for Labour Palestine, for which he came under bitter attack from the Jewish non-Zionist socialists – of all people – and as far as we were concerned, the atmosphere was very charged. Nonetheless despite everything that was happening around me, I took an hour off one day to try – aided by distance – to win Sheyna over and to convince her that I was not just a selfish and bad mother.

'I ask only one thing,' I wrote to her from Brussels, 'that I be understood and believed. My social activities are not accidental; they are an absolute necessity for me ... Before I left, the doctor assured me that Sarah's health permits my going, and I have made adequate arrangements for Menachem ... But in our present situation I could not refuse to do what was asked of me. Believe me, I know it will not bring the Messiah, but I think we must miss no opportunity to explain to influential people what we want and what we are ...' But though Sheyna herself was to go back to America shortly to study to become a dietitian, leaving her two older children in Palestine, she continued to accuse me of turning, as she put it, 'into a public person, not a homebody'. And my mother went on chastising me, too. I suppose that what really upset them so much was that I was away from home so often and that the children had to eat their midday meal without me in the

rather spartan but good communal dining-room that was part of the
workers' housing estate in which we lived on Hayarkon Street, facing
the sea in the north of Tel Aviv.

Actually we all managed quite well. I always let one of our three
rooms so that the children were never alone (for years I slept – and
very well – on a couch in what was our combined dining–living-room)
and whenever I had to go abroad I got someone to come in and take
care of them. But, of course, they saw less of me than they should have,
and I was constantly pressed for time and preoccupied by the conflict-
ing demands made on me by home and work.

Today the head offices of the *Histadrut* occupy an immense building
on one of Tel Aviv's main streets and are like a great beehive that hums
with the sound of hundreds of voices, typewriters and telephones, but
in those days things were very different. We had just a few rooms, a
couple of typists, only one telephone, and everybody knew everybody
else. We were, in the most literal sense of the word, *chaverim* (comrades),
and although we argued among ourselves all the time about details
and techniques, we shared the same basic outlook on life and the same
values. Most of the relationships I made then have lasted – in one way
or another – till today (although, of course, over the past few years I
have had to attend a great many funerals of colleagues who were young
when I and the *Histadrut* were also young).

Of that group, three or four were to become well known outside the
yishuv. About Ben-Gurion, who became – and with good reason – the
very personification of Israel throughout the world and who will almost
certainly be remembered as one of the truly great Jews of the twentieth
century, I shall write later. Of all of us, he was the only one of whom
it could be said that he was literally indispensable to the Jewish people
in its struggle for independence. But I hardly knew him at this point.
Among the people I was getting to know well were Shneur Zalman
Shazar, who was to become third president of the State of Israel;
Levi Eshkol, who became its third prime minister; David Remez and
Berl Katznelson; and Yosef Shprinzak, who was to become the first
speaker of the Knesset.

I met Shazar (whose name before he hebraized it was Rubashov)
for the first time just after we left Merhavia and returned to Tel Aviv.
It was on 1 May, the workers' holiday, and Morris and I went to a
rally sponsored by the *Histadrut* in the yard of the Herzlia High School.
I have never particularly enjoyed listening to long speeches – even if
they are about the Labour movement – and my mind was wandering

a bit when a young man got up to speak. I can see him now, a vigorous young man in a *rubashka* (the Russian type of blouse that workers wore in Palestine then), a sash fixed around his waist and khaki trousers. He spoke with such fervour and enthusiasm and in such marvellous Hebrew that I immediately asked who he was. 'That is Rubashov,' I was told rather reproachfully, as though I should have known. 'A poet and a writer. A *most* important man.' When I came to know him, I was also very impressed by him, and we eventually became extremely close friends.

Unlike some of us who were lent stature by the great challenge of Zionism and who might never have amounted to much under other circumstances and in other situations, Shazar had remarkable personal gifts. He was a true scholar, steeped in Jewish learning – as was only proper for a son of the famous Hassidic family of the Lubavitchers (his first names are those of the first Lubavitcher rabbi) – and a most talented journalist, essayist and editor. He died in 1974 at the age of eighty-five, about a year after he left the presidency of the state. When he was already a very old man, the young people in Israel tended to smile (though I think rather affectionately) at his emotion-charged, long and flowery speeches, which had changed very little in style since the 1920s.

But Shazar always had something relevant to say, even if it took him some time to say it. As president of the state he unfailingly stressed the essential unity of what he called 'the family of Israel', by which he meant all of the Jews in the country, those of European (his own) origin and those thousands upon thousands who came from Arabic-speaking countries and to whom Hassidism and Yiddish culture meant nothing at all. For many years Shazar edited *Davar*, the daily newspaper of the Labour movement, and I remember someone saying to me once: 'Zalman finds it much more enjoyable to correct mistakes in what others write than to write himself. He should really have been a teacher.'

He never did teach, but he did become Israel's first minister of education in 1948, a job that he undertook with enormous zest. I always liked the story of his first day at the ministry because I think it makes clear what a warm, unpretentious and dedicated man he was. When he arrived at the ministry he discovered that one room and one male secretary had been set aside for him, but no typewriter. This didn't bother Shazar much. He hung up his hat, sat down and said to his new secretary briskly: 'Please take a note. No typewriter? It doesn't matter. Take it in longhand. Ready? All Israeli children between the ages of

four and eighteen are to receive free education of the highest quality.'
When the secretary commented that this might have to wait a few
days before it could be carried out, since the state was only one day
old, Shazar said fiercely: 'When it comes to education, I want no
arguments. This is my first order as the minister responsible for it.' He
did, in fact, promulgate Israel's Education Act very soon afterwards.

When Shazar was president and I was prime minister, I used to see
him as often as I could. He hated the relative isolation of the presidency and I was always calling him up or visiting him to keep him from
involving himself in some explosive political situation, especially those
concerning the Labour movement. 'Don't forget you are the president
now, Zalman,' I used to say. 'You mustn't interfere.' Most of the time
Shazar would shake his head unhappily at my advice but take it
nonetheless.

Levi Eshkol (his original name was Shkolnik) was another of the
promising young men with whom I became friendly in the 1920s. He
was quite different from Shazar, though he also came from a Hassidic
family in Russia. But he was much more a man of action and much less
a man of words. He had come to Palestine when he was only nineteen
and after working as an agricultural labourer in various parts of the
country he joined the Jewish Legion together with Ben-Gurion and
Ben-Zvi (for years, he boasted that he had been made a lance corporal
before Ben-Gurion). When the war ended, he became a member of
Degania, from which he was coopted by the *Histadrut*, though his ties
with the kibbutz remained strong all his life. Eshkol was typical of the
practical idealists of that era: his great interests were land, water and
defence, though not necessarily in that order, and he was happiest
dealing with such down-to-earth and crucial problems. Politics in the
abstract didn't particularly attract him, and he hated bureaucratic
procedures; but give him a specific challenge and he met it with an
extraordinary combination of doggedness, ingenuity and shrewdness.
If you wanted a Jewish national home, you had to settle Jews on the
land – never mind how much the land cost or what obstacles the mandatory government put in the way of the Jewish institutions that wanted
to buy it. 'Not enough room to swing a cat in Palestine,' said the British
Colonial Office in 1929, by way of trying to excuse its inexcusable
policy of limiting Jewish immigration and land purchase. So Eshkol
spent the next thirty years looking for places in which new settlements
could indeed be established, and, as head of the Jewish Agency's
Land Settlement Department, he supervised the founding of nearly 400

new Jewish villages. You couldn't have settlements without irrigation
or irrigate without water, so Eshkol proceeded to organize an intensive
search for water. It was a very expensive search, so he also looked for
money, as well, and managed to find both – though not, needless to
say, in quantities that would last for ever. If you had land and water
and the misfortune of having extremely hostile neighbours, you also had
to acquire arms and train an army, and the story of Eshkol's contribution to Israel's armed strength from 1921 (when he joined the *Histadrut*'s first defence committee) all the way through his period as prime
minister and minister of defence which began in 1963 is a story in its
own right. As Israel's prime minister during the Six Day War, he was
much (and most unfairly) abused for what his critics called his hesi-
tancy – though surely a leader who is not hesitant about sending young
men into battle is a national disaster – and all kinds of malicious jokes
were circulated about his supposed inability to make up his mind. The
great drama and pain of Eshkol's last years, however (he died of a
heart attack – a polite name, I think, for a broken heart – in 1969),
was his rift with Ben-Gurion, whose absolutely loyal follower he had
been for decades and at whose request he reluctantly took over as
prime minister in 1963. That bitter conflict involved the entire Labour
movement and almost tore Israel apart, but it belongs to a much later
period, so I postpone writing about it for the moment.

Eshkol was not, to use the fashionable word, 'charismatic'. He had
no 'glamour', but he was an unusually creative person, a man who got
things done when they really needed doing, however hard the job was,
and a man to whom people and their feelings mattered a great deal.
From the start, I liked and trusted him, though who would have
dreamed when we worked together in Tel Aviv then that he would
eventually be a prime minister or that I would follow him in that office.
In the 1950s, when Eshkol was Israel's minister of finance and I was
minister of labour, we had a great many clashes – though they were
never in any way personal. Those were the years when the young
state was flooded with hundreds of thousands of poverty-stricken,
undernourished, homeless Jews from the DP camps of Europe and the
ghettos of the Arabic-speaking states and the only way that we could
house this torrent of people was by setting up camps of our own for
them.

One day Eshkol burst into my office. 'We've got to get them out of
these camps,' he shouted. 'We've got to spread them all over the
country. I don't know how we'll do it or what we'll use for money or

what they'll do for a living, but we've got to get them out of the camps.'
I told him that it was impossible to do now, out of the question, it
would take time, but he was adamant – and he was quite right. Looking back, I don't think Israel would have survived those first chaotic
years after 1948 if Eshkol hadn't insisted on taking close to 700,000
immigrants out of the reception centres at once and distributing them
throughout the country in the tent cities which covered the state like
toadstools within a few weeks – but which, in the end, made it possible
for them to be absorbed.

As minister of labour, it was my job to find these people work and
get them out of those miserable tents and I was forever plaguing
Eshkol for money to finance special projects and housing. But he had
other priorities and one slogan. 'Look,' he used to say to me, 'you can't
milk a house. But you can milk a cow. Right now if you want money
you can have it – but only for cows!' Once I got so angry that I went
to Ben-Gurion and told him I was resigning. I had undertaken to be
minister of labour and development (which included housing), not
minister of unemployment and tents! In the end, of course, I didn't
resign, and Eshkol found some more money from somewhere or other
for housing.

Another dear friend made in those first years after I went back to
work was David Remez, whom I have already mentioned. He had
Eshkol's warmth and sense of humour and, like Eshkol, he was drawn
to the solving of the practical problems of Zionism, in particular to
Solel Boneh and later to *Histadrut* projects that concerned transportation – roads, shipping and even attempts to encourage local aviation.
Remez belonged to the tail end of what we call the Second *Aliyah* (the
35,000 odd Jews who made their way to Palestine from about 1909
until the outbreak of the First World War), and to some extent he was
typical of that generation of pioneers. In his youth he wrote poetry,
read and talked about socialism, acquired a life-long interest in Hebrew
and studied law (for a while he attended the University of Constanti-
nople, where he met Ben-Gurion, Ben-Zvi and the young Moshe
Sharett). But when he arrived in Palestine, he put theory and book-
learning behind him, picked up the hoe and the spade and for five
tough years practised what he preached as a labourer in the Jewish
orange groves and vineyards of the country.

All his life (he died in 1951), Remez combined a passionate concern
for the content of the movement – the unity of the workers and the
future of socialism in the Jewish national home – with an equally

passionate concern for its form. He was as involved with the revival of
the Hebrew language as he was with Jewish shipping, and one of his
methods of relaxing was to create useful new Hebrew words from ancient
Hebrew roots. Even the words that Remez invented (probably the three
most important were the Hebrew for bulldozer, road sign and seniority) had to do characteristically with real life – rather than with
ideology – though he was extremely active in the leadership of the
Labour movement and served for many years as secretary-general of
the *Histadrut*. Incidentally, in 1948 Remez was among the drafters of
Israel's Declaration of Independence. When the state was established,
he became its first minister of transport and then minister of education. We saw a great deal of each other and we had much in common
in terms of our approach to things. Remez was one of the very few of
my comrades with whom I ever discussed any personal, non-political
matters, and I relied a great deal on his advice and guidance – and
miss them to this day.

Above all, there was Berl Katznelson. He died in 1944 and so he
never saw the State of Israel, though I have often wondered what he
would have thought of it – and of us. I have no doubt that many things
would have been different – and better – had Berl been with us over the
past thirty years. The Labour movement – whose undisputed spiritual
leader and guide he was, would have remained, I am sure, more loyal
to itself and its stated principles than it has, and maybe we would have
achieved a society blessed by greater equality. Berl played a unique
role in the movement, though he held few official posts in it, and I am
ashamed of the fact that despite the twelve volumes of his essays and
speeches that have been published, no one has yet written a real
biography of him. I am certainly no historian and I cannot (and will
not) presume to try to analyse or assess the extent of Berl's influence
upon all of us. But at least I can do something to introduce his name to
the world outside Israel's borders, for he was the one man whom all of
us, including Ben-Gurion, deeply revered and who served us all as an
unquestioned and much loved moral authority.

Berl was not at all physically impressive. He was small, his hair was
always untidy, his clothes always looked rumpled. But his lovely smile
lit up his face, and his eyes – always a little sad – looked right through
you, so that no one who ever talked to Berl forgot him. I think of him
as I saw him, hundreds of times, buried in a shabby old armchair in
one of the two book-lined rooms in which he lived in the heart of Tel
Aviv, where everyone came to see him and where he worked (because

he hated going to an office). 'Berl would like you to stop by' was like a command that no one disobeyed. Not that he held court or ever gave orders, but nothing was done, no decision of any importance to the Labour movement in particular or the *yishuv* in general, taken without Berl's opinion being sought first.

He sat in that chair, chin in hand, and talked and listened for hours; and his views were almost always decisive, although the only administrative offices he held in the Labour establishment were as editor of *Davar* and director of the Am Oved publishing house. I am quite sure that, had he lived until 1948, he would have refused to serve in the cabinet and that all of us would still have come to him for guidance and encouragement. It was nothing as cheap as false modesty that kept Berl from seeking power. It was his real disinterest in the machinery of politics, which he regarded as trivial, and his intense, almost burning preoccupation with the kernel of every issue. He was like an archeologist digging for the truth and, most of the time, he arrived at it – with no concern at all for what was fashionable or likely to make him popular. So throughout the twenties, thirties and the early forties, until he died, no one in the Labour movement made up their mind about anything that mattered without first asking 'but what does Berl think?'

He had at least two other outstanding attributes in addition to this unquenchable thirst for the truth. Berl was a man of penetrating intelligence and tremendous charm. It was impossible not to be impressed by his wisdom or deeply attracted by his personality. I remember that at party conferences he used to spend most of the time standing in the corridors talking to 'unimportant' people about important things, instead of sitting with the party's leaders at the high table, and when his turn would come to speak everyone would rush around looking for him. He was no orator. He never made formal speeches. He never spoke *at* anyone. He just stood on the platform and conversed – sometimes for hours – taking little sips of water now and then and weighing the pros and cons of everything with marvellous simplicity. He used that magnificent intellect to clarify and cut through confusion and examine. And no one ever wrote notes, whispered or left the room when Berl spoke – though often he talked for two or three hours at a single stretch.

What did he believe in? Like most of us – though we might have forgotten had Berl not reminded us so often – he believed that our kind of socialism had to be different; that we were creating a society, not

just a trade union; and that the class struggle had no significance in a
community that had no classes yet. He believed that Zionism was one
of the world's greatest revolutionary movements, and he described it as
'the plot on which contemporary Jewish history hinges'. It meant, he
said 'a total rebellion against the bondage of the Diaspora – in any
form', and 'the creation of a working Jewish population versed in all
branches of agriculture and industry'. He became the intellectual parent
of many of the *Histadrut*'s most important bodies. It was Berl who
formulated the need for a workers' bank, for a cooperative wholesale
society and for a workers' sick fund.

This concern with essentials led him also to father first the concept
of a large *unselective* immigration of Jews to Palestine (at a time when
there was a tendency in the Labour movement to advocate the support
primarily of pioneers who had already received some prior training in
agriculture abroad) and then the so-called 'illegal' immigration of Jews
into Palestine. 'From now on,' he said, 'not the pioneer but the refugee
will lead us,' and what he was talking about was the destiny of the
yishuv working itself out through heroic acts undertaken in small
stages, step by step – as indeed happened, though Berl didn't live long
enough to know it. One of those small stages for which he was also
responsible was the dropping of Palestinian Jews behind the Nazi
lines (within the framework of the Allied armies) in a desperate attempt
to reach the Jews of Europe during the Second World War, and he was
the first of us to formulate the urgent claim to statehood, though it was
Ben-Gurion who brought it before the world at a meeting in a New
York hotel in 1942.

Considering how truly erudite Berl was, it is interesting, I think,
that he had practically no formal schooling. He had been a rather
sickly child and was tutored at home, which gave him time to read. 'I
read everything I could lay my hands on,' he told me once, 'the Talmud
in Hebrew and Aramaic, Pushkin and Gorky in Russian, Mendele
Mocher Sforim in Yiddish and Goethe and Heine in German.' By the
time he was *bar mitzvah* at thirteen, his father was dead and he was helping to support the family by giving private lessons.

Since it took him so long to come to a conclusion about anything,
Berl was always a great admirer of people like Ben-Gurion, who could
make up their minds quickly and take action. He considered Ben-
Gurion to be the greatest statesman that the movement – and the
Jewish people – had 'in our time', and to his dying day Ben-Gurion
kept Berl's photograph on his desk. It is also the only photograph in my

living-room now. On at least one occasion, however, Berl's obvious lack of enthusiasm for policies favoured by Ben-Gurion led to a vote in the Labour party against Ben-Gurion. Not that Berl canvassed against him or tried to sway anyone in the opposite direction. It was enough for the Labour leadership to know that Berl was not in favour of something for that something to be reviewed very carefully, even if its proponent was B.-G. In 1937, when Ben-Gurion favoured the Royal (Peel) Commission proposal to partition Palestine, Berl opposed our giving our consent to the Peel plan on the grounds (which turned out to be correct) that the British would never go through with it, whereas our agreement would forever be on the record and would certainly be held against us.

He was a very loving man, quite without cynicism, and he gave a great deal of time and attention to young people – perhaps because he had no children of his own. Whenever I needed to talk to him, he took me for long walks. We would march back and forth on Rothschild Boulevard for half the night and thrash things out – what was happening in Russia (he hated the Bolsheviks), the place Hebrew had to occupy in the Zionist revolution, the importance of publishing good entertaining books in Hebrew and the need to maintain the unity of the Jewish people by observing the Sabbath and the dietary laws of Judaism (*kashrut*) in all the public institutions of the Jewish national home. He abhorred having to keep to a schedule, so he gave me all the time I wanted without once looking at his watch, and I loved him for that, too. He used to meet with groups of youngsters all over the country and listen to what they had to say. I remember a Saturday not long before he died when I took a bunch of young people (including Sarah) to a kibbutz where Berl was staying for the weekend and they sat on the lawn all afternoon – Berl and fifteen boys and girls – and talked and listened to each other. He organized a month's study course in Rehovot in 1943 with youngsters from all over Palestine, and I can see him now on the porch with them, his old grey cap pushed down on his head, concentrating on the not very original points some boy was making about the *Histadrut*.

And, of course, I shall never forget the dreadful night that Berl died, in Jerusalem, of a stroke. Years later, when President Kennedy was assassinated and the United States stood still in its shock and bereavement, I thought at once about that night thirty years ago when Berl died and we couldn't, any of us, imagine how anything would go on without him. I was in Tel Aviv. I had been to a play given by the

Habimah Theatre and on the bus going home I heard people whispering to each other as though something awful had happened. Awful things happened all the time in 1944, and I was a bit worried when I saw a knot of friends standing outside the house I lived in on Hayarkon Street. They were waiting for me. 'Berl is dead,' they said. There was nothing else to say. I left for Jerusalem at once. Ben-Gurion was in Haifa that night, but after he heard the news no one dared to talk to him. He just lay on his bed all night, shivering and crying. He had lost the only man whose opinion he ever really valued, perhaps his only real friend.

6

'We shall fight Hitler'

I WAS AWAY FROM Palestine often in 1929 and 1930. Once I returned to the United States on behalf of the Women's Labour Council and twice I visited England, also as a representative of the Labour movement. In those days, of course, one didn't just hop across the ocean in a plane (though I flew for the first time in 1929 – in the United States – and sat bolt upright all the way, frozen with fear but hoping that I looked more confident than I felt), and each trip abroad lasted for several weeks. I knew that Menachem and Sarah dreaded my long absences. On the rare occasions that I had to stay home from work in Tel Aviv because I had a headache, they were overjoyed and used to dance around me, singing a little song: 'Mommy's staying at home today! Mommy has a headache! Mommy's staying at home today!' It didn't help the headache any, and it hurt the heart a lot, but I was learning that you can get used to anything if you have to, even to feeling perpetually guilty.

It was very strange to be back in the States after seven years. It was like visiting a foreign country, and it took me some time to get my bearings, to find my way around New York, to cope with railway timetables and day coaches and even to get used to the sound of English all around me again, though in fact most of the women with whom I actually worked spoke Yiddish. The organization to which I was sent in the States, the Pioneer Women, had been founded only three or four years earlier by Rachel Yanait-Ben-Zvi and women whose husbands were active in the American Labour–Zionist movement. Almost all of these women were European born. They spoke Yiddish at home, and to people who didn't know them, I suppose they appeared very much like their own mothers, like typical working-class *Yiddishe mamas* whose main concern was feeding the family and maintaining the home. But, of course, they were different. These were idealistic, politically committed, liberal young women to whom what was happening in Palestine really mattered. They found time to involve themselves in organizational activities and fund-raising for farms that were training girls in agricultural work in Petach Tikvah, Nachlat Yehuda and Hadera, places that they had never seen and never expected to see. What's more, the ideals of Labour–Zionism were not particularly popular anywhere in 1929, least of all perhaps in the States, and the Pioneer Women's campaign for the Women's Labour Council was an uphill road, to put it mildly.

I did what I could to help and encourage them. I made speeches, answered hundreds of questions, explained the urgency of the working women's farms and talked for hours about the new society that was being created in Jewish Palestine by the Labour movement, with its guarantees of full emancipation for women. I talked also about the internal Zionist political scene in Palestine and was amazed and heart-warmed by the interest these women showed in the various shades of political belief that were represented in the Labour factions of the *yishuv* at that point. Within the year, two major Labour parties were to merge: *Hapoel Hatzair* (The Young Worker), which was greatly influenced by A. D. Gordon, and *Achdut Ha-Avodah* (to which I and they belonged), which was based on socialist ideology and considered itself part of the Socialist International. Despite the differences between them, they united into one party called *Mapai* (which stood for the Labour Party of the Land of Israel), while another party called *Hashomer Hatzair* (The Young Guard), made up mostly of kibbutzim members with a Marxist ideology, was on the rise.

Much later, in the 1940s, a group split off from *Mapai* and eventually joined up with *Hashomer Hatzair* to form a new party called *Mapam* (the United Workers Party) and even later, at the end of the 1960s, there were to be other fateful combinations and changes. But *Mapai* remained dominant throughout the years. Its history has been that of the country itself, and the State of Israel has never yet had a government without at least a *Mapai* majority, however small it has been sometimes. As for myself, *Mapai* was my party from the start, and I have never wavered in my loyalty to it or in my conviction that the only firm foundation for Labour–Zionism is the rule of one unified Labour party representing the various shades of opinion. In the years to come, I was lucky enough to be able to put this conviction to work, more than once.

At all events, the Pioneer Women were immensely concerned with whatever was going on in Palestine, and it gave me a great deal of satisfaction to know that I was playing a role in their work, though I was worried about the extent to which they seemed determined to remain a Yiddish-speaking group in a country in which the Jewish immigration from Europe was dwindling yearly. It was all very well for them to assure me that all their children spoke Yiddish and that the Yiddish newspapers and theatre were still flourishing in America. I came from a country of immigration, too, and just as I was sure that in Palestine Yiddish would eventually be replaced altogether by Hebrew, so I was sure that if it was to survive the next decade, the Pioneer Women would have to broaden its base and attract younger, more Americanized, English-speaking women to its ranks. And I talked about this, too, for days on end with my American comrades.

I also went to Cleveland to see Clara. She was married by then to a young man called Fred Stern and had a bright, handsome little boy, Daniel David. I hadn't seen Clara since she was a teenager, and although we sometimes wrote to each other (and, of course, my parents corresponded regularly with her) it took me a while to get used to her. We seemed – and were – worlds apart. Everything I cared for was in Palestine. Everything that Clara cared for was in the United States. I was totally committed to Zionism, and to the extent that I had embarked on a career (though I never thought in those terms) it was obviously within the ranks of the Labour movement of the *yishuv*. Clara and Fred were both sociologists and, by the time I met him, Fred already had a graduate degree. He was a very intelligent man, very well read and very cultured. He had grown up more or less on the streets of Milwaukee, selling newspapers from the time he was six, and he was entirely 'self-made'. They were just as involved with Jewish life as I was, but on the community and social-work level, rather than politically or nationally, and we spoke entirely different languages. I knew that Clara would stay in the States not because life was easier for her there (I was appalled by their poverty in Cleveland), but because that was where she felt she belonged. Although she was interested in Palestine, it was an academic interest, while Fred made it clear to me within a few hours that he disapproved of all nationalism and regarded Zionism as an extremely reactionary movement.

Clara and Fred planned to have only one child so they could give him everything but, as my mother used to say, '*a mensch tracht un Gott lacht*' (man proposes and God disposes), and Daniel David died when he was eighteen as the result of a severe illness while serving in the US army. After that, Fred became terribly ill. He lost a leg and was bedridden for years. But Clara never felt sorry for herself, never stopped working hard and managed – despite all the tragedies – to make a great success of her professional life. They moved to Bridgeport, Connecticut, prior to David's death and Fred's illness and she became executive director of the United Jewish Council there. But of course in 1929 all I knew was that my baby sister was not going to join the rest of us in Palestine, and it upset me.

In 1930 I was away again. I attended the Conference of Socialist Women in England. There were over 1,000 other delegates, and I think it was the first time that I understood how interested people outside Palestine, non-Jews, could become in what was already being called 'the Palestine problem'. I addressed the conference for only a few minutes, but afterwards I was asked to speak to smaller groups in various parts of England, and I met the British in their own country for the first time. The socialist women who bombarded me with questions about the *Histadrut*, the kibbutz, the Women's Labour Council, the way we lived and how we treated the Arabs were quite different from the one or two British ladies I had met in Palestine itself. There, the British regarded us as a singularly complicated breed of native, less charming than the humble and picturesque Arabs and much more pretentious and demanding. But in England itself, in London, Manchester and Hull, I talked to women who were genuinely fascinated by the Zionist 'experiment' and who, if not always sympathetic, were at least eager to learn the facts.

I didn't think that Zionist rhetoric would impress them much, and I decided that a few home truths would be more useful. There had been another wave of Arab riots in 1929, directed by the mufti of Jerusalem, Haj Amin el-Husseini (who was to become notorious for his pro-Fascist and Nazi agitation among the Arabs during the Second World War), and although the British had eventually restored peace, they did so in a manner calculated to impress upon the Arabs that no one would be punished very severely for murdering Jews or for looting Jewish property. I was only too glad, therefore, to have a chance to explain the real sequence of events to my socialist sisters in England.

On that same visit I met – also for the first time – women members of British cooperative societies and heard their glowing reports about the wonders of Soviet Russia. I remember thinking that perhaps if we brought them to Palestine and showed them what we had accomplished there, they might talk about us in that same breathless way. I have never changed my mind about that either, and to this day I believe that one visit to Israel is worth a hundred speeches.

I returned to London again that year for a week or two as a delegate to the Imperial Labour Conference. Ramsay MacDonald was then prime minister. Although he himself was sympathetic to, even concerned with, the *yishuv*'s progress, it was his government that issued the notorious White Paper of 1930 (known as the Passfield Paper) whittling down Jewish immigration and settlement in Palestine. Thirteen years after the Balfour Declaration, the British seemed to be more concerned with appeasing the Arabs than fulfilling their promise to the Jews. Someone in London said to me cynically: 'You Jews wanted to own a national home, but all you are getting is a rented flat!' The truth was even harsher, however. It was beginning to look as though our landlord now wanted to break the lease altogether, although in 1930, of course, no one imagined that it would only take eighteen more years for the British to declare that the Mandate was absolutely unworkable.

Perhaps it was because I had lived in America for so long that I didn't fall quite as thoroughly under the spell of the British as many of my colleagues did. I admired and liked the British people, including the leadership of the Labour Party, but I can't honestly say that I was really taken by surprise when we were so badly let down by them, then or later. Many, if not most, Palestinian Jews were afflicted in those years by what turned out to be the pathetic belief – all evidence to the contrary notwithstanding – that Britain would keep faith with us after all, regardless of increasing Arab pressure and the traditionally pro-Arab stand of the Colonial Office. I think that much of this reluctance to face up to the fact that the British government was in the process of changing its mind about its responsibility to the Zionists stemmed from the tremendous respect in which British democracy was held by Jews who had been brought up in nineteenth-century Eastern Europe.

On the whole, for many years, most of my colleagues tended to regard British parliamentary and civic institutions and procedures as only a little short of miraculous, while I, who had actually lived in a democracy, was rather less dazzled. Incidentally, it is remarkable that despite the long, stormy, and often terrible conflict between us and the

British, and the way in which that conflict ended in 1948, we Israelis still hold the British people in great and truly affectionate esteem and are more hurt by being let down by the British than by any other nation. There are various reasons for this. One is, of course, that it was Britain that gave us the Balfour Declaration. Another is that the Jews have never forgotten the lonely British stand against the Nazis, and yet another may be, I think, the in-born Jewish respect for tradition. At all events, throughout the thirty-odd years of the Mandate, the *yishuv* always made a clear-cut distinction between the Palestine mandatory government and the British people, between the man in the street in England and the officials of the Colonial and Foreign Offices, and went on hoping to win unqualified British support. But on the political level, at least, it remained mostly an unrequited love.

I probably would have been sent back to the States sooner or later in any case, but in 1932 Sarah became very ill indeed, and it was I who suggested that I return to America, with the children, so that she could get expert medical treatment there – though the doctors at home weren't even sure that she would survive the trip. She looked dreadful. Her little face was so swollen that sometimes I could hardly see her eyes, and she was running a fever. 'You'll kill her if you take her to the States,' our own doctor said. 'You mustn't cross the ocean with her,' and the specialists backed him up. She was virtually fasting by now; there were days when she could have only six or seven glasses of very sweet tea and no food at all. 'This is soup,' she would pretend. 'This is meat, this is bread, this is carrots and *this* is pudding.' One night, while Menachem and Sarah were asleep, Morris and I sat up on the balcony till morning trying to decide what should be done, and by the morning we had made up our minds. I went to the Women's Labour Council and asked if I could be sent as a *shlichah*, an emissary, to the Pioneer Women.

'If we don't take her, she may die here and we'll all know, for the rest of our lives, that we didn't do absolutely everything possible,' I explained to my parents, who thought it was madness to travel so far with such a terribly sick child. But I knew that we had no real alternative and that I couldn't sit by her bed with folded hands and watch her grow weaker, more swollen and paler every day until she just faded away.

It wasn't a simple trip to plan. Morris was going to stay and work in Haifa and I was going to travel alone with the children, first by train to Port Said, then on a French liner to Marseilles, then by train to

Cherbourg and finally on the S.S. *Bremen* to New York. It would take at
least two weeks, and who knew what would happen to Sarah during
those two weeks? But I felt there was no alternative, and we set out on
our dangerous voyage.

I don't think I relaxed for one minute during those two weeks.
Menachem was very good and kept himself busy, and Sarah – considering that she was only six and extremely ill – was amazing. It was
almost as though she knew how frightened I was and felt that she had
to reassure me. We had a cabin with two bunks on the *Bremen*, and at
night I brought in a deck-chair for myself and lay near Sarah, watching
her and, I suppose, in my own way, praying.

Fanny and Jacob Goodman, dear and old friends, put us up in their
apartment in Brooklyn, and I began at once to arrange for Sarah to be
admitted to the Beth Israel Hospital on Stuyvesant Square East. No one
who has ever hospitalized a child needs to be told what it is like to leave
a small son or daughter in a hospital ward. Not only was the hospital
strange, but Sarah, of course, knew no English at all, and for the first
two weeks she sobbed her heart out and begged me not to leave her.

It didn't take the Beth Israel doctors long to arrive at a diagnosis.
Sarah was indeed suffering from a kidney disease, but not the one for
which she had been treated in Palestine. There was no need for a strict
diet, no need for her to stay in bed. As soon as she regained her strength,
she could go to school, roller-skate and swim, walk down stairs and run
up them. She was given treatment, fattened up and, after six weeks,
released from the hospital 'in perfect health', as I wrote to Morris, tears
of relief streaming down my face.

Now I had time for my work and for Menachem, who hadn't been
allowed to visit Sarah in the hospital and who had therefore seen very
little of me since we arrived in New York. He was furious that she had
already learned some English from the nurses at Beth Israel while he was
still having to make himself understood in a mixture of Hebrew and
Yiddish. The children missed Morris very much and hated my travelling from city to city for the Pioneer Women, often not coming 'home' at
all for a month at a time. But I took them to meet Clara and Fred and
Morris's mother, to children's concerts, movies and the opera and hoped
that their exposure to a richer world than Tel Aviv would make up for
their having been uprooted again. Anyhow, they both flourished, and
Sarah was literally not to be recognized. This is not to say that either of
them ever admitted out aloud that anything in the States was better or
more imposing than in Palestine, or that they weren't confused by being

abroad. I remember, for instance, that for weeks Menachem couldn't understand why all our friends in New York said that they were going to vote for Roosevelt. 'Why not for Ben-Zvi or Ben-Gurion?' he asked.

As for myself, I worked very hard indeed during those two years. When I left, a rather exaggerated tribute was paid to me in the magazine of the Pioneer Women, which I had edited for a while. Headlined 'Goldie Meyerson's Tour', it read:

Goldie brought us a waft of fragrant orange blossoms, sprouting vegetables, budding trees, well-cared-for cows and chickens, stubborn territory conquered, dangerous natural elements vanquished, all the result of work, work, work. Work, not under pressure or for personal gain, but sweat and blood, field and plow, road and cement, barrenness and endurance, swamps and disease, dangers, deprivations, obstacles, tribulations, inspiration and work, just for work's own sake, just for the ecstasy of creation . . . Her eloquence and sincerity, her poise and simplicity have instilled in her hearers a reverence for our cause and respect for our organization. We will endeavor to enlist her admirers on behalf of our work and hope to be successful.

But what I recall most vividly of those months of touring (once I travelled for nearly eight weeks at a stretch, talking about Palestine and trying to raise money and bring in recruits for the organization) was the smell of railway stations and the sound of my own voice. The sums of money that were raised in those days bore no resemblance to the millions of dollars that are raised on similar tours nowadays, and the quotas set by each community were very rarely met. But each penny mattered as much then as it does now. If the Pioneer Women of Newark, New Jersey, had hoped to raise 165 dollars from October 1933 to July 1934 and had, in fact, only raised $17.40, or the Chicago West Side Club had undertaken to raise 425 dollars and had scraped together only 76 of them, it just meant that an extra effort had to be made by the membership. Yet another raffle or bazaar had to be scheduled, another masquerade dance (for which 25 cents could be charged) had to be planned, or another lecture delivered on 'The Role of the Woman in the Kibbutz' or 'The Life of Labour in Palestine'.

A typical letter (this one was from Winnipeg) sent to me at the Pioneer Women headquarters in New York read:

We have chairmen in charge of the various branches of the work, helped by committees. We meet every week and at every alternate meeting we have some prominent lectures. Last week we were addressed by Dr Hennell, who gave a very interesting talk on his visit to Palestine. Our first financial venture this year was a Silver Tea at which we raised 45 dollars. We are now planning a *Hanukkah* celebration, but are not certain as to which form it will take as yet. At present all our members are working enthusiastically on the 5-dollar-luncheon and are eagerly looking forward to your visit here.

In the same mail Cleveland asked for my help in organizing an outing with a treasure hunt and a meal cooked out of doors as well as a cultural programme tracing 'The Beginning and Development of Political Groups in Zionism' while from Kansas City came a request that I speak at a meeting and attend a Friday night social with a lecture 'on some Jewish topic'. I must have stayed overnight in dozens of homes throughout the United States and Canada and mapped out hundreds of programmes in Yiddish and English for study groups. Very often I was exhausted but I was never bored and, more important, I never doubted for a minute the significance or urgency of the work that the Pioneer Women were doing.

There are also lighter memories of the incessant travelling. Once, on a blustery winter morning, I arrived in Winnipeg on a train that came in early. Since I couldn't see any of the women who were supposed to meet me, I decided to go to a nearby hotel rather than wake any of the women at such an early hour. But no sooner had I unpacked than the telephone rang. A despairing voice said to me: 'Mrs Meyerson, we are all at the station. A large delegation has come to greet you. How can I tell them that we missed you? How can I deprive them of the excitement and the enthusiasm, of the special privilege of being among the first to press your hand in welcome? They will be so disappointed!' So I said, 'Don't worry. I'll be there in a few minutes.' I packed again, called a cab, and within fifteen minutes was back at the station, meeting the delegation, which happily escorted me to my hostess's home.

And I remember going to a big meeting in some eastern city where I was to speak three times, once on Saturday evening, again on Sunday morning and a third time on Sunday evening. On Sunday afternoon I was lying down in someone's home to rest for an hour when the president of the local Pioneer Women club came in, sat herself down on my bed and began a harangue. 'Look, Golda,' she said firmly, 'you speak very well but you don't speak like a woman. When Rachel Yanait-Ben-Zvi was here, she wept and we all wept with her. But you talk like a man, and no one weeps.' All I could say lamely was: 'I'm sorry, but I really can't talk any other way.' Although she could see that I was dead tired, she felt she had a mission, and she sat there for that precious hour repeating over and over again that I *must* learn to talk like a woman. What upset her, she explained, was that I spoke to the Pioneer Women not only about the Women's Labour Council but about the *Histadrut* in general, about the problems of immigration and the political situation, and she didn't think *that* would bring in any money!

On the other hand, I certainly didn't know all there was to know about fund-raising either. On one trip, I came to a small town in the Middle West to find all the members very excited. They had raised more money that year than ever before, although they were only a very small group. I said, 'How did you do it?' They said, 'Oh, by playing cards.' I hit the ceiling. 'For Palestine you play cards! *That's* the kind of money we need? If you want to play cards, play as long as you like, but not in our name.' No one said anything, except for one woman who said very quietly: '*Chavera* Goldie, in Palestine you don't play cards?' 'Certainly not,' I answered furiously. 'What sort of people do you think we are?' Then, when I came back to my flat in Tel Aviv a year later, I noticed that some of the members of the *Histadrut* sitting on their verandas in the evening playing cards – although not for money, thank God. I wanted to write to that woman and apologize but I didn't know her name.

Between tours of the country, I wrote editorials for the magazine and inaugurated the sale of products made or grown in Palestine. One project I started in the Bronx was the sale of *matzah* baked in Palestine for Passover. I set up headquarters in an enormous warehouse, where we first packed and then delivered the *matzah* ourselves to the entire neighbourhood. I have always been a great believer in not wasting time, so while we packed the *matzah* I taught the women the latest songs from the *yishuv*.

My editorials always dealt with the political issues that most closely concerned Labour–Zionism, and I can see now why that talkative lady accused me of not being sentimental enough – although, as Ben-Gurion once wrote to a colleague of his with whom he was quarrelling, 'Sentimentality is not a sin, either from the socialist or from the Zionist point of view.' I believed, and I still believe, that people who are involved in a cause deserve to be spoken to about it as seriously and as intelligently as possible, and tears don't have to be elicited from anyone in the Zionist movement. God knows, there is always enough to cry about!

One article that I wrote in the spring of 1933 was in answer to a charge made by a leader of *Hadassah* to the effect that the success of Labour–Zionism depended on the financial support of 'bourgeois-capitalist Jews':

We have always maintained that the success of the Zionist work depends mainly on two inner Jewish factors – workers to do the work, and money to make this work possible. We did not know that the money coming from large Jewish masses must be labelled as 'class money' . . . We consider the money for the Jewish National Fund and the *Keren Hayesod* [which was responsible for financing Jewish immigration and settlement in Palestine] as well as the manpower, the *Halutz* [pioneering] movement, to be a manifestation of the will and determination of the nation at large . . . Does this mean that we are opposed to private capital and private initiative? Indeed not. Labour-Zionists are primarily interested in mass immigration into Palestine. If we cannot achieve this end through national capital, we welcome private capital. It is true that we say that even private capital must serve the ends of Zionism. Private capital that does not employ Jewish labour does not help our cause . . . To our sorrow, it is only too often that we have witnessed private enterprise in Palestine used exclusively for private benefit, forgetting that Jewish immigration in Palestine depends primarily on possibilities of work created in the country. And we wish to state here again very emphatically : private capital that does not employ Jewish labour is *not* welcome in Palestine because private capital of such a character will not make possible the mass immigration which we – and the *Hadassah* – desire . . .

In the summer of 1934, we got ready to return home. I made a final round of the States, to part from the Pioneer Women clubs and chapters I had come to know so well. I was filled with respect for those hard-working, unfashionable, devoted women who had given me so much affection, and I wanted them to know how grateful I was. I knew that whatever happened in Palestine, they would always support and aid us – and, of course, time was to prove me right.

I had arrived in New York in 1932 with two small children, neither of whom spoke one word of English. I arrived back in Palestine in 1934 with two small children who now spoke both English and Hebrew – and who were beside themselves with joy at seeing Morris again. There were many disappointments in Morris's life, but it was a source of constant delight to him that Menachem was so profoundly interested in music and so obviously talented. Although, later on, it was usually I who had to carry the cello to and from Menachem's music lessons (until he was big enough to haul it around himself), it was Morris who, throughout the years, listened to Menachem practise at weekends, played records for him and strengthened and deepened his growing love for music.

But I had come back to Palestine to face an even greater challenge than serving as national secretary for the Pioneer Women in the United

States. Within a few weeks of our homecoming, I was asked to join the *Va'ad Hapoel* (the Executive Committee of the *Histadrut*).

To the extent that the *Histadrut* represented what was on the whole an extremely advanced form of Jewish self-government in Palestine, the *Va'ad Hapoel* was its 'cabinet' – within which, for the next very stormy fourteen years, I was assigned various portfolios and responsibilities. None of these, as I look back, were either easy to carry out or likely to make me particularly popular inside the *Histadrut* itself. But they did have one great asset: they all had to do with what in fact most concerned and interested me – the translation of socialist principles into the down-to-earth terminology of everyday life.

I suppose that if times had been good economically and politically – or at least better – in the Palestine of the mid-1930s and the 1940s, it would have been relatively easy to ensure a just sharing of burdens within the labour community. After all, other than what they did for a living, there really were no differences at all – either economic or social – between the so-called rank and file of the membership and the so-called *Histadrut* leadership. We were all paid a fixed basic living wage which varied only according to actual seniority and the number of dependants in each family, and there were no exceptions to this rule. I know that today people in Israel and elsewhere regard this kind of egalitarianism not only as old-fashioned but as downright unworkable. Perhaps it is, but I myself approved of it and have always approved of it. I still think that it made good sound socialist sense – which usually means good sound common sense – for the janitor of the *Histadrut* building in Tel Aviv who had nine children to support to get a considerably fatter pay envelope than I, who had only two children to support.

Socialism in practice involved much more than my calling this janitor Shmuel and his calling me Golda. It meant also that his obligations to the other members of the *Histadrut* were the same as mine, and the economic situation in Palestine, as well as everywhere else, being as difficult as it was then, this aspect of trade unionism became the focal point of most of my battles within the *Histadrut*.

Payment of *Histadrut* dues was fixed according to a sliding scale, like income tax. It was paid every month in a lump sum that covered trade union funds, pension funds and the *Kupat Holim* (the Workers' Sick Fund) and was known as the 'single tax'. I was convinced that this single tax should be assessed not according to basic wages or average earnings or some theoretical sum, but on the full pay that each worker actually received. Otherwise, where was the 'equality' we talked about so much? Was sharing to be the sole property of the kibbutzim, or could give-and-take be made the way of life among the workers of Tel Aviv, too? And what about the *Histadrut* membership's collective responsibility for comrades who were unemployed? Was it conceivable that the *Histadrut* should make its voice heard (and its presence felt) on each and every issue that vitally concerned the *yishuv* – immigration, settlement, self-defence – but avert its gaze from the men and women who were without jobs and whose children were barely getting enough to eat? If nothing else, mutual aid – one of the bases of the *Histadrut* – was certainly a prerequisite of socialism, however hard-up an *employed* member of the *Histadrut* might be and regardless of how painful it was to turn over a day's salary each month to a special unemployment fund. But I felt very strongly about these fundamental matters and persisted in setting up an unemployment fund, despite the very vocal opposition to it. We called it *Mifdeh*, which means 'redemption', and when the number of unemployed increased (at one point during the 1930s about 10,000 *Histadrut* members were out of work, I pressed for an increase in the unemployment tax and we established *Mifdeh B*.

Some of my friends charged me with 'destroying the *Histadrut*' and 'demanding the impossible', but Ben-Gurion, Berl Katznelson and David Remez all backed me, and the *Histadrut* nonetheless managed to remain intact. As a matter of fact, it turned out that the *Mifdeh* campaign served as a very important precedent for much heavier voluntary taxation that came not very long afterwards in the form of the *Kofer Hayishuv* ('ransom of the *yishuv*'), established when the toll in life and property of the Arab disturbances of 1936 became so high that we were forced to levy a defence tax on virtually the entire Jewish population. And even later, during the Second World War, when we set up a War Needs and Rescue Fund, we relied again on experience gained in the days of those loathed *Mifdeh* drives.

I was also involved in the bitter aftermath (it lasted many years) of a terrible tragedy that overtook the Labour movement when I was in the States. One of the brightest and best of the rising stars of *Mapai*, young Chaim Arlosoroff, who had just returned from what today would be called a fact-finding mission to the Germany in which Hitler had just come to power, was shot to death as he walked along the Tel Aviv beach with his wife. A member of the right-wing Revisionist Party, Abraham Stavsky, was accused and convicted of Arlosoroff's murder, though he was acquitted afterwards by a court of appeals for lack of evidence. The identity of the assassin will probably never be known, but at the time virtually the entire leadership of the shocked and bereaved Labour movement was convinced of Stavsky's guilt, as I myself was. Arlosoroff represented moderation, caution, a balanced approach to world problems and, of course, to our own, and his tragic death seemed the inevitable consequence of the kind of anti-socialist right-wing militarism and violent chauvinism that was being advocated by the Revisionists. I hadn't gotten to know Arlosoroff very well yet, but like everyone who knew him at all, I was greatly impressed by his intellectual powers and his political acumen, and I was deeply shaken by his murder, news of which had reached me in New York.

But even more, I was horrified by the very notion that in Palestine one Jew might be capable of killing another and that political extremism within the *yishuv* could lead to bloodshed. At all events, with Arlosoroff's murder, what had been for years a growing friction between the left and right wings of the Zionist movement turned into a breach that in some respects has not healed to this day – and perhaps will never heal entirely.

At the end of 1933 and the beginning of 1934, it looked as though battle lines had been drawn up within the *yishuv* – particularly on the labour front. The Revisionists accused the *Histadrut* of a 'blood libel' and of maintaining a stranglehold on the *yishuv* by keeping non-socialists out of work and thus literally starving out its political opponents, and there were constant, sometimes bloody, clashes between workers all over the country. Ben-Gurion thought that unity within the Jewish community of Palestine must be preserved at all costs, and many of us (myself included) agreed with him. He proposed a 'ceasefire' in the form of a labour agreement between left and right that would, he believed, help to put an end to the dissension. We spent weeks and weeks discussing the 'treaty', heatedly, sometimes even hysterically; but Arlosoroff's murder dominated all the discussions, and Ben-Gurion's proposal was turned down – most unfortunately, I think.

But unemployment, on the one hand, and internal conflict on the other, were only two of the problems we faced. There were even more serious issues at stake. Both in Palestine and abroad, storm clouds had gathered. Hitler had come to power in 1933, and however absurd his loudly proclaimed programme for world domination by the Aryan 'race' had seemed at first, the violent anti-Semitism which he had preached from the start was obviously not just a rhetorical device. One of Hitler's very first acts, in fact, was the passage of savage anti-Jewish legislation that stripped Germany's Jews of all usual civil and human rights. Of course, no one, myself included, dreamt then that Hitler's vow to destroy the Jews would ever be literally carried out. In a way, I suppose, it should be chalked up to the credit of normal decent men and women that we couldn't believe that such a monstrously evil thing would ever actually happen – or that the world would permit it to happen. It wasn't that we were gullible. It was simply that we couldn't conceive of what was then still inconceivable. Today, however, no horror is inconceivable to me any more.

But even before Hitler's 'Final Solution', the first results of Nazi persecution – legally enacted – were terrible enough. There was only one place on the face of the globe to which the Jews could come as a right, no matter what restrictions the British sought to impose on their immigration to Palestine and by 1934, thousands of up-rooted homeless refugees from Nazism were making their way to us. Some of them brought with them what few possessions they could rescue, but most of them came with nothing at all. They were highly educated, industrious, energetic people and their contribution to the *yishuv* was immense. But it meant that 60,000 men, women and children had to be absorbed at once by a population of less than 400,000 that was barely able to make ends meet in any case, and they all had somehow to survive not only growing Arab terror but also the indiffer-ence – not to say hostility – of the mandatory government.

Absorbing immigrants, particularly if they are refugees, is quite different from merely welcoming them. Those thousands of men, women and children who came to us then from Germany and Austria had to be housed, given jobs, taught Hebrew and helped to acclimatize. The lawyer from Berlin, the musician from Frankfurt, the research chemist from Vienna had to be turned, overnight, into a chicken farmer, a waiter and a bricklayer, otherwise they wouldn't have work at all. They also had to get used – again overnight – to a new and harder way of life and to new dangers and deprivations. It was not easy for them, or for us, and to this day I think it was remarkable that the *yishuv* weathered those years and emerged from them stronger than it had been before. But I suppose there are only two reasonable, or even possible, responses to national adversity. One is to collapse, to give in and to say: 'It just can't be done.' The other is to grit your teeth and to fight on as many fronts as necessary for as long as necessary – which is exactly what we did and, as it turns out, exactly what we are still doing now.

In fact, today I often think of how it was in Palestine in the 1930s and the 1940s and derive considerable encouragement from these memories, though certainly not all of them are pleasant. But when people say to me in 1975 'How can Israel possibly cope with everything – with the Arab determination to liquidate the state, with the over-whelming Arab superiority of money, men and arms, with the influx of thousands of immigrants from Russia, with the relative indifference, at best, of most of the world to these problems and with a critical economic situation that seems impossible to remedy?' I can only answer, and with perfect honesty, 'It was all much more difficult forty years ago, and we did manage somehow – though the price was always very high.' Sometimes, in fact, I think that only those of us who were active forty years ago can really understand how much was accomplished since then or how great our victories have really been, and maybe that is why the greatest optimists in Israel today tend to be the old people like myself, who take it for granted that nothing as tremendous as the rebirth of a nation can be accomplished rapidly, painlessly or effort-lessly!

Anyhow, we sorted out our priorities. The daily job had to be done, however acute the emergency. As far as I personally was concerned, this meant serving as chairman of the Board of Directors of the Workers Sick Fund, supervising the working conditions of *Histadrut* members employed on building British army camps all over the country, con-ducting a variety of other labour negotiations and getting the housework done and helping Menachem and Sarah with their homework. Those were the routine preoccupations.

But at the same time, we had to formulate and implement a series of major decisions about the overall situation of the *yishuv*. The first question that required an immediate reply was what were we going to do about the constant outbreaks of Arab terror? In 1936 alone they had resulted in the wanton destruction of hundreds of thousands of trees planted by the Jews with so much love, care and hope; the derailing of countless trains and buses; the burning of hundreds of fields; and, most dreadful of all, in some 2,000 armed attacks on Jews – eighty of whom were killed (and many more gravely wounded). By the time the 'Arab Revolt' was over in 1939, some 500 Jews had fallen victim to Arab violence.

The riots started in April 1936. By the summer it was no longer safe for Jews to travel from one city to another. Whenever I had to go from Tel Aviv to Jerusalem for a meeting – which was frequently – I kissed the children good-bye in the morning knowing that I might well never come home again, that my bus might be ambushed, that I might be shot by an Arab sniper at the entrance to Jerusalem or stoned to death by an Arab mob on the outskirts of Tel Aviv. The *Haganah* (the underground Jewish self-defence organization) was much better equipped and larger than it had been at the time of the Arab riots of 1929, but we had no intention either of turning it into an instrument of counter-terror against the Arabs just because they were Arabs or of providing the British with any excuse for further clamping down on Jewish immigration and settlement, as they tended to do whenever we visibly played too active a role in our own defence. Although it is always much harder to exercise self-restraint than it is to hit back, we had one paramount consideration: nothing must be done – even in the face of constant danger and harassment – that might provoke the British into slashing the number of Jews allowed to enter Palestine. The policy of self-restraint (*havlagah* in Hebrew) was rigidly enforced. Whenever and wherever possible, Jews defended themselves from attack, but there were virtually no acts of retaliation by the *Haganah* throughout the three years of what the British, with splendid understatement, chose to call 'the disturbances'.

This determination of ours to defend ourselves but not to retaliate was not, however, universally applauded in the *yishuv*. A minority clamoured for counter-terror and denounced the policy of *havlagah* as cowardly. I was always among the majority that was absolutely convinced that *havlagah* was the one and only ethical course we could follow. The notion of attacking Arabs indiscriminately, regardless of whether or not they were the particular perpetrators of an outrage, was morally abhorrent to me. A specific attack had to be repelled and a specific criminal had to be punished – well and good. But we were not going to kill Arabs just because they were Arabs or engaged in the kind of wanton violence that typified the Arab method of fighting us.

Let me at this juncture deal also – even if very briefly – with the ridiculous accusation that I have heard for so many years to the effect that we ignored the Arabs of Palestine and set about developing the country as though it had no Arab population at all. When the instigators of the Arab disturbances of the late 1930s claimed, as they did, that the Arabs were attacking us because they had been 'dispossessed', I did not have to look up British census figures to know that the Arab population of Palestine had doubled since the start of Jewish settlement there. I had seen for myself the rate of growth of the Arab population ever since I had first come to Palestine. Not only did the living standard of the Arabs of Palestine far exceed that of the Arabs anywhere else in the Middle East, but, attracted by the new opportunities, hordes of Arabs were immigrating to Palestine from Syria and other neighbouring countries all through those years. Whenever some kindly representative of the British government sought to shut off Jewish immigration by declaring that there was not enough room in Palestine, I remember making speeches about Palestine's larger absorptive capacity, complete with statistical references which I dutifully took from British sources, but which were based on what I had actually witnessed with my own eyes.

And let me add, there was no time during the thirties that I did not hope that eventually the Arabs of Palestine would live with us in peace and equality as citizens of a Jewish homeland – just as I kept on hoping that Jews who lived in Arab countries would be allowed to live there in peace and equality. This was another reason why our policy of self-restraint in the face of the Arab attacks seemed so important to me. Nothing, I felt, must be allowed to complicate or embitter the future. It didn't work out that way, but it took us all a long time to accept the fact that the reconciliation we expected was not going to take place.

Then, we decided to step into the economic vacuum that was created when the Arab Higher Committee, headed by the mufti, declared a General Strike in the hope of paralysing the *yishuv* altogether. No Arab anywhere in Palestine was to go to work, the mufti ordered, until all Jewish immigration ended and all land purchases by Jews came to a stop. To this we also had a simple reply. If the port in Jaffa no longer operated, we would open a port of our own in Tel Aviv. If Arab farmers no longer marketed their crops, then Jewish farmers would double and triple their efforts. If all Arab transport ceased on the roads of Palestine, then Jewish trucks and bus drivers would work extra shifts and armour plate their vehicles. Whatever the Arabs refused to do, we would get done – somehow or other.

There were, of course, many people whose judgement, opinions and personalities affected these decisions – including, to a very small extent, my own – but there was one man, above all others, upon whose remark-able qualities of leadership and stunning political intuition we all relied and were to continue to rely in the years that lay ahead. That man was David Ben-Gurion, the only one among us whose name, I profoundly believe, will be known to Jews and non-Jews alike even in a hundred years. Not long ago, I visited Ben-Gurion's grave in the Negev kibbutz of Sdeh Boker, where he spent the last years of his life and where he wished to be buried. Standing there alone, I suddenly recalled a con-versation I had with him in 1963, when he resigned (for the second and last time) as prime minister of Israel and several of us begged him to change his mind.

'Of course no one man is ever really indispensable,' I said to him. 'You know that and we know that. But I'll tell you one thing, Ben-Gurion. If we were to go to Times Square today, stop people in the street and ask them the names of the presidents and prime ministers of most of the important countries in the world, they wouldn't be able to answer us. But if we asked them: "Who is the prime minister of Israel?" they would all know.' It didn't make much of an impression on Ben-Gurion, but I think it was true; and what's more, I am sure that the names 'Israel' and 'Ben-Gurion' will be linked in men's minds for a very long time, maybe forever. No one, of course, can tell what or who the future may bring. But I very much doubt that the Jewish people will ever produce a greater leader or a more astute and courageous states-man.

What was he like as a person? It is a hard question for me to answer because it is so difficult to describe someone whom you have both admired and followed for long and have also opposed as strongly as I was eventually to oppose Ben-Gurion. But I will try – not that the way I saw him is necessarily the only way he can be seen or that my own perceptions are necessarily so sharp.

The first thing that occurs to me about Ben-Gurion when I sit down to write about him now is that he was not a man to whom one could be close. Not only to whom I was never really close, but to whom I don't think anyone was ever close, except perhaps his wife, Paula, and maybe his daughter, Renana. The rest of us – Berl, Shazar, Remez, Eshkol – were not only comrades-in-arms, we also liked each other's company, and we used to drop in on one another and talk about all sorts of things – not just the big political or economic issues, but about people, about ourselves and our families. But not Ben-Gurion. It never entered my mind, for instance, to call up Ben-Gurion and say 'Look, suppose I come over tonight?' Either you had something specific to talk about, some business to conduct with him, or you didn't go to him. He didn't need people the way the rest of us did. He was much more self-sufficient than we were, but of course he also didn't know much about people, though he used to get very angry with me indeed whenever I told him this.

I think part of his not needing anyone was due to the fact that he found it so difficult to talk to people. He had no small talk at all. I remember his telling me that when he first came to Palestine in 1906 he

once walked the streets of Jerusalem for almost an entire night with
Rachel Yanait without saying a single word to her. I could only com-
pare it to a story that Chagall once told me about himself years ago.
Chagall's father had been a poor water-carrier in Vitebsk. He carried
pails of water all day and only came home late at night. 'He would come
in, sit down, and my mother would give him something to eat,' Chagall
said. 'I never remember his talking to me or our having a single conversation together. My father would just sit at the table and tap on it with
his fingers all evening. So I grew up without knowing how to talk to
anyone.' Then Chagall fell in love with a girl and they went together for
years, but he couldn't ever talk to her. When he left Vitebsk, she waited
for him and he wanted to write to her and ask her to marry him, but he
couldn't write a letter, just as he couldn't converse with anyone. So she
stopped waiting and married someone else. Ben-Gurion was like that,
though he could write, but I can't imagine his ever talking to anyone
about his marriage or his children or anything like that. It would have
been a waste of time for him.

On the other hand, whatever interested him or mattered to him he
did with complete and total concentration – something that not everyone always appreciated or understood. Once – I think it was in 1946 –
he asked for a few months' leave from the Jewish Agency, which he
headed at that time, so that he could learn exactly what the *Haganah* had
at its disposal and what it was likely to need for the struggle he was so
sure lay ahead. Everyone laughed at the idea of what they called Ben-
Gurion's 'seminar'. Who took time off, in those days of incessant crisis,
'to study'? The answer, of course, is that Ben-Gurion did, and when he
came back to work he knew more about the real strength of the *Haganah*
than all of us put together. After he had been back at work for a few
days, he called me up. 'Golda,' he said, 'come over. I want to talk to
you.' He was walking back and forth in his big study upstairs, pacing
the floor. 'I tell you,' he said to me, 'I feel as though I were going mad.
What's going to happen to us? I'm sure the Arabs will attack us, and
we're not prepared for it. We have nothing. What's going to happen to
us?' He was literally beside himself with anxiety. Then we sat down and
talked, and I told him how frightened of the future one of our colleagues
in the Labour movement was, a man who had always been opposed to
Ben-Gurion's activism, and now, in the dark years of what we called
the *ma'avak* (our full-fledged struggle) against the British, was all the
more so. Ben-Gurion listened to me very attentively. Then he said, 'You
know, it takes a lot of courage to be afraid – and still more courage to

say so. But even Y. doesn't know how much there is to be afraid of.'
Fortunately, Ben-Gurion knew. He combined his fantastic intuition with
as much information as he could acquire and then he did something
about it. He went to the Jews of the United States – almost three years
before the War of Independence broke out in 1948 – and enlisted their
help in what he called 'the probable eventuality' of war with the Arabs.
He wasn't always right, but he was more often right than wrong – and
he was absolutely right about that.

Ben-Gurion wasn't a callous or a heartless man at all, but he knew
that sometimes it is necessary to make decisions that cost lives, and at a
time when many people in the *yishuv* thought it was impossible for us to
establish the State of Israel and defend it successfully, Ben-Gurion saw
no real alternative to doing so – and I, for one, agreed with him. Even
people like Remez had grave doubts. I remember we sat on my balcony
overlooking the sea one night early in 1948 talking about what the
future might bring, and Remez said to me solemnly: 'You and Ben-
Gurion will smash the last hope of the Jewish people.' Nevertheless,
Ben-Gurion brought the Jewish state into being. Not alone, of course,
but I doubt that without his leadership it would have been established.

From the start, we worked together very well. Ben-Gurion trusted
me and, I think, liked me. For years he never let anyone criticize me in
his presence, though there were times when I disagreed with him on
significant issues – such as the Peel Commission's proposal to partition
Palestine in 1937 or the importance of the 'illegal' immigration to
Palestine, which Ben-Gurion didn't take very seriously at first.

Was he dictatorial? Not really. It is a vulgarization to say that people
were frightened of him, but he was certainly not a man with whom
anyone disagreed lightly. Among the people who fell out of favour with
Ben-Gurion – and for whom he made life difficult – were two of the
prime ministers of Israel, Moshe Sharett and Levi Eshkol. But there
were also others.

He hated to be accused of running the party, and later the government, in an autocratic way. At one party meeting when this charge
was levelled at him, he appealed to a minister whom he regarded as
being beyond reproach from the point of view of intellectual honesty
and who, Ben-Gurion knew only too well, was not in the least scared of
him. 'Tell me, Naphtali,' he asked. '*Do* I conduct party meetings
undemocratically?' Peretz Naphtali looked at him for a minute, smiled
his charming smile and answered thoughtfully 'No, I wouldn't say that. I
would say rather that in the most democratic fashion possible, the party

always decides to vote the way you want it to.' Since Ben-Gurion had no sense of humour at all (I can't remember his ever having cracked a joke), he was quite satisfied with Naphtali's reply – and, by the way, it was not inaccurate.

The subject of government meetings and votes reminds me of a conversation I had a few years ago at a party held during a meeting of the Socialist International. I was sitting with Willy Brandt, Bruno Kreisky, one of the prime ministers of a Scandinavian country and Harold Wilson, who was not prime minister then. We were chatting about the processes of government when one of them turned to me and asked 'How do *you* conduct cabinet meetings?' I said 'We vote.' They were all horrified. 'You *vote* at cabinet meetings?' 'Well, of course,' I answered. 'What do you do?' Brandt explained that in Bonn he presented an issue, it was discussed, he gave a résumé of the discussion and then his decision. Kreisky nodded his head in agreement and added 'Any minister who dared say that he was opposed to the prime minister's summary and decision, well, he'd have to go home.' But that's not the way it is or ever was in Israel, even in Ben-Gurion's day. We always have long discussions and when necessary take a real vote. I don't think that I was ever in the minority when I was prime minister, but since we have coalition governments and therefore large cabinets – and most members of an Israeli cabinet think that they aren't performing their duty properly if they don't ask for the floor on each and every question – cabinet meetings often last for hours, even when the subjects discussed could be decided upon in half an hour. I shall never forget the astonishment on Brandt and Kreisky's faces when I patiently explained all this to them.

But to get back to Ben-Gurion, the really uncanny thing about him for most of his political life was that even when in theory he was quite wrong, he would usually be proven right in practice, and that, after all, is the difference between a statesman and a politician. Although I never forgave him the wounds he inflicted upon us over the Lavon Affair, the abuse he heaped on his former comrades or the damage he did to the Labour movement in the last ten years or so of his life, I still feel the way I felt once when I sent him a cable on his birthday from one of my missions abroad. 'Dear Ben-Gurion,' I wrote. 'We have had many arguments in the past and doubtless will have many more, but no one, regardless of what the future may hold, will ever be able to take away from me my sense of the enormous privilege I have had in working side by side, for tens of years, with the one man who, more than any other

single person, was responsible for the establishment of the Jewish state.'
I believed it then, and I still believe it.

In 1937 I was sent back to the United States, this time to raise funds
for a *Histadrut* project that held tremendous appeal for me (and, as a
fringe benefit, also fascinated my children). It was a campaign to launch
a shipping enterprise called *Nachshon* (after the first of the Children of
Israel to obey Moses's command and jump into the Red Sea during the
Exodus from Egypt), and I liked everything about it. It was a brainchild
of David Remez, born in the wake of the Arab general strike. The
ancient Jews in Palestine had been a sea-faring people, of course, but the
art was lost in the course of the 2,000 years of land-locked exile and it was
only just being revived. Then the strike of the Jaffa port workers in 1936
served as the starting signal for a major effort on the part of the *yishuv*
to train people, as I told audiences throughout the States, 'to work on
the sea as we had trained them for so many years to work on the soil'.
This meant opening a port of our own, buying ships, training seamen
and generally becoming a sea-faring nation again.

The day that the port of Tel Aviv opened for business was, in every
sense of the words, a national holiday for the Jews of Palestine. It still
moves me to remember how the waiting crowds on the shore rushed into
the sea to help the longshoremen – all of them Jews from Salonika – to
unload the sacks of cement from the Yugoslav ship that was the first to
anchor in Tel Aviv. We all knew that a wooden jetty was not really a
harbour yet, certainly no Rotterdam or Hamburg, but it was ours, and
we were very proud of it and very excited. Later it was replaced by an
iron jetty, and every evening (if the British didn't slap a curfew on
Tel Aviv), the whole town came to see how work was progressing. Poets
wrote poems about the port, songs were composed in its honour and,
more important, ships actually used it!

There was something about the idea of the return of the Jews to the
sea that had always attracted me, and I sailed whenever I could on
'Jewish' ships, of which the first was the S.S. *Tel Aviv*, on whose decks
the details of *Nachshon* were first worked out when Remez, Berl
Katznelson and I once travelled together to a Zionist Congress in
Switzerland. Of course, there were sceptics who couldn't understand
what difference it made that almost all of Palestine's sea-borne traffic
was in non-Jewish hands, but I saw *Nachson* as one more stage towards
Jewish independence, and for a while I ate, drank, slept and talked
shipping and fishing – and made yet another fund-raising trip to the
United States on their behalf. But in a sense, that was just a romantic

interlude. Sometimes in the evenings, when I was finished with cooking for the next day and whatever mending and any other work I had to do in the house and if there were no meetings of the *Va'ad Hapoel* and nobody needed to see me for anything, I used to sit on my veranda, cool off in the breeze and look out at the sea, wondering what it would be like if we had a navy of our own, a flourishing merchant fleet and passenger liners, flying the Star of David, going to Europe, Asia and Africa. It was a form of relaxation for me, just as Ben-Gurion secretly went to the movies and devoured detective stories, or other people collected stamps. I knew all the time that for us the real meaning of the sea was much grimmer, for it was only by sea that Jewish refugees from Nazi Europe could make their way to Palestine, provided that the British would let them in. And by 1939, with a world war looming, it was clear that the British Colonial Office was going to give way completely to Arab pressure and virtually stop all immigration of Jews to Palestine.

The Peel Commission, which had toured Palestine in 1936, had recommended that the country be partitioned into two states, a Jewish state to occupy all of 2,000 square miles, and an Arab state occupying the rest of the country, with the exception of an international enclave for Jerusalem and a corridor from it to the coast. The proposed Jewish state was not my idea of a viable national home for the Jewish people. It was far too small and far too cramped. I thought it was a grotesque proposal and I said so, though most of my colleagues, led by Ben-Gurion, reluctantly decided to accept it in the end. 'Some day, my son will ask me by what right I gave up most of the country and I won't know how to answer him,' I said at one of the many party meetings at which the Peel proposal was debated. I was not entirely alone in my party, of course. Berl, as I have already mentioned, and a few other ranking members of the Labour movement agreed with me. But we were wrong and Ben-Gurion, in his greater wisdom, arguing that any state was better than none, was right.

Thank God it was not because of me that we didn't get that state in 1937 but because of the Arabs, who flatly turned down the partition plan – though had they accepted it, they could have had a 'Palestinian' state forty years ago. The guiding principle behind the attitude of the Arabs in 1936 and 1937, however, was exactly what it has been ever since: decisions are made not on the basis of what is good for them but on the basis of what is bad for us. And in retrospect, it is clear that the British themselves never intended to implement the Peel plan. At all events, I certainly couldn't have lived with myself all these years if I had thought – in the light of what happened afterwards – that it was I who was to blame for its collapse. If we had had even a tiny little mockery of a state only a year before the war broke out, hundreds of thousands of Jews – perhaps many more – might have been saved from the ovens and gas chambers of the Nazis.

Although the question of immigration was quickly turning into a matter of life or death for the Jews of Europe, we seemed to be the only people in the world who understood this – and who was going to listen to us? What were we? A few hundred thousand Jews who were very far from being masters of their own fate, stuck away in some small corner of the Middle East, not even an integral part of the British Empire and lacking so much as the elementary right to say to the threatened Jews of Europe: 'Come to us now before it is too late.' It was the British who held the keys to the gates of the Jewish homeland, and they were clearly about to lock them – regardless of what was already happening.

But if Palestine was to be out of bounds for the Jews of Europe, then what about other countries? In the summer of 1938 I was sent to the International Conference on Refugees that was called by Franklin Delano Roosevelt in Évian-les-Bains. I was there in the ludicrous capacity of 'the Jewish observer from Palestine', not even seated with the delegates but with the audience, although the refugees under discussion were my own people, members of my own family, not just inconvenient numbers to be squeezed into official quotas, if at all possible. Sitting there in that magnificent hall and listening to the delegates of thirty-two countries rise, each in turn, to explain how much they would have liked to take in substantial numbers of refugees and how unfortunate it was that they were not able to do so, was a terrible experience. I don't think that anyone who didn't live through it can understand what I felt at Évian – a mixture of sorrow, rage, frustration and horror. I wanted to get up and scream at them all, 'Don't you know that these "numbers" are human beings, people who may spend the rest of their lives in concentration camps, or wandering around the world like lepers, if you don't let them in?' Of course I didn't know then that not concentration camps but death camps awaited the refugees whom no one wanted. If I had known that, I couldn't have gone on sitting there silently hour after hour being disciplined and polite.

I remember at one point thinking back to the Socialist International I had attended the year before, when I had watched the Spanish delegation, weeping and imploring for help so Madrid might be saved. All that Ernest Bevin could find it in his heart to say to them was 'British labour is not prepared to go to war for you.' Much later, I was to learn lessons of my own about socialist brotherhood, but at Évian I realized – perhaps for the first time since I was a little girl in Russia listening in terror to the hooves of Cossack horses thundering through town – that it is not enough for a weak people to demonstrate the justice of its demands.

To the question 'To be or not to be?' each nation must make its own reply in its own way, and Jews neither can nor should ever depend on anyone else for permission to stay alive. A great deal has happened to the world, to the *yishuv* and to me personally since 1938, and much of what has happened has been terrible. But at least the words 'Jewish refugees' are no longer heard anywhere because now there is a Jewish state that is prepared and able to take in every Jew – skilled worker or not, old or young, sick or healthy – who wants to live there.

Nothing was accomplished at Évian except phraseology, but before I left I held a press conference. At least the journalists wanted to hear what I had to say, and through them we could reach the rest of the world and try again to get its attention. 'There is only one thing I hope to see before I die,' I told the press, 'and that is that my people should not need expressions of sympathy any more.'

But in May 1939, despite the escalating persecution and murder of Jews in Austria and Germany, the British decided that the time was ripe, after all, for finally slamming Palestine's gates shut. The Chamberlain government gave way to Arab blackmail in much the same fashion that it was giving way to the Nazis. If appeasement was the solution to the 'problem' of Czechoslovakia, then it could certainly serve the same purpose in Palestine – about which no one seemed to care very much in any case. The 1939 White Paper on Palestine, in effect, ended the British Mandate, though the death throes were to go on for another nine years. A Palestinian state was to be created within a decade, based on a constitution that guaranteed 'the rights of minorities' and a canton system. Jewish land purchases in Palestine were to end altogether – except in some 5 per cent of the country – and Jewish immigration into Palestine was first to be restricted to a maximum of 75,000 Jews over the forthcoming five years and then stopped for ever 'unless the Arabs of Palestine are prepared to acquiesce in it'.

A day or two before the White Paper was published, I had written an article for the magazine put out by the Women's Labour Council. I had stayed up almost all night to write it, and I remember telling Menachem that even if no one read it, it had given me some relief to do it. Today, reading it again, I am struck by the irony of the timing.

Every day brings forth new edicts that engulf hundreds of thousands of people. We know, we mothers, that Jewish children are scattered everywhere in the world, and that Jewish mothers in many countries ask for only one thing: 'Take our children away. Take them wherever you choose. Only save them from this hell!'

Children cross from Germany to Austria, from Austria to Czechoslovakia, from Czechoslovakia to England – and who can assure their mothers that by getting them out of one hell, they have not got them into another?

Here, however, our children will be safe for the Jewish people. And I cannot conceive that we shall fail in our work here, in our defence of every single settlement, even the smallest, if we keep before us the picture of the thousands of Jews in the concentration camps of Europe. Therein lies our strength . . . our fundamental faith is alive. What has been done to other peoples and to other countries will not be done to us.

Little did I know that what would be done to the Jews would be indescribably worse.

Obviously, the White Paper was unacceptable. We held protest meetings and strikes and signed manifestos. But also decisions had to be taken. It was not enough to bemoan our betrayal at the hands of the British or to march, sick at heart and with bowed heads, down the main streets of Tel Aviv, Jerusalem and Haifa. What were we going to do? Were we going to defy the British, and if so, how? Towards what goal was the Zionist movement going to direct its activities now that the British had chosen – in the hour of our greatest need – to wipe their hands of the national aspirations of the Jews?

In August, I wearily explained to the children that I had to go abroad again, this time to the Zionist Congress in Geneva, where monumental issues that concerned the life of the *yishuv* were going to be thrashed out. They were terribly disappointed, I could see, but although sometimes they argued and asked if it was really necessary, this time they didn't argue at all. Actually, by the time I left for Geneva, *Mapai* policy had already been formulated. Whatever position Zionist delegates from abroad would take, we were clear about our own. Immigration would go on, even if it came to armed clashes with the British, and we would also continue to settle and defend the land. This meant, in fact, that we were committing ourselves to waging war against the British – if we had to. We, who were not even important enough to be represented fully and formally at an International Conference on Refugees? But there seemed to be no alternative, unless we, too, adopted a quota system and thus joined the society of nations that 'deeply regretted' their inability to participate in the rescue of Jews.

By the time war broke out in September 1939, Ben-Gurion had defined our position, tersely but very lucidly. 'We shall fight Hitler as if there were no White Paper and fight the White Paper as if there were no Hitler.'

7 The struggle against the British

I SUPPOSE I must have tried a thousand times since 1939 to explain to myself – let alone to others – just how and why it happened that during the very years that the British stood with so much courage and determination against the Nazis, they were also able (and willing) to find the time, energy and resources to fight so long and bitter a war against the admittance to Palestine of Jewish refugees from the Nazis. But I have still not found any rational explanation – and perhaps there is none. All I know is that the State of Israel might not have come into being for many years if that British war-within-a-war had not been waged so ferociously and with such insane persistence.

As a matter of fact, it was only when the British government decided – in the face of all reason or humanity – to place itself like an iron wall between us and whatever chance we had of rescuing Jews from the hands of the Nazis that we realized that political independence was not something that we could go on regarding as a distant aim. The need to control immigration because human lives depended on such control was the one thing that pushed us into making the sort of decision which might otherwise have waited for much better (if not ideal) conditions. But the 1939 White Paper – those rules and regulations laid down for us by strangers to whom the lives of Jews were obviously of secondary importance – turned the entire subject of the right of the *yishuv* to govern itself into the most pressing and immediate need that any of us had ever known. And it was out of the depth of this need, essentially, that the State of Israel was founded, only three years after the end of the war.

What was it that we demanded of the British and that they so stubbornly refused to give us? Today the answer seems incredible, even to me. The truth is that all that the *yishuv* wanted from 1939 to 1945 was to take in as many Jews as could be saved from the Nazis. That was all. Just to be allowed to share the little that we had with men, women and children who were fortunate enough not to have been shot, gassed or buried alive yet by the very people to whose downfall the entire British Empire was in any case totally committed.

We didn't ask for anything else: not for privileges of any kind, not for power, not for promises relating to the future. We just begged – in view of the death sentence that had been passed on millions of European Jews by Hitler and was being carried out – to be permitted to try and rescue as many of them as possible before they all perished and bring them to the one place where they were wanted. When the British first turned a deaf ear to this request and then answered that they couldn't 'cope' with it for all sorts of technical and absolutely invalid reasons (for instance, a 'lack of ships', though ships were produced in abundance when in 1940 it became 'necessary' to haul 'illegal' immigrants from Palestine to Mauritius), we stopped making requests and began to insist.

But nothing – no pleas, no tears, no demonstrations, no intervention by friends, however influential – did any good. The British White Paper remained in force, and the gates of Palestine opened only long enough and wide enough to let in the exact number of Jews stipulated in that shameful document and not one more. It was then that we all knew what many of us had always suspected: no foreign government could or would ever feel our agonies as we felt them, and no foreign government would ever put the same value on Jewish lives that we did. It wasn't a very complicated lesson to learn, but once learnt it wasn't likely that any of us would forget it, though just as incredibly the rest of the world, with very few exceptions, seems by now to have done so. It was not, mind you, as though any real choices were involved or as though a long line of other nations was queuing up in front of the British Colonial Office and clamouring to receive refugees and shelter, feed and rehabilitate them. A few countries were prepared – to their eternal credit – to take in some of the Jews if and when they managed to escape the Holocaust. But nowhere on the face of the earth except in Palestine was there a single country that was anxious to receive the Jews, prepared to pay any price for them, to do anything, and take any risks required to save them.

The British remained adamant. They went on fighting like lions against the Germans, the Italians and the Japanese, but they couldn't or wouldn't stand up to the Arabs at all – though much of the Arab world was openly pro-Nazi. For the life of me, I cannot understand to this day, in the light of what was happening to the Jewish people, why the British found it impossible to say to the Arabs: 'You have nothing at all to worry about. Once the war is over, we will see to it that each and every clause of the White Paper is fully enforced, and if they defy us, we will send the British army, navy and air force to subdue the Jews of Palestine. But right now what is at stake is not the future of the Middle East or of the Mandate or of national aspirations of any kind. It is the lives of millions of human beings and we, the British, will not stand in the way of the rescue of Hitler's victims. The White Paper will have to wait until after the war.'

And, after all, what would have happened if the British had issued a declaration of this sort? A few Arab leaders might have made threatening speeches. Perhaps there would have been a protest march or two. Maybe there would even have been an additional act of pro-Nazi sabotage somewhere in the Middle East. And maybe it would have been too late to save most of the Jews of Europe anyway. But thousands more of the six million might have survived. Thousands more of the ghetto fighters and Jewish partisans might have been armed. And the civilized world might then have been freed of the terrible accusation that not a finger was lifted to help the Jews in their torment.

As it was, in all those long, tragic years of the war and its immediate aftermath, I did not once encounter – or even hear of – a single Palestinian Jew who hesitated for one moment to offer whatever personal or national sacrifices might be needed in order to reach out to the Jews of Europe and bring them into safety. Not that there was always unanimity among us as to how this could best be done. But to the best of my knowledge, the question of whether it should be done or not never once arose. If no one else was going to help us, then we were going to have to try and go it alone – which is just what we did.

In Geneva, at that Zionist Congress of 1939, I had spent most of my time closeted with the delegates of the Labour movement's European youth organizations, planning the ways in which we could stay in touch with each other when and if war broke out. Of course neither I nor they knew then about Hitler's 'Final Solution', but I remember looking into their eyes as we shook hands and said '*shalom*' to each other and wondering what awaited each of them when they returned to their homes.

I have often replayed in my mind those relatively optimistic conversations we had in my room in Geneva towards the end of August
1939. All but a few of those dedicated young people perished later in
Auschwitz, Majdanek and Sobibor, but among them were the leaders
of the Jewish resistance movements of Eastern Europe who fought the
Nazis inside the ghettos, outside them with the partisans and finally
behind the electrified barbed wire of the death camps. I can hardly
bear to think of them now, but I believe with all my heart that one of
the things that made it possible for them to go on fighting against such
odds to the very end was the knowledge that we were with them all the
time and so they were never really alone. I am not particularly given to
mysticism, but I hope I will be pardoned for saying that in our darkest
hours, it was the memory of their spirit that gave us heart, inspired us to
go on and, above all, lent validity to our own refusal to be wiped out
to make life easier for the rest of the world. In the final analysis, it was
the Jews of Europe, trapped, doomed and destroyed, who taught us
once and for all that we must become the masters of our own undertaking, and I think it can be said that we have kept faith with them.

'We shall fight Hitler as if there were no White Paper and fight the
White Paper as if there were no Hitler' was a ringing slogan, but not
simple to implement. Actually, not one but three closely linked (though
still separate) struggles were under way in Palestine during the first years
of the war and, as a member of the *Va'ad Hapoel*, I participated in each
of them. There was the desperate struggle to get as many Jews as
possible into Palestine; the humiliating and inexplicable battle we were
forced to fight in order to persuade the British to let us take part in
military action against the Nazis; and finally there was the struggle – in
the face of almost total British indifference – to preserve the *yishuv*'s
economy so that we could somehow emerge from the war strong enough
and healthy enough to absorb a large immigration – providing there
were any Jews left to immigrate.

Since then, I have sometimes wondered how we got through those
years without going to pieces, but perhaps physical and emotional
stamina are mostly a matter of habit, and whatever else we lacked, we
didn't lack opportunities for testing ourselves in times of crisis. People,
especially my own family, have charged me for almost as long as I can
remember with driving myself too hard, whatever that really means.
Even now, when my life is relatively easy, the children are forever at me
because I don't 'rest' enough. But during those war years, I learned a
very important lesson: one can always push oneself a little bit beyond

what only yesterday was thought to be the absolute limit of one's endurance. Anyhow, I don't recall ever having felt 'tired' then, so I must have gotten used to fatigue. Like everyone else, I was so driven by anxiety and anguish that no day (or night, for that matter) was long enough for everything that had to be done. The main reason for this, of course, was that regardless of how difficult others found it to believe that the Nazis were in the process of liquidating the Jews of Europe, most of us believed it at once; and when you know that the clock is ticking away the lives of your people, there is no such thing as too much to do.

I remember quite distinctly the day that those first awful reports reached us about the gas chambers and the soap and lampshades that were being made from Jewish bodies. We held an emergency meeting in the offices of the *Histadrut* and decided on the spot to send someone to Ankara to try to make contact with the Jews from there. The curious and the terrible thing was that none of us questioned the information we had received. We all believed the reports immediately and in their entirety. The next day I had an appointment over some minor routine matter with a British official whom I had always liked, and naturally I told him what we had just learned about the Nazi atrocities. After a few minutes, he looked at me with an odd expression and said, 'But Mrs Meyerson, surely you don't believe all that, do you?' Then he went on to explain to me about the atrocity propaganda of the First World War and how utterly outlandish it had been. I couldn't explain to him how or why I knew that this was different, but I could see in his worried, rather kind blue eyes that he thought I had gone quite mad. 'You mustn't believe everything you hear,' he said to me gently before I left.

Anyhow, we did our regular jobs during the day, and in between and at night we did whatever we could about the war against the Jews. Since I had worked in the field of labour negotiations before, I went on with this work – though now I dealt almost exclusively with the British military authorities. The British, as I have mentioned, were dead set against letting the Jews of Palestine volunteer for the army (though 130,000 did so) and invented a series of complicated schemes (most of which failed) for keeping enlistment in the *yishuv* down to the bare minimum, including insistence upon equal numbers of Jewish and Arab recruits. But when the war spread to the Middle East, the Allies found themselves increasingly dependent on the one source of highly skilled (and, of course, politically completely reliable) manpower in the area. Tens of thousands of young Palestinian Jews who were barred from serving in British combat units worked throughout the war as army drivers, in the ordnance service corps and with the medical corps. They were known, needless to say, as 'Palestinians', not as Jews, and they were treated as 'natives', but at least they were part of the army. The *yishuv*'s civilian labour force, however – both skilled and unskilled – was not only treated as 'native' but also paid at Egyptian rates of pay. Since this was not acceptable to the *Histadrut*, I spent months and months arguing and negotiating with GHQ Middle East. A great many Palestinian Arabs eventually joined us in those stormy representations, though one of them – a charming man from Haifa – was to pay with his life for that united front when he was assassinated by Arab terrorists in 1947.

One typical episode of that period was the talks I conducted for weeks with a firm that had operated in Burma and was then appointed as transport agents for the Palestine mandatory government. I don't think it had ever occurred to these gentlemen before that they couldn't just hire and fire individual drivers when and as they saw fit, but I was determined to get them to acknowledge the existence of trade unions and the importance of collective bargaining. 'In Burma', they told me airily when we first met, 'we didn't need any workers' cooperatives. We had our own "cooperative" of 80,000 labourers.' But in the end, they agreed to negotiate with the *Histadrut*, and I think they also may have learned something concerning the *yishuv* and what it was all about.

As the military situation in the Middle East went from bad to worse, more and more Palestinian Jews were absorbed in the war effort, and the mandatory government began to feel itself obliged to create some kind of public body with which it could consult on economic matters. It set up a War Economic Advisory Council, of which I was a member until the war ended.

These were things that had to be done and that were important, but they were very far indeed from being central. My real preoccupations were different. The man we had sent to Ankara (Mellech Neustadt, today Noy) came back to the *Va'ad Hapoel* one day with news that made us tremble. It was as though he had returned with a message from another planet. He had found people in Turkey who could establish contact with the Jewish underground in Poland. He warned us that they were not angels, of course. In addition to asking a great deal of money for their services, he thought they would probably take for themselves huge cuts out of anything they undertook to deliver to the ghettos, and some of them were almost certainly Nazis. But we weren't hiring office workers. We were looking for emissaries who could move more-or-less freely in Nazi-occupied Europe, and their *curricula vitae* didn't matter. That very day, we began to organize a secret fund. We set what was then a staggering goal for ourselves – 75,000 pounds sterling – though we already knew that only a fraction of this sum – if we ever raised it – would get to its destination. But with that fraction Jews might be able to secure arms and food – not much of either under any circumstances, but enough, perhaps, to keep the Jewish resistance movements going, however briefly.

That was the real beginning of our desperate attempts to batter our way into Nazi-occupied Europe and throw a life-line to the Jews. By the time the war ended, there was no route we hadn't explored, no opening we hadn't pursued, no possibility we hadn't investigated at once. For years we beseeched the Allies to help us send our young men into the very heart of Europe – on foot, by submarine and finally by air. And in the summer of 1943, with great reservations, the British at last agreed. They consented to let us drop not hundreds, as we had asked, but thirty-two Palestinian Jews into Axis-held territory, where they would be able to perform a two-fold task: aid Allied prisoners of war (mostly captured airmen) to escape, and go to the aid and encouragement of the Jewish partisans.

As I write these lines, I see before me the faces of two men, neither of whom are alive today. They were very different from each other in background, personality and manner, but both of them were dear to me, and I think of them now – with a piercing pain – as typifying those dark and agonizing times. One was Eliahu Golomb, the other was Enzo Sereni; and since it must be left to writers and historians to tell the detailed story of what the Jews of Palestine tried to do – and did – during the Holocaust, I shall write only about them, though there were many many others – men and women alike – who gave to their people as much as Eliahu and Enzo did.

I knew Eliahu better and for longer than Enzo. He was part of a remarkable family – four brothers-in-law who played a major role in the upbuilding of the *yishuv* and its Labour movement. About one of them – Moshe Sharett – I shall tell even more later, because our lives and work were to become closely intertwined. But the other three were no less important at the time of the war. Each of the four (or all of them together) could well be the subject of a book that would, I think, inevitably become a saga of the entire *yishuv* – and I very much hope that one day someone will write it.

Moshe Sharett was then the head of the Political Department of the

Jewish Agency. He had inherited Chaim Arlosoroff's mantle in 1933 and always thought of himself (even then, I suspect) as the obvious candidate for foreign minister – if a Jewish state should ever come in being. He was the most 'man-of-the-world' of the four brothers-in-law, intelligent, able and a brilliant linguist. But he was also formalistic and very pedantic. Despite his considerable talents, he was no Ben-Gurion or Berl Katznelson. But he served for years, with great distinction, as Israel's foreign minister and even, for a short, bitterly unhappy period between the first and second of Ben-Gurion's resignations, as prime minister. During the war, it was Sharett, more than anyone else, who threw himself heart and soul into the maddening battle for the establishment of the Jewish Brigade, which was finally created in the last year of the war, just in time to see action in Italy.

One of Sharett's sisters was married to Dov Hos, who for years served the *Histadrut* as its 'man in London' and had developed extremely warm personal ties with many of the leaders of the British Labour Party. He was not a particularly imposing figure physically, but he had tremendous charm, and he understood and liked the British. So we often chose Dov to represent us with the mandatory authorities. His pet project was the development of aviation in Palestine, and he was a pilot himself, which the rest of us thought was very dashing. In 1940 he was killed in Palestine, together with Rivkah his wife, and daughter, in a traffic accident, and when he died we lost one of our real pillars of strength. I used to spend a lot of time with Dov whenever I was in London before the war, and afterwards we had much to do together concerning the recruiting of volunteers for the British army.

Service in the British army was not, by the way, something about which everyone in the *yishuv* felt as we did. There were people – and not a few – who argued that by putting all of our eggs into one basket, so to speak, we were endangering the actual security of Jewish towns and settlements in the event of a British defeat in the Middle East. 'It is all very well to campaign for volunteers for the army to fight the Nazis abroad, but what will happen to the *yishuv*,' they asked, 'if the Axis is victorious? Who will be left to defend Tel Aviv or Degania or Rehovot? A handful of poorly equipped members of the *Haganah*?' They had a point, of course, but not a good one in my opinion. The idea of waiting to fight Hitler until the Germans approached the borders of Palestine was absurd. We wanted to help overthrow the Nazis wherever they were, and we spent days upon days trying to persuade our opponents both inside and outside the *Histadrut* and *Mapai* that they were wrong.

Another of Sharett's in-laws (Zipporah Sharett's brother) was that fantastic man Shaul Avigur, who is still alive, thank God. No one passing Shaul today, or even then, on the streets of Tel Aviv or working in the garden of Kibbutz Kinneret (of which he is still a member) would ever guess from his rather rumpled and very ordinary appearance that for all the years preceding the establishment of the State of Israel he was, in effect, our underground minister of defence. Shaul was the man who set up the *Haganah*'s legendary intelligence service and who, when the war ended, stood at the head of what we called the '*Mossad*' (the 'Institution'), organizing and directing the intricate and dangerous 'illegal' immigration to Palestine of the remnants of European Jewry. Nothing about Shaul's exterior or manner of speech reveals the fact that unlike Sharett, Dov, Eliahu or myself, for that matter, he was a born conspirator. I have never known Shaul to write an unnecessary note or say an unnecessary word. Whatever he did or ordered to have done was carried out with maximum secrecy – and everyone was suspect, in his eyes, of possible indiscretion. Sometimes we laughed at him for what we thought was his exaggeratedly cautious attitude. I remember that when his daughter was in England for a while, she asked him to send her a bundle of Hebrew newspapers and wasn't at all surprised when her father automatically wrote 'Strictly Confidential' on the wrapper! But we all immensely respected him and still do. His authority on any matter that had to do with the underground – the secret purchase of arms in Europe in 1947, the bringing in to Palestine of Jewish refugees from Arab countries at the height of the war, the essential compilation of dossiers about the British CID – was unquestioned. Typically, Shaul was the first to devote himself, years and years ago, to the cause of Jewish emigration from Russia.

But it was the fourth brother-in-law, Eliahu Golomb, who was at the heart of everything in those days. It was his house in Tel Aviv and his office (Room 17) in the *Histadrut* building that were our real nerve centres. I don't think the light was ever turned off in Eliahu's home during the entire war or that the house was ever empty. If we had any kind of headquarters of our own then, that was it. Whatever time of the day or night you turned up to consult Eliahu (and we always walked through the kitchen, for some reason) you found his mother-in-law (Sharett's mother, whom we all called 'Mamochka') calmly ironing away, even at midnight, and Ada Golomb unfailingly ready with a glass of tea. Ben-Gurion, Sharett, Dov Hos and others were the policy-makers, the negotiators, the spokesmen of the *yishuv* to the world outside, while Eliahu Golomb – not unlike Berl in the sphere of pure ideology – was our commander-in-chief, the effective head of the *Haganah* from 1931 until he died in 1945. Like Berl, he never saw the State of Israel for himself, and also like Berl, his absence from the scene during Israel's first years was a great, I would even say constant, deprivation for all of us, because in many ways Eliahu was one of its real founders.

What did our 'commander-in-chief' look like? Well, what did any of us look like? Other than Ben-Gurion with his flying white hair, I can't think of a single one of the 'founding fathers' of the State of Israel who cut much of a figure, and Eliahu was certainly no exception. He was a small, short man with a very high forehead that was always wrinkled, and deep-set rather beautiful eyes. Like Berl, he wore a sort of uniform – a *rubashka* that buttoned down the side and a pair of creased khaki trousers. I don't remember ever having seen him in a suit. He spoke very quietly, very slowly and very persuasively, and was astonishingly well read. Actually, he was probably the least military-looking man I knew and had none of the mannerisms or affectations that leaders of underground movements often develop in order to impress their followers. In fact, there was nothing at all distinctive about him, except for his strong personality, and even that was not revealed except to the people with whom he worked most closely. But the *Haganah*, its philosophy and its strength were very largely Eliahu's creation. He had come to Palestine from Russia in 1909 and, together with Sharett, was among the first graduates of Tel Aviv's Herzlia High School. In the Jewish Legion, during the First World War, he had made friends with Berl, and under Berl's influence he began to develop his concept of Jewish self-defence in Palestine.

From the start, Eliahu conceived of the *Haganah* not as a guerrilla movement or as any kind of elite force, but as the most broadly based possible national response to the need of the *yishuv* to protect itself and as an integral part of the Zionist movement. Self-defence, he believed, was neither less nor more important than the conquest of the desert or the ingathering of the exiles. This being so, the *Haganah* had both to grow out of and belong to the entire Jewish population and therefore it had to function under the supreme authority of the *yishuv*'s national institutions, regardless of how secret its specific functions might have to be. From this concept stemmed also Eliahu's attitude towards the two dissident military organizations that eventually came into being – the *Irgun Zvai Le'umi* (IZL) and *Lehi* (the Stern Group), which evolved primarily because they disapproved of the *Haganah*'s policy of self-restraint, non-retaliation and avoidance, not to say abhorrence, of Jewish terrorism. But from the very beginning, Eliahu understood the need to prepare the *Haganah* for its ultimate role in the struggle for independence, and he always regarded it as the nucleus of a Jewish army able and entitled to defend the right of the Jews to come to Palestine, to settle in it and to lead a free life in it.

Defined in these terms, the *Haganah* had a truly unique role to play. Self-defence, in Eliahu's eyes, meant that the *yishuv* used its always-meagre resources wherever and whenever they were needed most. The same young men and women who brought Jews to Palestine 'illegally' also guarded settlers putting up stockades and water towers in areas forbidden to Jewish settlement under the White Paper, manufactured and tried to stockpile arms against future attack and even parachuted into Nazi-occupied Europe. He moulded the *Haganah* into a true instrument of national redemption, always keeping its component parts interchangeable and readying it so that in 1948, when it proved necessary, it could become *the* instrument of national redemption. He guarded and cherished this ultimate purpose so that it never became contaminated. But, of course, he could do this because he was basically a pioneer, an idealist, a socialist and a good Jew, as well as being an underground leader.

It is bitter to write about Eliahu now, in a world that has chosen to endow Arab terrorism with glamour and to admit to the so-called council of nations a man like Yassir Arafat, who has not one constructive thought or action to his credit and who, to put it quite plainly, is only a costumed multiple murderer heading a movement dedicated solely to the destruction of the State of Israel. But it is my most profound conviction – and consolation – that the seeds of the inevitable failure of Arab terrorism lie in the very concept of terrorism itself. No movement, regardless of the money available to it or the appeasement upon which it feeds – and in this case it is the sort of appeasement that has always brought disaster upon the world – can succeed for long if the calibre of its leadership is shoddy and if its only commitments are to blackmail and bloodshed. It is not by killing and maiming children, hijacking aircraft or murdering diplomats that real movements of national liberation accomplish their aims. They must also have content, goals that will serve them long after the immediate crisis has passed, and they must – to use an old-fashioned word – have some claim to intellectual and moral purity.

In the end, Eliahu's greatest gift to the *yishuv* was not the skill with which the *Haganah* carried out its operations, but its fundamental purpose, which, when the time came, was taken over almost intact into the ranks of Israel's army. Of course, there were mistakes (sometimes costly ones) and breakdowns and many disappointments. But from its first day the mission of the *Haganah* was to serve the Jewish people, not to terrorize or to dominate others, and because it gave equal weight to development and to self-determination, it prevailed and its spirit endured.

Although I myself had nothing to do with the selection of the *Haganah* volunteers who parachuted into Europe, I met all of them because each came to the *Histadrut* to take their leave of us. It was on one of these occasions that I even tried to argue Enzo Sereni out of going at all. One afternoon, I was working in my room at the *Va'ad Hapoel* when the door opened and Enzo came in. Behind his glasses, his eyes looked brighter than usual. 'I've come to say good-bye,' he said. 'I'm off.' 'Don't go,' I told him. 'First of all, you are really much too old and much too valuable here. Please be reasonable, for everyone's sake, and stay.' I knew I would never persuade him, though I tried very hard for about a quarter of an hour. But when I was through, he took my hand and said: 'Golda, you must understand. I can't possibly stay behind when it is I who sent so many of the others. Just don't worry. I give you my word of honour that we'll meet again.' But we never did. In 1945, I stood on a beach in Palestine one windy night and watched a *Haganah* ship called the *Enzo Sereni* spill a thousand or more survivors of the death camps on to the sand, having brought them safely through the British blockade. I remember thinking then that each nation honours its heroes as best it can, in its own way, and that this was ours – and Enzo would have liked it.

Enzo came from a background that was strikingly different from that of most of my colleagues. He had been born and raised in Italy, where his father had been a personal physician to the king. His was a well-to-do, very assimilated, highly cultured family. One of his uncles was a famous lawyer, and a brother became a leading communist senator. There was nothing that connected Enzo with Zionism, except for his great interest in socialism and his fascination with the kibbutz movement, about which he read and thought a great deal. In the late 1920s, after a major clash with the fascists, he came to Palestine, helped to found a kibbutz (Givat Brenner, not far from Tel Aviv, which is where I met him) and became very active in the Labour movement. He believed in a special brand of socialism that was mixed with a strong feeling for religion and, typically, he was a confirmed pacifist. We got along very well, though we always argued a lot, particularly during the 1936–9 riots, when Enzo insisted on moving around Arab villages at night, unarmed, because he said it was his duty to try and calm the Arab population. But no one could ever get him to change his mind about anything that involved principles. If something was worth doing, then he himself had to do it. So we weren't very surprised when, almost at once after the outbreak of war, he volunteered for the army.

Volunteering was one thing, but parachuting behind enemy lines was something else. He was already forty years old, had a family, was badly needed in Palestine itself and had no chance whatsoever of surviving fascist imprisonment if he were captured. It wasn't as though he was not already participating fully in the war effort. He broadcast regularly to Italy on behalf of the Allies and edited an anti-fascist newspaper that was read by thousands of Italian POWs. Nor did he lack adventure. The real story of Enzo's exploits in Iraq in 1941 has still to be told, but one of the things he did was lead young Jews out of the ghettos of Iraq, across the desert into Palestine at tremendous personal risk. All the time, however, he was haunted by the suffering of Italian Jewry and determined to go to its rescue, or at least be with it in its misery. So, having helped Eliahu to choose the parachutists, he insisted on training with them and being dropped into Italy. He was caught almost immediately, shipped in a transport of Jews to Dachau and killed there by the Nazis. He was only one of the thirty-two parachutists – the most famous of whom was the young poet Hanna Senesh – but somehow for me he symbolized all of them and the basic helplessness of our situation.

Interviewers have sometimes asked me what I feel about the Germans, and perhaps this is the time and place to answer that question. Post-war Germany was something with which the State of Israel had to deal, make contact and work. That was one of the facts of life after the Second World War, and facts of life have to be faced, however painful they are. It should go without saying that nothing will ever diminish the impact of the Holocaust. Six million murdered Jews are also a fact of life, a fact that must never be erased from the memory of man, and certainly that no Jew – or German – should ever forget. But although it took years before I forced myself – in 1967 – to set foot on German soil again, I was always in favour of reparations, of taking money from the Germans so that we could build up the State of Israel, for I believe that they owed us that much so that we could absorb the Jews who had remained alive. I also believe that Israel itself is the strongest guarantee against another Holocaust.

And when the time was ripe, years later, I was in favour also of diplomatic relations with Germany, though I violently opposed that government's choice of an ambassador and was outraged when I learned that Rolf Pauls had fought and even been wounded (he lost an arm) in the war. 'Never mind that he is a brilliant career diplomat,' I said, 'and never mind that he was not a member of the Nazi party. Let the Germans at least send an ambassador who has no war record at all.' But the German government refused to change its mind Rolf Pauls came to Israel and there were demonstrations against him, and I was sure he would have to be recalled. Fortunately, however, I was wrong. Today, he is Bonn's ambassador to Peking, but he is still one of Israel's staunchest and best friends.

When Pauls first presented his credentials in Jerusalem, I was Israel's foreign minister. Since I assumed that he had been told and thus knew exactly how I felt about his appointment, it was not an easy moment, but at least, I thought, it was a moment for truth. 'You have a most difficult task before you,' I said to him. 'This is a country made up, to a large extent, of the victims of the Holocaust. There is hardly a family that does not live with nightmare recollections of the crematorium, of babies used as targets for Nazi bullets, of Nazi "scientific" experiments. You cannot expect a warm reception. Even the women who will wait at table, if you ever come to me for a meal, have Nazi numbers tattooed on their arms.'

'I know,' Pauls answered. 'I have come to you now from Yad Vashem (Israel's memorial to the six million) and there is already one thing I can promise you. For as long as I serve here, I shall make it my business to see that any German who comes to this country goes first – as I did today – to that memorial.' And he kept his word.

Once I told Pauls about my twenty-four-hour visit to Germany, and I remember how white his face was as he listened to me. I had gone to Germany right after the Six Day War, when I was out of government. I had been attending a socialist conference in Paris with an old comrade of mine, Reuven Barkatt. One morning the phone rang and it was Abba Eban, our foreign minister, calling from New York. He was at the United Nations, fighting what looked at that point like a losing battle against a so-called Yugoslav (really Russian) resolution, one of those standard resolutions that condemned us as 'aggressors' and demanded our immediate unconditional withdrawal from the occupied territories. The French, who supported this resolution, were putting tremendous pressure on the representatives of the French-speaking African states,

Eban said, in an attempt to get them to vote for it, too. The leading French-speaking African delegation was that of the Ivory Coast, whose foreign minister was most sympathetic to Israel and whose president, Félix Houphouët-Boigny, was and is a dear personal friend of mine. Would I go, Eban asked, to see Houphouët-Boigny, who was somewhere in Europe at the time – he didn't know exactly where – and talk to him at once about that resolution?

It turned out that Houphouët-Boigny was resting at a German resort before starting an official visit to Germany. I would have given my right arm not to go there, but Eban kept pressing and, of course, I fully understood why. So I went and I talked to the president, but I barely ate or drank and I left as soon as I could. When I returned to Paris, Barkatt, who knew how hard it had been for me to go to Germany, said to me, 'Nothing else you have ever done for Israel was quite as difficult as that trip, was it?' But I didn't answer him. I couldn't even put into words for Barkatt then or Pauls later the horror and revulsion I had felt during those twenty-four hours. All I could think of were the faces of the people I had seen at the Eichmann trial, Adolf Eichmann himself and the eyes of the men, women and children whom we had brought out of that hell in the 1940s.

Although nothing ever can or will bring the slaughtered back to life, the trial of Adolf Eichmann in Jerusalem in 1961 was, I believe, a great and necessary act of historic justice. It took place two decades after those desperate years in which we tried in every way possible to deny him his prey, but it is part and parcel of the record of the Holocaust nonetheless. I was (and I am) absolutely convinced that only the Israelis were entitled to try Eichmann on behalf of world Jewry, and I am deeply proud that we did so. It was not, in any sense, a question of revenge. As the Hebrew poet Bialik once wrote, not even the devil himself could dream up an adequate revenge for the death of a single child, but those who remained alive – and generations still unborn – deserve, if nothing else, that the world know, in all its dreadful detail, what was done to the Jews of Europe and by whom.

For as long as I live, I shall never forget sitting huddled in that court-room with Sheyna, hearing the evidence of the survivors. Many of my friends had the strength to attend the trial day after day, but I must confess that I only went twice. There are not many things in life that I have knowingly dodged, but those living testimonies of torture, degra-dation and death – given in the chill presence of Eichmann himself – were literally unbearable for me, and instead I listened to the trial on the radio, as did most people in Israel. But that, too, made it impossible to go on normally with life. I worked, of course, went to the office every day, ate my meals, brushed my hair, but my inner attention was always fixed on what was happening in the courtroom, and the radio was always on, so that the trial dominated everything for weeks, for me and for everyone else. I remember listening to the people who gave evidence and wondering how and where they had found the will to live, to rear new families, to become human beings once more. I suppose the answer is that all of us, finally, crave life – regardless of what the past has held – but just as I cannot really know what it was like in the death camps, so I cannot really ever know what it was like to start all over again. That knowledge belongs to the survivors.

In 1960, standing before the Security Council to answer the charges of illegality brought against Israel by the government of Argentina (from which Eichmann had been plucked by Israeli volunteers), I tried to explain at least what the trial meant to the Jews. Of all the public addresses I have made, that was the one that most drained me, because I felt I was speaking for millions who could no longer speak for themselves and I wanted each word to have meaning – not just to be moving or horrifying for a minute or two. It is always much easier, I have discovered, to make people cry or gasp than to make them think.

It wasn't a long statement, but I shall only quote part of it here. I do so not in order to see my own words in print, but because to my sorrow there are still people who do not understand that we are committed to live and act so that those Jews who were killed in the gas chambers will have been the last Jews ever to die without defending themselves. And because they do not or cannot understand *this*, such people have also never understood what is called our 'obstinacy'.

In the record of the Nuremberg trial, we read what Dieter Wisliceny, Eichmann's aide, said about the process of the 'Final Solution':

Until 1940 the general policy within the section was to settle the Jewish question in Germany and in areas occupied by Germany by means of a planned emigration. The second phase, after that date, was the concentration of all Jews, in Poland and in other territories occupied by Germany in the east, in ghettos. This period lasted approximately until the beginning of 1942. The third period was the so-called "Final Solution" of the Jewish question, that is, the planned extermination and destruction of the Jewish race; this period lasted until October 1944, when Himmler gave the order to stop their destruction.

Further, in answer to a question whether in his official connection with Section IV A4 he learned of any order which directed the annihilation of all Jews, he said: 'Yes, I learned of such an order for the first time from Eichmann in the summer of 1942.'

Hitler did not solve the Jewish question according to his plans. But he annihilated six million Jews – Jews of Germany, France, Belgium, Holland, Luxembourg, Poland, the USSR, Hungary, Yugoslavia, Greece, Italy, Czechoslovakia, Austria, Rumania, Bulgaria. With these Jews were destroyed over 30,000 Jewish communities which for centuries had been the centre of Jewish faith, learning and scholarship. From this Jewry stemmed some of the giants in the field of arts, literature, and science. Was it only this generation of Jews of Europe that was gassed? One million children – the future generation – were annihilated. Who can encompass this picture in all its horror and its consequences for the Jewish people for many generations to come and for Israel? Here was destroyed the natural reservoir for all that is needed for a new country – learning, skill, devotion, idealism, a pioneering spirit.

I spoke also of Eichmann himself and of his direct personal responsibility, and went on:

I am convinced that many in the world were anxious to bring Eichmann to trial, but the fact remains that for fifteen years nobody found him. And he could break laws of who knows how many countries, by entering them under a false name and forged passport and abuse the hospitality of countries which, I am sure, recoil in horror from his deeds. But Jews, some of whom personally were the victims of his brutality, found no rest until they located him and brought him to Israel – to the country to whose shores hundreds of thousands of the survivors of the Eichmann horror have come home; to the country that existed in the hearts and minds of the six million, as on the way to the crematoria they chanted the great article of our faith: '*Ani ma'amin be'emuna shlema beviat ha-Mashiah*' (I believe with perfect faith in the coming of the Messiah).

And then, I ended with a question:

Is this a problem for the Security Council to deal with? This is a body that deals with threats to the peace. Is this a threat to peace – Eichmann brought to trial by the very people to whose total physical annihilation he dedicated all his energies, even if the manner of his apprehension violated the laws of Argentina? Or did the threat to peace lie in Eichmann at large, Eichmann unpunished, Eichmann free to spread the poison of his twisted soul to a new generation?

My hands shook for hours afterwards, but I hoped I had partly explained why we had brought Eichmann to trial.

That was fifteen years after the Holocaust ended. But in the early

1940s, no one knew how or when it would end – or even whether it would end at all. Despite the tightening of the British blockade, one *Haganah* ship after another (there were over sixty in all) was purchased, filled with Jews and sent on its way to Palestine. Each time, the British patrols were more alert, and the voyage in those barely seaworthy, crowded, filthy ships became more dangerous. It was not, however, only Jews escaping the European camps that the British hunted down so obsessively. It was also the *Haganah* and whatever arms it managed to accumulate – though now and then there was a lull in the British pursuit until some new restriction or anti-Jewish measure forced the *Haganah* deeper underground.

Two years stand out particularly in my memory, both for personal and political reasons. In 1943, Sarah informed me that she was leaving high school – though she only had one more year to go – and going with her youth movement group for agricultural training on a kibbutz, as well as joining the *Palmach* (the *Haganah* shock troops). (At the end of the war, this group joined Kibbutz Revivim, in the Negev, where Sarah has been a member to this day.) She had grown up to be a sweet, very shy, very serious girl and a better student than Menachem, who was absorbed in his music and had already decided to be a professional cellist. Both the children, like nearly all the teenagers in the *yishuv*, were involved in *Haganah* activities, though the subject was never openly discussed at home. But even if they said nothing, parents and school teachers knew that youngsters had often been up till late serving as couriers for the underground or circulating *Haganah* posters and leaflets. I remember actually writing one of those posters at home, though of course I took great care not to let the children see what I was doing. A day or two afterwards, Sarah said: '*Ima*, I'll be back late tonight, maybe even very late.' Naturally I wanted to know why. 'I can't tell you,' she said, and walked off with a parcel under her arm. I knew perfectly well what was in that parcel and I also knew that pasting up 'illegal' posters was a very risky business in those days. I stayed awake till dawn that night waiting for her to come home, but we observed all the rules and I didn't as much as touch on the subject next morning, though I was dying to say something.

Like Menachem, Sarah had belonged for years to one of the Labour movement's pioneer youth organizations, so I wasn't really taken aback when she made her announcement about the kibbutz. To begin with, I had wanted to live permanently on a kibbutz and I thought it was a wonderful way of life. Secondly, I could quite understand her desire to participate more directly in what was happening in the country.

The British had dismissed 85 per cent of the Negev as 'entirely unculti-
vable', though it accounted in area for almost one-half of Palestine. But
the Jewish Agency had worked out a detailed long-range plan for trying
to irrigate at least part of those two million acres of scorched sand in the
belief that hundreds of thousands of immigrants could be settled there,
and Sarah and her friends in the youth movement had decided that they
were going to take part in the great experiment. The plan called for the
establishment of three settlements – observation posts really – south of
Beersheba, which was then just a dusty little Arab town. 'If we manage
to prove now that people can live and raise crops in the Negev, we will
be doing much more for the country than if we just finish school,' Sarah
proclaimed, and in my heart of hearts, I thought she might be right.
But perhaps it could wait one year? Graduating from high school was
such an important step, and very few people, having once left school,
ever went back to it, I argued. Besides, was she absolutely sure that the
whole scheme wasn't a method of avoiding the last difficult year of high
school and final exams? Because if it was, then I certainly disapproved
of the idea.

We talked on and on. Morris was furious at the very idea of her leaving school. Eliahu Golomb, whose orphaned niece had come home with
a similar announcement, begged me to join him in a collective stand
against the youngsters. Sheyna told me that if I gave in, I would regret
it all my life and so would Sarah. But, though this may come as a surprise to some people, I have never believed in inflexibility – except
when Israel is concerned. On matters that have to do with my country, I
have never conceded an inch, but people are something else. Anyhow, I
thought it was unlikely that Sarah would surrender, so *I* did, though not
lightheartedly.

The first time I went to visit her in Revivim, I really thought I would
die. For miles around there was nothing, not a tree, not a blade of
grass, not a bird, nothing but sand and glaring sun. There was practically nothing to eat either, and the precious water which the settlers
drilled from the ground was so salty that I couldn't drink it – though
they had managed to raise some vegetables, which, mercifully, were less
fussy about the water than I was! The 'settlement' consisted of a pro-
tective wall, a watch tower and a few tents. It was intolerably hot during
most of the year but freezing cold in the winter, and I thought it was the
last place in the universe for a girl who had once almost died of a kidney
disease. But I said nothing about that either. Whenever I could, I
drove down and spent a few hours with Sarah listening to reports on the
kibbutz's progress, looking at the sluiceways and reservoir they were

building to catch the winter rains and sometimes talking to a very nice young man, Zechariah Rehabi, a Yemenite boy from Jerusalem, of whom Sarah seemed extremely fond. I often thought to myself, that life in Revivim (which means 'dewdrops' in Hebrew) might have been made more comfortable with only a little effort – despite its surroundings. But then I recalled how irritated everyone in Merhavia had been with me for such advice, and I held my tongue.

In September 1943 I appeared as a witness in an arms trial that became something of a *cause célèbre* in Palestine. Two young Jews were accused by the British of stealing arms from the army in order to turn them over to the *Haganah* and, as a member of the *Va'ad Hapoel*, I was called upon to testify in the military court. The prosecutor was a disagreeable gentleman called Major Baxter, who was obviously not nearly as interested in the two boys as he was in portraying the Jewish self-defence organization as a widespread movement of terrorists who menaced public security in Palestine. He also permitted himself to slander the *yishuv* by saying that one of the reasons for the rate of Jewish enlistment was so that the Jews could lay their hands on weapons. It was more than merely an unjust charge, it was wicked. (Nobody could have been as astonished as I was in 1975 when I got a letter from Major Baxter, written from Ireland, congratulating me on having been named 'Woman of the Year' in an American poll. 'If you are ever looking for a job,' he wrote, 'I can get you one here in Ulster, where your talents would be valuable!')

To tell the truth, I was rather glad of the chance to show Major Baxter what I thought of him, though I had to watch my step carefully. I knew that Baxter wanted more than anything else to prove that the Jewish Agency, an official institution, and the *Haganah*, which was illegal, were working hand in glove. I swore to myself that Baxter would get nothing from me except what he deserved, and I took as my motto one of my mother's favourite sayings: 'When you say no, you never regret it.' I think that excerpts of that cross-examination by Major Baxter tell more about the British attitude and behaviour towards us in 1943 than anything I could write about it now. Here is part of the report that appeared in the English-language *Palestine Post* (now the *Jerusalem Post*) on 7 September 1943. One word of explanation: Ben Shemen is a youth village that was turned upside down by the British in their frenzied search for arms there.

Major B.:   You are a nice, peaceful, law-abiding lady, are you not?
G.M.:   I think I am.

Major B.: And you have always been so?

G.M.: I have never been accused of anything.

Major B.: Well, listen to this from a speech of yours on 2 May 1940 (*reading out of a file*): 'For twenty years we were led to trust the British government but we have been betrayed. The Ben Shemen case is an example of this. We have never taught our youth the use of firearms for offence but for defensive purposes only. And if they are criminals, then all the Jews in Palestine are criminals.' What about that?

G.M.: If it is a question of defence, then I, like every Jew in Palestine, am for defence.

Major B.: Were you yourself trained in the use of arms?

G.M.: I do not know whether I am required to answer that question. In any case I have never used firearms.

Major B.: Have you trained the Jewish youth in the use of firearms?

G.M.: Jewish youth will defend Jewish life and property in the events of riots and the necessity to defend life and property. I, as well as other Jews, would defend myself.

President
of the Court: Please reply only to the questions.

Major B.: Do you have an intelligence service in the *Histadrut*?

G.M.: No.

Major B.: What?

G.M. You heard me: No!

Major B.: Have you heard of '*Haganah*'?

G.M. Yes.

Major B.: Do they have arms?

G.M.: I don't know, but I suppose so.

Major B.: Have you heard of '*Palmach*'?

G.M.: Yes.

Major B.: What is it?

G.M.: I first heard of the *Palmach* as groups of young people, organized with the knowledge of the authorities, who were specially trained at the time that the German army was drawing near to Palestine. Its function was to help the British army in any way necessary should the enemy invade the country.

Major B.: And are these groups still in existence?

G.M.: I don't know.

Major B.: Is this a legal organization?

G.M.: All I know is that these groups were organized to help the British army and with the knowledge of the authorities.

(After witness stated that a member of the *Histadrut* might be a member of the *Haganah* and *Palmach*, Major Baxter asked if they were prepared to do what she had said in her speech [in 1940].

G.M.: They are prepared to defend themselves when attacked. We have had very bad experiences in this country. When I say we are ready to defend, I want to make myself clear. This defence is not theoretical. We still remember the riots of 1921, 1922 and 1929 and the four years of disturbances from 1936 to 1939. Everybody in Palestine knows, as do the authorities, that not only would there have been nothing left, but Jewish honour would have been blemished had there not been people ready for defence, and if brave Jewish youths had not defended the Jewish settlements.

Major B.: Don't you know that the government has provided 30,000 Jewish armed special constables?

G.M.: Yes, I know, and I know that before 1936 the government was also providing for us. But no one in the government can deny the fact that if the Jews had not been prepared to defend themselves, terrible things would have happened to us. Furthermore, we are proud of the Jews of the Warsaw Ghetto who stood up against their persecutors, practically unarmed, and we are certain that they took their example from the Jewish self-defence in Palestine.

Major B.: What about this business of stealing 300 rifles and ammunition from the army?

G.M.: We are interested in this war and in the victory of the British forces, and stealing from the army is a crime in our eyes.

Major B.: But these arms might be useful for the *Haganah*?

G.M.: There is not a Jew who is not interested in this war and in the victory of the British forces.

Major B.: You wouldn't say, would you, that the rifles walked off by themselves?
(*showing the witness the exemption card of one of the defendants'*): This exemption card seems to indicate that you had conscription?

(The witness stated that it was no secret that the Jewish Agency had for some time been conducting a campaign for enlistment and that every able-bodied Jew was ordered to place himself in the armed forces. 'We have been at war with Hitler since 1933,' she said.)

President: Don't you think that the government is the best judge of whether there should be conscription or not? Would it not have been wiser to follow loyally the government decision not to have conscription in this country?

G.M.: We are not in a position to impose conscription in Palestine, but on the other hand both the government and the army asked for Jews to go into the forces and asked the Agency to help, and we thought it right to tell the Jews that this was their war.

Major B.: Do you call it volunteering when a man is dismissed from his job on account of his refusal to enlist?

G.M.: It is only moral pressure. This war means more to the Jews than to anybody else.

(Re-examined by the defence counsel, Dr Joseph, Mrs Meyerson said that even high-ranking British army officers had taken part in the Jewish Agency recruiting campaign and that some of them had come to the *Histadrut* to ask for its advice and help in recruiting Jews to the British army.)

Dr Joseph: Is it true that there was a terrible massacre and almost all the Jewish population killed in Hebron only because there was no Jewish self-defence there?

G.M.: Yes, that was in 1929, and the same thing happened that year in Safad; in 1936 there was a night of terrible slaughter in the Jewish quarter of Tiberias, and all this only because there was no *Haganah* in those places.

Major B.: Did *Haganah* also have arms before the outbreak of war?

G.M.: I do not know, but I suppose so. There were also riots before the war.

President: I ask you to limit yourself only to what concerns this case and not to go backwards, or otherwise we'll soon be back two thousand years ago.

G.M.: If the Jewish question had been solved two thousand years ago . . .

President: Keep quiet!

G.M.: I object to being addressed in that manner.

President: You should know how to conduct yourself in court.

G.M.: I beg your pardon if I interrupted you, but you should not address me in that manner.

Next day I went to visit my parents in Herzlia. My mother opened the door and said: 'Your father has been out all morning showing the newspapers to the neighbours and saying "You see, my Golda!" to everyone.'

Still, it seemed probable to most of us that when the war ended in an

Allied victory, as it obviously would, the British would rethink their catastrophic Palestine policy. At the very least, we were sure in 1945 that whatever Jews had stayed alive in Europe would be let into Palestine. In the dawn of a new post-war era, the White Paper would certainly be abrogated, particularly since there was now a Labour government in Britain. For thirty years, the British Labourites had condemned the restrictions on Jewish immigration to Palestine and issued one pro-Zionist statement after another. It may have been extremely naïve of us to have believed that now everything would change, but it was certainly not unreasonable – especially in the light of the horrifying spectacle of hundreds of thousands of emaciated survivors tottering out of the death camps into the arms of the liberating British forces.

Of course, we were quite wrong. British policy certainly did change, but it changed for the worse. Not only did Mr Attlee's government not revoke the White Paper, but it announced that it saw no need to honour any of the pledges it had made about Palestine – pledges made, even worse, not only to us but to millions of British workers and soldiers. Ernest Bevin, the new British foreign secretary, had a 'Final Solution' of his own for the problem of the Jews of Europe, who were now becoming known conveniently as 'displaced persons'. If they pulled themselves together and made a real effort, they could settle down quietly in Europe again. Never mind that the continent was one great cemetery for millions of murdered Jews or that there was only one place in the whole world to which the wretched DPs wanted to go – Palestine.

It was hard, almost impossible, for me to believe that instead of helping us – as it had solemnly promised to do for so long – to lay the foundations for Jewish independence in Palestine, a British Labour government, come to power in the wake of a world war, was now prepared to send British soldiers to wage war against innocent people who asked only one thing: that they be allowed to live out their days among other Jews in Palestine. All things considered, it was not much of a request, but Bevin turned it down with unprecedented harshness and with a lunatic stubbornness, as though the fate and future of the entire British Empire depended on keeping those few hundred thousand half-dead Jews from entering Palestine. I couldn't account then – and even today I cannot account – for the blind fury with which the British government pursued those Jews – and us. But it was that fury which left us with no alternative at all other than to take up the challenge, though we certainly weren't well equipped to do so. Between the summer of 1945 and the winter of 1947, we transported some 70,000 Jews from the DP camps of Europe on those thoroughly inadequate ships of ours and got them through a blockade ferociously maintained by a government made up of men to whose stirring proclamations on Zionism I myself had listened at countless Labour Party conferences.

The real struggle – the *ma'avak* itself – should be dated from 1945, but 1946 was, I think, the year of decision. The immediate background was the British government's astonishing refusal to agree to an appeal made by no less a person than President Truman, who asked that 100,000 Jewish refugees from Germany and Austria be allowed to enter Palestine – exclusive of the White Paper – in a one-time gesture of mercy and humanity. But Mr Attlee and Mr Bevin, who apparently thought that the 'problem' of European Jews was created only in order to embarrass the British government, said no to President Truman, too. They added, however, that if the US government was so worried about the Jews, perhaps it would help find some solution for the Palestine question. An Anglo-American Committee of Inquiry was duly formed. It visited the DP camps, heard the Jews there declare that they wanted to go only to Palestine, talked to the leaders of British and American Jewry and then came to Palestine in the early spring of 1946 to hold hearings there.

On 25 March 1946 I appeared before the Committee as a representative of the *Histadrut*. Once again, the facts (which one might have been forgiven for supposing that everyone already knew by now) had to be restated, including a capsule history of the Jews and their effort in Palestine. I tried to explain what it was like to have watched from Palestine the slaughter of millions of Jews and to have been able to do nothing about it. I also tried to warn the Committee that we were determined to put an end to what the great Hebrew poet Chaim Nachman Bialik had called 'the senseless living and senseless dying' of our people.

'I am authorized,' I said, 'on behalf of the close to 160,000 members of the *Histadrut* to state here in the clearest terms that there is nothing that Jewish labour is not prepared to do in this country in order to receive large masses of Jewish immigrants, with no limitations and with no conditions whatsoever . . .' But did the honourable members of the committee really understand what I meant? I wanted to be very sure that the issue was not confused, so I decided to tell them how it actually felt to stand in a courtroom and have to 'testify' on such matters. It couldn't hurt and it might even help. After all, they were civilized and learned men.

I don't know, gentlemen, whether you who have the good fortune to belong to the two great democratic nations, the British and the American, can, even with the best of will to understand our problems, *realize what it means to be the member of a people whose very right to exist is constantly being questioned*: our right to be Jews such as we are, no better, but no worse than others in this world, with our own language, our culture, with the right of self-determination and with a readiness to dwell in friendship and cooperation with those near us and those far away. Together with the young and the old survivors in the DP camps, the Jewish workers in this country have decided to do away with this helplessness and dependence upon others within our generation. We want only that which is given naturally to all peoples of the world, to be masters of our own fate – *only* of our fate, not of the destiny of others; to live as of right and not on sufferance, to have the chance to bring the surviving Jewish children, of whom not so many are left in the world now, to this country so that they may grow up like our youngsters who were born here, free of fear, with heads high. Our children here don't understand why the very existence of the Jewish people as such is questioned. For *them*, at last, it is natural to be a Jew.

But I couldn't guess from the expression on their faces whether they had, after all, understood or not. At least three members of the Committee, however, were to become firm friends of ours – Bartley Crum, Richard Crossman and James G. McDonald, who served as the first US ambassador to the State of Israel.

By now, Palestine was in a state of great unrest. Ship after ship brought refugees to its shores only to have the British subtract the number of 'illegal' immigrants from that month's quota of certificates of entry, and when the *Haganah* refused to halt this immigration, the British issued emergency regulations that amounted to martial law.

In April, while the committee was preparing its report, the British took one more step in their war against the refugees. It wasn't enough that the Royal Navy, the Royal Air Force and thousands of British soldiers were engaged in patrolling the coast of Palestine and trying to trap the 'dangerous political offenders' who were helping to bring the DPs out of Europe. Now, the battle spread to another country. Two *Haganah* ships (one, the *Fede*, was renamed the *Dov Hos* and the second named the *Eliahu Golomb*) were caught at La Spezia, on the Italian Riviera, just before they were due to leave for Palestine with 1,014 refugees on board. Under British pressure, the Italians refused to let the ships sail, while the refugees, for their part, refused to disembark. They declared a hunger strike and said that if force was used against them, they would kill themselves and sink the ships.

I had no doubt at all that they were desperate enough to do it, and I couldn't bear the thought of those poor exhausted people, jammed together like sardines, depriving themselves of even the little food we managed to give them. If we couldn't bring the boats in ourselves, at least we could show the immigrants – and the rest of the world – how profoundly outraged we were. I went first to the *Va'ad Hapoel* and then to the *Va'ad Le'umi* (the Jewish National Council, which represented the entire *yishuv* and of which Remez was then chairman) and suggested that we declare a hunger strike to relieve the refugees in La Spezia. We made two conditions: that each major group in the *yishuv* send not more than one representative to the *Va'ad Le'umi* in Jerusalem, where the strike was to take place, and that only fifteen people in good health would be allowed to participate.

I was on rather shaky ground here because I had just been rather ill and I wasn't really surprised when my doctor told me that it was out of the question for me to join the strikers. 'O.K.,' I said to him. 'You can choose. Either I sit with them in the *Va'ad Le'umi* or I'll sit at home and fast. You can't expect me not to be in on the strike at all.' He wasn't pleased, but he eventually gave in and handed me the precious medical certificate. I wasn't the only person to have trouble with doctors. Shazar had been ill too, but he went to a gynaecologist friend of his in Rehovot and got a certificate from him without any trouble! (Though after the strike, by the way, he was taken straight to hospital, where he stayed for nearly a month.)

We set up beds in the *Va'ad Le'umi* offices, drank tea without sugar when we were parched but ate nothing for 101 hours, though I had decided, thank God, that smoking was permissible. One difficulty that presented itself was that the third day of the hunger strike coincided with the beginning of Passover, and Chief Rabbi Herzog informed us that we must end our strike, since according to Jewish law all Jews must eat at the *seder*. So we had a consultation: the experts among us said that we need not eat more than a piece of *matzah* (no larger than an olive), and we went on with the strike. The *seder* that night was very moving. Then, and for the duration of our hunger strike, Jews filled the court-yard below us, praying and chanting, and delegations came from all over the country to wish us well. One day, to my delight, Menachem and Sarah appeared, and Ben-Gurion was with us often, though he had been against the strike for some reason. In theory, people were only allowed to visit us once a day between 12 and 1 p.m., but in fact we were very rarely alone.

I remember that a few minutes before we began the strike, we decided to visit the chief secretary of the Palestine government and make one last plea that the people at La Spezia be allowed in. He listened, then he turned to me and said: 'Mrs Meyerson, do you think for a moment that His Majesty's Government will change its policy because *you* are not going to eat?' I said, 'No, I have no such illusions. If the death of six million didn't change government policy, I don't expect that my not eating will do so. But it will at least be a mark of solidarity.'

Nonetheless, the hunger strike made an impression. On 8 May, the *Dov Hos* and the *Eliahu Golomb*, under heavy British escort, sailed for Palestine – 1,014 certificates having been duly deducted from the May quota. That month, the Anglo-American Committee published its report. It proposed that 100,000 immigrants be admitted to Palestine at once and the land-sale regulations of the White Paper be abolished. There was also a long-term suggestion that the Mandate be extended into a UN trusteeship. But Mr Bevin said no again. If 100,000 refugees entered in the face of Arab opposition, it would take an entire British division to restore order in Palestine, he said. 'In that case,' I told a party conference in Haifa that week, 'we shall have to prove to Mr Bevin that unless his policy is altered, he will have to send an army division to fight *us*.' Mr Bevin was, in fact, quite anxious to do just that – and did.

On Saturday, 29 June 1946, the British government in effect declared war on the *yishuv*. One hundred thousand British soldiers and nearly 2,000 policemen broke into dozens of kibbutzim and villages; raided the national institutions, such as the Jewish Agency, the *Va'ad Le'umi* and the *Va'ad Hapoel*; slapped a curfew on all the cities in the country that had a Jewish population; and imprisoned over 3,000 Jews, including most of the *yishuv's* leaders. The purpose of this was at least threefold. It was intended to demoralize and punish the *yishuv*, to destroy the *Haganah* and to put a stop – once and for all – to 'illegal' immigration by jailing the people who were responsible. It failed on all three counts, but from that 'Black Saturday' (as it is known today in Israel) on, Palestine became, quite literally, a police state.

Luckily, we had been tipped off that an operation of this kind was in the making. Dozens of *Haganah* commanders went into hiding, arms were moved to new caches and new codes were invented. Ben-Gurion was abroad in any case, but Remez, Sharett and virtually all the members of the Jewish Agency and the *Va'ad Le'umi* were rounded up and sent to a detention camp in Latrun. I wasn't arrested, however –

though there were people who said unkindly that this was the worst thing the mandatory government ever did to me! Perhaps I really wasn't important enough – or perhaps they couldn't accommodate women in Latrun. At all events, it was considered by many to be a mark of honour to have been rounded up that day, and one of my colleagues was so anxious to be jailed with everyone else that instead of hiding, he walked around the streets all day until a policeman finally told him to go home. I remember Paula Ben-Gurion (a lady not known for her tact) phoning me every few hours: 'Golda, you are still at home? They didn't come to take you?' I'd say no and hang up. Then she'd call again: 'Golda, they haven't come yet?' All this on the phone as though nobody else could listen in.

The British didn't only arrest people and search for arms and documents, they caused enormous wanton damage. One of the big kibbutzim, Yagur, was occupied for a whole week. The British had found a *Haganah* arsenal there and they tore the kibbutz apart. The settlers, assumed by the British to be members of the *Haganah*, refused to identify themselves by name, only as 'Jews in Palestine', and the men were all dragged off to detention camps so that only the women and children were left in Yagur when the troops took over. As soon as the soldiers left, I went there to see the damage, and I shall never forget picking up snapshots of kibbutz children with the eyes poked out of the photographs.

Since Sharett was in Latrun, I became acting head of the Jewish Agency's Political Department, and in that capacity I suggested that the *yishuv*'s response to the mass arrest of thousands of people could only be civil resistance. Not only was it impossible to take what had happened lying down, but unless we did something effective I was sure that the *Irgun Zvai Le'umi* and the Stern Group would take the matter into their own hands.

There is a time and place for everything, and this book is not the place nor this the time for going into the full, detailed and on the whole tragic story of the two dissident underground organizations that existed in the *yishuv* then, or of their relationship with the *Haganah*. I leave that to others and the future. But I feel that it would be dishonest for me not to make crystal clear my own attitude to the methods (and philosophy) of the *Irgun Zvai Le'umi* and the Sternists. I was and always have been unalterably opposed – both on moral grounds and tactically – to terror of any kind, whether waged against Arabs because they are Arabs or against the British because they were British. It was and has remained my firm conviction that, although many individual members of these

dissident groups were certainly extremely brave and extremely dedicated, they were wrong (and thus dangerous to the *yishuv*) from start to
finish. And I was positive in the summer of 1946 that if we did not react
effectively to the events of 'Black Saturday', they would do so, and
bring even greater disasters upon us. As soon as I could, I went to see
Dr Chaim Weizmann in Rehovot in the hope of persuading him to call
for this kind of massive demonstration. At that time, Dr Weizmann was
president of the World Zionist Organization and chairman of the
Jewish Agency. He was, without question, the leader and the premier
spokesman of world Jewry.

A noted scientist, he was Russian born but had lived and worked in
England for many years and had played a major role in the securing
of the Balfour Declaration. He was a majestic man, tall, good looking
and regal in bearing. Jews throughout the world thought and spoke of
him as 'king of the Jews', and although he belonged to no one
political party, he was always deeply involved with the kibbutz movement in particular and close to the Labour movement in general –
though inevitably there was friction between Weizmann the gradualist
and Ben-Gurion the activist. Their relationship worsened during the
war, when Ben-Gurion felt that Dr Weizmann was not doing enough to
press for the creation of a Jewish Brigade and even proposed to the party
that we ask Weizmann to resign from office. We didn't go along with
Ben-Gurion, of course, but later, at the Zionist Congress of 1946 in
Basle, Weizmann received a vote of no confidence.

Despite stories that are told in Israel today regarding the real
relationship between these two men, so entirely different from each other
in temperament and approach, Ben-Gurion, like the rest of us, admired
and loved Weizmann, though he never shared Weizmann's trusting and
optimistic attitude about the British. Weizmann believed – even after
1946 – that the British would come to their senses one day, and he found
it impossible to accept the extent of their betrayal of us. But whether in
or out of office, he was, for the thirty years of the Mandate, the one man
who embodied Zionism for the world outside Palestine, and his influence was immense.

It was only Weizmann who could have persuaded President Truman,
at zero hour in 1948, to recognize a Jewish state of which the Negev was
a part. He was old and frail then and nearly blind, but when Truman
did authorize the recognition of Israel by the United States on the
afternoon of 14 May 1948, it was of Dr Weizmann that he thought and
spoke. 'The old Doctor will believe me now,' he said. And there was

never any doubt in Ben-Gurion's mind that when we had a state of our own, Chaim Weizmann would be its first president.

I used to visit Weizmann quite often in Rehovot, where he and his wife, Vera, had built a house in the 1930s (it was to serve as the presidential residence from 1948 to 1952, when Dr Weizmann died). Every now and then he would call me up and say, 'Come and have a meal with us,' and I would spend an evening with him, gossiping and talking politics. He grew very bitter towards the end of his life. He spoke of himself as the 'prisoner of Rehovot' and felt that he was being deliberately excluded from policy-making. I remember once I had lunch with him and he spoke very sadly about de Gaulle and the fact that when de Gaulle wanted to, he could attend cabinet meetings and even preside over them, whereas our parliamentary system was different. I think that perhaps it was a mistake that Weizmann went on living in Rehovot, though he wanted, of course, to be near the Weizmann Institute of Science – that wonderful centre of scientific research that grew out of the Daniel Sieff Research Institute, which he had founded in 1934. If Weizmann had lived in Jerusalem and opened his house to the people of Israel – as Ben-Zvi and Shazar did when they were presidents – he would have been and felt less isolated. And if Mrs Weizmann had been less elegant and aloof, that might have helped too. At any rate, he was a very great man, and I was deeply honoured when the chancellor of the Weizmann Institute, my friend Meyer Weisgal, asked me to serve as honorary world chairman of the Weizmann Centenary Celebrations in 1974.

But when I went to see him that day in 1946, he was still in his prime and very powerful. 'If you call upon the *yishuv* to adopt a policy of civil disobedience towards the government of Palestine,' I said, 'it will show the world that we cannot acquiesce in what has happened. Only you have the necessary authority to make this proclamation effective.'

'Alright,' he said. 'But I must be assured by the *Haganah* that nothing will be done – no actions taken – until the Jewish Agency meets in Paris in August.' I promised him to make every effort to secure such an assurance from the five people (I was not yet one of them) who decided these matters, and I went to Eshkol at once to find out whether this could be done. In actual fact, action had already been decided upon by a vote of three to two, but when Eshkol heard what Weizmann wanted he immediately said that he would change his vote. He, too, realized that if the national institutions failed to react, the *Irgun Zvai Le'umi* would certainly do something. Then Weizmann backed down. I think probably his friends in England talked him out of leading a civil disobedience campaign, but whatever his reason was, I was very upset and angry.

In August the Jewish Agency meeting took place in Paris as scheduled. We didn't want Ben-Gurion, who was still abroad, to return to Palestine, because he probably would have been arrested, so we went to France and heard the details of a new proposal made by Mr Bevin. This time, Bevin suggested the cantonization of Palestine with one Jewish canton. At this point, the British were already deporting 'illegal' immigrants from Palestine to camps on Cyprus and pouring more and more troops into the country. There seemed no point at all to any proposal except one that would result in the creation of a Jewish state, but Weizmann was carrying on conversations with the British which were not exactly along these lines.

Ben-Gurion was ready to tear the world apart, but I suggested that we fly to London and talk to Weizmann ourselves. Poor man, he had lost a son in the war, his eyesight was going and his heart was being broken by the British and by his anxiety lest, in our rejection of a British cantonization plan, we plunge the *yishuv* into total war. But I couldn't stand the charge that we were being 'irresponsible' and I lost my temper – which is something I very rarely do. I got up and walked out of the room, and it took years before Dr Weizmann forgave my opposition to him then, and later that year in Basle.

Incidentally, it was not the only time I walked out of a room in that period. Only a few months earlier I had gone to see the government's chief secretary about something and was astounded to hear him say pleasantly: 'Mrs Meyerson, you must agree that if the Nazis persecuted the Jews, they must have had some reason for it.' I got up and walked out without a word and refused to see him again. Afterwards, I was told that he couldn't imagine why I was so enraged.

The Twenty-second Zionist Congress in Basle was the first to be convened after the war. It was like the gathering of a terribly bereaved family mourning the death of multitudes, but rallying itself – despite its great grief – to save the remnants and to face the problems of the present. Now we talked openly to the world about a Jewish state. Speaking in Yiddish, I recalled the dark days of the war and the events that had followed it, and I talked about our youth, the young *sabras* born in Palestine, about whom we had once asked each other: 'What is to bind these children of ours to the Jewish people throughout the world?' I wanted the Zionist delegates to know that these youngsters who had not long ago been so unfamiliar with the Diaspora were no less committed to the free immigration of Jews than we were.

The time came when the *sabras* themselves gave us the answer. They are strangers to casuistry and abstract precepts. They are plain and pure as the sun of Palestine. For them, matters are simple, clear, and uncomplicated. When the catastrophe descended upon the Jews of the world, and Jews began coming to Palestine in 'illegal' ships, as they still do, we saw these children of ours go down to the seas and risk their lives – this is no rhetoric, but literally so – to ford the waves and reach the boats and bear the Jews ashore on their shoulders. This, too, is no rhetoric, no flowery speech, but the literal truth: sixteen- and eighteen-year-old Palestinian girls and boys carried the survivors on their backs. From the mouths of Jews borne on those shoulders I have heard how they shed tears for the first time – after all they had been through in Europe for seven years – when they saw Palestinian youngsters bearing grown men and women to the soil of the homeland. We have been blessed in this youth, which sets out to offer its life not on behalf of its own particular kibbutz, or of the *yishuv* in Palestine in general, but for the sake of every Jewish child, or old man, seeking entry.

One miracle was that the Jews still came, in the face of British gas bombs and truncheons, knowing that some might be killed and that all would be shipped off to detention in Cyprus. But the other miracle was that our own children were with us in the struggle.

As to the future, these blows have strengthened our determination to demand that full measure of political independence which can only be attained through the establishment of a Jewish state.

What I did not say to the congress, because I did not yet know it myself, was that the blows awaiting us in the twenty-one months that were to pass before Israel was born were to be crueller by far than any that we had experienced in Palestine before.

8

We have our State

IF 1946 WAS DIFFICULT, then I can only describe 1947 as the year in which the situation in Palestine got completely out of hand as far as the British were concerned. In the course of that year, the battle against Jewish immigration turned into open warfare not only against the entire *yishuv* as such, but also against the refugees themselves. It was as though Ernest Bevin had nothing else whatsoever on his mind except how to keep Jewish refugees out of the Jewish homeland. The fact that we refused to solve this problem for him apparently infuriated him so that he eventually lost control altogether, and I honestly believe that some of the decisions he made regarding Palestine could only have been the result of his intense personal rage against the Jews because they could not and would not accept the judgement of the British foreign secretary as to how or where they should live.

I don't know (nor really does it matter any more) whether Bevin was a little insane, or just anti-Semitic, or both. What I do know is that he insisted on pitting the strength of the British Empire against the will of the Jews to live and that by so doing he not only brought great suffering to people who had already suffered enormously, but also forced upon thousands of British soldiers and sailors a role that must have filled them with horror. I remember staring at some of the young Englishmen who guarded the DP detention camps on Cyprus – when I went there myself in 1947 – and wondering how on earth they managed to reconcile themselves to the fact that not so long ago they were liberating from Nazi camps the very same people whom they now kept penned behind barbed wire on Cyprus only because these people found it impossible to go on living anywhere except Palestine. I looked at those nice young English boys and was filled with pity for them. I couldn't help but think that they were no less victims of Bevin's obsession than the men, women and children on whom their guns were now trained night and day.

I had gone to Cyprus to see what – if anything – could be done about the hundreds of children who were being kept there. At that point, about 40,000 Jews were living in the Cyprus camps. Each month, with great precision, the British allowed exactly 1,500 Jews to enter Palestine: 750 from the camps of Europe and 750 from Cyprus. The principle under which this policy operated in Cyprus was 'first in, first out', which meant that, inevitably, many small children were doomed to live under very difficult conditions for months. Our doctors in the Cyprus camps were very concerned about this, and one day a delegation of physicians appeared in my office in Jerusalem.

'We can take no further responsibility for the health of the infants if they stay in the camps for one more winter,' they informed me. So I began to negotiate with the Palestine government. What we suggested was some scheme that would permit DP families with a child under the age of one year to leave Cyprus 'out of turn' and then subtract their number from the DPs who left 'in turn'. This meant persuading the Palestine government to be both flexible and reasonable – at a time when it was neither – and also persuading the DPs themselves to set up a special system of priorities. It took quite a time for me to work something out with the government, but in the end I managed to do so and even got permission for orphaned children to leave as soon as possible.

The next step was obviously for me to go to Cyprus and talk to the DPs. 'They'll never listen to you,' my friends warned me. 'You will only be sticking your neck out and asking for trouble. The one thing that these people are waiting for is to get out of Cyprus, and now you want to ask them to agree to let some people who may have only been there for a week or two jump to the head of the queue. It won't work!' But I couldn't see it that way. I thought that at least it had to be tried, so I went.

When I got to Cyprus, I immediately reported in to the office of the British commandant of the camp, an elderly, tall, thin Englishman who had served for years with the army in India. It was what you might call a courtesy call. I told him briefly who I was and what I wanted and asked whether he had any objection to my touring the camps on the next day. He listened to me very stiffly and then said: 'I know all about the families with babies, but I haven't received any instructions about orphans.' 'But that was part of the agreement I made with the chief secretary,' I said. 'Well, I'll have to check it,' he answered, rather unpleasantly. Nonetheless, we went on talking, and after a while he said suddenly, 'Oh, very well, then. Include the orphans.' I couldn't understand why he had surrendered so quickly, but in the morning I discovered that he had received a telegram from the chief secretariat in Jerusalem that read: 'Beware of Mrs Meyerson. She is a formidable person!' And, I suppose, he decided on the spot to take the advice seriously.

The camps themselves were even more depressing than I had expected, in a way worse than the camps for DPs that were being run in Germany by the US authorities. They looked like prison camps, ugly clusters of huts and tents – with a watch tower at each end – set down on the sand, with nothing green or growing anywhere in sight. There wasn't nearly enough water for drinking and even less for bathing, despite the heat. Although the camps were right on the shore, none of the refugees were allowed to go swimming, and they spent their time, for the most part, sitting in those filthy, stifling tents, which, if nothing else, protected them from the glaring sun. As I walked through the camps, the DPs pressed up against the barbed wire fences that surrounded them to welcome me, and at one camp two tiny little children came up with a bouquet of paper flowers for me. I have been given a great many bouquets of flowers since then, but I have never been as moved by any of them as I was by those flowers presented to me in Cyprus by children who had probably forgotten – if they ever knew – what real flowers looked like, and who had been helped in making those pathetic bouquets by nursery-school teachers whom we had sent to the camps. Incidentally, one of the Palestinians Jews in Cyprus then – though she later escaped – was an attractive girl named Aya, a young radio operator from a captured *Haganah* ship who is today a child psychiatrist in Tel Aviv and my daughter-in-law.

At any rate, the first item on the agenda was a meeting at which I explained my mission to the committee representing all the detainees. This was followed by an open-air meeting with most of the detainees themselves. I told them that I was sure they would not have to remain on Cyprus for long and that eventually everyone would be released; but until this time came, I needed their cooperation in order to save the children. The *Irgun Zvai Le'umi* sympathizers in the camps objected violently to the agreement I had made with the British. It was all or nothing, they shouted, and there was even an attempt to attack me physically. But finally they calmed down, and we made the necessary arrangements.

There was still one problem bothering me. We had asked that 'orphans' be allowed to enter Palestine 'out of turn', but what about the children on Cyrpus who had only one surviving parent? When I got back to Jerusalem, I went to see the high commissioner, Sir Alan Cunningham, and thanked him for what he had done. Then I said: 'But there is one very tragic aspect of our agreement. It seems terribly unfair that a child whose mother or father was killed in Europe should have to stay on Cyprus when a friend who may have been "lucky" enough to have lost both parents is able to leave. Is there anything at all that we can do about this?' Cunningham – who was to be the last British high commissioner to Palestine and who was an extremely kind and decent man – shook his head rather unhappily. Then he heaved a resigned sigh, smiled and said, 'Don't worry. I'll take care of that at once, Mrs Meyerson.' I used to see him from time to time, and however tense or chaotic the situation in Palestine was, he and I were always able to talk to each other like friends. After Cunningham left Palestine on 14 May 1948 I didn't expect to hear from him ever again. But one day several months after I became prime minister I got a letter from him. It was written by hand from the country place in England to which he had retired, and its essence was that however great the pressures upon us, Israel should not budge from any of the territories we had taken in the Six Day War, unless and until we were guaranteed secure and defensible borders. I was very touched indeed by his letter.

A less pleasant reminder of those days was the ceremony I attended in Haifa in 1970, when the bodies of 100 children who had died in those dreadful camps were brought to Haifa for reburial in the lovely foothills of Mount Carmel. I tried to shake off the thought but I couldn't help wondering if the two little girls who had so solemnly handed me those flowers in 1947 were not among them. On the other hand, I often bumped into people who had attended that meeting in Cyprus and remembered it well. About five years ago, for instance, I was visiting a kibbutz in the Negev when a middle-aged woman came up to me very hesitantly. 'Excuse me for bothering you,' she said, 'but this is the first opportunity I have had in all these years to thank you.' 'For what?' I asked. 'I was on Cyprus with a baby in 1947,' she replied, 'and you saved us. Now I'd like you to meet that "baby".' The 'baby' was a sturdy, pretty girl of twenty who had just finished her military service and obviously thought I had taken leave of my senses when I gave her a great big kiss in front of everybody – without a word of explanation.

At the Zionist Congress in Basle in 1946, it had been decided that Moshe Sharett should head the Political Department of the Jewish Agency from Washington and that I should remain its head in Jerusalem. But by 1947, living in Jerusalem was like living in a city occupied by an extremely hostile foreign power. The British shut themselves up in what was actually an improvised fortress – a heavily guarded compound (we called it Bevingrad) right in the middle of town, sent their tanks rumbling through the streets at the slightest provocation and forbade their troops to have anything to do with the Jews. Whenever the *Irgun Zvai Le'umi* and the Stern Group took the law into their own hands – which, most unfortunately, they did fairly regularly – the British responded with retaliatory actions that were aimed at the entire *yishuv*, particularly at the *Haganah*, and hardly a week went by without some sort of crisis – arms searches, mass arrests, curfews that lasted for days and paralysed everyday life and, finally, the deportation of Jews without even a charge, let alone a trial. When the British began flogging members of the *Irgun* or Sternists whom they caught, the two dissident organizations responded by kidnapping and even executing two British soldiers – and all this while our battle for free immigration and land settlement was in full force.

Looking back at that period, I can see, of course, that almost any other colonial power imposing itself on a rebellious 'native' population (which is how the British saw us) would probably have behaved in an even harsher manner. But the British were harsh enough. It wasn't only their often very cruel punitive measures that made the situation so intolerable, it was also our knowledge that, whenever possible, they aided and abetted the Arabs, not to speak of inciting them against us. On the other hand, the idea of a perpetual bloodbath in Palestine was also not very appealing to Britain – least of all in her post-war mood – and in February 1947 Mr Bevin himself decided that his government was tired of the whole thing and said so in the House of Commons. Let the United Nations deal with the Palestine problem. The British had had enough. I can't imagine that the United Nations was overjoyed at having this responsibility dumped on it, but it couldn't very well refuse to accept it.

The UN Special Committee on Palestine (UNSCOP) arrived in the country in June. According to its terms of reference, it was to report back to the UN General Assembly by 1 September 1947 with some sort of concrete proposal for a solution. The Palestinian Arabs, as usual, refused to cooperate with it in any way, but everyone else did, though a little wearily: the leaders of the *yishuv*, the Palestine government and later even the leaders of some of the Arab states. I spent a lot of time with the eleven members of the committee and was horrified to discover how little they knew of the history of Palestine, or of Zionism, for that matter. But since it was essential that they learn – and as quickly as possible – we began to explain and expound as we had done so often before, and eventually they started to grasp what all the fuss was about and why we were not prepared to give up our right to bring the survivors of the Holocaust to Palestine.

Then, for reasons which will never be understood by me – nor, I suspect, by anyone else – just before UNSCOP was scheduled to leave Palestine, the British chose to demonstrate in the most unmistakable way just how brutally and tyrannically they were dealing with us and with the question of Jewish immigration. Before the shocked eyes of the members of UNSCOP, they forcibly caged and returned to Germany the 4,500 refugees who had come to Palestine aboard the *Haganah* ship *Exodus 1947*, and by so doing I think that they actually contributed considerably to UNSCOP's final recommendations. If I live to be a hundred, I shall never erase from my mind the gruesome picture of hundreds of British soldiers in full combat dress, bearing and using clubs, pistols and grenades against the wretched refugees on the *Exodus*, 400 of whom were pregnant women determined to give birth to their babies in Palestine. Nor will I ever be able to forget the revulsion with which I heard that these people were actually going to be shipped back, like animals in their wire cages, to DP camps in the one country that symbolized the graveyard of European Jewry.

Speaking at a meeting of the *Va'ad Le'umi* only a few days before the passengers of the *Exodus* left on their grim journey to Hamburg, I tried to express the disgust and grief of the *yishuv*, as well as its flickering hope that somehow someone, somewhere would intervene to save the refugees from this new torment:

The British hope that through deportation of the *Exodus 1947* they will succeed in frightening the Jews of the DP camps and terrify us. There can be only one answer on our part: this flow of boats will not cease. I am aware that the Jews seeking to immigrate to Palestine and those assisting them now face terrible difficulties, with all the forces of the British Empire concentrated for one purpose: to attack these creaking boats laden with human suffering.

Nevertheless, I believe that there can be only one effective answer: the unin-
terrupted flow of the 'illegal' ships. I have no doubts about the stand of the
Jews of the camps; they are ready for all perils in order to leave the camps.
The Jewish survivors of many European countries cannot remain where they
are.

If we in Palestine, together with American, South African, and British
Jewry, do not let ourselves be frightened, the boats will continue to come.
With much travail, greater than in the past – but come they will. I do not, for
one moment, disregard what the thousands of these boats will face in the
coming days. I know that each one of us would deem himself happy if he
could be with them. Each one of us worries over what may happen when the
Jews on the *Exodus* are brought to Germany . . . with the British forces completely free to teach these lawbreakers a lesson. There can be no doubt that
they will be steadfast, as they have been until now. The question is only
whether there is no hope for some last-minute change of heart on the part of
the British.

Since we are incapable of despair, we wish at this moment, from this place,
once more to address our call to the world, to the nations – to the many who
suffered so much during the war, to those on many of whose fronts Jews fought
and helped in their liberation. To these nations we issue this last-minute
appeal. Is it possible that no voice will be raised, that the British government
will not be told: remove the whip and the rifle from over the heads of the
Jews on the *Exodus*? And to Britain we must say: it is a great illusion to
believe us to be weak. Let Great Britain with her mighty fleet and her many
guns and planes know that this people is not so weak and that its strength will
yet stand it in good stead . . .

But the fate of the *Exodus* had already been sealed, and the ship returned
to Germany.

The summer of 1947 dragged on and on. Despite the fact that the
Tel Aviv–Jerusalem road was increasingly coming under the control
of armed Arab bands who shot at all Jewish transport from the hills
above it, there was no alternative other than for me to ferry back and
forth between the two cities and rely on the young *Haganah* guards who
accompanied me. What was really at stake was not whether I would be
killed or wounded travelling to Tel Aviv and back but whether the
Arabs would succeed in their proclaimed intention of cutting the road
altogether and thus starving out the Jews of Jerusalem. And I was
certainly not about to help them achieve this aim by refraining from
using the one road that connected Jerusalem to the Jewish centres of the
country. Once or twice a bullet whizzed through the window of the
Jewish Agency car in which I used to travel, and once we took a wrong

turn and arrived in an Arab village that I knew to be a nest of cut-throats, but we escaped without a scratch.

Sometimes there were also 'adventures' of a different nature. For instance, one time British soldiers searched my car for arms just after I had been promised by the chief secretary himself that these searches would end, in view of the growing danger to Jewish traffic on the roads. My protests did no good at all. A gun was found on one of the *Haganah* escorts and she was promptly arrested. 'Where are you dragging her to?' I asked the officer in charge of this great operation. 'To Majdal,' he said. Majdal, an Arab town, was certainly no place for a young girl to spend the night, and I told the captain that if she were taken there, I would insist on going with her. By then he knew who I was, and I don't think he looked forward at all to explaining to his superiors why a member of the Jewish Agency Executive had gone to sleep in Majdal, so he changed his mind, and we all went off to a police station in a near-by Jewish town. By then it was midnight, but I still had to get to Tel Aviv – which I duly did, royally escorted by British policemen and the *Haganah* girl who was hastily released. Others, however, were not so lucky. The death toll on the roads rose weekly, and by November 1947 the Arabs – in full view of the British – had begun to lay siege to Jerusalem.

On 31 August – only a minute or two before their deadline expired – the eleven gentlemen of UNSCOP, convened in Geneva, turned in their report on Palestine. Seven members of the committee recommended – as the Peel Commission had done – that the country be partitioned into an Arab state and a Jewish state plus an international enclave that would take in Jerusalem and its immediate vicinity. The minority (consisting, among others, of the representatives of India, Iran and Yugoslavia – all of which had large Moslem populations) suggested a federal Arab–Jewish state. It was now up to the UN General Assembly to decide. In the meantime, all the parties concerned made their responses known, and I can't say that any surprises awaited the United Nations in this respect. We accepted the plan, of course – without much elation but with great relief – and demanded that the Mandate come to an end at once. All the Arabs said that they would have nothing to do with either set of recommendations and threatened war unless all of Palestine was made an Arab state. The British made clear that they would not cooperate with the implementation of any partition plan unless both the Jews and the Arabs were enthusiastic about it, and we all knew what that meant. And the Americans and the Russians each published statements in favour of the majority recommendation.

On the next day I held a press conference in Jerusalem. In addition to thanking the committee for having worked so rapidly, I stressed that 'we could hardly imagine a Jewish state without Jerusalem' and that 'we still hoped that this wrong would be rectified by the UN Assembly'. We were also very unhappy, I said, about the exclusion of western Galilee from the Jewish state and assumed that this would be taken up at the Assembly too. But the most important point I wanted to make was that we were extremely anxious to establish a new and different relationship with the Arabs – of whom, I thought, there would be some 500,000 in the Jewish state. 'A Jewish state in this part of the world,' I told the press, 'is not only a solution for us. It should and can be a great aid for everyone in the Middle East.' It is heart-rending now to think that we were using those words – to no avail – as long ago as 1947!

The voting took place at Lake Success in New York on 29 November. Like everyone else in the *yishuv*, I was glued to the radio, with pencil and paper, writing down the votes as they came through. Finally, at about midnight our time, the results were announced: thirty-three nations, including the United States and the Soviet Union, were in favour of the partition plan; thirteen, including all the Arab states, opposed it; ten, including Great Britain, abstained. I went immediately to the compound of the Jewish Agency building, which was already jammed with people. It was an incredible sight: hundreds of people, British soldiers among them, holding hands, singing and dancing, with truckloads of more people arriving at the compound all the time. I remember walking up to my office alone, unable to share in the general festivity. The Arabs had turned the plan down and talked only of war. The crowd, drunk with happiness, wanted a speech, and I thought it would be wicked to dampen the mood by refusing. So from the balcony of my office, I spoke for a few minutes. But it was not really to the mass of people below me that I talked; it was, once again, to the Arabs.

'You have fought your battle against us in the United Nations,' I said. 'The United Nations – the majority of countries in the world – have had their say. The partition plan is a compromise; not what you wanted, not what we wanted. But let us now live in friendship and peace together.' That speech was hardly the solution for our situation. Arab riots broke out all over Palestine on the very next day (seven Jews were killed in an Arab ambush on a bus) and on 2 December an Arab mob set the Jewish commercial centre in Jerusalem on fire, while

British police stood by, interfering only when the *Haganah* tried to take action.

We were, of course, totally unprepared for war. That we had managed for so long to hold the local Arabs at bay, more or less, didn't mean that we could cope with regular armies. We needed weapons urgently – if we could find anyone willing to sell them to us; but before we could buy anything, we needed money – not the sort of money which had helped us to afforest the country or bring in refugees, but millions of dollars. And there was only one group of people in the whole world that we had any chance of getting these dollars from: the Jews of America. There was simply nowhere else to go and no one else to go to.

It was, of course, out of the question for Ben-Gurion to leave Palestine then. His role was absolutely central. I think that he himself felt that no one else could possibly raise the kind of money that was being discussed in the series of secret meetings we held in Tel Aviv in December 1947 and the early part of January 1948, and I certainly agreed with him. But he *had* to stay in the country. So who would go? At one of these meetings, I looked around the table at my colleagues, so tired and harassed, and wondered for the first time whether I ought not to volunteer for the mission. After all, I had done some fund-raising in the States before, and I spoke English fluently. My services in Palestine could certainly be dispensed with for a few weeks, and though I wasn't used to proposing myself, I began to feel that I should suggest this to Ben-Gurion. At first, he wouldn't hear of it. He was going, he said, and was taking with him Eliezer Kaplan, the treasurer of the Jewish Agency.

'But no one can take your place here,' I argued, 'while I may be able to do what you can do in the United States.'

'No. I need you here.' He was adamant.

'Then let's put it to the vote,' I said. He looked at me for a second, then nodded. The vote was in favour of my going. 'But at once,' Ben-Gurion said. 'Don't even try to get back to Jerusalem.' So I flew to the States that day – without any luggage, wearing the dress I had worn to the meeting with a winter coat over it.

The first appearance I made in 1948 before American Jewry was unscheduled, unrehearsed and, of course, unannounced. Also, I was quite unknown to the people I addressed. It was in Chicago on 21 January, at the General Assembly of the Council of Jewish Federations and Welfare Funds, which were non-Zionist organizations. Palestine, in fact, was not on the agenda at all. But this was a meeting of professional fund-raisers, of the tough experienced men who controlled the Jewish fund-raising machinery in the United States, and I knew that if I could get through to them, there was some chance of getting the money that was the key to our ability to defend ourselves. I didn't speak for long, but I said everything that was in my heart. I described the situation as it had been the day I left Palestine, and then I said:

The Jewish community in Palestine is going to fight to the very end. If we have arms to fight with, we will fight with them. If not, we will fight with stones in our hands.

I want you to believe me when I say that I came on this special mission to the United States today not to save 700,000 Jews. During the last few years the Jewish people lost six million Jews, and it would be audacity on our part to worry Jews throughout the world because a few hundred thousand more Jews are in danger.

That is not the issue. The issue is that if these 700,000 Jews in Palestine can remain alive, then the Jewish people as such is alive and Jewish independence assured. If these 700,000 people are killed off, then for centuries we are through with the dream of a Jewish people and a Jewish homeland.

My friends, we are at war. There is no Jew in Palestine who does not believe that finally we will be victorious. That is the spirit of the country . . . But this valiant spirit alone cannot face rifles and machine guns. Rifles and machine guns without spirit are not worth very much, but spirit without arms can, in time, be broken together with the body.

Our problem is time . . . The question is what can we get immediately. And, when I say immediately, I do not mean next month. I do not mean two months from now. I mean now . . .

I have come here to try to impress Jews in the United States with the fact that within a very short period, a couple of weeks, we must have in cash between twenty-five and thirty million dollars. In the next two or three weeks we can establish ourselves. Of that we are convinced.

The Egyptian government can vote a budget to aid our antagonists. The Syrian government can do the same. We have no governments. But we have millions of Jews in the Diaspora, and exactly as we have faith in our youngsters in Palestine so I have faith in the Jews of the United States; I believe that they will realize the peril of our situation and do what they have to do.

I know that we are not asking for something easy. I myself have sometimes been active in various campaigns and fund collections, and I know that collecting at once a sum such as I ask is not simple. But I have seen our people at home. I have seen them come from the offices to the clinics when we called the community to give their blood for a blood bank to treat the wounded. I have seen them lined up for hours, waiting so that some of their blood can be added to this bank. It is blood plus money that is being given in Palestine . . .

We are not a better breed; we are not the best Jews of the Jewish people. It so happened that we are there and you are here. I am certain that if you were in Palestine and we were in the United States, you would be doing what we are doing there, and you would ask us here to do what you will have to do.

I want to close by paraphrasing one of the greatest speeches that was made during the Second World War – the words of Churchill. I am not exaggerating when I say that the *yishuv* in Palestine will fight in the Negev and will fight in Galilee and will fight on the outskirts of Jerusalem until the very end.

You cannot decide whether we should fight or not. We will. The Jewish community in Palestine will raise no white flag for the mufti. That decision is taken. Nobody can change it. You can only decide one thing: whether we shall be victorious in this fight or whether the mufti will be victorious. That decision American Jews can make. It has to be made quickly, within hours, within days.

And I beg of you – don't be too late. Don't be bitterly sorry three months from now for what you failed to do today. The time is now.

They listened and they wept and they pledged money in amounts that no community had ever given before. I stayed in the United States for as long as I could bear to be away from home – for about six weeks – and the Jews all over the country listened, wept and gave money – and when they had to, took loans from banks in order to cover their pledges. By the time I came back to Palestine in March, I had raised fifty million dollars, which was turned over at once for the *Haganah*'s secret purchase of arms in Europe. But I never deceived myself – not even when upon my return Ben-Gurion said to me 'some day when history will be written, it will be said that there was a Jewish woman who got the money which made the state possible'. I always knew that these dollars were given not to me, but to Israel.

That journey to the States, however, was only one of the journeys I made that year. In the six months that preceded the establishment of the state, I met twice with King Abdullah of Transjordan, who was King Hussein's grandfather. Although both those talks remained closely guarded secrets for many years – long after Abdullah's assassination by his Arab enemies (probably the mufti's henchmen) in Jerusalem in 1951 – no one knows to this day to what extent rumours about them were responsible for his death. Assassination is an endemic disease in the Arab world, and one of the first lessons that most Arab rulers learn is the connection between secrecy and longevity. Abdullah's murder made a lasting impression on all subsequent Arab leaders, and I remember that Nasser once said to an intermediary whom we despatched to Cairo: 'If Ben-Gurion came to Egypt to talk to me, he would return home as a conquering hero. But if I went to him, I would be shot when I came back.' And I am afraid that is still the situation.

The first time I met Abdullah was early in November 1947. He had agreed to meet me – in my capacity as head of the Political Department of the Jewish Agency – in a house at Naharayim (on the Jordan), where the Palestine Electric Corporation ran a hydroelectric power station. I came to Naharayim with one of our Arab experts – Eliahu Sasson. We drank the usual ceremonial cups of coffee and then we began to talk. Abdullah was a small, very poised man with great charm. He soon made the heart of the matter clear: he would not join in any Arab attack on us. He would always remain our friend, he said, and, like us, he wanted peace more than anything else. After all, we had a common foe, the mufti of Jerusalem, Haj Amin el-Husseini. Not only that, but he suggested that we meet again, after the United Nations vote.

Another of our Arab experts, Ezra Danin, who had met with Abdullah often before, filled me in on the king's general concept of the role of the Jews. It was that Providence had scattered the Jews throughout the Western world in order that they might absorb European culture and bring it back to the Middle East with them, thus reviving the area. As to his reliability, Danin was dubious. At any rate, he said, Abdullah was certainly sincere in his expressions of friendship, though they would not necessarily be at all binding upon him.

Throughout January and February, we maintained contact with Abdullah, as a rule through the good offices of a mutual friend, through whom I was able to send direct messages to the king. As the weeks passed, my messages became more worried. The air was thick with conjecture, and there were reports that, despite his promise to me, Abdullah was about to join the Arab League. 'Was this indeed so?' I asked. The reply from Amman was prompt and negative. King Abdullah was astonished and hurt by my question. He asked me to remember three things: that he was a Bedouin and therefore a man of honour; that he was a king and therefore doubly an honourable man; and finally, that he would never break a promise made to a woman. So there could not possibly be any justification for my concern.

But we knew differently. By the first week of May, there was no doubt that, for all of his assurances, Abdullah had, in fact, thrown his lot in with the Arab League. We debated the pros and cons of requesting another meeting before it was too late. Perhaps he could be persuaded to change his mind at the last minute. If not, perhaps we could at least find out from him just how deeply he had committed himself and his British-trained and -officered Arab Legion to the war against us. A great deal hung in the balance: not only was the Legion by far the best Arab army in the area, but there was also another vital consideration. If, by some miracle, Transjordan stayed out of the war, it would be much harder for the Iraqi army to cross over into Palestine and join in the attack on us. Ben-Gurion was of the opinion that we could lose nothing by trying again, so I requested a second meeting, and asked Ezra Danin to accompany me.

This time, however, Abdullah refused to come to Naharayim. It was too dangerous, he told us through his emissary. If I wanted to see him, I would have to come to Amman, and the risk would have to be entirely mine. He could not be expected, he informed us, to alert the Legion to the fact that he awaited Jewish guests from Palestine, and he would take no responsibility for anything that might happen to us en route. The first problem was to get to Tel Aviv, which at that time was almost as difficult as getting to Amman itself. I waited in Jerusalem from early in the morning until about 7 p.m. for a plane to arrive from Tel Aviv, and when it finally turned up, it was so windy that we could hardly take off. Under normal conditions, I would have tried to postpone the trip for another day, but there were no days left. It was already 10 May and the Jewish state would be proclaimed on 14 May. This was our very last chance to talk to Abdullah. So I insisted that we try to reach Tel Aviv – even in that Piper Cub, which looked as though it would collapse in a strong breeze, let alone a gale. After we left, a message arrived at the airstrip in Jerusalem to say that the weather was far too bad for us to attempt the flight, but we were already well on our way by that time.

Next morning I set out by car for Haifa, where Ezra and I were to meet. It had already been decided that he would not disguise himself other than by wearing traditional Arab headgear. He spoke fluent Arabic, was familiar with Arab customs and could easily be taken for an Arab. As for me, I would travel in the traditional dark and voluminous robes of an Arab woman. I spoke no Arabic at all, but as a Moslem wife accompanying her husband, it was most unlikely that I would be called upon to say anything to anyone. The Arab dress and veils I needed had already been ordered, and Ezra explained the route to me. We would change cars several times, he said, in order to be sure that we were not followed; and at a given point that night someone would turn up not far from the king's palace to lead us to Abdullah. The major problem

was to avoid arousing the suspicions of the Arab Legionnaires at the
various check posts we had to pass before we got to the place where our
guide was to meet us.

It was a long, long series of rides through the night. First into one car,
then out of it, into another for a few more miles and then, at
Naharayim, into a third car. We didn't talk to each other at all during
the journey. I had perfect faith in Ezra's ability to get us through the
enemy lines safely, and I was much too concerned with the outcome of
our mission to think about what would happen if, God forbid, we were
caught. Luckily, though we had to identify ourselves several times, we
got to our appointed meeting place on time and undetected. The man
who was to take us to Abdullah was one of his most trusted associates, a
Bedouin whom the king had adopted and raised since childhood and
who was used to running perilous errands for his master.

In his car, its windows covered with heavy black material, he drove
Ezra and myself to his house. While we waited for Abdullah to appear, I
talked to our guide's attractive and intelligent wife, who came from a
well-to-do Turkish family and complained to me bitterly about the
terrible montony of her life in Transjordan. I remember thinking that I
could have done with some monotony myself at that point, but I only
nodded my head sympathetically.

Then Abdullah entered the room. He was very pale and seemed under
great strain. Ezra interpreted for us and we talked for about an hour. I
started the conversation by coming to the point at once. 'Have you
broken your promise to me, after all?' I asked him. He didn't answer
my question directly. Instead he said: 'When I made that promise, I
thought I was in control of my own destiny and could do what I thought
right. But since then I have learned otherwise.' Then he went on to say
that before he had been alone, but now, 'I am one of five,' the other
four, we gathered, being Egypt, Syria, Lebanon and Iraq. Still, he
thought war could be averted.

'Why are you in such a hurry to proclaim your state?' he asked me.
'What is the rush? You are so impatient!' I told him that I didn't think
that a people who had waited 2,000 years should be described as being
'in a hurry', and he seemed to accept that.

'Don't you understand,' I said, 'that we are your only allies in this
region? The others are all your enemies.' 'Yes,' he said, 'I know that.
But what can I do? It is not up to me.' So then I said to him: 'You must
know that if war is forced upon us, we will fight and we will win.' He
sighed and again said 'Yes. I know that. It is your duty to fight. But

why don't you wait a few years? Drop your demands for free immigration. I will take over the whole country and you will be represented in my parliament. I will treat you very well and there will be no war.'

I tried to explain to him that his plan was impossible. 'You know all that we have done and how hard we have worked,' I said. 'Do you think we did all that just to be represented in a foreign parliament? You know what we want and to what we aspire. If you can offer us nothing more than you have just done, then there will be a war and we will win it. But perhaps we can meet again – after the war and after there is a Jewish state.'

'You place much too much reliance on your tanks,' Danin said. 'You have no real friends in the Arab world, and we will smash your tanks as the Maginot Line was smashed.' They were very brave words, particularly since Danin knew exactly what the state of our armour was. But Abdullah looked even graver and said again that he knew that we had to do our duty. He also added, unhappily I thought, that events would just have to run their course. All of us would know eventually what fate had in store for us.

There was obviously no more to say. I wanted to leave but Danin and Abdullah had begun a new conversation.

'I hope we will stay in touch even after the war starts,' Danin said. 'Of course,' Abdullah answered. 'You must come to see me.' 'But how will I be able to get to you?' asked Danin. 'Oh, I trust you to find a way,' Abdullah said with a smile. Then Danin chided him for not taking adequate precautions. 'You worship at the mosque,' he said to Abdullah, 'and permit your subjects to kiss the hem of your garments. One day some evil-doer will harm you. The time has come for you to forbid the custom, for safety's sake.' Abdullah was visibly shocked. 'I shall never become the prisoner of my own guards,' he said very sternly to Danin. 'I was born a Bedouin, a free man, and I shall remain free. Let those who wish to kill me try to do so. I will not put myself in chains.' Then he bid us farewell and left.

Our host's wife invited us to eat. At one end of the room, there was an enormous table laden with food. I wasn't at all hungry, but Danin told me that I must fill my plate – whether I ate or not – because otherwise it would appear that I was abstaining from accepting Arab hospitality. So I heaped the plate but only toyed with the food. There was no doubt left in my mind that Abdullah would wage war against us. And for all of Danin's bravado, I knew that the Legion's tanks were no joke, and my heart sank at the thought of the news I would have to bring back to

Tel Aviv. It was now nearly midnight. We still had a long and dangerous trip ahead of us – and this time we wouldn't be bolstered by any false hopes.

After a few minutes, we also took our leave and departed. It was a very dark night and the Arab driver who was to take us back to Naharayim (from there we would drive to Haifa) was terrified each time the car was stopped at a Legion check post. In the end, he made us get out some distance before we reached the power station. By now it was two or three o'clock in the morning, and we were faced with having to find our way back alone. Neither of us was armed, and I must admit that I was very frightened, as well as very depressed. From the windows of the car, we had seen the Iraqi forces massing at Camp Mafrak and had talked in whispers of what would happen on 14 May. I remember my heart pounding when Danin said, 'If we are lucky – and victorious – we will only lose 10,000 men. If we are unlucky, we may have up to 50,000 casualties.' I was so upset by this that by common consent we changed the subject, and for the rest of the trip we talked about Moslem tradition and Arab cuisine. But stumbling around in the dark, we couldn't talk at all. In fact, we didn't even dare to breathe too loudly. I was badly hampered by the clothes I was wearing, not at all sure that we were going in the right direction and unable to shake off my depression and sense of failure about the talk with Abdullah.

I suppose Danin and I must have been walking for about half an hour when the young *Haganah* member from Naharayim – who had been waiting for us in a fever of anxiety all night – suddenly spotted us. I couldn't see his face in the dark but I don't think I ever held on to anyone's hand so tightly or with such relief. Anyhow, he led us effortlessly over the hills and across the *wadis* back to Naharayim. I saw him again only a few years ago when a middle-aged man came up to me in the lobby of a Jerusalem hotel. 'Mrs Meir,' he said, 'don't you recognize me?' I searched my mind but couldn't place him at all until he grinned at me very sweetly and said: 'It was I who showed you the way back to Naharayim that night.'

But I never saw Abdullah again, though after the War of Independence there were prolonged negotiations with him. Later I was told that he said about me: 'If any one person was responsible for the war, it was she, because she was too proud to accept the offer I made her.' I must say that when I think of what would have befallen us as a 'protected' minority in the kingdom of an Arab ruler who was himself murdered by Arabs within just over two years, I can't bring myself to regret the fact that I disappointed Abdullah so much that night. But I wish that he had been brave enough to stay out of the war. It would have been so much better for him – and for us – if *he* had been a little prouder.

At all events, I was driven straight back from Naharayim to Tel Aviv. The next morning there was to be a meeting at the headquarters of *Mapai* – almost incessant rounds of meetings were going on, of course, all that week – and I knew that Ben-Gurion would be there. When I entered the room, he lifted his head, looked at me and said: '*Nu?*' I sat down and scribbled a note. 'It didn't work,' I wrote. 'There will be war. From Mafrak, Ezra and I saw the troop concentrations and the lights.' I could hardly bear to watch Ben-Gurion's face as he read the note, but, thank God, he didn't change his mind – or ours.

Within two days, the final decision had to be taken: should a Jewish state be proclaimed or not? After I had reported on my conversation with Abdullah, a number of people on the *Minhelet Ha-Am* (literally the People's Administration), made up of members of the Jewish Agency, the *Va'ad Le'umi* and various small parties and groups which later became the provisional government of Israel, pressed Ben-Gurion for one last evaluation of the situation. They wanted to know what the *Haganah*'s assessment was at zero hour. So Ben-Gurion called in two men: Yigael Yadin, who was the *Haganah*'s chief of operations, and Yisrael Galili, who was its *de facto* commander-in-chief. Their answers were virtually identical – and terrifying. We could be sure of only two things, they said: the British would pull out and the Arabs would invade. And then? They were both silent. But after a minute, Yadin said: 'The best we can tell you is that we have a fifty-fifty chance. We are as likely to win as we are to be defeated.'

So it was on that bright note that the final decision was made. On Friday, 14 May 1948 (the 5th of Iyar 5708, according to the Hebrew calendar), the Jewish state would come into being, its population numbering 650,000, its chance of surviving its birth depending on whether or not the *yishuv* could possibly meet the assault of five regular Arab armies actively aided by Palestine's one million Arabs.

According to the original plan, I was to return to Jerusalem on Thursday and remain there for the duration. Needless to say, I very much wanted to stay in Tel Aviv, at least for long enough to attend the proclamation ceremony – the time and place of which were being kept secret (except for the 200-odd invitees) until about an hour before the event. All day Wednesday I hoped against hope that Ben-Gurion would relent, but he was adamant. 'You must go back to Jerusalem,' he said. So on Thursday, 13 May, I was back in that little Piper Cub again. The pilot's orders were to take me to Jerusalem and return to Tel Aviv at once with Yitzhak Gruenbaum, who was to be minister of the interior in the provisional government. But as soon as we got past the coastal plain and reached the Judean Hills, the engine began to act up in the most alarming way. I was sitting next to the pilot (those tiny planes – which we affectionately called Primuses – only boasted two seats), and I could see that even he was very nervous. The engine began to sound as though it was about to break away from the plane altogether, and I wasn't really surprised when the pilot said, apologetically: 'I'm awfully sorry, but I don't think I can clear the hills. I'll have to go back.' He turned the plane around, but the engine went on making dreadful sounds, and I noticed that the pilot was looking around below. I didn't say a word. After a while the engine picked up a bit and he asked me: 'Do you know what is happening?' 'Yes,' I replied. 'I was looking,' he said, 'for the most likely Arab village where we could land.' This was on 13 May, mind you. Then he added, 'But now I think I can put down in Ben Shemen.' At that point the engine improved a bit more. 'No,' he said, 'I think we can make it back to Tel Aviv.'

So I was able to attend the ceremony after all, and poor Yitzhak Gruenbaum had to stay in Jerusalem and couldn't sign the Declaration of Independence until after the first ceasefire.

On the morning of 14 May, I participated in a meeting of the National Council at which we were to decide on the name of the state and on the final formulation of the declaration. The name was less of a problem than the declaration because there was a last-minute argument about the inclusion of a reference to God. Actually the issue had been brought up the day before. The very last sentence, as finally submitted to the small sub-committee charged with producing the final version of the proclamation, began with the words: 'With trust in the Rock of Israel, we set our hands in witness to this Proclamation . . .' Ben-Gurion had hoped that the phrase 'Rock of Israel' was sufficiently ambiguous to satisfy those Jews for whom it was inconceivable that the document which established the Jewish state should not contain any reference to God – as well as those who were certain to object strenuously to even the least hint of clericalism in the proclamation.

But the compromise was not so easily accepted. The spokesman of the religious parties, Rabbi Fishman-Maimon, demanded that the reference to God be unequivocal and said that he would only approve of the 'Rock of Israel' if the words 'and its Redeemer' were added, while

Aaron Zisling of the left wing of the Labour Party was just as determined in the opposite direction. 'I cannot sign a document referring in
any way to a God in whom I do not believe,' he said. It took Ben-
Gurion most of the morning to persuade Maimon and Zisling that the
meaning of the 'Rock of Israel' was actually twofold: while it signified
'God' for a great many Jews, perhaps for most, it could also be considered as a symbolic and secular reference to the 'strength of the Jewish
people'. In the end, Maimon agreed that the word 'Redeemer' should
be left out of the text, though, funnily enough, the first English-language
translation of the proclamation, released for publication abroad that
day, contained no reference at all to the 'Rock of Israel', since the military
censor had struck out the entire last paragraph as a security precaution,
because it mentioned the time and place of the ceremony.

The argument itself, however, though it was perhaps not exactly
what one would have expected a prime minister-designate to be spending
his time on only a few hours before proclaiming the independence of a
new state – particularly one threatened by immediate invasion – was
far from being just an argument about terminology. We were all deeply
aware of the fact that the proclamation not only spelled the formal end
to 2,000 years of Jewish homelessness, but that it also gave expression
to the most fundamental principles of the State of Israel. For this reason,
each and every word mattered greatly. Incidentally, my good friend
Zeev Sharef, the first secretary of the government-to-be (who laid the
foundations for the machinery of government), even found time to
see to it that the scroll we were about to sign that afternoon should be
rushed to the vaults of the Anglo-Palestine Bank after the ceremony,
so that it could at least be preserved for posterity – even if the state and
we ourselves did not survive for very long.

At about 2 p.m., I went back to my hotel on the seashore, washed my
hair and changed into my best black dress. Then I sat down for a few
minutes, partly to catch my breath, partly to think – for the first time in
the past two or three days – about the children. Menachem was in the
United States then – a student at the Manhattan School of Music. I
knew that he would come back now that war was inevitable, and I
wondered when and how we would meet again. Sarah was in Revivim,
and although not so very far away, as the crow flies, we were quite cut
off from each other. Months ago, gangs of Palestinian Arabs and armed
infiltrators from Egypt had blocked the road that connected the Negev
to the rest of the country, and were still systematically blowing up or
cutting most of the pipelines that brought water to the twenty-seven

Jewish settlements that then dotted the Negev. The *Haganah* had done its best to break the siege. It had opened a dirt track, parallel to the main road, on which convoys managed, now and then, to bring food and water to the 1,000-odd settlers in the south. But who knew what would happen to Revivim or any other of the small, ill-armed, ill-equipped Negev settlements when the full-scale Egyptian invasion of Israel began, as it almost certainly would, within only a few hours? Both Sarah and her Zechariah were wireless operators in Revivim, and I had been able to keep in touch with them up till then. But I hadn't heard about or from either of them for several days and I was extremely worried. It was upon youngsters like them, their spirit and their courage, that the future of the Negev and therefore of Israel depended, and I shuddered at the thought of their having to face the invading troops of the Egyptian army.

I was so lost in my thoughts about the children that I can remember being momentarily surprised when the phone rang in my room and I was told that a car was waiting to take me to the museum. It had been decided to hold the ceremony at the Tel Aviv Museum on Rothschild Boulevard, not because it was such an imposing building (which it wasn't) but because it was small enough to be guarded easily. One of the oldest buildings in Tel Aviv, it had originally belonged to the city's first mayor, who had willed it to the citizens of Tel Aviv for use as an art museum. The grand total of about 200 dollars had been allocated for decorating it suitably for the ceremony; the floors had been scrubbed, the nude paintings on the walls modestly draped, the windows blacked out in case of an air raid and a large picture of Theodor Herzl hung behind the table at which the thirteen members of the provisional government were to sit. Although supposedly only the 200-odd people who had been invited to participate knew the details, a large crowd was already waiting outside the museum by the time I arrived there.

A few minutes later, at exactly 4 p.m., the ceremony began. Ben-Gurion, wearing a dark suit and tie, stood up and rapped a gavel. According to the plan, this was to be the signal for the orchestra, tucked away in a second-floor gallery, to play '*Hatikvah*'. But something went wrong and there was no music. Spontaneously, we rose to our feet and sang our national anthem. Then Ben-Gurion cleared his throat and said quietly: 'I shall now read the Scroll of Independence. It took him only a quarter of an hour to read the entire proclamation. He read it slowly and very clearly, and I remember his voice changing and rising a little as he came to the eleventh paragraph:

Accordingly we, the members of the National Council, representing the Jewish people in the Land of Israel and the Zionist movement, have assembled on the day of the termination of the British Mandate for Palestine, and, by virtue of our natural and historic right and of the resolution of the General Assembly of the United Nations, do hereby proclaim the establishment of a Jewish state in the Land of Israel – the State of Israel.

The State of Israel! My eyes filled with tears and my hands shook. We had done it. We had brought the Jewish state into existence – and I, Golda Mabovitch Meyerson, had lived to see the day. Whatever happened now, whatever price any of us would have to pay for it, we had recreated the Jewish national home. The long exile was over. From this day on, we would no longer live on sufferance in the land of our forefathers. Now we were a nation like other nations, masters – for the first time in twenty centuries – of our own destiny. The dream had come true – too late to save those who had perished in the Holocaust, but not too late for the generations to come. Almost exactly fifty years ago, at the close of the First Zionist Congress in Basle, Theodor Herzl had written in his diary: 'At Basle, I founded the Jewish state. If I were to say this today, I would be greeted with laughter. In five years, perhaps, and certainly in fifty, everyone will see it.' And so it had come to pass.

As Ben-Gurion read, I thought again about my children and the children that they would have, how different their lives would be from mine and how different my own life would be from what it had been in the past. And I thought about my colleagues in besieged Jerusalem, gathered in the offices of the Jewish Agency, listening to the ceremony through static on the radio while I, by sheer accident, was in the museum itself. It seemed to me that no Jew on earth had ever been more privileged than I was that Friday afternoon.

Then, as though a signal had been given, we rose to our feet, crying and clapping, while Ben-Gurion, his voice breaking for the only time, read:

'The State of Israel will be open to Jewish immigration and the ingathering of exiles.' This was the very heart of the proclamation, the reason for the state and the point of it all. I remember sobbing out aloud when I heard those words spoken in that hot, packed little hall. But Ben-Gurion just rapped his gavel again for order and went on reading:

'Even amidst the violent attacks launched against us for months past, we call upon the sons of the Arab people dwelling in Israel to keep the peace and to play their part in building the state on the basis of full and equal citizenship and due representation in all its institutions, provisional and permanent.'

And 'We extend the hand of peace and good neighbourliness to all the states around us and to their peoples, and we call upon them to co-operate in mutual helpfulness with the independent Jewish nation in its land. The State of Israel is prepared to make its contribution in a concerted effort for the advancement of the entire Middle East.'

When he finished reading the 979 Hebrew words of the proclamation, he asked us to stand and 'adopt the scroll establishing the Jewish state', so once again we rose to our feet. Then, something quite unscheduled and very moving happened. All of a sudden, Rabbi Fishman-Maimon stood up and, in a trembling voice, pronounced the traditional Hebrew prayer of thanksgiving. 'Blessed be Thou, O Lord our God, King of the Universe, who has kept us alive and made us endure and brought us to this day. Amen.' It was a prayer that I had heard often, but it had never held such meaning for me as it did that day.

Before we came up, each in turn, in alphabetical order, to sign the proclamation, there was one other point of 'business' that required our attention. Ben-Gurion read the first decrees of the new state. The White Paper was declared null and void while, to avoid a legal vacuum, all the other mandatory rules and regulations were declared valid and in temporary effect. Then the signing began. As I got up from my seat to sign my name to the scroll, I caught sight of Ada Golomb, standing not far away. I wanted to go over to her, take her in my arms, and tell her that I knew that Eliahu and Dov should have been there in my place, but I couldn't hold up the line of signatories so I walked straight to the middle of the table, where Ben-Gurion and Sharett sat with the scroll between them. All I recall about my actual signing of the proclamation is that I was crying openly, not able even to wipe the tears from my face, and I remember that, as Sharett held the scroll in place for me, a man called David Zvi Pincus, who belonged to the religious *Mizrachi* Party, came over to try and calm me. 'Why do you weep so much, Golda?' he asked me. 'Because it breaks my heart to think of all those who should have been here today and are not,' I replied, but I still couldn't stop crying.

Only twenty-five members of the People's Council signed the proclamation on 14 May. Eleven others were in Jerusalem and one was in the States. The last to sign was Moshe Sharett. He looked very controlled and calm compared with me – as though he were merely performing a standard duty. Later, when once we talked about that day, he told me that when he wrote his name on the scroll, he felt as though he were standing on a cliff with a gale blowing up all around him and nothing to hold on to except his determination not to be blown over into the raging sea below – but none of this showed at the time.

After the Palestine Philharmonic Orchestra played the '*Hatikvah*', Ben-Gurion rapped his gavel for the third time: 'The State of Israel is established. This meeting is ended.' We all shook hands and embraced each other. The ceremony was over. Israel was a reality.

Not unexpectedly, the evening was filled with suspense. I stayed in the hotel, talking to friends. Someone opened a bottle of wine and we drank a toast to the state. A few of the guests and their young *Haganah* escorts sang and danced, and we heard people laughing and singing in the street. But we knew that at midnight the Mandate would terminate, the British high commissioner would sail away, the last British soldier would leave Palestine, and we were certain that the Arab armies would march across the borders of the state we had just founded. We were independent now, but in a few hours we would be at war. Not only was I not gay, I was very frightened – and with good reason. Still, there is a great difference between being frightened and lacking faith, and though the entire Jewish population of the reborn state numbered only 650,000, I knew for certain that night that we had dug in and that no one would be able to disperse or displace us ever again.

But I think it was only on the following day that I really grasped what had happened in the Tel Aviv Museum. Three separate but very closely linked events brought the truth home to me as nothing else could have done, and I realized, perhaps for the first time, that nothing would ever be the same again. Not for me, not for the Jewish people, not for the Middle East. To begin with, just before dawn on Saturday, I saw for myself through the windows of my room what might be called the formal start of the War of Independence: four Egyptian Spitfires zooming across the city on their way to bomb Tel Aviv's power station and airport in what was the first air raid of the war. Then, a little later, I watched the first boatload of Jewish immigrants – no longer 'illegals' – enter the port of Tel Aviv, freely and proudly. No one hunted them down any more or chased them or punished them for coming home. The shameful era of the 'certificates' and the human arithmetic had ended, and as I stood there in the sun, my eyes fixed on that ship (an old Greek vessel called the S.S. *Teti*), I felt that no price demanded of us for this gift could possibly be too high. The first legal immigrant to land in the State of Israel was a tired, shabby old man called Samuel Brand, a survivor of Buchenwald. In his hand he clutched a crumpled slip of paper. It said only 'The right to settle in Israel is hereby given', but it was signed by 'the Immigration Department' of the state, and it was the first visa we ever issued.

And then, of course, there was the wonderful moment of our formal entry into the family of nations. A few minutes after midnight on the night of 14 May, my phone rang. It had been ringing all evening, and as I ran to answer it, I wondered what bad news I would hear now. But the voice at the other end of the phone sounded jubilant. 'Golda? Are you listening? Truman has recognized us!' I can't remember what I said or did, but I remember how I felt. It was like a miracle coming at the time of our greatest vulnerability, on the eve of the invasion, and I was filled with joy and relief. In a way, though all Israel rejoiced and gave thanks, I think that what President Truman did that night may have meant more to me than to most of my colleagues because I was the 'American' among us, the one who knew most about the United States, its history and its people, the only one who had grown up in that great democracy. And although I was as astonished as everyone else by the speed of the recognition, I was not at all surprised by the generous and good impulse that had brought it about. In retrospect, I think that like most miracles this one was probably triggered by two very simple things: the fact that Harry Truman understood and respected our drive for independence because he was the sort of man who, under different circumstances, might well have been one of us himself; and the profound impression made upon him by Chaim Weizmann, whom he had received in Washington and who had pleaded our cause and explained our situation in a way that no one had ever done in the White House before. Weizmann's work was of incalculable value. American recognition was the greatest thing that could have happened to us that night.

As for the Soviet recognition of Israel, which followed the American recognition, that had other roots. There is now no doubt in my mind that the primary Soviet consideration was to get the British out of the Middle East. But all through the debates that had taken place at the United Nations in the autumn of 1947, it had seemed to me that the Soviet bloc was supporting us also because of the terrible toll that the Russians themselves had paid in the world war and their resultantly deep feeling that the Jews, who had also suffered so bitterly at the hands of the Nazis, deserved to have their state. However radically the Soviet attitude has changed in the intervening two and a half decades, I cannot now falsify the picture as I saw it then. Had it not been for the arms and ammunition that we were able to buy in Czechoslovakia and transport through Yugoslavia and other Balkan countries in those dark days at the start of the war, I do not know whether we actually could have held out until the tide changed, as it did by June 1948. For the first six weeks of the War of Independence, we relied largely (though not, of course, entirely) on the shells, machine guns, bullets – and even planes – that the *Haganah* had been able to purchase in Eastern Europe at a time when even the United States had declared an embargo on the sale or shipment of arms to the Middle East. One cannot and must not try to erase the past merely because it does not fit the present, and the fact remains that although the Soviet Union was to turn so savagely against and upon us in the years to come, the Soviet recognition of the State of Israel on 18 May was of immense significance for us. It meant that the two greatest powers in the world had come together, for the first time since the Second World War, to back the Jewish state, and though we were still in deadly danger, we knew, at last, that we were not alone. It was in that knowledge – combined with sheer necessity – that we found the spiritual, if not the material, strength that was to lead us to victory.

Also, while I am on this subject, let me say – for the record – that the second state to offer recognition to Israel on the day of its birth was little Guatemala, whose ambassador to the United Nations, Jorge Garcia Granados, had been one of the most active members of UNSCOP.

So now we were an accepted fact. The only question that remained – and incredibly enough, remains to this very day – was how we would stay alive. Not 'if', but 'how'. By the morning of 15 May, Israel was already under armed attack by the Egyptians from the south, the Syrians and Lebanese from the north and the north-east, the Jordanians and the Iraqis from the east. On paper, it seemed that week as though there might be some grounds for the Arab boast that within ten days Israel would be crushed.

The most relentless advance was that of the Egyptians – though of all the invading armies, the Egyptians certainly had least to gain. Abdullah had a reason. It was a bad one, but it was there, and he was able to define it: he wanted the whole country and especially Jerusalem. Lebanon and Syria also had a reason: they hoped to be able to divide up Galilee between themselves. Iraq wanted to participate in the blood-letting and – as a fringe benefit – acquire an outlet to the Mediterranean, through Jordan if necessary. But Egypt had no real war aim at all – except to loot and destroy whatever the Jews had built. As a matter of fact, it has never ceased to astonish me that the Arab states have been so eager to go to war against us. Almost from the very beginning of

Zionist settlement until today, they have been consumed by hatred for us. The only possible explanation – and it is a ridiculous one – is that they simply cannot bear our presence or forgive us for existing, and I find it hard to believe that the leaders of *all* the Arab states are and always have been so hopelessly primitive in their thinking.

On the other hand, what have we ever done to threaten the Arab states? True, we have not stood in line to return territory we won in wars they started, but territory, after all, has never ever been what Arab aggression is all about – and in 1948 it was certainly not a need for more land that drove the Egyptians northwards in the hope of reaching and destroying Tel Aviv and Jewish Jerusalem. So what was it? An overpowering irrational urge to eliminate us physically? Fear of the progress we might introduce in the Middle East? A distaste for Western civilization? Who knows? Whatever it was, it has lasted – but then so have we – and the solution will probably not be found for many years, though I have no doubt at all that the time will come when the Arab states will accept us – as we are and for what we are. In a nutshell, peace is – and always has been – dependent entirely upon only one thing: the Arab leaders must acquiesce to our being here.

In 1948, however, it was understandable that the Arab states – given in any case to chronic flights of fancy – saw themselves as racing through what was now Israel in a matter of days. To begin with, they had begun the war, which gave them great tactical superiority. Secondly, they had easy, not to say effortless, overland access to Palestine, with its Arab population that had been incited against the Jews for years. Thirdly, the Arabs could move without any problems from one part of the country to the other. Fourthly, the Arabs controlled most of the hilly regions of Palestine from which our lowland settlements could be attacked without much difficulty. Finally, the Arabs had an absolute superiority of manpower and arms and had been given considerable help by the British in various ways, both direct and indirect.

And what did we have? Not much of anything – and even that is an exaggeration. A few thousand rifles, a few hundred machine guns, an assortment of other firearms, but on 14 May 1948 not a single cannon or tank, though we had all of nine planes (never mind that only one had two engines!) The machinery for making arms had been bought abroad – thanks to Ben-Gurion's amazing foresight – but couldn't be brought into Israel until the British had left, and then it had to be assembled and run in. Our trained manpower situation was also most unimpressive, as far as statistics were concerned. There were about 45,000 men, women and teenagers in the *Haganah*, a few thousand members of the two dissident underground organizations and a few hundred recent arrivals who had been given some training – with wooden rifles and dummy bullets – in the DP camps of Germany and the detention camps of Cyprus (and after independence, another few thousand Jewish and non-Jewish volunteers from abroad). That was all. But we couldn't afford the luxury of pessimism either, so we made an altogether different kind of calculation based on the fact that the 650,000 of us were more highly motivated to stay alive than anyone outside Israel could be expected to understand, and that the only option available to us, if we didn't want to be pushed into the sea, was to win the war. So we won it. But it wasn't easy, it wasn't quick and it wasn't cheap. From the day that the UN resolution to partition Palestine was passed (29 November 1947) until the day that the first armistice agreement was signed by Israel and Egypt (24 February 1949), 6,000 young Israelis were killed, one per cent of our entire population, and although we couldn't have known it then, we hadn't even bought peace with all those lives.

For me to have had to leave Israel the moment the state was established was more difficult than I can say. The very last thing I wanted to do was to go abroad, but on Sunday, 16 May, a cable came from Henry Montor, vice-president of the United Jewish Appeal. American Jewry had been profoundly moved by what had happened. There were no limits to its excitement or its pride. If I came back, even for a short tour, he thought we might raise another 50 million dollars. No one knew better than I what that kind of money would mean to Israel, how desperately we needed the arms it would buy, or how much it would cost to move and settle the 30,000 Jews penned up in Cyprus who had waited so long to come to Israel. My heart sank at the thought of tearing myself away from the country, but there was no real choice at all. After discussing the matter with Ben-Gurion, I cabled back at once that I would leave on the first plane. Luckily, there were no preparations to make for the trip. My clothes, such as they were, were all in Jerusalem, as out of reach as though they were on the moon, so all I had to 'pack' was a hairbrush, a toothbrush and a clean blouse, though when I got to New York I discovered that the veil I had worn to Amman was still in my bag! I managed to speak to Sarah briefly and tell her that I would be back in a month at the very most, and to receive a hastily produced *laissez-passer* which was, in fact, the first travel document to be given to any citizen of the State of Israel. Then I left on the very first plane that was available.

In the States, I was greeted as though I were the personification of Israel. Over and over again I told the story of the proclamation, of the beginning of the war, of the continuing siege of Jerusalem, and over and over again I assured the Jews of America that with their help Israel would prevail. I spoke in city after city throughout the States, at UJA lunches, dinners and teas and at parlour meetings in people's homes. Whenever I felt overwhelmed by fatigue – which was often – all I had to do was to remind myself that I was now talking as an emissary of a Jewish state, and my tiredness simply drained away. It even took me weeks to accustom myself to the sound of the word 'Israel' and to the fact that I now had a new nationality. But the purpose of my journey was not in the least sentimental. I had come to raise money, as much money as possible, as quickly as possible, and my message was as blunt in May as it had been in January. The State of Israel, I told Jews all over America, could not survive on applause. The war would not be won by speeches or declarations or even tears of happiness. And time was of the essence, or there would be nothing to applaud.

'We cannot go on without your help,' I said in dozens of public and private appearances. 'What we ask of you is that you share in our responsibility, with everything that this implies – difficulties, problems, hardships and joys. Surely what is happening in the Jewish world today is so important and so vital that you, too, can change your way of life for a year, or two, or three until together we have put Israel on its feet. Make up your minds and give me your answers.'

They answered me with unprecedented generosity and speed, with their whole hearts and souls. Nothing was too much or too good, and by their response they re-affirmed their sense of partnership with us, as I had hoped they would. Although there was as yet no separate drive for Israel, and although less then 50 per cent of the 150 million dollars raised for the UJA in 1948 actually went to Israel (the rest was turned over to the Joint Distribution Committee for aid to Jews in European countries), that 50 per cent unquestionably helped us to win the war. and it also taught us that the involvement of American Jewry in the State of Israel was a factor upon which we could count.

As I travelled, I met many people who were themselves later to become 'spokesmen' of the state, men who had not been intimately involved in the Zionist effort before 1948 but who now were moved to make Israel their life's work – and who were to be my close associates in the founding of the Israel Bond Organization in 1950. In the past, whenever I had come to the United States, it had been on missions for the *Histadrut*, and I had spent my time almost entirely with Labour-Zionists. But in 1948 I met a new kind of American Jew – well to do, super-efficient and totally committed. In the first instance there was, of course, Henry Montor himself, brusque, gifted and deeply concerned with Israel, a slave driver who mercilessly drove himself as well as others in the attempt to raise ever larger sums of money. But there were also businessmen, hard-headed experienced industrialists like Bill Rosenwald, Sam Rothberg, Lou Boyar and Harold Goldenberg, to name just a few of the men with whom I found time to talk hurriedly on that whirlwind tour about the possibility of selling bonds for Israel as well as making appeals for philanthropy.

But all the time, I waited anxiously for the moment when I could return home, though I already knew that the newly created Foreign Office, and particularly the new foreign minister, Moshe Sharett, had other plans for me. The day before I left for the States, Sharett and I had met in my hotel and he had spoken to me of the problems of manning the embassies and consulates that Israel would have to establish in those countries that had either already recognized her or were likely to do so within a few weeks.

'I have no one for Moscow,' he said in a very worried voice. 'Well, thank God, you can't offer it to me,' I replied. 'My Russian is almost non-existent.' 'As a matter of fact, that isn't what matters,' he answered. But he didn't pursue the topic, and I tried to dismiss it as a good joke. Although I sometimes thought about the conversation when I was flying from one place to another in the States, I fervently hoped that Sharett himself had forgotten all about it.

One day, however, a cable came from Tel Aviv. I glanced at the signature before I read the text to make sure that it wasn't about Sarah or Menachem (already with his brigade and in combat). But when I saw the name 'Moshe', I knew that it was about Moscow and I had to steel myself to read the message. The State was not even a month old. The war was not over. The children were not safe yet. I had a family and dear friends in Israel, and it seemed to me that it was grossly unfair to ask me to pack my bags again so soon and take off for such a remote and essentially unknown post. 'Why is it always me?' I thought, in a burst of self-pity. There are plenty of other people who could do the job as well, better in fact. And Russia, of all places, the country I had left as a little girl and of which I had not a single pleasant memory. At least in America I was doing something real, concrete and practical, but what did I know or care about diplomacy? Of all my comrades, I thought, I was surely the least suited to diplomatic life. But I also knew that Sharett must have secured Ben-Gurion's consent to the appointment, and Ben-Gurion was certainly not likely to be swayed by any personal appeals. And then there was the matter of discipline. Who was I to disobey or even demur at a time when each day brought news of fresh casualties? One's duty was one's duty – and it had nothing to do with justice. So what if I longed to be in Israel? Other people longed for their children to be alive or whole again. So after a few more cables and telephone calls, I answered Sharett's cable, not very enthusiastically but affirmatively. 'When I get back to Israel, I will try to persuade Moshe and Ben-Gurion that they have made a mistake,' I promised myself. At the end of the first week of June, however, my appointment as Israel's minister to Moscow was made public.

I took a day off to see old friends in New York and say good-bye to new ones. I was determined to visit Fanny and Jacob Goodman before I left. Neither the children nor I had ever lost touch with them, and I thought it would cheer me up to spend an hour or two with them, telling them about Sarah and Zechariah, and Sheyna's children, whom they hadn't seen for so long. But I never got to their house after all. On the way to Brooklyn, a car crashed into my cab, and the next thing I knew I had a badly fractured leg enveloped in a gigantic plaster cast and my address for the next few weeks was neither Moscow nor Tel Aviv but the New York Hospital for Joint Diseases! Looking back at the times and at my mood, I think that nothing (including the blessing of the phlebitis and blood clots I developed) could have kept me in that hospital had it not been for the fact that on 11 June the fighting had temporarily ended in Israel.

By 11 June, the progress of the Arab invasion had been halted. The Egyptian attempt to conquer Tel Aviv and Jerusalem had failed, though the Jordanians were still battering away at Jerusalem from the east and the north, and the Jewish Quarter of the Old City had fallen to Abdullah's Arab Legion. The Syrians, though their advance in the north had been stopped, still held a bridgehead on the Jordan River, and the Iraqis were still poised against the very narrowest part of the country in Samaria. The United Nations had been trying for weeks to impose a truce, but as long as they had some hope of defeating Israel, the Arabs were not at all interested. However, as soon as it became quite clear to them, as well as to us, that this was not about to happen, they agreed to a ceasefire – to the first truce, which was to last for twenty-eight days and give us a chance to rest, rally, and plan the major offensives that in July removed the last threats to Tel Aviv and the coastal plain, lifted the siege on Jerusalem and destroyed all of the major Arab bases in Galilee.

So in theory, pain or no pain, I might have caught my breath a bit in the hospital – both physically and emotionally – but actually I was under enormous pressure there all the time. To begin with, there were the television cameras and the newspapermen. A woman ambassador to Moscow would have been a novelty in any case in 1948, but a woman minister to Moscow who represented the tiny embattled State of Israel and who was totally immobilized in New York must have been a real bargain. I suppose I could have refused to be interviewed – and today, of course, that is just what I would do under such circumstances. But at that time I thought it would be good for Israel if we got a lot of publicity, and I felt that I mustn't turn down a single request from the press – though the various members of the family, especially Clara, were absolutely appalled by the three-ring circus going on in my room.

What was much worse, though, was the pressure I was under to get to Moscow. I was literally bombarded with cables from Israel. 'When can you leave New York?' 'When can you take over?' 'How do you feel?' Rumours had spread in Israel that this was a 'diplomatic' illness and that nothing was really wrong with me except that I didn't want to go to Russia. But as if this disgusting whispering campaign were not bad enough, there were also indications that the Soviet government itself was offended by my supposed 'malingering', which was 'actually' a tactic designed to delay the exchange of ministers so that the US ambassador to Israel could arrive first and thus become doyen of the diplomatic corps. All this was something which I had to take very seriously, regardless of my state of health. So there was nothing I could do except start tormenting my doctors for permission to leave the hospital. It was, need I say, the wrong thing to have done. I should have remained in New York until I was completely well. Both our Foreign Office and the Soviet Ministry of Foreign Affairs would have survived without me for a few more weeks, and I would have spared myself a great deal of misery and at least one operation later on. But one of the penalties of public office is that one loses one's sense of proportion in certain respects, and I was convinced that there would be some kind of terrible crisis unless I turned up in Moscow as soon as possible.

I did make one attempt, when I got back to Israel, to talk Sharett out of the whole thing, but by then it wasn't a very wholehearted attempt. One day I heard an interesting story that cheered me up: Ehud Avriel, one of the *Haganah* men who had done most to secure arms for us in Czechoslovakia and who later became Israel's first minister to Prague, had been invited for a talk with the Soviet ambassador in that city. In the course of the conversation, the Russian said to Avriel: 'I suppose your people are looking around for someone to send to Moscow. Don't feel that it has to be a person whose Russian is fluent or who is an expert on Marxism and Leninism. Neither of these qualifications are important.' Then, after a while, as though à propos of nothing, he said to Avriel: 'By the way, what is happening to Mrs Meyerson? Is she going to stay in Israel or does she have other plans?' From this my friends – including Sharett – gathered that the Russians had more or less asked for me, in their own way, and I began to feel differently about going.

Also, one of the few pleasant things that had occurred while I was in the hospital was that one morning I got a cable from Tel Aviv: 'Do you have any objection to appointment of Sarah and Zechariah as radio operators in Moscow embassy?' I was very touched – and grateful. To have Sarah and Zechariah with me in Russia was almost worth the exile from Israel. One of my first projects when I came back to Tel Aviv was to ask Sheyna if Sarah and Zechariah could be married in the small house which Shamai and she had bought years ago. We decided it would be a real family wedding, with only a few 'outside' guests. My father had died in 1943 – another of the people who were most dear to me and who had not lived to see the state – and my mother, poor soul, had been incapacitated for several years, her memory gone, her eyesight bad, her personality quite faded away, leaving almost no trace of the critical, energetic, peppery woman she had been. But Morris was there, as gentle as ever and beaming with pride, and so were Zechariah's parents. His father had come to Palestine from Yemen when the Turks still ruled the country. He was very poor, very religious and not formally educated, except in the *Torah*, but he had brought up a wonderful and loving family – though Zechariah himself by now was quite removed from Yemenite customs and traditions.

I settled in again at the hotel on the seashore. Sarah flew from Revivim to Tel Aviv and moved in with me for a few days, and Zechariah, who had been very ill and in a hospital near Tel Aviv for weeks, was finally discharged. Of our immediate family, only Clara and Menachem were missing at the wedding in Sheyna's garden. I couldn't help thinking how different my own wedding had been – under what different circumstances it had taken place and how differently Morris and I had started out on life together. There was no point to wondering now who had been to blame, or why our marriage had fallen apart, but I felt (and rightly it turned out) that Sarah and Zechariah, though they were the same age that we had been when we stood under that bridal canopy in Milwaukee, were more mature and better suited to each other and that they would succeed where Morris and I had failed.

In between rushing around to party meetings, being briefed about the Soviet Union and making plans for our departure, I concentrated on thinking about the kind of representation that Israel should have in the Soviet Union. How did we want to show ourselves abroad? What did we want the world in general and the USSR in particular to think about Israel? What sort of state were we in the process of creating and how could we best reflect its quality? The more I thought about it, the less I thought that our legations should mimic those of other countries. Israel was small, poor and still at war. Her government was still a provisional government (the first elections to the Knesset took place only in January 1949), but the majority of its members would certainly represent the Labour movement. The face we turned to the world, I was convinced, needed no make-up at all. We had established a pioneering state in a sorely beleaguered country devoid of natural resources or any wealth, a state to which hundreds of thousands of DPs – who also had nothing – were already streaming in the hope of making a new life for themselves. If we wanted to be understood and respected by other states, we would have to be abroad what we were at home. Lavish entertaining, grand apartments, conspicuous consumption of any kind was not for us. Austerity, modesty and a sense of our own worth and purpose were what we had to offer, and anything else would be false.

There was something at the back of my mind all the time that I was thinking along these lines, and then one day I found it. The legation in Moscow would be run in the most typically Israeli style I knew: like a kibbutz. We would work together, eat together, get the same amount of pocket money and take turns doing whatever chores had to be done. As in Merhavia or Revivim, people would do the work that they were trained for and suited to in the opinion of our Foreign Office, but the spirit of the legation, its atmosphere and flavour would be that of a collective settlement – which, apart from any other consideration, ought, I believed, to be especially attractive to the Russians (not that their own brand of collectivism was or is anything to write home about). We were to be twenty-six people in all, including Sarah, Zechariah and myself, and the legation's counsellor, Mordechai Namir, a widower who brought his fifteen-year-old daughter, Yael, with him. (Namir afterwards served as Israel's ambassador to the USSR, then as minister of labour and for ten years as mayor of Tel Aviv.) As my personal assistant, I chose a most charming woman, Eiga Shapiro, who not only spoke Russian but also knew much more about the niceties of life than I did and who could be entrusted, I was sure, with such (to me terrifying) missions as deciding what furniture and clothing legation personnel and the minister would need.

Even before I returned to Tel Aviv, I wrote to Eiga to ask her to join me – if and when I indeed went to Moscow – and to my delight she agreed at once. One of the notes she sent to New York at the end of June is before me now, and it tells something, I think, of what was involved in sending a woman to a top diplomatic post – particularly a woman like myself who was so determined to live in Russia in much the same way she lived at home.

'I have had a talk with Ehud,' Eiga wrote. 'He tells me that we shall have to be very *comme il faut*. So please, Golda, what about a fur coat for yourself? It is very cold in the place to which you are travelling, and most people there wear fur coats in the winter. You need not buy yourself mink, but a good Persian lamb will be very serviceable ... You will also need a few evening dresses, and buy yourself woollies – warm nightgowns, woollen stockings and woollen underwear. And please get yourself a pair of good snow shoes.'

The question of dress was obviously not uppermost in my mind, but for a while I regretted that we had no national costume – which would have solved at least one problem for me, as it did for Mrs Pandit, the only other woman diplomat in Moscow, who wore her sari, of course, on all ceremonial occasions. In the end, Eiga and I agreed that when I presented my credentials, I would wear a long black dress sewn for me in Tel Aviv and that, when necessary, I would wear a small black velvet turban with it. As far as furnishing the legation was concerned, Eiga undertook to do that in Scandinavia as soon as we found permanent accommodation in Moscow. In the interim, we would establish our 'kibbutz' in a hotel. There was also the question of finding and taking with us to Russia someone whose French was absolutely perfect, since it had been decided that French would be Israel's diplomatic language. Eiga introduced me to a bright, amusing, painfully thin young woman called Lou Kaddar, who was born in Paris, whose French was beyond reproach and who had lived in Jerusalem all through the siege and had been badly wounded. I liked her the moment I set eyes on her – and it was just as well that I did, because for the better part of the next twenty-seven years Lou was my close friend, my indispensable assistant and, more often than not, my travel companion. At all events, she agreed to go with us to Russia.

I stayed in Israel long enough that summer to welcome the first US ambassador to Israel, that delightfully frank and warm gentleman James G. McDonald, whom I had met before, and to meet the Russian minister, Pavel I. Yershov. It was typical of the newness of the state – and of its lack of proper housing – that the American and Soviet missions in Tel Aviv made their first home in the same hotel, not far from mine, and I never quite got used to seeing the Stars and Stripes fly from one end of the hotel roof and the Hammer and Sickle from the other. There were all sorts of 'incidents' during the first weeks of this 'co-existence'. I remember, for instance, a 'gala' performance of the Israel National Opera at which the orchestra opened with first the '*Hatikvah*' and then, in McDonald's honour, the 'Star-Spangled Banner' but not the 'Internationale', though Yershov's counsellor was present – at least until the intermission, when he and his party rather noisily walked out. Everyone in our Foreign Office was reduced to trembling in his boots until Yershov himself agreed to accept our explanation that, had he been there, the Soviet anthem would have certainly been played. Today, these minor disasters seem funny, but at the time we all took them very seriously. Nothing ever appeared unimportant to us, and Sharett, by nature, was both exacting and sensitive to a remarkable degree and felt – as did the Russians themselves, by the way – that protocol was of the utmost importance, though I could never see why it mattered so much.

A second truce began on 19 July, signalling the start of a long, painful round of negotiations over the Negev which Count Folke Bernadotte, the Swedish UN mediator, recommended be handed over to the Arabs. Considering the fact that he was really a referee, his position was amazingly lacking in neutrality, and he became extremely unpopular – particularly when he added insult to injury by advocating also that Jerusalem be torn away from the Jewish state and that the UN supervise Israel's air and sea ports. God knows that these recommendations were unacceptable and that they proved only that Bernadotte really never understood what the State of Israel was all about. But it is certainly no crime to be obtuse, and I was horrified when, on 17 September, only two weeks after I arrived in Moscow, I learned that Bernadotte had been shot to death on a quiet street in Jerusalem (although his assailants were never identified, we knew it would be assumed that they were Jews). I thought the end of the world had come, and I would have given anything to have been able to fly home and be there during the ensuing crisis. But by then I was already deeply involved in a totally new and very demanding way of life.

9

Minister to Moscow

We arrived in Moscow (via Prague) on the grey rainy afternoon of 2 September 1948. The first thing I was told by the officials of the Soviet Ministry of Foreign Affairs who welcomed me at the airport was that we might have some difficulty getting to the hotel because at that very moment the funeral of Andrei Zdanov, one of Stalin's closest associates, was taking place in the city. My first impressions of the Soviet Union, therefore, were the length and solemnity of that funeral and the hundreds of thousands – perhaps millions – of people whom we saw in the streets on our way to the Hotel Metropole. The hotel, which was reserved for the use of foreigners, looked like something from another era. The rooms were huge with great cut-glass chandeliers, long velvet curtains, overstuffed plush armchairs and, in one room, even a grand piano. On each landing sat a stern old lady to whom one handed one's keys when leaving the hotel, but whose job obviously was to report to the KGB on the guests, though it was very unlikely that she was the sole source of information. We never found any microphones in our rooms, though we conducted regular searches for them, and more veteran members of the diplomatic corps in Moscow took it for granted that every word I said in the two-bedroom suite I shared with Sarah and Zechariah was being recorded.

By the time we had been in the hotel for a week, I realized that we would have to start our kibbutz-style life as soon as possible or else we would run out of money. The cost of living was unbelievably high, and the first hotel bill we got staggered me. 'There is only one way we can manage on our very modest budget,' I told my staff, 'and that is if we

all eat only one meal a day in the hotel dining-room. I will provide
food for breakfasts and suppers, and on Fridays we'll have our main
meal together in the evening.' The very next day Lou Kaddar and I
went out to buy electric plates, which I then distributed to each of our
rooms together with crockery and cutlery that I borrowed from the
hotel – since there was still none to be had in any shop in post-war
Moscow. As for food, once or twice a week Lou and I loaded up our
baskets with cheese, sausages, bread, butter and eggs (which we bought
at a market that was slightly cheaper than any shop in town) and
placed them between the big double windows of our rooms to keep
from spoiling. On Saturdays I prepared a sort of brunch for my own
family (and the 'bachelors' of the staff, including Eiga and Lou), cooked
on a hot plate in the dining-room of my suite.

I think those trips to market so early on frosty winter mornings were
perhaps the most pleasant single thing I did during my seven months
in the Soviet Union. Neither Lou nor I could speak Russian, but the
peasants at the market were very nice to us and waited patiently,
smiling and gesturing that we needn't hurry while we nibbled and
made up our minds about what to buy. Like most people, I was charmed
by the politeness, sincerity and warmth of the ordinary Russian,
though, of course, as a socialist, I was constantly shocked by what I
saw of the supposedly classless Soviet society. I couldn't believe my eyes
when I used to drive through the streets of Moscow and see middle-aged
women digging ditches and sweeping the roads with only rags bound
around their feet when it was 40 degrees below zero, while other women
in furs and high heels stepped into enormous shiny cars.

From the beginning, we had 'open house' in my rooms on Friday
evenings. I had hoped that local people would drop in – as people do
in Israel – for a piece of cake and a cup of tea with us, but it was a
very naïve hope – though the Friday night tradition was to continue
long after I left Moscow. Newspapermen came, Jews and non-Jews
from other embassies came, visiting Jewish businessmen (such as fur-
riers from the States) came, but never any Russians, and never, never
any Russian Jews, but of that more later.

My first official job was to write a formal letter of condolence to
Mr Molotov, the Soviet foreign minister, on Zdanov's death, and then
to present my credentials. The president of the USSR, Mikhail
Shvernik, was away, so the ceremony took place in the presence of the
deputy president. I won't deny that I was very nervous. Suppose I did
or said the wrong thing? The consequences for Israel might be critical.

Or suppose I disappointed the Russians? I had never done anything remotely like this before, and I was filled with a sense of responsibility. But Eiga soothed me, persuaded me to wear her string of pearls and, accompanied by Namir, Arieh Levavi (our first secretary) and Yohanan Rattner (our military attaché), I went off more or less calmly to participate in the brief ritual that actually marked the start of the official existence of the Israeli mission to the USSR. After my credentials were read, I delivered a little speech in Hebrew (we had sent it earlier to the Soviet chief of protocol so he could prepare a translation) and then there was a modest, rather pleasant reception in my honour.

Now that the major formality was over, I desperately wanted to make contact with the Jews. I had already told my staff that just as soon as I presented my credentials, we would all visit the synagogue. There, if nowhere else, I was sure we would meet the Jews of Russia, from whom we had been separated for thirty years – since the Revolution – and about whom we knew almost nothing. What were they like? What had remained of their Jewishness after so many years of life under a regime that had proclaimed war not only against all religions as such, but also specifically against Judaism, and regarded Zionism as a crime for which the only appropriate punishments were penal servitude in a forced-labour camp or exile to Soviet Asia. Although Hebrew was banned, Yiddish had been tolerated for a while, and there had even been official sponsorship of a Yiddish-speaking Jewish autonomous region, Birobidzhan, on the Chinese border. But it had never really gotten off the ground, and after the Second World War (in which millions of Russian Jews perished), the Soviet authorities saw to it that most Yiddish schools and newspapers never re-opened. By the time we arrived in the USSR, there was not only overt repression but also a vicious brand of government-directed anti-Semitism which was to 'blossom' within a few years into the wholesale and ruthless persecution of Jews and the imprisonment of Jewish intellectuals – actors, doctors, writers – accused of 'cosmopolitanism' and 'Zionist imperialism'. The situation was already so tragic that those members of the legation who had close relatives in Russia – brothers, sisters, even parents – were in an agony of doubt throughout my stay in Moscow as to whether or not they should contact people whom they longed to see, but whom they knew might be condemned to deportation if their relationship with any Israeli were to be revealed.

It was an excruciating dilemma, and we often spent days trying to decide the 'pros' and 'cons' of getting in touch with X's sister or sending food and money to Y's aged and ill mother, and usually came to the conclusion that whatever we did would harm their relatives, so for their sake it would be better to do nothing at all. Of course, there were exceptions, but even now I dare not write freely about this, because to do so might place Jews who are still in Russia in terrible danger. Today, the entire civilized world is aware of what happens to Soviet citizens who ignore the perverted rules and regulations by which their leaders seek to control them. But 1948 was still a 'honeymoon' year, and it was very hard for us either to understand or to accept a system of things in which it was an offence against the state for an old woman to meet the son she had not seen for three decades – particularly when that son was a recognized member of the diplomatic corps and his presence presumably welcome in the Soviet Union.

At all events, on the first Saturday following the presentation of credentials, we set off on foot for the Great Synagogue (Moscow's other two synagogues were only small wooden structures), each of the legation's men carrying a prayer shawl and a *siddur*. In the synagogue, we found only about 100 or perhaps 150 elderly Jews who, of course, had no idea that we were coming, though we had notified Rabbi Schliefer that we hoped to attend the Sabbath services. As was customary, towards the end of the service a blessing was recited for the good health of the heads of the state – and then, to my surprise, for me. I was sitting in the women's gallery (in orthodox synagogues, men and women are separated), and when my name was mentioned, the whole congregation turned to stare at me as though it was memorizing my face. No one said anything. They just looked and looked at me.

After the service was over, I introduced myself to the rabbi and we chatted for a few minutes. Meanwhile, the rest of the legation staff had gone on ahead, and I began to walk to the hotel alone, my head filled with thoughts about the service and the few weary-looking, shabby old men and women who still went to synagogue every week in Moscow. I hadn't gone very far when an elderly man brushed up against me in a way that I knew at once was not accidental. 'Don't say anything,' he whispered to me in Yiddish. 'I'll walk on and you follow me.' When we were near the hotel, he suddenly stopped, turned around to face me and, standing there on that windy Moscow street, he recited the thanksgiving prayer, '*Shehehiyanu*', that I had last heard intoned by Rabbi Fishman-Maimon in Tel Aviv on 14 May. Before I could say or do anything, the old Jew had slipped away, and I entered the hotel alone, my eyes brimming, wondering if that strange pathetic encounter had really taken place or whether I had dreamed it.

A few weeks later, it was *Rosh Hashanah*, the Jewish New Year. I had been told that on the High Holidays many more people came to synagogue than on Saturdays, and I decided, once again, that the entire legation would attend the *Rosh Hashanah* service. Then, a day or two before the holiday, a long article appeared in *Pravda*, written by Ilya Ehrenburg, the well-known Soviet journalist and apologist who was himself a Jew. Were it not for Stalin, Ehrenburg wrote piously, there would be no such thing as a Jewish state. 'Nonetheless, let there be no mistake about it,' he explained, 'the State of Israel has nothing to do with the Jews of the Soviet Union, where there is no Jewish problem and therefore no need for Israel. That is for the Jews of the capitalist countries, in which, inevitably, anti-Semitism flourishes. And in any case there is no such entity as the Jewish people. That is as ridiculous a concept as if one claimed that everybody who had red hair or a certain shape of nose belongs to one people.' Not only I but the Jews of Moscow read this article. And like me, because they were used to reading between the lines, they understood what it was all about and knew that they were being warned to keep away from us! The response which thousands upon thousands of these Jews deliberately and courageously chose to make to that sinister warning was something which shattered and overwhelmed me at the time I witnessed it and has inspired me ever since. There is not a detail about what happened on that New Year's Day that I do not remember as vividly – and with as much emotion – as if it had taken place only a few hours ago.

As we had planned, we went to the synagogue on *Rosh Hashanah*. All of us – the men, women and children of the legation – dressed in our best clothes, as befitted Jews on a Jewish holiday. But the street in front of the synagogue had changed. Now, it was filled with people, packed together like sardines, hundreds and hundreds of them, of all ages, including Red Army officers, soldiers, teenagers and babies carried in their parents' arms. Instead of the 2,000-odd Jews who usually came to synagogue on High Holidays, a crowd of close to 50,000 people was waiting for us. For a minute, I couldn't grasp what had happened – or even who they were. And then it dawned on me. They had come – those good, brave Jews – in order to be with us, to demonstrate their sense of kinship and to celebrate the establishment of the State of Israel. Within seconds, they had surrounded me, almost lifting me bodily, almost crushing me, saying my name over and over again.

Eventually, they parted ranks and let me enter the synagogue; but there, too, the demonstration went on. Every now and then, in the women's gallery, someone would come to me, touch my hand, stroke or even kiss my dress. Without speeches or parades, without any words at all really, the Jews of Moscow were proving their profound desire – and their need – to participate in the miracle of the establishment of the Jewish state, and I was the symbol of the state for them.

I couldn't talk, or smile, or wave my hand. I sat in that gallery like a stone, without moving, with those thousands of eyes fixed on me. No such entity as the Jewish people, Ehrenburg had written. The State of Israel meant nothing to the Jews of the USSR! But his warning had fallen on deaf ears. For thirty years we and they had been separated. Now we were together again, and as I watched them, I knew that no threat, however awful, could possibly have stopped the ecstatic people I saw in the synagogue that day from telling us, in their own way, what Israel meant to them. The service ended, and I got up to leave, but I could hardly walk. I felt as though I had been caught up in a torrent of love so strong that it had literally taken my breath away and slowed down my heart. I was on the verge of fainting, I think. But the crowd still surged around me, stretching out its hands and saying 'Nasha Golda' (our Golda) and 'Shalom, shalom', and crying.

Out of that ocean of people, I can still see two figures clearly. A little man who kept popping up in front of me and saying 'Goldele, leben zolst du. Shana Tova!' (Goldele, a long life to you and a Happy New Year) and a woman who just kept repeating: 'Goldele! Goldele!' and smiling and blowing kisses at me.

It was impossible for me to walk back to the hotel, so although there is an injunction against riding on the Sabbath or on Jewish holidays, someone pushed me into a cab. But the cab couldn't move either because the crowd of cheering, laughing, weeping Jews had engulfed it. I wanted to say something, anything, to those people, to let them know that I begged their forgiveness for not having wanted to come to Moscow and for not having known the strength of their ties to us. For having wondered, in fact, whether there was still a link between them and us. But I couldn't find the words. All I could say, clumsily, and in a voice that didn't even sound like my own, was one sentence in Yiddish. I stuck my head out of the window of the cab and said: 'A dank eich vos ihr seit geblieben Yidden' (Thank you for having remained Jews), and I heard that miserable inadequate sentence being passed on through the enormous crowd as though it was some wonderful prophetic saying.

Finally, after a few more minutes, they let the cab move forward and leave. In the hotel, everyone gathered in my room. We had been shaken to our very depths. Nobody talked. We just sat there. It had been far too great a revelation for us to discuss it, but we needed to be together. Eiga, Lou and Sarah were sobbing as though their hearts would break, and several of the men held their faces in their hands. But I couldn't even cry. I just sat, my face drained of colour, staring in front of me. And that was how we stayed, for hours, flooded with emotions so powerful that we couldn't even communicate them to each other. I can't pretend that I knew for sure then that within twenty years I would see many of those Jews in Israel. But I did know one thing: I knew that the Soviet Union had not succeeded in breaking their spirit; that Russia, with all its power, had failed. The Jews had remained Jews.

Someone took a photograph of that *Rosh Hashanah* crowd and I suppose that thousands of copies were made of it because, later, people passing me in the street would whisper to me, so quietly that at first I didn't understand what they were saying: 'We have the picture.' Of course, I knew that they would have showered the same love and pride on a broomstick, if it had been sent to them to represent Israel. But all the same, I was very touched when years later Russian immigrants to Israel brought me either yellowing twenty-year-old prints of that photograph or of a photograph showing me presenting my credentials in the Kremlin, which appeared in 1948 in a Soviet periodical and had also been lovingly saved for two decades.

On *Yom Kippur* (the Day of Atonement), which comes ten days after the Jewish New Year, thousands of Jews once again crowded the synagogue, and this time I stayed there with them all day. I remember that when the rabbi recited the closing sentence of the service, '*Leshanah ha-ba'ah b'yerushalayim*' (Next year in Jerusalem), a tremor went through the entire synagogue, and I said a little prayer of my own. 'God, let it happen. If not next year, then let the Jews of Russia come to us soon.' But even then, I didn't really expect that it would happen within my lifetime.

Not long afterwards, I was also given the privilege of meeting Mr Ehrenburg. One of the foreign correspondents stationed in Moscow, an Englishman who used to drop in on Friday nights, asked me once if I wanted to meet Ehrenburg. 'As a matter of fact, I do,' I said. 'There are one or two things I'd very much like to talk to him about.' 'I'll arrange it,' promised the Englishman, but he never did. Then, a few weeks later, there was an Independence Day party in the Czech embassy and this same journalist came up to me. 'Mr Ehrenburg is here,' he said. 'Shall I bring him over to you?' Ehrenburg was quite drunk – not an unusual condition for him, I was told – and, from the start, very aggressive. He began speaking to me in Russian. 'I'm sorry, but I can't speak Russian,' I said. 'Do you speak English?' He looked at me nastily and replied. 'I hate Russian-born Jews who speak English.' 'And I am sorry for Jews who don't speak Hebrew or at least Yiddish!' I answered. Of course, lots of people milling around overheard this exchange, and I don't think it increased anyone's respect for Mr Ehrenburg.

I had a much more interesting and rewarding encounter with another Soviet citizen at the reception given by Mr Molotov on the anniversary of the Russian Revolution, to which all diplomats in Moscow are invited each year. The heads of legations were received by the foreign minister in a special room. After I had shaken hands with Molotov, his wife, Ivy Molotov, came up to me. 'I am so pleased to meet you, at last,' she said with real warmth and even excitement. Then she added: 'I speak Yiddish, you know.' 'Are you Jewish?' I asked in some surprise. 'Yes,' she said, answering me in Yiddish, '*Ich bin a Yiddishe tochter*' (I am a daughter of the Jewish people). We talked together for quite a long time. She knew all about the events at the synagogue and told me how good it was that we had gone. 'The Jews wanted so much to see you,' she said. Then we touched on the question of the Negev, which was being debated at the United Nations. I made some remark about not being able to give it up because my daughter lived there, and added that Sarah was with me in Moscow. 'I must meet her,' said Mrs Molotov. So I introduced Sarah and Yael Namir to her, and she talked to them about Israel and asked Sarah dozens of questions about the kibbutzim, who lived in them and how they were run. She spoke Yiddish to the girls and was overjoyed when Sarah answered in the same language. When Sarah explained that everything in Revivim was owned collectively and that there was no private property, Mrs Molotov looked troubled. 'That's not a good idea,' she said. 'People don't like sharing everything. Even Stalin is against that. You should acquaint yourself with Stalin's thoughts and writings on the subject.' Before she returned to her other guests, she put her arm around Sarah and, with tears in her eyes, said: 'Be well. If everything goes well with you, it will go well for all Jews everywhere.'

I never saw or heard from Mrs Molotov again. Many years later, in

New York, Henry Shapiro, the veteran United Press correspondent in Moscow, told me that after her conversation with us, Ivy Molotov had been arrested, and I remembered that anniversary celebration and how, earlier that day, we had watched the military parade in Red Square. I had so envied the Russians all those weapons on display – the tiniest fraction of which was beyond our means – and, as if he had read my thoughts, Molotov had raised a glass of vodka to me later and said: 'Don't think we got it in a single day. The time will come when you, too, will have these things. It will all be alright.'

But by January 1949 it was apparent that Russian Jewry was going to pay a heavy price for the welcome it had given us, for the 'treachery' to Communist ideals that was – in the eyes of the Soviet government – implicit in the joy with which we had been greeted. The Yiddish theatre in Moscow was closed. The Yiddish newspaper *Enigkeit* was closed. The Yiddish publishing house Emes was closed. It didn't matter that all of these had faithfully followed the Communist line. The fact remained that Russian Jewry had shown far too great an interest in Israel and the Israelis to please the Kremlin. Within five months there was practically no single Jewish organization left in Russia, and the Jews kept their distance from us.

In the meantime, I dutifully went on the necessary rounds of courtesy calls to the heads of other Moscow legations and embassies and waited for permanent quarters. At last we were given a house, a two-storey villa that boasted a large courtyard containing a few small buildings which could be used for housing. It was very hard for me to keep my mind off what was happening in Israel and on the dinner parties and teas I had to attend – not to speak of the matter of furnishing the new house. But the sooner we moved, the better, so I asked Eiga to go to Sweden to buy the furniture, curtains and lamps we needed for it. It took her several weeks to find the things we wanted at the prices we could afford, but she did a wonderful job and furnished our seven bedrooms, reception hall, dining-room, kitchen and all the offices both inexpensively and attractively. Incidentally, when she left for Stockholm, she stuck all the mail we wanted to send to Europe with her into her suitcase, but on the way she decided that Israel really needed a diplomatic pouch, and she had one designed for us in a Stockholm department store. She also bought warm clothing for everyone and tinned food.

I went back to Israel twice during my seven months in Moscow and each time I felt as though I had come from another planet, from a vast

cold land of suspicion, hostility and silence into the warmth of a small
country – still at war and facing immense hardships, but open, hopeful,
democratic and my own – and I could hardly bear to tear myself away
from it again. On the first of those two visits – which was after our
elections in January 1949 – Ben-Gurion asked me if I would join the
cabinet he was forming. 'I want you to serve as minister of labour,' he
said. *Mapai*, the largest Labour party in Israeli, had won an overwhelming victory at the polls by receiving 35 per cent of the total vote
(20 per cent more than *Mapam*, its nearest rival) in an election in
which 87 per cent of all the eligible voters in Israel had gone to the polls.
The state's first government was formed by a coalition which included
the United Religious Front, the Progressive Party (made up largely of
middle-class professionals who were *Mapai* oriented, though they
stressed a non-partisan point of view) and the *Sephardim* (a tiny party
that represented the interests of the so-called oriental Jews).

The religious bloc balked a bit at the idea of a woman minister, but
eventually accepted the argument that in ancient Israel Deborah had
been a judge – which was at least equivalent to, if not more important
than, being a cabinet minister! The religious bloc's objection to my
holding office, based on my being a woman, came up again in the 1950s,
when I was a candidate for the mayoralty of Tel Aviv, though on that
occasion it was not overcome as it was in 1949. Anyhow, I was overjoyed by Ben-Gurion's offer. At last I would be where I wanted to be,
doing what I most wanted to do and what, for a change, I felt completely qualified to do. Not that I, or anybody else in the government,
knew at that point exactly what fell within the jurisdiction of a Ministry
of Labour. But I couldn't imagine a more constructive and gratifying
task than one which – whatever else it encompassed – would certainly
have much to do with employing and housing the hundreds of thousands
of immigrants who were already arriving in Israel. I said yes to Ben-
Gurion at once, without a moment's hesitation, and I never regretted it.
My seven years in the Ministry of Labour were, without doubt, the
most satisfying and the happiest of my life.

But before I could plunge into my new job, I had to return to Moscow
for another few weeks. It didn't take long for the effects of my trip home
to wear off. The obvious social inequalities, the general anxiety and fear
of the population, the isolation in which the diplomatic corps went
through its paces all depressed me unspeakably, and I felt very guilty
knowing that I would soon be out of it while Namir, Levavi and the
rest of the staff stayed on. Sarah and Zechariah were both dying to

leave, as was Lou, but they still had to serve several more months in the legation. I embarked on a round of farewell parties and said good-bye to the few Soviet officials with whom I had dealt directly – all of whom had been unfailingly courteous, though also unfailingly evasive about nine out of every ten requests or queries we had. Still, we had been treated no worse (if no better) than other legations and, like other legations, we too became accustomed to the practically total absence of affirmative replies – or of any replies at all, for that matter. Most of all, of course, I wanted to say not good-bye but *au revoir* to the Jews, but almost none of them dared come to the legation any more, and there were no more crowds at the synagogue.

On 20 April 1949 I returned to Israel. At this point, I think it is important to describe what was happening there, because in the course of 1949 and 1950 Israel underwent a process that no other country has ever undergone in quite the same way, and that was to result in the doubling of our population within only two years. The War of Independence ended (to the extent that it ever ended) in the spring of 1949, and armistice agreements – though not peace treaties – had been signed with Egypt, Lebanon, Jordan and Syria through the good offices of Dr Ralph Bunche (who had taken Count Bernadotte's place as UN mediator). Unfortunately, however, their signatures didn't mean that the Arab states were now reconciled to our existence. On the contrary, it meant that the war they were so anxious to wage against us and which they had lost on the battlefield would now be fought differently and in a manner less likely to result in their defeat but just as likely, they hoped, to destroy the Jewish state. Having been trounced in battle, the Arabs now switched from military weapons to economic ones. They boycotted any companies or individuals that traded with her. They closed the Suez Canal to Israeli shipping, in the face of the international convention which stipulated that the Canal must be open to all nations at all times.

But they didn't stop killing Jews altogether. For years there was a steady infiltration across our borders of armed Arab gangs that murdered and robbed Israelis, set fields and orchards on fire, stole cattle and generally made life a misery in our border settlements. Whenever we protested or tried to convince the United Nations that these constant raids were, in fact, a continuation of the war and a major violation of the armistice agreements, the Arab states, loudly proclaiming their innocence, said that there was nothing whatsoever they could do about these 'incidents' – although we knew that they were providing the

money, arms and backing and, what's more, we could prove our allegations. Under normal circumstances, I suppose this continuous, malicious
and very dangerous harassment would have so enraged us that we
would have retaliated in a way, and on a scale, appropriate to a sovereign state. But since, at that point, we were all so preoccupied with the
problem of feeding, housing and employing the 684,201 Jews from
seventy countries who arrived in Israel between 14 May 1948 and
the end of 1951, all we did, at first, was to complain to the United
Nations about the raids and hope that something would be done
about them.

It may be difficult today to imagine what that flood of human beings
was like. These were not immigrants of the kind that had come when
Sheyna and I did – sturdy young idealists in good physical condition
who couldn't wait to settle on the land and who regarded the discomforts of pioneering as part of the great Zionist experiment in which
they had so eagerly involved themselves. Nor were they the professionals, tradesmen or artisans who came in the 1930s with some
means of their own, and whose contribution to the *yishuv*'s economy
began as soon as they reached Palestine. The hundreds of thousands of
Jews who streamed into Israel in those early years of statehood were
utterly destitute. They had nothing at all except the will to live and
the desire to get away from their past. Most of them were broken in
body, if not in spirit, and many thousands were broken in both. All of
the Jews of Europe had suffered crippling tragedies; as for the Jews
from the Arab lands of the Middle East and North Africa, they had
lived, for the most part, uneducated, poverty-stricken and terrorized
in the ghettos and casbahs of some of the most repressive countries on
earth, and they knew little or nothing about twentieth-century life. It
was, in short, a flood of Jews from opposite ends of the earth who spoke
different languages, came from widely contrasted backgrounds, ate
different foods and were frequently quite ignorant of each other's
traditions and customs. The one thing they had in common was
that they were all Jews; but that was a great deal – everything, in
fact.

I know that statistics make dull reading – at least they do for me –
but perhaps I will be forgiven for citing a few in order to illustrate the
scope of the problems we faced – problems which, to some extent,
Israel's minister of labour was called upon to solve. By 1949, 25,000
European Jews had come to Israel from the camps on Cyprus and
75,000 from the DP camps of Germany and Austria. Of the 80,000

Jews living in Turkey at the beginning of 1948, 33,000 were in Israel by the end of 1950. Czechoslovakia was letting its surviving Jews leave at the rate of 20,000 a year, and 37,000 Bulgarian Jews plus 7,000 Yugoslav Jews – almost all that were left after the Holocaust – had made their way to Israel by the autumn of 1950. The news of the birth of the Jewish state gave rise to the immigration of 35,000 Jews from Morocco, Tunis and Algiers in less than three years, and 5,000 Jews came from China. At first Poland and Rumania would not let their Jews go, but towards the end of 1949 their governments had a brief change of heart, and between December 1949 and February 1951 28,000 Jews came from Poland, and in 1950 and 1951 88,000 Rumanian Jews were gathered in. In 1950 a movement of 3,000 Jews per month began from Hungary, and emigration from Persia, once a clandestine trickle, turned into a wave, carrying along with it refugees who had congregated in Persia from surrounding countries. Nineteen-fifty was also the year that a law was passed in Iraq permitting Jewish emigration within a twelve-month period, and a grand total of 121,000 Iraqi Jews were airlifted into Israel while there was still time!

Each of these migrations, of these mass responses to the establishment of the State of Israel, had its own special history, and each was different. But certainly the airlift of the Jews of Yemen from south-west Arabia to the Jewish state was the most remarkable migration of all. No one knows exactly when the Jews first came to Yemen. It may have been in the days of King Solomon, or perhaps there were Jews who crossed the mountains of Arabia with the Roman troops that fought there at the beginning of the Christian era. At any rate, Jews had lived in Moslem Yemen for many centuries, cut off from the rest of the Jewish world, persecuted, deprived of political rights and impoverished, but always loyal to their faith and to the Bible, which served as their only source of knowledge and learning for hundreds of years. They survived as serfs, as the property of the ruler of Yemen, forbidden to work in trades that were open to others, or even to walk on the same side of the street as Moslems. In that backward, bigoted and poverty-stricken country, the Jews were the poorest and lowest of citizens; but unlike the rest of the population, they were literate. In their synagogues and schools, they taught their male children to read and write Hebrew, and I remember that one of my first impressions of the Yemenite Jews was that they were able to read upside down. Because books were so rare, the children, who sat in a circle in the mud-baked huts that

served as schools in the Jewish quarters of Yemen, had to learn to read
the Bible from every possible angle.

How did they keep themselves alive? They became master craftsmen,
silversmiths, jewellers, weavers and carpenters. All over Israel today
you can see – and buy – their delicate, exotic filigree work. Of course,
those who couldn't keep their families alive by craftsmanship became
itinerant workmen and pedlars, but for all of them life was more than
degrading; it was also very precarious. Out of every 1,000 Jewish
children born in Yemen, nearly 800 died, and all orphaned Jewish
boys were forced to convert. But somehow the Jewish community of
Yemen never disappeared, and every now and then Yemenite Jews
either were given permission by the imam to leave Yemen or they
escaped from it across the desert into Aden, hoping from there to reach
the Holy Land – though very few ever did.

Still, when I came to Palestine in 1921, there were already some
Yemenite Jews there. They had learned of the renewed settlement
activity in Palestine from Shmuel Yavnieli, an East European Jew who
had made his way through Yemen as early as 1908, finding these 'lost
remnants' of his people and bringing them the message of the return
to Zion. I was fascinated by them. I knew that they were capable of
great feats of strength, but to me they looked like dark-skinned, fragile
dolls in their colourful traditional clothing (in Yemen they were not
allowed to wear the same clothes as Arabs). Most of the Yemenite
women in Palestine then wore lovely hooded garments and dresses
over narrow, beautifully embroidered trousers, while the men, all of
whom had long earlocks, were dressed in loose striped robes. During
the war years, a few thousand Yemenite Jews who received permission
from the British to leave Aden and enter Palestine sailed up the Red
Sea and through the Suez Canal. But the majority were still trapped.
In 1947, a few days after the UN vote on partition, there were dreadful
Arab riots in Aden, and the situation of the Jews inside Yemen itself
also worsened. In their despair and terror, thousands of Yemenite
Jews – hearing that the State of Israel was at last coming into being –
finally took their lives in their own hands and fled. They left their few
possessions behind, gathered up their families and – like the biblical
Children of Israel – began to walk out of slavery into freedom, believing
implicitly that somehow or other they would get to the Holy Land.
They walked in groups of thirty or forty, set upon by Arab brigands,
eating only the *pitta* (flat Arab bread), honey and dates they could
carry and paying exorbitant ransoms to the various desert sultanates

they passed en route for each man, newborn baby and Bible. Most of them did reach Aden and the camps organized for them there by the Joint Distribution Committee and staffed by Israeli doctors and social workers, where they rested, prayed and read their Bibles. But since the Egyptians had closed the Suez Canal to Israeli shipping, there was only one way for them to reach Israel – and that was by air. Each day, 500 or 600 Yemenite Jews were flown to Israel packed into giant converted transport planes that flew them along the Red Sea route in what soon became known as 'Operation Magic Carpet'! That airlift went on all through 1949 and, by the time it ended, it had brought 48,000 Yemenite Jews to Israel.

Sometimes I used to go to Lydda and watch the planes from Aden touch down, marvelling at the endurance and faith of their exhausted passengers. 'Had you ever seen a plane before?' I asked one bearded old man. 'No,' he answered. 'But weren't you very frightened of flying?' I persisted. 'No,' he said again, very firmly. 'It is all written in the Bible. In Isaiah. "They shall mount up with wings of eagles."' And standing there on the airfield, he recited the entire passage to me, his face lit with the joy of a fulfilled prophecy – and of the journey's end. Today there are virtually no more Jews in Yemen, and the scars of their long exile have begun to fade. Ben-Gurion used to say that his happiest day would come when a Yemenite Jew would be appointed chief-of-staff of the Israel Defence Forces, and I myself think that day is not far off now.

Reading over what I have just written I am still amazed by the sheer number of the immigrants we absorbed. But we weren't dealing with abstract numbers then. It wasn't the arithmetic of the Law of the Return – the bill passed by the Knesset in July 1950 giving the right of immigration to all Jews and automatic Israeli citizenship to all Jewish immigrants – that most concerned us. What worried us was how were we ever going to feed, clothe, house, educate and generally care for those thousands of immigrants. How and with what? By the time I arrived back in Israel, there were 200,000 people living (if that's the word) in tents all over the country, more often than not two families to a tent – and not necessarily families from the same country or even the same continent. Apart from the fact that none of the services we improvised in such a rush really worked well or were geared for so many thousands of people, there were also a great many sick, undernourished and handicapped people who might have managed better had they been housed differently but who just couldn't cope at all under the circumstances. The man who had lived through years of Nazi slave labour, survived the DP camps and braved the trip to Israel and who was, at best, in poor health and, at worst, badly damaged physically and entitled to the best possible conditions, found himself and his family (if he still had one) living in unbearable proximity with people with whom he didn't even have a common language. Nine times out of ten, he even regarded his new neighbours as primitive because they had never seen a flush toilet. Even then, he might have pulled himself together faster if we had been able to give him a job at once or move him into more adequate housing or somehow give him the sense of permanence for which, like all refugees, he longed. Or consider the illiterate woman from Libya or Yemen or the caves of the Atlas Mountains who was stuck with her children in a draughty, leaky tent with Polish or Czech Jews who prepared their food differently, ate things that made her feel sick and, by her standards, weren't even Jews at all, either because they weren't observant or else because their prayers and rituals were totally unfamiliar to her.

In theory, none of this should have mattered. In theory, no overcrowding, no misery, no cultural or intellectual differences should have been at all important for people who had experienced the Holocaust or for those who had literally walked out of Yemen through the robber-infested, scorching desert. But theory is for theoreticians. People are people, and the tensions and discomforts of those hideous tent cities that I saw everywhere in 1949 were really unbearable. Something had to be done at once about housing, and jobs had to be created for those unhappy people as soon as possible. Their health and their nutrition were taken care of more or less adequately: the TB, trachoma, ringworm, malaria, typhoid, dysentery, measles and pellagra that the immigrants brought with them were all being coped with, though I don't know how our overworked and exhausted doctors and nurses did it. And all of the tent cities had 'schools' of some sort where Hebrew was being taught intensively. But in 1949 housing seemed an insurmountable problem.

As for our resources, despite the magnificent response of world Jewry, there was never enough money. Thanks to our neighbours, our defence budget had to stay sky high, and anyhow all the other essential needs of the state had to be met somehow. We couldn't close down our schools or our hospitals or our transport or our industries (such as they were) or put too tight a rein in any way on the state's development. So everything had to be done at the same time. But there were things that we could do without after all – so we did without them. We rationed almost everything – food, clothing and shoes – and got used to the idea of an austerity that lasted for years. Recently I came across one of my own ration books, a drab little booklet issued by the Ministry of Commerce and Industry in 1950, and I recalled the hours I stood in line for a few potatoes or three eggs or the frozen fish on which we feasted so gratefully – when we got it. Luckily, I still had clothes from my stay in Russia. But most Israelis had a very hard time indeed. Their standard of living dropped drastically. Whatever had been sufficient for one family in 1948 now had to be shared with two or three other families. Oldtimers, who had just emerged from months of a terrible war, might have been forgiven for rebelling against the new demands made on them. But no one rebelled. A few people said that perhaps the immigrants should wait wherever they were until times were better here. But no one, no one at all, ever suggested that the burden was too heavy or that the infant state might collapse under it. The national belt was tightened – and tightened again – and still we all managed to breathe. And about one thing we were all in agreement: without those Jews, Israel wasn't worth having.

But there had to be priorities, and for me, at least, housing and jobs for the immigrants headed the list. Not all of my colleagues agreed with me. A barrage of experts explained to me in detail, with charts and graphs, why a housing programme of the kind I envisaged was not a good idea. It would only lead to inflation, they said. It would be far wiser to put the little money at our disposal into factories or streamlined methods of agriculture. But I couldn't accept or support any recommendation that didn't deal with the absorption of immigrants, first and foremost, from the human point of view. And I certainly didn't believe that anything could ever be as 'productive' – in terms of Israel's future – as decent housing. To me it seemed absolutely clear that good citizenship, a real sense of belonging, the beginning of integration – in other words, the creation of a good society – depended to an overwhelming degree on how people lived, and there was no point in our talking loftily about social responsibility, education or even public health unless we got at least some of the new immigrants out of those dreadful tents and into proper housing as soon as possible.

A few weeks after I returned from Moscow, I went to the Knesset with a plan for building an initial 30,000 housing units and got it through, despite the objections. But we couldn't make houses out of milk and honey (not that those commodities were available either), so I took myself off to the States in search of the necessary funds and once again asked the Jews of America for help – this time 'not to win a war but to maintain life'.

I went to our Parliament two weeks ago last Tuesday, and presented a project for 30,000 housing units by the end of this year. Parliament approved it, and there was great joy in the country. But actually I did a strange thing: I presented a project for which I didn't have the money.

What we want to do is to give each family a luxurious apartment of one room; one room which we will build out of concrete blocks. We won't even plaster the walls. We will make roofs, but no ceilings. What we hope is that since these people will be learning a trade as they build their houses, they will finish them, and eventually, one day, add on another room. In the meantime, we will be happy, and they will be happy, even though it means putting a family of two, three, four or five into one room. But this is better than putting two or three families in a single tent . . .

It is an awful thing to do – to forge a signature to a cheque, but I have done it. I have promised the people at home and the people in the camps that the government is going to put up these 30,000 units, and we have already started to do so with the little money we have. But there isn't enough for these 30,000 units. It is up to you either to keep these people in camps and send them food packages, or to put them to work and restore their dignity and self-respect.

I got the money and we began to build those units. Of course, at first we made all kinds of mistakes – some of them serious – both in planning and in execution. We miscalculated, sited badly, fell behind the flow of immigration. In the end, we couldn't build quickly enough or well enough, and by October 1950 we had only constructed a third of the units we had undertaken to build because an unusually severe winter forced us to divert funds earmarked for building to the emergency purchase of thousands of metal huts, which were better than tents in the winter but like roasting ovens all through Israel's long, hot summer. Still, not a single family that entered Israel in those great waves of immigration ever lacked shelter of some kind. Somehow we found or invented accommodation for everyone. When the corrugated metal huts ran out, we used canvas and nailed it to wooden frames and created tens of thousands of fabric shacks; when these ran out we went unhappily back to tents for a while. But no one slept out of doors, and we never stopped building.

By the end of 1950, however, we knew that we couldn't go on thinking of those 'temporary camps' as reception centres that could be neatly folded away within a few months. They were obviously going to have to do for several years, and, that being the case, their entire character would have to change. They would have to be turned into work villages and moved to the outskirts of towns and cities, so that the new immigrants could live near places where labour was in demand. They would have to be so organized that the people in them could become more or less self-sufficient, cooking for themselves, rather than eating in public kitchens, and participating in the upkeep of public services. We couldn't levy rates and taxes on penniless men and women, but we could prevent them from feeling that they were the objects of charity.

The new camps were called *ma'abarot*, the plural of the Hebrew word *ma'abara* (place of transit), and by November 1951 we had set up 112 *ma'abarot*, housing a total population of 227,000 new immigrants. But if we were not to create two classes of Israelis – the relatively well-established 'oldtimers', on the one hand, and the new immigrants in their crowded, ugly *ma'abarot* on the other – we would have to supply a lot more than just housing. We would have to see to it that the new immigrants worked and got paid for their work, and I believed that there was only one way of doing this: a public works programme would have to be established.

That was not easy either. The majority of the so-called oriental Jews (those from the Middle East and North Africa) had virtually no skills that were applicable to their circumstances in the new state. We feared that many of them would get used to doing nothing but living on a dole for years and years, while the gap between them and us widened. But social welfare, however enlightened, certainly wasn't the answer. Employment opportunities had to be created, and we would have to create them, so we set in motion a chain of special projects that offered work to people who had never used drills or held bricks in their hands or even worked in fields. The Ministry of Labour launched a massive road-building scheme throughout the country, and hundreds upon hundreds of acres of stony, stubborn land were cleared, terraced and afforested, by hand. And all the time we went on building and training the immigrants, though the tide of immigration didn't slow down until 1952.

The real problem, of course, wasn't the difficulty of creating a labour force or building houses or absorbing thousands of immigrants into our economy. Those were all urgent matters, but they were never at the core of our concern. What really preoccupied us in those days – and what, in part, still preoccupies all thinking Israelis – was how to weld together people who, on the surface, had so little in common and found it so hard to understand each other. But, again because we had no alternative, we often succeeded where success seemed impossible. I remember, for instance, how pessimistic – not to say disapproving – some of my colleagues were about the road-building. Not only didn't we need all those approach roads, but importing the building materials was in itself a luxury, and anyhow the roads would be no good because we didn't have the kind of workers we needed. But I relied on three things: the dedication and ingenuity of the oldtimers; the growing desire of the new immigrants to earn an honest day's wage and not to be turned into perpetual wards of the state or the Jewish Agency; and the understanding and generosity of world Jewry, which responded again and again to our endless pleas for help. Looking back, I must say that I was very rarely disappointed, though anyone watching the way in which those roads were built in 1949 and the early 1950s would have been justified in considering us all to be a little mad. We used to take one skilled construction worker from Jerusalem or Tel Aviv, turn him overnight into the foreman of a road-building crew somewhere in the south and leave him to cope with the problem of supervising ten men who spoke ten different languages, came from ten different countries and had only been in Israel for a few intolerably confusing months. But somehow or other, though perhaps inefficiently and too expensively, the roads (wryly nicknamed 'the golden roads' in my honour) were built.

In 1952, when the immigration began to taper off at last – to 1,000 a day – we started to direct newcomers away from the *ma'abarot* into regular quarters in new development areas and border villages all over Israel and stress agriculture rather than public works. We gave each immigrant family not only a tiny house but also a plot of land, livestock and lessons in farming. We made mistakes about that, too. We tried, probably too soon, to turn the pressure cooker into a melting pot. We created villages populated by combinations of people like the road-building crews. They had nothing much in common with each other and found it difficult (sometimes impossible) to live together in a totally isolated part of the country, and they usually had neither any experience nor any taste for farming. Many of them rebelled and drifted away to the towns, where they settled into slums. But most of them stayed and became first-rate farmers whose children today grow the Israeli fruit, flowers and vegetables that are bought around the world.

I'm not at all sure that my constant visits to building sites, the new
roads and the new settlements were always appreciated by the engineers
and architects responsible for them. I couldn't walk into one of those
tiny houses and not notice that the wall between what was to be the
eating area and the kitchen only made the whole house smaller than
necessary; or not see that the kitchen counter was so designed that no one
could keep it clean, least of all women who had never cooked in an
indoor kitchen before; or not observe that two steps leading to a house
built on a slope weren't enough and that a third step was essential –
especially for families that comprised eight or nine small children, a
pregnant mother and at least one (if not two or three) grandparents.
'But it will cost much more,' was the inevitable response to my
suggestions.

Of course, it would have been easier to accept the argument that
most of the immigrants – particularly those from Yemen and North
Africa – were better off even in badly designed houses than they had
been before. 'They don't know how to live in the kind of houses you
want them to have,' I was told often. 'They don't know what bathrooms
or flush toilets are. They'll just turn the space into storage rooms for
junk.' It was true. They didn't know what bathrooms were or how to
use showers, but that didn't mean that they weren't entitled to them or
shouldn't be taught how to use them. And the same applied to kitchens,
to schools, and to the state itself, for that matter. But it was also true
that we couldn't do anything without money.

So, though I begrudged every minute that I was away from Israel, I
went on with my fund-raising speeches abroad, travelling often to
Europe, the United States and South America. But fund-raising, too,
had to be suited to our new circumstances. The United Jewish Appeal
had become a magnificent instrument for the raising of money, but it
was still an appeal and the money was still 'gift' money. I had been
troubled for years by the picture of a Jewish state that relied on charit-
able funds which, apart from everything else, could never begin to meet
our growing needs for development capital. I wasn't an economist any
more than I was a construction engineer, but just as I didn't need to be
able to use a slide rule in order to understand how high a kitchen sink
should be, so I didn't require years of experience as a financier in order
to know that a fall-off in philanthropic funds was inevitable. But it
wasn't only the amount of money that worried me, it was also the kind
of money we were getting. It seemed to me that a continued dependence
on philanthropy violated the most elementary concepts of Zionism, of

self-reliance and self-labour, to say nothing of national independence, and I began to think of other possible sources of funds, sources that would make world Jewry fuller partners in the Zionist enterprise and in the 'ingathering of the exiles'. After my 1948 visits to the United States, I had corresponded steadily on this subject in dozens of letters and cables with Henry Montor, and whenever he and I and Eliezer Kaplan (Israel's first minister of finance) met, we talked in depth about the feasibility of entering into a new economic activity that would express itself in the floating of an Israel bond issue.

The first time that the bond idea surfaced in public was September 1950 at a special three-day conference convened in Jerusalem by Ben-Gurion, and attended by the leaders of the major Jewish communities in the United States. At the beginning there was very little enthusiasm for the idea. What if the sale of bonds undermined the efforts of the UJA? And who wanted either to make money out of Israel or, as seemed more likely and worse, lose it? Philanthropic contributions were tax-deductible, but the bonds would not be. And anyhow, what if the US government did not look with favour on a bond issue? Underlying all these reservations and anxieties, I felt, was a general unease about an altered relationship with Israel. No one came out and bluntly said that Israel wasn't a good financial risk, but I couldn't help sensing a feeling that the whole notion of an assumption of indebtedness by us at this time was most undesirable. The bonds, however, found one very powerful champion – far more influential than Ben-Gurion, Kaplan, Montor and myself put together. Henry J. Morgenthau, the former US secretary of the treasury, with whom I had travelled to so many communities in 1948 and who had served as general chairman of the UJA, understood at once and immediately approved. He did more than that. He went to see President Truman at the White House and we discovered that the president also understood and approved. So another conference was convened – this time in Washington, DC – and I was handed the 'choice' assignment of trying to convert the non-believers and turn their scepticism and resistance into support and cooperation.

I didn't waste much time on preliminaries or phraseology. If Israel was to develop, to grow and to thrive, even to be able to feed itself, we needed 1½ billion dollars over the next three years! We ourselves – all 1 million of us – would be responsible, I said, for a third of that staggering sum. But a billion dollars would have to be provided by the Jews of America in various ways, including the purchase of bonds.

Part of that money will have to be given as donations, but part of it, the major part, must be money we can invest profitably, money that will be returned, money that can bear interest. In addition to a large, strong UJA, we want investment capital; we want to sell bonds; we want you to lend us money. I don't know what security we can give you, or what security you can ask for. There is only one kind of security that I think I can offer you on behalf of the government of Israel. I can offer you the gilt-edged security of the people of Israel, the hundreds of thousands of Jews who will still come to Israel and the tens of thousands of Jews in Israel who live in tents. But also I can offer you our children, the children of the oldtimers and the little Yemenite children and the Iraqi children and the Rumanian children who are growing up in Israel – proud, safe, self-respecting Jews. They will pay back this debt, which they are honour-bound to pay back, with interest.

As I spoke, I saw before my eyes those children – and their fathers' in the long processions that left the tents, the wooden barracks and the canvas huts early each morning to plant trees on hillsides or build roads. They were not all young men, their clothes were tattered, their bodies were frail, but only a few months ago they had walked with bent backs and downcast heads in the streets of Yemen or sat, despondent and listless, in the DP camps of Europe. Now, their heads were up and their backs were straight and they held picks and shovels in their hands. I knew that they were a sound investment – and, thank God, I was right. From the time that the first Israel Bond Campaign was launched in May 1951 up to the present, close to three billion dollars' worth of bonds have been sold, of which one billion has already been repaid. Flowing into Israel's economy by way of a development budget, the bonds helped substantially and dramatically to establish the new state's economic viability.

But work was not everything for me during that period. There were also the private joys and sorrows of every life. One day in 1951, when I was away from home on one of those interminable trips to raise money, a cable arrived informing me that Morris was dead. I flew back to Israel at once to attend his funeral, my head filled with thoughts about the life we might have lived together if I had only been different. It was not a bereavement that I either could or wanted to talk about with other people, even my own family. Nor am I prepared to write about it now, except to say that although we had been apart for so long, standing at his graveside I realized once again what a heavy price I had paid – and made Morris pay – for whatever I had experienced and achieved in the years of our separation.

There was also Sarah's pregnancy, illness and stillborn first baby and the days of unbearable worry about her recovery when Zechariah and I tried to force the doctors to tell us that everything would be alright and, instead, heard with horror that there was little hope for her life. I couldn't believe it, perhaps because I had heard those same words so many years before, or perhaps because they are words one never really believes. But she pulled through this time, too, and, characteristically, insisted on returning to Revivim as soon as she could and starting another baby. It took me months, however, to recover from the fright I had had, and every time I remembered how desperately ill she had been, I wanted to rush down to Revivim and drag her back to Jerusalem with me so that I could take care of her myself. But I knew that my mission would fail and that I had to let her live her own life where and how she chose, regardless of how much I worried about her.

One of the greatest personal pleasures of my life during the time that I was minister of labour was the flat in which I lived in Jerusalem. I had never been particularly interested in my immediate surroundings, as long as they were clean, neat and reasonably attractive. After all, a house is only a house, and I have lived in a number of houses since the state was born: the official residence of the foreign minister, that of the prime minister, and now the small semi-detached house in a garden suburb of Tel Aviv in whose other half live Menachem, Aya, their three sons and a cocker spaniel called Daisy – who is a lot fonder of me than I am of her. But none of those houses has ever meant as much to me as the lovely flat that was mine from 1949 to 1956. Its story is far more than just the tale of a piece of real estate.

At the end of 1949, on Ben-Gurion's instructions, the Knesset and most of the government offices moved from Tel Aviv to Jerusalem. It was not a simple decision for Ben-Gurion to make, but it was entirely typical of him. Although the opening session of the Knesset had taken place in Jerusalem, and Dr Weizmann had been sworn in as Israel's president there, only the Israelis themselves seemed aware of the absolutely unique place that Jerusalem had occupied throughout the ages in the hearts of Jews everywhere. The rest of the world managed to disregard the tie that has always existed between us and the City of David. Both the Peel Commission and UNSCOP had taken the position that Jerusalem must not be included either in the proposed Jewish or Arab state, and the UN General Assembly decided that Jerusalem should be internationalized, administered through a special council and its own governor and guarded by an international police force. The point of all this, ostensibly, was to protect the holy places so that 'order and peace' might reign in Jerusalem forever. The Arabs, of course, rejected this plan lock, stock and barrel, along with the entire partition proposal. But we accepted it, though very unhappily, and comforted ourselves with the UN promise that at the end of ten years there would be a referendum 'leading to certain modifications'. Since there were 100,000 Jews and only 65,000 Arabs in Jerusalem in 1948, it seemed not impossible that, in the end, Jerusalem would be ours. Not that we ever intended to expel its Arab population (as has, I think, been amply proven by the events in that city since the Six Day War), nor that we didn't bitterly resent the implication that we were likely to disturb the 'order and peace' of a city that has been sacred to us for over 2,000 years. After all, we knew by heart – even if others had forgotten it – the record of Arab disturbances and violence in Jerusalem ever since 1921, and we knew that not one incident there had ever been caused by Jews.

That special council never came into existence, but Jerusalem came – and remained for months – under Arab fire. During that siege of Jerusalem, when the city was mercilessly shelled by the Egyptians and Jordanians, all of the great international concern for the holy places just vanished into thin air. Apart from a few feeble resolutions at the United Nations, no one, except the Jews, said or did anything to halt the Arab assault on the city, and no one, except the Jews, moved to rescue either its people or its ancient sites. The Arab Legion occupied the Old City, and every single Jew in it who remained alive was thrown out. In fact, we became the only people to be denied access to the holy places, but still no one, except the Jews, said a word. Nobody even asked: 'How is it that the Jews can no longer go to synagogue in the Jewish Quarter of the Old City or pray at the Western Wall?' In view of the deafening silence, we could hardly be expected ever again to rely on anyone else to protect Jerusalem or take seriously any Christian or Moslem protestations of anxiety about the holy places. Anyhow, we were perfectly capable of guarding them ourselves, along with all the other historical and religious sites in Israel. And what's more, there was no longer any reason for us to wait for a referendum about Jerusalem. We had had a war forced on us instead.

Nonetheless it took considerable courage on Ben-Gurion's part – in the face of a UN resolution passed in December 1949 calling for the internationalization of Jerusalem at once – to decide to move the government there before any such resolution could be implemented.

Even in Israel there were voices raised against the possible perils – both political and military – of the move, but Ben-Gurion's inner voice was stronger yet; and although most of the foreign missions (and therefore our Foreign Ministry) stayed on in Tel Aviv, my ministry and most of the others packed up and moved to Jerusalem, the capital.

This meant that I had to find somewhere to live in Jerusalem, and I certainly didn't want to settle in an hotel or take a room with a strange family. So even though I knew better than most people just how scarce housing was, I implored my co-workers at the Ministry of Labour to scour the city in search of a room for me. 'All that I need,' I said, 'is one room with a private entrance. Surely that is available.' It took some time, but finally my phone rang. 'Golda, we have found a room with a private entrance, but we don't think it is at all suitable for you. Still, if you'd like to see it . . .' I went to look at the room immediately, of course. It was in the Talbieh section of the city, in a house called the Villa Haroun al-Raschid (of all things), which had once served as a British headquarters. The house had two floors and an enormous roof with one broken-down room on it, and it was all indescribably dirty. The engineer was quite right. The whole house, let alone the roof-top room, was not only unsuitable, it was impossible. Nonetheless, I went up to see the roof. I spent five minutes looking around me at the spectacular view of Jerusalem and then came down with an announcement. 'This is it. I'll make myself comfortable in that filthy little room while you go ahead and fix up a small flat for me on another part of the roof.' There was an instant barrage of disapproval. It wasn't large enough for a minister. It was too near the border. It would take too long to build a small flat for me, and I'd have to live in that dreadful room for months. But I just smiled and said that I would move in as soon as the room was cleaned up. It did take several months before the flat was finished, but it was well worth waiting for. From its one big bay window, I could see the whole of Jerusalem perched on the Judean Hills, and I never got tired of looking at it. It didn't matter how hard or how long the day had been, how many new settlements I had visited or how many meetings I had attended. When I closed the door of that roof-top flat, made myself a cup of tea and sat down at last, with the lights of the city spread out before me, I was as happy as I have ever been. I could – and did – sit like that for hours sometimes, with or without friends dropping in, just feasting my eyes on Jerusalem's beauty. Later, Menachem and Aya were married in that flat, and it became part of our family history.

As I write about that period in my life, I can't help but reflect on how lucky I was to have been in on the beginnings of so many things – not that I influenced the course of events, but that I was so much a part of what was happening all around me, and sometimes my ministry and I were even able to play a decisive role in the upbuilding of the state. I suppose that if I were to limit myself – as I must – to singling out the two or three developments that were the most rewarding and most meaningful for me during those seven years, I would have to start with the legislation for which the Ministry of Labour was responsible. For me, that, more than anything else, symbolized the kind of social equality and justice without which I couldn't imagine the state functioning at all. Old age, pensions, widows' and orphans' benefits, maternity leaves and grants, industrial accident insurance, disability and unemployment insurance were essentials in any self-respecting society, and whatever else we lacked or postponed, these were basic.

Even if we couldn't afford to cover all of the Labour movement's achievements by law at once, we were at least duty-bound, I felt, to legislate as many as possible as soon as possible, and it meant a great deal to me to be able to present Israel's first National Insurance Bill – based largely on the voluntary insurance schemes of the *Histadrut* – to the Knesset in January 1952, thus paving the way for the National Insurance Act that came into effect in the spring of 1954. National Insurance wasn't a magical remedy. It didn't eliminate poverty in Israel, or close the educational or cultural gap between our citizens, or solve our security problems. But it did mean, as I told the Knesset that day, 'that the State of Israel will not tolerate within it poverty that shames human life, the possibility that the happiest hours of a mother's life will be marred by worry about food or the possibility that men and women who reach old age will curse the day they were born'. A drain on our resources? Of course it was – which was why we had to do it in stages. But it had economic as well as social significance and the merit of accumulating capital and withdrawing money from circulation, which helped us to fight inflation. Above all, it equalized the financial burden, made one age group responsible for the other and spread the risk. It also had another by-product that mattered to me: because the percentage of babies born in hospital rose as a result of the maternity benefits (which included the cost of hospitalization), infant mortality – which was high among the new immigrants and the Arabs – dropped. I went to Nazareth myself to hand the first cheque to the

first Arab woman who had her baby in hospital there, and I think I
was more excited than she was.

Another of the Ministry of Labour's projects with which I became
very involved had to do with vocational training, both for adults and
for youngsters. Again, it wasn't a question of waving a wand and
turning new immigrants into craftsmen or skilled technicians overnight.
It took years to qualify people for new professions or trades, and hundreds of the new immigrants never became fully employable, either
because they were already too old, too sick, too psychologically addicted
to not working or simply unable to adjust to the demands of modern
life. But thousands of other men and women attended vocational
schools and courses, learnt to handle machinery, raise poultry, become
plumbers and electricians, and I never got tired of watching the trans-
formation take place. Everyone pitched in to make the vocational
training programme a success; the Ministry of Labour joined forces
with the Ministry of Social Welfare, the Ministry of Education, the
army, the *Histadrut* and veteran voluntary organizations such as ORT
(Organization for Rehabilitation through Training), *Hadassah* and
WIZO (Women's International Zionist Organization), which were
financed by Jews abroad. We pushed and pulled together until we
turned out workers who made knitwear, polished industrial diamonds,
became part of assembly line teams and drove tractors. And this was
quite apart from the really titanic efforts that were required to battle
plain ordinary illiteracy and teach Hebrew.

Then there were the new towns that began to mushroom in those
years all over Israel. They didn't all live up to the promise of the
drawing board, and some of them failed altogether. But some of them
sprouted and bloomed and did great credit both to their planners and
their inhabitants, and in all of them the building was carried out mostly
by the government. One of those new towns was Kiryat Shmonah in
the extreme north, the Upper Galilee, which always held a special
appeal for me, perhaps because it was located in such breathtaking
surroundings or because I was so sure from the start that, despite all the
obstacles, Kiryat Shmonah would make it. Anyhow, my connection
with it from 1949 on was never merely formal.

It began life as a transit camp, a *ma'abara* made up of tin huts and
bewildered immigrants who had been taken there directly from the
planes or ships and who didn't really know where they were or why
they were there. It was a very far cry from the enticements of Tel Aviv.
There were no towns in the vicinity at all, just a few kibbutzim with

their fields and orchards, and the nearby swamps of the Huleh Valley
that we were just starting to reclaim. But the government had decided
to found an urban centre there that would be the dynamic core of a
newly populated region, and we sat for weeks poring over maps and
blueprints and trying to anticipate the needs of the future. The
ma'abara was replaced by the rudiments of a town. Schools, a community centre, light industry – even a swimming pool – were built in
Kiryat Shmonah, and everything was planned down to the last nail –
except the reaction of the new immigrants to life there. Yes, the scenery
was wonderful and, yes, the climate was bracing, and yes, the spick-
and-span new houses were fine, they told me; but it was very lonely
and there weren't enough jobs for everyone. The European Jews said
that we had dumped them down in the middle of nowhere, and the
oriental Jews made it clear that we were forcing new ways upon them
too quickly, disrupting their mode of life and treating them like second-
class citizens.

There was a constant turnover of population, and each time I went
to Kiryat Shmonah I listened to the complaints and saw the discontent
and came back to Jerusalem with a list of new suggestions, which there
usually wasn't enough money to implement. It broke my heart to see
houses that we had built with such difficulty sitting there empty. But
we increased the subsidies, and new batches of immigrants came – and
most of these stayed. They stayed even when, after the Six Day War,
Kiryat Shmonah was picked as a favourite target for the rockets of
Arab terrorists operating across the Lebanese border, and even, much
more recently, when the terrorists entered and killed people in the
town itself. Whenever I can, I go back to Kiryat Shmonah to sit in the
city square with some of the old hands and exchange stories with them
about the days when they and I thought that the town might never
develop. Not that I don't still come back with a list of new suggestions
or that even today there is enough money for everything that should
be done there.

Something else may come as a surprise to certain of Israel's 'constructive critics', particularly those of the so-called New Left. Along with
all the rest of the building and settlement we did in those hectic seven
years, we also built for the Arabs, because when we talked about the
citizens of Israel, we meant *all* the citizens of Israel. Whenever I had
arguments with local people in Kiryat Shmonah and similar places,
there was always someone in the crowd who shouted that the Arabs
were better off. It wasn't true, of course, but it is equally untrue – and

far more wicked – to claim that we ignored the Arabs altogether. The truth is that we used the houses of those Arabs who ran away from the country in 1948 for new immigrant housing whenever we could, although the properties remained under the supervision of a special custodian. At the same time, we allocated more than 10 million pounds for new Arab housing and rehoused hundreds of Arabs who remained in Israel but were displaced as a result of the fighting. There was such an outcry about the way we used absentee property – as though there were a better way to use it – that in 1953 we passed a Land Acquisition Law under which at least two-thirds of all the Arabs who put in claims were paid compensation, given back their property or given other property in its place – and none of them was asked to take a loyalty oath before his claim was honoured.

Whenever I read or hear about the Arabs whom we allegedly dealt with so brutally, my blood boils. In April 1948, I myself stood on the beach in Haifa for hours and literally beseeched the Arabs of that city not to leave. Moreover, it was a scene that I am not likely to forget. The *Haganah* had just taken over Haifa, and the Arabs were starting to run away – because their leadership had so eloquently assured them that this was the wisest course for them to take and the British had so generously put dozens of trucks at their disposal. Nothing that the *Haganah* said or tried did any good – neither the pleas made via loud-speakers mounted on vans nor the leaflets we rained down on the Arab sections of the town ('Do not fear!' they read in Arabic and Hebrew. 'By moving out you will bring poverty and humiliation upon yourselves. Remain in the city which is both yours and ours.' They were signed by the Jewish Workers' Council of Haifa. To quote the British general Sir Hugh Stockwell, in command of the troops then, 'The Arab leaders left first and no one did anything to halt what began as a rush and then became a panic.' They were determined to go. Hundreds drove across the border, but some went to the seashore to wait for boats. Ben-Gurion called me in and said: 'I want you to go to Haifa at once and see to it that the Arabs who remain in Haifa are treated properly. I also want you to try to persuade those Arabs on the beach to come back. You must get it into their heads that they have nothing to fear.' So I went immediately. I sat there on the beach and I begged them to return to their homes. But they had only one answer. 'We know that there is nothing to fear but we have to go. We'll be back.' I was quite sure that they went not because they were frightened of us but because they were terrified of being considered traitors to the Arab 'cause'. At all events, I talked myself blue in the face, but it didn't help.

Why did we want them to stay? There were two very good reasons: first of all, we wanted to prove to the world that Jews and Arabs could live together – regardless of what the Arab leadership was trumpeting; secondly, we knew perfectly well that if half a million Arabs left Palestine at that point, it would create a major economic upheaval in the country. This brings me to another issue with which I might just as well deal now. I should very much like, once and for all, to reply to the question of how many Palestinian Arabs did, in fact, leave their homes in 1947 and 1948. The answer is: at the very utmost, about 590,000. Of these, some 30,000 left right after the November 1947 UN partition resolution; another 200,000 left in the course of that winter and the spring of 1948 (including the vast majority of the 62,000 Arabs of Haifa); and after the establishment of the state in May 1948 and the Arab invasion of Israel, yet another 300,000 Arabs fled. It was very tragic indeed, and it had very tragic consequences, but at least let everyone be clear about the facts as they were – and still are. The Arab assertion that there are 'millions' of 'Palestinian refugees' is as dishonest as the claim that we made the Arabs leave their homes. The 'Palestinian refugees' were created as a *result* of the Arab desire (and attempt) to destroy Israel. They were not the *cause* of it. Of course, there were some Jews in the *yishuv* who said, even in 1948, that the Arab exodus was the best thing that could have happened to Israel, but I know of no serious Israeli who ever felt that way.

Those Arabs who stayed in Israel, however, had an easier life than those who left. There was hardly an Arab village with electricity or running water in all of Palestine before 1948, and within twenty years there was hardly an Arab village in Israel that wasn't connected to the national electric grid, or a home without running water. I spent a lot of time in those villages when I was minister of labour, and I felt as delighted with what we were doing for them as I was when the *ma'abarot* disappeared. Hearsay and propaganda are one thing; facts are another. It was I – and not members of the New Left – who as minister of labour opened roads and visited new housing units in Arab villages all over Israel. One of my favourite recollections of that era, by the way, is of the village in Lower Galilee that needed a road because it was on a hill, while the village well was below and carrying water uphill was no joke. So we built the road, and when it was done, there was a celebration with refreshments, speeches and flags. Then, all of a sudden, a young woman got up to speak – which is not customary among Arabs. She looked very pretty, in a long purple dress, and made a very charming speech. 'We want to thank the Ministry of Labour and the minister for easing the burden of the feet of our men,' she said. 'But now we would like to ask the minister if she could ease the burden also of the heads of our women.' She put it poetically, but what she meant was that she wanted running water so that she needn't carry those heavy jars on her head any more, even on the new road. So, a year later, I went to another celebration there, and this time I turned on tens of taps!

It was during that time that I almost lost my job as minister of labour. In 1955 elections were coming up. *Mapai* was very anxious to have a labourite mayor in Tel Aviv and Ben-Gurion decided that I was the only candidate who had a chance. I wasn't very pleased because I didn't want to give up the ministry, but since that was the party's decision, I felt I had no choice. 'You must understand, though, that it will mean leaving the cabinet,' I said to Ben-Gurion. 'That is out of the question,' he retorted. 'We'll make you a minister without portfolio.' 'No,' I said. 'If I am going to be mayor, then I'm going to be a full-time mayor.' He was very angry, but, fortunately for me, we didn't get a majority on the Tel Aviv Council. And since my election by the Council depended on the votes of two men belonging to the religious bloc, one of whom refused to vote for a woman, I didn't become a mayor and went on with the Ministry of Labour – which, I devoutly hoped, I would be allowed to do for many years more.

Although, personally, I was very relieved, I was enraged by the fact that the religious bloc had managed – at the last minute – to exploit the fact that I was a woman, as if the women of Israel hadn't done their full share – and more – in the building of the Jewish state. There wasn't a settlement in the Negev or the Galilee that hadn't, from its first days, included women. And it wasn't as if the representatives of the religious bloc weren't at that very minute sitting together with women in the Knesset, just as they had accepted the presence of women in the Jewish Agency and the *Va'ad Le'umi*. To have objected to my being mayor of Tel Aviv because I was a woman was a political tactic for which I had great contempt, and I said so without mincing any words.

The religious question – by which I mean the extent to which the clerical parties had their way – flared up sporadically all through the 1950s. We were determined not to be drawn (if it could be avoided) into open conflict with the religious bloc because we had troubles enough without that particular headache. Nonetheless, every now and then there were explosions which brought cabinet crises in their wake. Suffice it to say that no easy way was ever found of getting around the place of religion in the Jewish state. It bedevilled us then and, to some degree, it still bedevils us now.

One of the jokes which Israelis told in those days was about the man who sighed: 'Two thousand years we waited for a Jewish state, and it had to happen to me!' I think that all of us probably felt that way – though very fleetingly – at one time or another during those first years of statehood. At all events, since nothing in Israel ever stays static, in 1956 Ben-Gurion had a new plan for me.

10

The right to exist

Before I go on to tell about that plan and what became of me, I must explain that it was while I was minister of labour that Ben-Gurion – physically and spiritually worn-out – decided to resign as prime minister and minister of defence. The past twenty years had utterly exhausted him, and he asked for a two-year leave of absence. He needed a change of scene, and he was going off to a small Negev kibbutz, Sdeh Boker, not far from Beersheba. There, he told us, he would live as a pioneer again, devoting himself to reclaiming the wilderness as a member of a collective settlement. It was like a thunderclap. We begged him not to go. It was far too soon; the state was only five years old; the ingathering of the exiles was far from completed; Israel's neighbours were still at war with her. It was no time for Ben-Gurion to desert the country that had looked to him for guidance and inspiration for so many years – or us. It was inconceivable that he should leave. But he was determined to go, and nothing we said had any effect on him. Moshe Sharett, retaining the portfolio of foreign affairs, became Israel's prime minister, and in January 1954 Ben-Gurion went off to Sdeh Boker (where he stayed until 1955, when he returned to public life first as minister of defence and then as prime minister, while Sharett went back to being a full-time foreign minister).

As prime minister, Sharett was the same intelligent, cautious, man he had been before. However, I must admit that although the leadership of *Mapai* had tremendous respect and affection for him – most of us were fonder of Sharett than of Ben-Gurion – whenever there was a really difficult problem to be solved, it was to Ben-Gurion that people still turned for advice – and that included Sharett himself. There was a steady stream of visits and correspondence to Sdeh Boker – which became one of the most famous places in Israel overnight – and although Ben-Gurion liked to think of himself as a simple philosopher-shepherd who tended the kibbutz sheep for half the day and spent the other half reading and writing, he still kept his hand very near, if not actually on, the helm of the ship of state. That, I think, was inevitable under the circumstances, but what made for trouble was that Ben-Gurion and Sharett never really got on together, despite all the years of their partnership. They were too different in their basic personalities, though they were both ardent socialists and ardent Zionists.

Ben-Gurion was an activist, a man who believed in doing rather than explaining and who was convinced that what really mattered in the end – and what would always really matter – was what the Israelis did and how they did it, not what the world outside Israel thought or said about them. The first question he asked himself – and us – about almost any issue that came up in those days was: 'Is it good for the state?' And what he meant was: '*In the long run*, is it good for the state?' Ultimately, history would judge Israel on the record of its deeds, not its statements or its diplomacy and certainly not on the number of favourable editorials that appeared in the international press. Being liked or not – or even being approved of or not – was not the kind of thing that interested Ben-Gurion. He thought in terms of sovereignty, security, consolidation and real progress, and he regarded world opinion, or even public opinion, as relatively unimportant compared to these.

Sharett, on the other hand, was immensely concerned with the way in which policy-makers elsewhere reacted to Israel and what was likely to make the Jewish state look 'good' in the eyes of other foreign ministers or the United Nations. Israel's image and the verdict of his own contemporaries – rather than history or future historians – were the criteria he tended to use most often. And what he really wanted most for Israel, I think, was for it to be viewed as a progressive, moderate, civilized European country of whose behaviour no Israeli, least of all himself, ever need be ashamed.

Luckily, for many years, until the 1950s in fact, the two worked together very well. Sharett was a born diplomat and negotiator. Ben-Gurion was a born national leader and fighter. And the Zionist movement in general, as well as the Labour movement in particular, benefited tremendously from their combined talents and even, I would say, from their very different temperaments and attitudes. They weren't similar and they weren't really friends, but they did complement each other and, of course, they did share the same fundamental aims. But after the establishment of the state, their basic incompatibility grew – or maybe it simply became more obvious and more significant. At all events, when Ben-Gurion came back from Sdeh Boker in 1955 (for reasons which I shall go into a little later on), the tension and disagreements grew to such a point that they became intolerable.

One major area of conflict between them then was the question of Israeli retaliation for terrorist activities. Sharett was just as convinced as Ben-Gurion that the incessant incursions across our frontiers by gangs of Arab infiltrators had to end, but they disagreed sharply on the method that should be used. Sharett did not rule out retaliation. But he believed more strongly than most of us did that the most effective way of dealing with this very acute situation was by continuing to put maximum pressure on the powers-that-be so that they, in turn, would put maximum pressure on the Arab states to stop aiding and abetting the infiltrators. Well-worded protests to the United Nations, skilful and informed diplomatic notes and clear, repeated presentation of our case to the world would, he was sure, eventually succeed, whereas armed reprisals by Israel could only result in a storm of criticism and make our international position even less comfortable than it was. He was 100 per cent right about the criticism. It was more than just a storm, it was a tornado. Whenever the Israel Defence Forces retaliated against the infiltrators – and sometimes, unavoidably, innocent Arabs were wounded or killed along with the guilty – Israel was promptly and very severely censured for 'atrocities'.

But Ben-Gurion still saw his primary responsibility not to the statesmen of the West or to the world tribunal, but to the ordinary citizens who lived in the Israeli settlements that were under constant Arab attack. The duty of the government of any state, he believed, was first and foremost to defend itself and to protect its citizens – regardless of how negative the reaction abroad might be to this protection. There was also another consideration of great importance to Ben-Gurion: the citizens of Israel – that conglomeration of people, languages and cultures – had to be taught that the government, and *only* the government, was responsible for their security. It would obviously have been much simpler to have permitted the formation of a number of anti-terrorist vigilante groups, shut an official eye to private acts of retaliation and vengeance and then loudly disclaim all responsibility for the resultant 'incidents'. But that was not our way. The hand extended in peace to the Arabs would remain extended, but at the same time the children of Israeli farmers in border villages were entitled to sleep safely in their beds at night. And if the only way of accomplishing this was to hit back mercilessly at the camps of the Arab gangs, then that would have to be done.

By 1955 dozens of such Israeli punitive raids had been carried out, all of them in answer to our growing death toll, the mining of our roads and the ambushing of our traffic. They didn't end the terror, but they did put a very high price on the lives of our settlers, and they did teach the Israelis that they could rely on their own forces. In fact, they underlined, at least for the new half of the population, the real difference between living in a country on sufferance and living in a country that belonged to one. But, unfortunately, they also served to widen the breach between Ben-Gurion and Sharett, who continued to disapprove of some of the reprisals.

After a while, Ben-Gurion stopped calling Sharett by his first name and began to talk to him as though he were a stranger. Sharett was terribly hurt by Ben-Gurion's coldness, but he never said anything about it in public, though he would sit at home at night and fill the pages of his diary with furious analyses of Ben-Gurion's character and maltreatment of him. In 1956 it so happened that *Mapai* was looking for a new secretary-general. Ben-Gurion decided that this would be an ideal job for me and he asked me what I thought about it, suggesting that we meet with some of our colleagues at his Jerusalem home to talk about the idea. Not everybody was equally enthusiastic, but although it meant that I would have to part from the cabinet and the Labour Ministry, I was prepared to leave the decision up to the party, and I listened with great interest to the ensuing discussion. I certainly didn't want to turn my ministry over to anyone else, but, on the other hand, I was extremely concerned about the future of *Mapai* (which had suffered in the July 1955 elections). I thought that its membership should and, what's more, could be substantially broadened and that the threat to *Mapai* – both from the extreme left and the extreme right – could be overcome, providing that an intensified effort was made on the part of *Mapai* the leadership (which tended, not unnaturally I suppose, to rely on Ben-Gurion to do much of its work for it). All of a sudden I heard Sharett say, jokingly: 'Well, maybe *I* should become the secretary-general of the party.' Everyone laughed – except Ben-Gurion, who jumped at Sharett's little joke. I don't think he would ever have brought himself to ask Sharett to leave the cabinet, but here the opportunity had unexpectedly presented itself – and Ben-Gurion was certainly never one to ignore opportunities.

'Marvellous,' he said at once. 'A wonderful idea! It will save *Mapai*.' The rest of us were a bit taken aback and embarrassed, but on second thought it did seem like a very good idea to the party, too. Cabinet meetings were increasingly turning into open disputes on policy between Ben-Gurion and Sharett; and though it wasn't an elegant solution, it was – or at least it looked like – a way of lessening the growing strain on all of us created by the perpetual wrangling between the two men. 'Don't *you* think it is a good idea for Moshe to become secretary of the party?' Ben-Gurion asked me a day or two later. 'But who will be foreign minister?' I wanted to know. 'You,' he said calmly. I couldn't believe my ears. It had never occurred to me, even as the remotest possibility, and I wasn't at all sure that I could or wanted to cope with it. In fact, I was only sure of one thing: I didn't want to leave the Ministry of Labour, and I told this to Ben-Gurion. I also told him that I didn't want to step into Sharett's shoes in this manner. But Ben-Gurion wouldn't listen to my objections. 'That's that,' he said – and it was.

Sharett was very bitter. I think he always imagined that had I refused to take over his beloved Foreign Ministry, Ben-Gurion would have acquiesced in his staying on indefinitely. But he was wrong. The tension between Ben-Gurion and Sharett would never have merely blown over; it was far too late for that, although Sharett didn't seem to realize this for a long time. It was only when two very close friends of his, Zalman Aranne and Pinchas Sapir, told him in so many words that unless he resigned from the cabinet Ben-Gurion might bid us all farewell once more that Sharett gave in. Levi Eshkol once said, 'As prime minister, Ben-Gurion is worth at least three army divisions to Israel'; and in a way, it is as good a measure as any of Ben-Gurion's prestige and personal strength at that time that Sharett, too, agreed with this assessment. Of course, later on some of Ben-Gurion's opponents charged him with having rid himself of Sharett so that he could go ahead and plan the Sinai Campaign without being burdened by Sharett's lack of sympathy for it; but I myself am sure that there was no such 'plot'. The story of their relationship didn't end then. Sharett removed himself from public life for a while and later became the chairman of the Jewish Agency. In 1960, when the so-called 'Lavon Affair' exploded, Sharett – already stricken by the illness that was to kill him in 1965 – became one of the most outspoken critics of Ben-Gurion's refusal to let the 'Affair' die a natural death.

As a matter of fact, since I've raised the subject of the Lavon Affair, I might as well go into it now, though I hardly intend to write an exhaustive tract on it. The original issue dated back to a security blunder related to an espionage mission in Egypt in 1954 (disastrous in its very conception, to say nothing of its execution). That was at the time when Sharett was prime minister and foreign minister. The new minister of defence, who had been handpicked by Ben-Gurion himself, was Pinchas Lavon, one of the most capable if least stable members of *Mapai*, a handsome, complicated intellectual who had always been a great 'dove' but who turned into the most ferocious sort of 'hawk' as soon as he began to concern himself with military matters. Many of us thought that he was extremely unsuitable for that very sensitive ministry. He had neither the necessary experience nor, we thought, the necessary powers of judgement. Not only I but Zalman Aranne, Shaul Avigur and various other colleagues had tried – in vain – to argue Ben-Gurion out of his choice of successor. As usual, he wouldn't change his mind. He went off to Sdeh Boker and Lavon took over the Defence Ministry. But he couldn't get along with the bright young men who had been Ben-Gurion's most devoted disciples – among them Moshe Dayan, who was Israel's chief-of-staff then, and Shimon Peres, who was director-general of the Defence Ministry. They neither liked nor trusted Lavon and they made this quite clear to him, while he, for his part, made it equally clear that he was not going to live in Ben-Gurion's shadow and that he was going to make his own mark. So the seeds of trouble were already sown.

When the security blunder which was the start of the whole affair occurred, a committee was appointed to look into its whys and wherefores. I am not free to go into any details about the actual mishap, nor do I want to. It is enough, I think, to say that Lavon claimed to have known nothing at all about the operation and accused the head of intelligence of having planned it behind his back. The committee didn't come up with any really conclusive findings one way or the other, but it also did not fully absolve Lavon of responsibility for what had happened. At all events, the public was unaware of the entire top-secret episode, and the few people who did know about it assumed that it was now a closed chapter. Nonetheless – and regardless of who was to blame – a terrible mistake had been made. Lavon had no alternative other than to resign, and Ben-Gurion was summoned back to the Defence Ministry from Sdeh Boker.

Then, six years later, the whole thing flared up again – and this time it turned into a major political scandal with the most tragic after-effects inside *Mapai* itself. It upset and confused the Israeli public for months, and it led, indirectly, to my own break with Ben-Gurion and to his second and final resignation as prime minister. In 1960 Lavon claimed that false evidence had been given at the initial enquiry and even that documents had been forged. Lavon therefore demanded that Ben-Gurion publicly clear his name. Ben-Gurion refused; he had not accused Lavon of anything, he said, and therefore he couldn't acquit him. That would have to be done by a court of law. A committee was formed at once to enquire into the conduct of the army officers whom Lavon had charged with conspiring against him. But before it could complete its work, Lavon had brought the entire matter to the attention of an important Knesset committee, and it eventually reached the press.

The rest of the Lavon–Ben-Gurion battle was fought out largely in public. Levi Eshkol, characteristically, undertook to try and calm everyone concerned, but Ben-Gurion was adamant about the need for a juridical enquiry. He was evidently quite prepared to injure his closest colleagues and the party he led in order to solve the problem in the only way he believed was right – and to prevent anyone from casting any aspersions either on the army or on the Defence Ministry. He went on demanding legal procedures while Eshkol, Sapir and I tried to get the conflict resolved at the cabinet level – decently and discreetly. Seven ministers were appointed to a special committee of investigation, and we were all thankful that Ben-Gurion raised no objection to this. But, in due course, the ministerial committee, which Ben-Gurion hoped would back him in his demand for legal proceedings, announced that nothing further need be done: Lavon had not been responsible for giving the order that led to the blunder and there was no need to go on pursuing the matter. Ben-Gurion was furious and argued that if the committee was sure that Lavon had not given the order, then the blame could only fall on the head of military intelligence. Since, however, there was no proof of this, only a judicial committee could decide who had been responsible. Furthermore, he said, the ministerial committee had behaved most improperly. It had not done what it was supposed to do; it had covered up for Lavon and, generally, it was a disgrace. In January 1961, Ben-Gurion resigned again, Levi Eshkol became prime minister at Ben-Gurion's suggestion and Ben-Gurion started up his campaign for a judicial enquiry all over again. But Eshkol had had enough of the Lavon Affair. He rejected the idea. Ben-Gurion was like a man possessed. He had counted on Eshkol to obey him, and Eshkol had refused. So now poor Eshkol and all his supporters within the party became the prime targets of Ben-Gurion's fury.

I couldn't forgive Ben-Gurion either for the ruthless way in which he was pursuing Eshkol or for the way in which he treated and spoke about the rest of us, myself included. It was as though all the years that we had worked together counted for nothing. In Ben-Gurion's eyes we had turned into personal enemies, and that was how he behaved towards us. We didn't see each other for years after that. I even thought that, feeling as I did, it wouldn't be right for me to attend Ben-Gurion's eightieth birthday party in 1969 (from which Eshkol had been excluded), though Ben-Gurion had sent a special emissary to invite me. I knew that it would hurt him very much if I refused, but I just couldn't say yes. He had injured all of us too badly, and I couldn't get over it. If we were really as stupid as he had said we were, well, when people are born stupid, not much can be done about it, and it isn't anyone's fault. But no one is born corrupt, and that is a terrible accusation! If other party leaders were willing to overlook the fact that Ben-Gurion thought, or at any rate said, that they were corrupt, well and good. Eshkol wasn't, and neither was I. I couldn't pretend that it never happened. I couldn't rewrite history, and I wouldn't lie to myself. I didn't go to that birthday party.

In 1969, when I presented my first cabinet to the Knesset, Ben-Gurion – who in the meantime had broken away from *Mapai* to form *Rafi* (the Israel Workers List), together with Dayan and Peres – abstained from voting. But he did make a statement. 'There is no doubt at all,' he told the Knesset, 'that Golda Meir is capable of being a prime minister. But it must never be forgotten that she lent her hand to something immoral.' And he went on and on again about the Lavon Affair. Towards the end of his life, however, we made up. I went down to Sdeh Boker on his eighty-fifth birthday, and though we didn't have a formal reconciliation, we were friends again. He, in turn, made a point of coming to Revivim when Sarah's kibbutz gave me a seventy-fifth birthday party in 1973. Of course, by then Ben-Gurion wasn't really Ben-Gurion any more. Still, we had at least repaired that awful and unnecessary breach – for which I have no adequate explanation to this day. That, in a very small nutshell indeed, was the Lavon Affair, the first instalment of which was already behind us in 1956, when I became Israel's second foreign minister.

Although it is customary for the formal handing-over of a ministry to be performed by the outgoing minister in the presence of the incoming one, Sharett took leave of his ministry differently. He went there alone, called in the heads of departments and said good-bye to them. Then he asked me to come and see him, and for three days he briefed me about as thoroughly as I have ever been briefed on anything by anybody. It was typical of Sharett that he knew everything down to the last detail about the ministry, including the name, family status and personal problems of everyone who worked there. He even knew the names of all their children. But he said he was not going to accompany me to the ministry on my first day. I would have to go there alone. So one day I made my appearance at the Foreign Ministry all by myself, feeling and probably looking miserable and fully aware of the fact that I was succeeding a man who had not only founded the ministry but had headed it ever since 1948.

My first few months as foreign minister were not much happier. It wasn't only that I was a novice among experts. It was also that Sharett's style was so different from mine, and the kind of people he had chosen to work with him – though they were all remarkably competent and genuinely dedicated – were not necessarily the kind of people with whom I was accustomed to work. Many of the more senior ambassadors and officials had been educated at British universities, and their particular brand of intellectual sophistication, which Sharett admired so much, was not always my cup of tea. Nor, to be honest, could I have any illusions about the fact that some of them obviously didn't think I was the right person for the job. I was certainly not known either for my subtle phraseology or for my great concern with protocol, and seven years at the Ministry of Labour wasn't their idea of the most suitable background for a foreign minister. But after a while we all got used to each other, and I must say that on the whole we worked very well together, perhaps because there was always so much at stake.

I had entered the Foreign Ministry in the summer of 1956, when the activities of the Arab terrorists – especially of the *fedayeen* (the bands of armed raiders supported and trained by Egypt)—had reached an intolerable peak. The *fedayeen* operated mainly from the Gaza Strip but they also had bases in Jordan, Syria and Lebanon, and Jews were being killed by them right in the centre of Israel, in such places as Rehovot, Lydda, Ramle and Jaffa. The Arab states had long ago explained their position. 'We are exercising a right of war,' an Egyptian representative had said in 1951 in defence of Egypt's refusal to let Israeli ships go through the Suez Canal. 'An armistice does not put an end to a state of war. It does not prohibit a country from exercising certain rights of war.' That these 'rights' were still being fully upheld in 1955 and 1956 we knew all too well. Colonel Gamal Abdel Nasser, who had to come to power in Egypt in 1952 and was now the most powerful figure in the Arab world, openly applauded the *fedayeen*. 'You have proven,' he told them, 'that you are heroes upon whom our entire country can depend. The spirit with which you enter the land of the enemy must be spread.' Cairo Radio also praised the murderers endlessly in language that was crystal clear: 'Weep, O Israel,' was one refrain, 'the day of extermination draws near.'

The United Nations did nothing effective to put a halt to the *fedayeen* outrages. The UN secretary-general, Dag Hammerskjöld, did succeed in arranging a ceasefire that lasted for a few days in the spring of 1956, but when the *fedayeen* went back to crossing the border, he let it go at that and didn't return to the Middle East. I know that today a small cult has grown up around the personality and fine perceptions of Mr Hammerskjöld, but I am not a party to it. I used to meet with him often, after he had seen Ben-Gurion and talked to him for an hour or two about Buddhism and other philosophical topics, in which they had a common interest. Then he and I would discuss such commonplace subjects as a clause in the armistice agreement with Jordan that was being contravened or some complaint we had against the United Nations. No wonder Hammerskjöld thought that Ben-Gurion was an angel and that I was impossible to get along with. I never considered him to be a friend of Israel and although I tried hard not to show it, I expect he sensed my feeling that he was less than neutral as far as the situation in the Middle East was concerned. If the Arabs said no to something – which they did all the time – Hammerskjöld never went any further. Not that U Thant (the Burmese statesman who followed him at the United Nations) was a great improvement. Despite all the years of Burmese–Israeli friendship and his own really warm personal relationship with the country, and with us, the moment that U Thant became secretary-general we were in for a very hard time. He also found it absolutely impossible, apparently, to be firm either with the Russians or with the Arabs, though he had no trouble at all being exceedingly firm with Israel.

But that is all by the way. Certainly it was not the UN secretary-general who was responsible for the almost daily murder, robbery and sabotage carried out by the *fedayeen*. In one of those attacks, a group of archaeologists working in Ramat Rachel near Jerusalem were fired upon from the Jordanian border. Four people were killed and many

others wounded. One of the four was part of my family. He was Menachem's father-in-law, Aya's father, a distinguished and gentle scholar
who had never harmed anyone in his whole life, and I remember thinking to myself bitterly that there was something crazy about a world
that calmly accepted the concept of 'rights of war' but was so indifferent
about the 'rights of peace'. But the real responsibility lay – not for the
last time – with the Russians.

In 1955 an agreement was concluded between Czechoslovakia (read
the Soviet Union) and Egypt as a result of which Egypt was receiving
an almost unending supply of arms – ranging from submarines and
destroyers to tanks and troop carriers. It may well be asked how it
happened that the Soviet Union suddenly decided to arm a state that
was making no bones whatsoever about its intention of 'reconquering
Palestine', as Colonel Nasser put it. The answer is that it was not really
sudden at all. In the global struggle of the 1950s, known (not very
accurately as far as *we* were concerned) as the Cold War, both the
United States and the Soviet Union were busy outbidding each other
for the favours of the Arab states, especially those of Egypt. The United
States and Britain may have felt a little uneasy about their courtship
of Nasser's Egypt, but the Soviet Union had no qualms at all. The fact
that the USSR was making possible the fulfilment of the Egyptian
dream of a second round of war against Israel was justified – to the
extent that the Russians ever feel that they have to justify themselves –
on the grounds that Zionism, which was such an evil thing, had to be
suppressed everywhere. And to prove how evil it was, the so-called
Doctors' Plot was invented in Moscow in 1953. The Russian people
were informed that nine doctors (no less than six of whom were Jewish)
had tried to murder Stalin, as well as a number of other Soviet leaders,
and an infamous trial was staged as part of an anti-Jewish campaign
set in motion throughout the Soviet Union.

Then, one night a small bomb exploded in the garden of the Soviet
legation in Tel Aviv. The Russians at once accused the government of
Israel of having engineered the incident and broke off diplomatic relations. But even when diplomatic relations were renewed a few months
later, the anti-Semitic propaganda campaign in the USSR, with its
constant references to Zionism, went on; and the chant about the
'Zionist stooges of imperialist warmongers' was taken up in Czechoslovakia, which mounted its own despicable campaign against the
Jews.

Despite all this – and the unconcealed Soviet–Arab preparations for another war – the United States and Britain refused to sell us arms. It didn't matter how often or how loudly we knocked on their doors. The answer was always negative, though at the very beginning of 1956 the United States – still refusing to sell us arms – indicated to France and Canada that it didn't mind if *they* did so. But France hadn't waited for US permission. For her own reasons, she had decided to come to Israel's aid, and while there was no possibility of matching the boundless Soviet 'generosity' to Egypt, we were now at least no longer totally defenceless nor alone.

In the summer of 1956, just as I was settling into my new office and getting used, among other things, to being called Mrs Meir – the closest I could get to a Hebrew version of Meyerson and still obey Ben-Gurion's order that I take a Hebrew name ('Meir' means 'illuminate' in Hebrew) – the noose tightened a bit more around our necks. Nasser made his most dramatic gesture. In July he nationalized the Suez Canal! No Arab leader had ever done anything so spectacular before, and the Arab world was profoundly impressed. There was, indeed, only one more thing that Nasser needed to do in order for the Egypt he ruled to be acclaimed as the supreme Moslem power, and that was to annihilate us. Elsewhere in the world, the nationalization of the Canal was anxiously discussed in terms of big power politics. But we in Israel were more worried about the increase in the military strength of Egypt and Syria, which had signed a pact to unite their high commands. There was no longer any doubt that war was inevitable and that the Egyptians had once again fallen prey to a fantasy of victory over Israel – a self-glorifying fantasy, incidentally, which Nasser himself had developed in his *Philosophy of a Revolution*.

There is already so much literature (some of it fact and some of it fiction) about the Sinai Campaign that I think my own contribution can be quite modest. But I must stress one fact. Regardless of the abortive French and British attempt to seize the Suez Canal, Israel's own strike against the Egyptians in 1956 had one goal and one goal only: to prevent the destruction of the Jewish state. The threat was unmistakable. As I later said at the UN General Assembly, 'Even if no one else chose to do so, *we* recognized the symptoms.' We knew that dictatorships – including those given disarmingly to informing the world of their plans – usually keep their promises, and no one in Israel had forgotten the lesson of the crematoria or what total extermination really meant. Unless we were prepared to be killed off, either piecemeal or in one sudden attack, we had to take the initiative – though, God knows, it wasn't an easy decision to make. Nonetheless, it was made. We began secretly to plan the Sinai Campaign (known in Israel as Operation Kadesh).

The French offered us arms and began making their own secret plans for the joint Anglo-French assault on the Suez Canal. In September they invited Ben-Gurion to send a delegation to France for talks with Guy Mollet (who headed the French socialist government), Christian Pineau (the French foreign minister) and Maurice Bourges-Manoury (the French minister of defence), and he asked me, as Israel's foreign minister, to join the group. It included Moshe Dayan, Shimon Peres and Moshe Carmel (our minister of transport, who had served with great distinction as a brigadier-general during the War of Independence). Needless to say, I couldn't even hint to Sarah that I was going abroad. As a matter of fact, you could count on the fingers of one hand the number of people, other than those who were actually travelling, who knew anything about the whole idea at that stage. It was a truly water-tight secret. Even the cabinet was told about the interaction with the French and British, and decided on the details of the campaign, only a few days before it started, on Monday, 29 October, and the opposition leaders were informed by Ben-Gurion even later than the cabinet. Everybody, in short, was taken by surprise – not only Nasser!

We flew to France from a secret airfield in a rickety old French army plane that was very badly lit. We were all very silent and, of course, tense. And no one's frame of mind was helped much when Moshe Carmel, while walking through the plane, almost fell out of the bomb bay, which was not properly closed. Fortunately, he managed to pull himself back into the plane, but broke three ribs in the process!

Our first stop was in North Africa, where we were put up at a very pleasant French guest house and given a marvellous meal. Our hosts had no idea of our identity, and I remember how astonished they were when they discovered that the mysterious mission included a woman. Anyhow, we flew on from there to a military airfield outside Paris and to our meetings with the French. I didn't even venture into Paris, and I remember being furious with Dayan, who did – though luckily no one recognized him. The main point of those talks was to work out various details of the military aid the French had promised us, especially the essential French undertaking to protect our skies, should we request it. But this was only the first of a series of such conferences, one of which was attended by Ben-Gurion himself.

On 24 October, in total secrecy, we began to mobilize our reserves. The public – and, by the same token, I suppose, Egyptian intelligence – was given the impression that because Iraqi troops had ominously moved into Jordan (which had recently joined the unified Egyptian–Syrian command), we were preparing for an assault against that country, and our troops massing on the Jordanian border helped to lend authenticity to the rumour. A week before the Sinai Campaign was to start, a conference of Israeli ambassadors took place at the Foreign Ministry, partly so that I could meet with some of our more important representatives abroad before the UN General Assembly convened. They went back to their respective posts four days before the war broke out not knowing anything about it. Sharett, who had gone to India as soon as I took over at the ministry, was actually talking to Nehru when they got word that the Sinai Campaign had begun, and Nehru couldn't believe that his guest knew nothing about it. But total secrecy was vital.

Every now and then during the last week or two before the campaign began, working at the Foreign Ministry or trying to get organized in the foreign minister's residence (to which I had moved in the summer), I found myself longing to talk to someone about what I knew was going to happen on 29 October. There is nothing lonelier or less natural for a human being than to have to keep a secret that affects the lives of every one around her, and one can only do it, I think, by an enormous, almost superhuman, effort. Wherever I went and whatever I did, I was never, for one instant, unaware of the fact that within a few days we would be at war. I had no doubt that we would be victorious, but however great our victory might be there would still be great suffering and danger. I used to look at the young men in the Foreign Ministry or at the boy who delivered my newspapers or at the builders working across the street from my home and wonder what would happen to them when the war started. It was not at all a good feeling, but there was no other way for us to get rid of the *fedayeen* or force the Egyptians to understand that Israel was not expendable. I spent the last weekend during that long hot October with Sarah and Zechariah at Revivim. I tried not to think about the war on my way to the kibbutz, but it was impossible. If something went wrong, it was through the Negev and through Revivim itself that the Egyptian army would smash its way into Israel, bent on destruction. I played with the children, sat with Sarah and Zechariah in the shade of the young trees of which Revivim was so proud, spent an evening with friends of theirs (and mine), talking, as Israelis always do, about 'the situation' – which means, whatever the year, the current danger to Israel's survival. And all the time I thought to myself: 'Must we really go on like this for ever, worrying about children and grandchildren and fighting, killing and being killed?' But I couldn't even warn them of what was ahead.

Just before I left Revivim to return to Jerusalem, a young man came up to me. I knew his face (he was one of the 'oldtimers' in the kibbutz), but I couldn't recall his name. He introduced himself to me, explained that he was in charge of security at Revivim and said that he already knew that something was about to happen. He didn't use the world 'mobilization', but we understood each other perfectly. 'I know that you can't tell me anything,' he said very apologetically, 'and that I ought not even to ask you this. But should we start to dig trenches?' I looked around at the little kibbutz, so exposed and vulnerable in the middle of the Negev, and into the grave eyes of the young man. 'I think perhaps I would if I were you,' I replied and got into my car. All the way back to Jerusalem I saw signs of the call-up that was already under way by word of mouth, telegram and telephone; at almost every bus stop men in civilian clothes were lining up for buses to take them to their units.

The Sinai Campaign began as scheduled, after sunset on 29 October, and ended as scheduled, on 5 November. It took the Israel Defence Forces, made up mainly of reservists travelling in a crazy assortment of military and civilian vehicles, less than 100 hours to cross and capture from the Egyptians the whole of the Gaza Strip and the Sinai Peninsula – an area two and a half times larger than Israel itself. We had counted on surprise, speed and utterly confusing the Egyptian army, but it was only when I myself flew to visit Sharm el-Sheikh at the southernmost tip of Sinai and toured the Gaza Strip by car afterwards that I really understood the extent of our victory – the sheer size and desolation of the territory through which those tanks, half-tracks, ice-cream trucks, private cars and taxis had raced in under seven days. The Egyptian defeat was absolute. The nests of the *fedayeen* were cleaned out. The elaborate Egyptian system to defend Sinai – the fortresses and the battalions concealed in the desert – was put totally out of commission. The hundreds of thousands of weapons and the millions upon millions of rounds of ammunition – mostly Russian – stock-piled for use against us were worthless now. A third of the Egyptian army was broken. Of the 30,000 Egyptian soldiers whom we found pathetically wandering in the sand, 5,000 were taken as prisoners to save them from dying of thirst (and eventually exchanged for the one Israeli the Egyptians had managed to capture).

But we hadn't fought the Sinai Campaign for territory, booty or prisoners, and as far as we were concerned, we had won the only thing we wanted: peace, or at least the promise of peace for a few years, perhaps even for longer. Although our casualties were 'light', we desperately hoped that the 172 Israelis who were killed (some 800 were wounded) would be the last battle casualties we would ever have to mourn. This time, we would insist that our neighbours come to terms with us and with our existence.

Of course, things didn't turn out that way. Although we had won our war against Egypt, the French and the British had lost theirs – due to some extent to their ineptness but mostly to the overwhelmingly negative public reaction in France and Great Britain to what was viewed as an imperialist assault on an innocent third party. I have always thought that had the Anglo-French attack on Suez been more swift and efficient, the storm of protest in those countries would have died down in the face of a *fait accompli*. But as it was, the combined assault failed, and the French and British backed down as soon as the United Nations, under intense US and Soviet pressure, demanded that they withdrew their troops from the Suez Canal zone. It also demanded Israel's withdrawal from the Sinai Peninsula and the Gaza Strip.

That was the beginning of the four and a half heart-breaking months of diplomatic battle that we waged – and lost – at the United Nations in our attempt to persuade the nations of the world that if we retreated to the armistice lines of 1949, war would again break out in the Middle East one day. Those people, those millions of people who even today have still not quite grasped the realities of Israel's struggle to stay alive, and who are so quick to condemn us for not being 'more flexible' and for not retreating pleasantly to our former borders each time we are forced to go to war, might do well to ponder the course of events following 1956 and ask themselves what was gained by the fact that we *did* reluctantly withdraw then from Sinai and the Gaza Strip. The answer is: only more wars, each one bloodier and far more costly than the Sinai Campaign had been. Had we been allowed to stay where we were until the Egyptians agreed to negotiate with us, the recent history of the Middle East would certainly have been very different. But the pressure was intense, and in the end we gave in. President Eisenhower, who had been kept totally in the dark by his European allies, was furious and said that unless Israel withdrew at once, the United States would support sanctions against her at the United Nations.

The source of the greatest pressure, however, was the Soviet Union, which had not only witnessed a complete Egyptian defeat – all the Soviet support notwithstanding – but was also now able to becloud the issue of the recent Soviet invasion of Hungary by screaming to high heaven about the terrible colonialist conspiracy against Egypt and, most of all, about Israel's 'unrestrained aggression'. In retrospect, it is unlikely that Soviet Prime Minister Nikolai Bulganin's threats of direct Soviet intervention in the Middle East would have resulted in a third world war, but at the time that was what was being read into his grim warnings. It looked as though virtually the whole world was against us, but I didn't believe that we should give in without a fight.

In December 1956 I left for the United Nations filled with forebodings. But before I went, I wanted to see Sinai and the Gaza Strip for myself, and I am glad that I did, because otherwise I would never have really comprehended the full gravity of the situation we had been in prior to the Sinai Campaign. I shall never forget my first sight of the elaborate Egyptian military installations – built in defiance of the United Nations itself – at Sharm el-Sheikh for the sole purpose of maintaining an illegal blockade against our shipping. The area of Sharm el-Sheikh is incredibly lovely; the waters of the Red Sea must be the bluest and the clearest in the world, and they are framed by mountains that range in colour from deep red to violet and purple. There, in that beautiful tranquil setting, on an empty shore, stood the grotesque battery of huge naval guns that had paralysed Eilat for so long. For me, it was a picture that symbolized everything. Then I toured the Gaza Strip, from which the *fedayeen* had gone out on their murderous assignments for so many months and in which the Egyptians had kept a quarter of a million men, women and children (of whom nearly 60 per cent were Arab refugees) in the most shameful poverty and destitution. I was appalled by what I saw there and by the fact that those miserable people had been maintained in such a degrading condition for over eight years only so that the Arab leaders could show the refugee camps to visitors and make political capital out of them. Those refugees could and should have been resettled at once in any of the Arab countries of the Middle East – countries, incidentally, whose language, traditions and religion they share. The Arabs would still have been able to continue their quarrel with us, but at least the refugees would not have been kept in a state of semi-starvation or lived in such abject terror of their Egyptian masters.

I couldn't help comparing what I saw in the Gaza Strip to what we had done – even with all the mistakes we had made – for the Jews who had come to Israel in those same eight years, and I suppose that is why I began my statement to the UN General Assembly on 5 December 1956 by talking not about the war we had won, but about the Jewish refugees we had settled:

Israel's people went into the desert or struck roots in stony hillsides to establish new villages, to build roads, houses, schools and hospitals; while Arab terrorists, entering from Egypt and Jordan, were sent in to kill and destroy. Israel dug wells, brought water in pipes from great distances; Egypt sent in *fedayeen* to blow up the wells and the pipes. Jews from Yemen brought in sick, undernourished children believing that two out of every five would die; we cut that number down to one out of twenty-five. While we fed those babies and cured their diseases, the *fedayeen* were sent in to throw bombs at children in synagogues and grenades into baby homes.

Then I went on to those celebrated 'rights of war', to that discredited excuse of a 'belligerent status' against Israel, the screen behind which Colonel Nasser had trained and unleashed the *fedayeen*:

A comfortable division has been made. The Arab states unilaterally enjoy the 'rights of war'; Israel has the unilateral responsibility of keeping the peace. But belligerency is not a one-way street. Is it then surprising if a people labouring under this monstrous distinction should finally become restive and at last seek a way of rescuing its life from the perils of the regulated war that is conducted against it from all sides?

The real point of that address, however, was not to make the familiar accusations – however justified they were – or even to try to bring home again to the so-called family of nations the immediate background to the Sinai Campaign. It was not even to put on the record what we knew to have been the very well-laid Egyptian plans for the annihilation of Israel. It was something else, something far more important: to try once again, and in public, to explore the source of the hatred the Arab leaders bore towards Israel and to make some concrete proposals for a possible peace. I want to emphasize the fact that I made this speech at the end of 1956, twenty years ago. If it is in any way familiar, that is only because we have gone on saying the same thing ever since, with about as much success as we had in 1956!

The fundamental problem in the whole situation is the systematically organized Arab hostility against Israel. This Arab enmity is not a natural phenomenon. It is artificially fostered and nurtured. It is not, as has been alleged here, Israel which is an instrument of colonialism. It is the Israel–Arab conflict which keeps the area at the mercy of dangerously contending outside forces. Only by the liquidation of that conflict will the people of the region be able to work out their own destinies in independence and hope. Only in that prospect lies hope for a brighter future of equality and progress for all the peoples concerned. If hatred is abandoned as a principle of Arab policies, everything becomes possible.

Over and over again the Israeli government has held out its hand in peace to its neighbours. But to no avail. At the ninth session of the General Assembly, the Israeli representative suggested that if the Arab countries were not yet ready for peace, it would be useful, as a preliminary or transitory stage, to conclude agreements committing the parties to policies of non-aggression and pacific settlement. The reply was outright rejection. Our offer to meet the representatives of all or any of the Arab countries still stands. Never have we heard an echo from across our borders to our call for peace.

The concept of annihilating Israel is a legacy of Hitler's war against the Jewish people, and it is no coincidence that Nasser's soldiers had an Arabic translation of *Mein Kampf* in their knapsacks. Those concerned sincerely with peace and freedom in the world would, I think, have been happier had some more ennobling literature been offered these men as a guide. Still, we are convinced that these dangerous seeds have not yet succeeded in corrupting the Arab peoples. This fatal game is one which the Arab political leaders should halt in the interests of the Arab peoples themselves . . .

What ought to be done now? Are we to go back to an armistice regime which has brought anything but peace and which Egypt has derisively flouted? Shall the Sinai Desert again breed nests of *fedayeen* and be the staging ground of aggressive armies posed for the assault? Must the tragedy again be re-enacted in the tinderbox of the Middle East? The peace of our region and perhaps of more than our region hangs on the answers which will be given to these questions.

Or, I asked, would the General Assembly now apply itself to thinking of the future 'with the same vigour and insistence' with which it was calling upon us to withdraw our troops from across a boundary that could not continue to be 'open to the *fedayeen* but closed to Israeli soldiers'? Surely, peace was not only necessary but also possible. Only a few days before my speech, I had heard the representative of Egypt, speaking from the same rostrum, make a speech which – though it was perhaps not very original – at least sounded a note that, for a change, was not war-like. Listening to him I had for a minute seen a picture of the Middle East as it might be if the barriers (they had actually become barricades) between the Arabs and ourselves ever fell. When the time came for me to speak, I thought I could do a lot worse than to repeat his words:

> With the great majority of the peoples of the world, Egypt has been saying, and will continue to say, that all nations can and should, for their own good, moral as well as material, live together in equality, freedom and fraternity, and with modern science and its vast potentialities at the service of man, enabling him, carried by the momentum of liberty and faith, to live an infinitely more productive and honourable life.

I had asked for a transcript of that speech, and now I read those lines out aloud to the General Assembly and continued:

> With that statement we wholeheartedly concur. We are ready to make it a practical reality . . . The countries of the Middle East are rightly listed in the category of the 'underdeveloped': the standard of living, disease, the illiteracy of the masses of people, the underdeveloped lands, desert, and swamp – all these cry out desperately for minds, hands, financial means, and technical ability. Can we envisage what a state of peace between Israel and its neighbours during the past eight years would have meant for all of us? Can we try to translate fighter planes into irrigation pipes and tractors for the people in these lands? Can we, in our imagination, replace gun emplacements by schools and hospitals? The many hundreds of millions of dollars spent on armaments could surely have been put to a more constructive purpose.
>
> Substitute cooperation between Israel and its neighbours for sterile hatred and ardour for destruction and you will give life and hope and happiness to all its people.

But walking back to my seat, I could see that no one else in that vast hall had shared the brief vision of the future with me, and I remember how surprised I was when a delegate sitting somewhere behind me applauded me as I sat down. The seating at the United Nations is always alphabetical; lots are drawn at the first meeting of each session as to which country should be seated first, and all the others are then seated in alphabetical order. At that session, Holland happened to be behind us. I nodded my head very gratefully to the Dutch delegate – one of the few not to vote against us – but I still took my place with a sense of great emptiness and utter disbelief. I had spoken to the United Nations and one would have thought from the expression on the faces of most of the delegates that I had asked for the moon, when in fact all

I had done – all that Israel has ever done at the United Nations – was to suggest that the Arabs, fellow-members of that organization, recognize our existence and work together with us towards peace. That no one had jumped up to seize the opportunity, to say: 'Alright, let's talk. Let's argue it all out. Let's make an effort to find a solution' was like a physical blow to me – not that I had many illusions left about the kind of family that family of nations was. Anyhow, I promised myself then that before the session was over, whatever else happened, I would try once again to reach the Arabs, to make a person-to-person appeal to them, because unless something was done soon, the future, as I saw it, looked pretty grim.

Those were terrible months. Our phased withdrawal from the Gaza Strip and Sinai was going on all the time, but nothing was being said or done to force the Egyptians to agree to enter into negotiations with us, to guarantee the lifting of the blockade of the Straits of Tiran or to solve the problem of the Gaza Strip. The four questions we had asked in November 1956 were still unanswered in February 1957. And I still couldn't get through to the Americans – least of all to the US secretary of state, that cold, grey man, John Foster Dulles – that our very life depended on adequate guarantees, real guarantees with teeth in them, and that we couldn't return to the situation which had existed before the Sinai Campaign. But nothing helped. None of the arguments, none of the appeals, none of the logic, not even the eloquence of Abba Eban, our ambassador to Washington. We just didn't talk the same language, and we didn't have the same priorities. Dulles was obsessed by his own 'brinkmanship', by his fear of a looming world war, and he told me in so many words, and more than once, that Israel would be responsible for that war, if it broke out, because we were so 'unreasonable'.

There were many days during that period when I wanted to run away, to run back to Israel and let someone else go on hammering away at Dulles and Henry Cabot Lodge, the head of the US delegation at the United Nations. I would have done anything just not to have to face another exhausting round of talks that always seemed to end in recriminations. But I stayed where I was, tried to swallow my bitterness and sense of betrayal, and at the end of February we arrived at a compromise of sorts. The last of our troops would leave the Gaza Strip and Sharm el-Sheikh in return for the 'assumption' that the United Nations would guarantee the right of free passage for Israeli shipping through the Straits of Tiran and that Egyptian soldiers would not be allowed back in the Gaza Strip. It wasn't much, and it certainly wasn't what we had been fighting for, but it was the best we could get – and it was better than nothing.

On 3 March 1957, having first had each last comma of it checked and cleared by Mr Dulles in Washington, I made our final statement.

The government of Israel is now in a position to announce its plans for full and prompt withdrawal from the Sharm el-Sheikh area and the Gaza Strip. In compliance with Resolution 1 of 2 February 1957, our sole purpose has been to ensure that on the withdrawal of Israeli forces, continued freedom of navigation will exist for Israel and international shipping in the Gulf of Aqaba and the Straits of Tiran.

And then, as I had promised myself I would do, I said:

Now may I add these few words to the states in the Middle East area and, more specifically, to the neighbours of Israel? Can we from now on, all of us, turn a new leaf, and instead of fighting among each other can we all, united, fight poverty, disease, illiteracy? Can we, is it possible for us to pool all our efforts, all our energy, for one single purpose – the betterment and progress and development of all our lands and all our peoples?

But no sooner had I taken my seat than Henry Cabot Lodge got up. To my astonishment, I heard him reassure the United Nations that while the rights of free passage for all nations through the Straits of Tiran would indeed be safeguarded, the future of the Gaza Strip would have to be worked out within the context of the armistice agreements. Perhaps not everyone at the United Nations that day understood what Cabot Lodge was saying, but *we* understood all too well. The US State Department had won its battle against us, and the Egyptian military government, with its garrison, was going to return to Gaza. There was nothing I could do or say. I just sat there, biting my lip, not even able to look at the handsome Mr Cabot Lodge while he pacified all those who had been so worried lest we refuse to withdraw unconditionally. It was not one of the finest moments of my life.

But reality had to be faced, and we had not lost everything. For the time being, the *fedayeen* terror was over; the principle of freedom of navigation through the Straits of Tiran had been upheld; the UN Emergency Force moved in to Gaza and the Sharm el-Sheikh area and we had won a victory that had made military history, proving again our ability – if needs be – to take up arms in our own defence.

I went back to the United Nations later that year, in October, and once again tried to break the ten-year-old deadlock between the Arab states and ourselves. I spoke to them out of the very depths of my conviction that the time had come for us to deal directly with each other, and I spoke on the spur of the moment, without any preparation and without a text.

Israel is approaching her tenth anniversary. You did not want it to be born. You fought against the decision in the United Nations. You then attacked us by military force. We have all been witnesses to sorrow, destruction and the spilling of blood and tears. Yet Israel is here, growing, developing, progressing . . . We are an old, tenacious people and, as our history has proved, not easily destroyed. Like you, the Arab countries, we have regained our national independence, and as with you, so with us, nothing will cause us to give it up. We are here to stay. History has decreed that the Middle East consists of an independent Israel and independent Arab states. This verdict will never be reversed.

In the light of these facts, what is the use or realism or justice of policies and attitudes based on the fiction that Israel is not here or will somehow disappear? Would it not be better for all to build a future for the Middle East based on cooperation? Israel will exist and progress even without peace, but surely a future of peace would be better both for Israel and for her neighbours. The Arab world with its ten sovereignties and 3 million square miles can well afford to accommodate itself to peaceful cooperation with Israel. Does hate for Israel and the aspiration for its destruction make one child in your country happier? Does it convert one hovel into a house? Does culture thrive on the soil of hatred? We have not the slightest doubt that eventually there will be peace and cooperation between us. This is an historic necessity for both peoples. We are prepared; we are anxious to bring it about now . . .

I could have saved my breath. Our few friends in the General Assembly clapped their hands politely, maybe even enthusiastically, but the Arabs didn't as much as look up.

During my term of office as foreign minister, I visited the United Nations often. I was there at least once a year as head of Israel's delegation to the General Assembly, and there wasn't a single time that I didn't make an attempt to contact the Arabs somehow – or, to my sorrow, a single time that I succeeded. I remember once, in 1957, seeing Nasser there from a distance and wondering what would happen if I just went over to him and began to chat. But he was surrounded by his bodyguards, and I had my bodyguards, and it obviously wouldn't work. But Tito was at that same session, and I thought perhaps I could talk to him and he would arrange something. So I asked someone in our delegation to talk to a member of the Yugoslav delegation and try to set up a meeting between Tito and me. I waited and waited and waited. I even postponed my return to Israel, but there was no reply.

Then, the day after I had left New York, we got an answer: Tito would meet me in New York. But I was already back home. We tried again – there was silence again.

There wasn't one possible intermediary whom I didn't approach during that period. At one Assembly session, I became quite friendly with the wife of the acting head of the Pakistani delegation, that country's ambassador to London. One day, she approached me, of her own accord, and said: 'Mrs Meir, if we women are in politics, *we* ought to try and make peace.' Well, that was just what I had been waiting for. I said to her: 'Let me tell you something. Never mind about peace. Invite a few of the Arab delegates to your home and invite me. I promise you, on my word of honour, that as long as the Arabs don't want anyone to know about our meeting, no one will know. And I don't want to meet them for peace negotiations. Just to talk. Just to sit in one room together.' She said: 'That's wonderful. I'll do it. I'll start to organize it at once.' So I waited and waited, but nothing happened. One day I asked her to have a cup of coffee with me in the Delegates' Lounge, and we were sitting there when the foreign minister of Iraq came in. (He was the gentleman who had once pointed at me from the General Assembly rostrum and said: 'Mrs Meir, go back to Milwaukee – that's where you belong.') She turned white. 'My God,' she said, 'he'll see me talking to you,' and she got up in a panic and left. That was the end of that.

And so it went, even down to the casual meetings we might have had at diplomatic luncheons. Every head of a UN delegation learned very quickly that if he wanted the Arabs to come, then he mustn't invite us. There was one foreign minister who was new to the game and who did invite both the Arabs and the Israelis. He not only invited us, he even seated an Iraqi delegate across the table from me. Well, the Arab sat down, started to eat his smoked salmon, raised his eyes, saw me, stood up and left. Of course, at the large receptions or the cocktail parties for hundreds of people, it was possible for a host to invite Arabs and Israelis, but for a dinner or a luncheon – never! As soon as an Arab delegate caught sight of one of the Israelis, he would walk out of the room, and there was nothing we could do about it.

But there were brighter moments during those years and some very memorable meetings. The most interesting and most memorable, perhaps, were those with John F. Kennedy, Lyndon Johnson and Charles de Gaulle. I met Kennedy twice. The first time was right after the Sinai Campaign, when he was a senator from Massachusetts. The

Zionists of Boston had organized a tremendous demonstration and a gala dinner in support of Israel, which was attended by the entire Consular Corps, the state's two senators – and the Israeli foreign minister. I was seated next to Kennedy, who was one of the speakers, and I remember being tremendously impressed by him, by how young he was and how well he spoke, though he was not really easy to talk to. I had a feeling that he was very shy, and we only exchanged a few words. The next time I met him was shortly before he was assassinated. I went down to Florida, where he was vacationing, and we talked for a very long time – and very informally. We sat on the porch of the big house in which he was staying, and I can still see him, in his rocking chair, without a tie, with his sleeves rolled up, listening very attentively as I tried to explain to him why we so desperately needed arms from the United States. He looked so handsome and still so boyish that it was hard for me to remember that I was talking to the president of the United States – though I suppose he didn't think I looked much like a foreign minister either! Anyhow, it was a strange setting for such an important talk. There were two or three other people with us, including 'Mike' Feldman, one of Kennedy's right-hand men, but they didn't participate in the conversation.

At first, I went into the current situation in the Middle East. Then, suddenly, it occurred to me that this bright young man might not understand very much about the Jews and what Israel actually meant to them, and I decided that I ought to explain that to him before I went on talking about why we had to have arms. So I said: 'Mr President, let me tell you in what way Israel is different from other countries.' To do so, I had to go back a long way, because the Jews are such an ancient people. They came into being more than 3,000 years ago and lived alongside nations that have long since disappeared – the Ammonites, the Moabites, the Assyrians, the Babylonians and others. In ancient times, they were all subject to oppression from foreign powers at one time or another, and in the end they all accepted their fate and became part of whatever the dominant culture was. All of them, that is, except the Jews. 'Like these other peoples,' I said, 'the Jews had their land occupied by foreign powers. But the fate of the Jews was very different, because – of all these nations – only the people of Israel were determined to remain what they were. The people of other nations stayed in their lands but abandoned their identity, while the Jews, who were dispersed among the nations of the world and lost their land, never let go of their determination to remain Jewish – or of their hope of returning to Zion. Well, now we are back there, and that places a very special burden on the leadership of Israel. In many ways, the government of Israel is no different from any other decent government. It cares for the welfare of the people, for the development of the state, and so on. But, in addition, there is one other great responsibility, and that is for the future. If we should lose our sovereignty again, those of us who would remain alive – and there wouldn't be very many – would be dispersed once more. But we no longer have the great reservoir we once had of our religion, our culture, and our faith. We lost much of that when six million Jews perished in the Holocaust.'

Kennedy didn't take his eyes off me and I went on: 'There are five and a half or six million Jews in the United States. They are wonderful, generous, good Jews, but I think that they themselves would be the first to agree with me if I say that I doubt very much whether they would have the tenacity which those lost six million had. And if I am right, then what is written on the wall for us is: "Beware of losing your sovereignty again, for this time you may lose it forever." If *that* should happen, then my generation would go down in history as the generation that made Israel sovereign again, but didn't know how to hold on to that independence.'

When I finished, Kennedy leaned over to me. He took my hand, looked into my eyes and said very solemnly, 'I understand, Mrs Meir. Don't worry. *Nothing* will happen to Israel.' And I think that he did truly understand.

I met Kennedy again at a formal UN reception where he was greeting the heads of delegations, but we only said hello to each other then, and I never saw him again. But I did go to his funeral and afterwards – with all the other heads of delegations – I went to shake Mrs Kennedy's hand. I never saw her again either, but I can't forget how she stood there, pale and with tears in her eyes, but still finding something special to say to each one of us. It was also at Kennedy's funeral – or, more accurately, at the state dinner given that evening by the new president – that I met Lyndon B. Johnson. I had met him before, during the General Assembly of 1956–7, when he was the Democratic majority leader of the Senate and came out, strongly and publicly, against President Eisenhower's threat of sanctions against us, so I already knew how he felt about Israel. But when I came up to him that night in the receiving line, he put his arm around me, held it there for a minute and said: 'I know that you have lost a friend, but I hope you understand that I, too, am a friend', which he certainly proved himself to be.

Often, throughout the period of the Six Day War, when President

Johnson backed our refusal to return to the pre-1967 lines unless we could do so within the framework of a peace settlement – and helped us achieve the military and economic means to maintain that position – I used to think back to the night of Kennedy's funeral and to the words that he said to me then, when he had so much else to think and worry about. I never saw him again either, though I wasn't at all surprised that he got along so well with Levi Eshkol when he was prime minister. They were very similar in many ways – open, warm and easy to establish contact with. I know how unpopular Johnson eventually became in the United States, but he was a very staunch friend indeed, and Israel owes a lot to him. I think he was one of the very few leaders abroad who understood what a mistake had been made by the Eisenhower administration after the Sinai Campaign, when we were forced to retreat before any negotiations with the Arabs got under way.

When Johnson died in 1973, I was prime minister and, of course, I wrote a letter of condolence to Mrs Johnson. I have her reply before me now. It, too, moved me greatly, particularly since I knew how sincere it was.

'Dear Mrs Meir,' she wrote. 'You must know how much my husband looked forward to your forthcoming visit here. Often he talked of visiting Israel some day. His concern for your country was real and deep and his respect for your people came from the depths of his heart . . .'

Another of the personalities who were to have such a decisive effect on Israel's future and whom I met at President Kennedy's funeral was General de Gaulle. I had seen him for the first time in 1958, when the French ambassador to Israel, Pierre Gilbert (who is a whole story unto himself) made up his mind that I must visit the general. Gilbert was as ardent a Gaullist as he was a Zionist, and there was no talking him out of this plan, though I must say that I was very nervous about meeting de Gaulle. Everything I had heard about him – including the fact that he expected everyone to know French perfectly, while I didn't know it at all – scared me. But once Gilbert had set my visit in motion, there was no pulling back, and I went to Paris for a few days. First, I met with the then French foreign minister, Maurice Couve de Murville, the most British Frenchman I ever encountered. He had served in various Arab countries. He was very correct, very cold and, on the whole, unfriendly – none of which helped me look forward to meeting de Gaulle the next day. I was received at the Elysée Palace with all the standard pomp and circumstance. Walking up the steps, I felt as though

I was reviewing the entire French army, and I wondered what those splendid French guards in their red cloaks thought of me as I trudged up to the general's office, feeling very ill at ease. And there he was, in all his height and glory, the legendary Charles de Gaulle. Jacob Tzur, who was the director-general of our Foreign Ministry then and who afterwards served as our ambassador to France, had come with me, and between de Gaulle's interpreter and Tzur, the general and I managed to converse. He was remarkably cordial and very kind. It only took a few minutes for me to feel quite relaxed, and we had a most satisfactory talk about the problems of the Middle East, with his assuring me of his undying friendship for Israel.

Then at Kennedy's funeral I saw him again, first at the cathedral (the only people who were not kneeling, I believe, were de Gaulle, Zalman Shazar – who was president of Israel – and myself) and later at the dinner which I've already mentioned. Before we went into dinner, I spotted de Gaulle (not a great feat, considering how he towered over everyone) at the other end of the room. I was just considering whether I ought to go over to him or not when he moved in my direction. There was a great flurry all around. *Who* was de Gaulle going to? 'He never goes over to anyone himself; people are always summoned to him,' someone standing next to me explained. 'He must be going to talk to a very important person.' It was like the Red Sea parting so that the Children of Israel could get through; de Gaulle walked straight ahead and everyone scuttled out of his way. I almost fell over when he stopped in front of me and did something that was really unprecedented for him: he spoke to me in English. 'I am enchanted to see you again, even on this so tragic occasion,' he said and bowed. It made an enormous impression on everyone, but most of all on me. In the course of time, I even became very good friends with Couve de Murville, who used to tell me that de Gaulle had a soft spot in his heart for me. I only wish it had stayed that way, but we didn't do what he told us to do (which was to do nothing) in 1967, and he never forgave us for that disobedience. In those dreadful days before the Six Day War he told Abba Eban that there were two things Israel should know: 'If you are in real danger, you can depend upon me; but if you move first, you will be destroyed, and you will bring a catastrophe on the entire world.' Well, de Gaulle was wrong. We weren't destroyed and there wasn't a world war, but our relationship with him – and with the French government – was not the same from that day on. The same de Gaulle who, in 1961, toasted 'Israel, our friend and ally' summed up his attitude towards the Jews after the Six Day War by describing us as 'an elitist, self-confident and domineering people'.

The most exciting and, I think, the most important contribution I made as foreign minister, however, was in a totally different sphere. It had to do with Israel's new role in the developing countries of Latin America, Asia, and in particular, perhaps, Africa, and it opened up an entirely new chapter in my own life, too.

11 African and other friendships

I SUPPOSE THAT as far as my personal feelings were concerned, at least some of the impetus for my initial involvement with Africa and with the Africans in the late 1950s came as an emotional response to the situation in which we found ourselves after the Sinai Campaign – in many respects entirely alone, less than popular and certainly misunderstood. France was an ally and a good friend, and one or two other European countries were sympathetic to us; but our relationship with the United States was strained, with the Soviet bloc it was worse than strained and in Asia – despite all our efforts to secure real acceptance – we had, for the most part, come up against a stone wall. True, we had established missions in Burma, Japan and Ceylon and consular offices in the Philippines, Thailand and India; but though we were among the first nations to recognize the People's Republic of China, the Chinese were not at all interested in having an Israeli embassy in Peking, and Indonesia and Pakistan, as Moslem states, were openly hostile to us. The 'Third World', in which Nehru, on the one hand, and Tito, on the other, played such a decisive role, looked towards Nasser and the Arabs – and away from us. And when in the spring of 1955 a conference of Asian and African nations took place at Bandung, though we had greatly hoped to be invited, the Arab states threatened to boycott it if Israel participated, and we were excluded from that 'club' as well. I used to look around me at the United Nations in 1957 and 1958 and think to myself: 'We have no family here. No one who shares our religion, our language or our past. The rest of the world seems to be grouped into blocs that have sprung up because geography and history have

combined to give common interests to their peoples. But our neighbours – and natural allies – don't want to have anything to do with us,
and we really belong nowhere and to no one, except to ourselves.' We
were the first-born of the United Nations, but we were being treated
like unwanted step-children, and I must admit that it hurt.

Still, the world was not made up exclusively of Europeans and Asians.
There were also the emerging nations of Africa, then on the verge of
achieving independence, and to the black states-in-the-making there
was a great deal that Israel could and wanted to give. Like them, we
had shaken off foreign rule; like them, we had had to learn for ourselves how to reclaim the land, how to increase the yields of our crops,
how to irrigate, how to raise poultry, how to live together and how to
defend ourselves. Independence had come to us, as it was coming to
Africa, not served up on a silver platter but after years of struggle, and
we had had to learn – partly through our own mistakes – the high cost
of self-determination. In a world neatly divided between the 'haves' and
the 'have-nots', Israel's experience was beginning to look unique
because we had been forced to find solutions to the kinds of problems
that large, wealthy, powerful states had never encountered. We couldn't
offer Africa money or arms but, on the other hand, we were free of the
taint of the colonial exploiters because all that we wanted from Africa
was friendship. Let me at once anticipate the cynics. Did we go into
Africa because we wanted votes at the United Nations? Yes, of course
that was one of our motives – and a perfectly honourable one – which
I never, at any time, concealed either from myself or from the Africans.
But it was far from being the most important motive, though it certainly
wasn't trivial. The main reason for our African 'adventure' was that
we had something we wanted to pass on to nations that were even
younger and less experienced than ourselves.

Today, in the wake of the post-Yom Kippur War rupture of diplomatic relations between most of the African states and Israel, the chorus
of cynics also includes disillusioned Israelis. 'It was all a waste of money,
time and effort,' they say, 'a misplaced, pointless, messianic movement
that was taken far too seriously in Israel and that was bound to fall
apart the moment that the Arabs put any real pressure on the Africans.'
But, of course, nothing is cheaper, easier or more destructive than that
sort of after-the-fact criticism, and I must say that in this context I
don't think it has the slightest validity. Things happen to countries as
they do to people. No one is perfect and there are setbacks, some more
damaging and painful than others, but not every project can be ex-

pected to succeed fully or quickly. Moreover disappointments are not failures, and I have very little sympathy indeed for that brand of political expediency that demands immediate returns. The truth is that we did what we did in Africa not because it was just a policy of enlightened self-interest – a matter of *quid pro quo* – but because it was a continuation of our own most valued traditions and an expression of our own deepest historic instincts.

We went into Africa to teach, and what we taught was learned. No one regrets more bitterly than I that, for the time being, the African nations – or many of them – have chosen to turn their backs on us. But what really matters is what we – and they – accomplished together; what the thousands of Israeli experts in agriculture, hydrology, regional planning, public health, engineering, community services, medicine and scores of other fields actually did throughout Africa between 1958 and 1973, and what the thousands of Africans who trained in Israel during those years took home with them. Those benefits can never be lost, and those achievements should never be minimized. They are of enduring worth, and nothing can erase them, not even the current loss to Israel of whatever political or other benefits we derived from our ties with the governments of the African states. Ungrateful those governments most certainly have been, and it will take a great deal of effort on their part to remove the bad taste left by their desertion of us in a time of crisis. But that is no excuse for disowning, or belittling, what I honestly believe to have been a profoundly significant, not to say unprecedented, attempt on the part of one country to better human life in other countries, and I am prouder of Israel's International Cooperation Programme and of the technical aid we gave to the people of Africa than I am of any other single project we have ever undertaken.

For me, more than anything else, that programme typifies the drive towards social justice, reconstruction and rehabilitation that is at the very heart of Labour-Zionism – and Judaism. The philosophy of life that impelled the men and women of Merhavia in the 1920s to dedicate themselves to pioneering within a cooperative framework, that led my daughter and her comrades to continue in that same demanding pattern in the Revivim of the 1940s and that is responsible today for each new kibbutz established in Israel is identical, I believe, with the vision that took Israelis into African countries for years to share with the Africans the practical and theoretical knowledge that alone could answer Africa's needs in a changing world in which it was, at last, responsible for its own destiny. Not that all those who took part in the sharing of our national experience with the Africans were socialists. Far from it. But for me, at least, the programme was a logical extension of principles in which I had always believed, the principles, in fact, which gave a real purpose to my life. So, of course, I can never regard any facet of that programme as having been 'in vain', and equally I cannot believe that any of the Africans who were involved in it, or reaped its fruits, will ever regard it in that light either.

One other thing: we shared with the Africans not only the challenges posed by the need for rapid development but also the memory of centuries of suffering. Oppression, discrimination, slavery – these are not just catchwords for Jews or for Africans. They refer not to experiences undergone hundreds of years ago by half-forgotten ancestors but to torment and degradation experienced only yesterday. In 1902 Theodor Herzl wrote a novel in which he described the Jewish state of the future as he imagined it might be. The novel was called *Altneuland* ('Old-New Land'), and on its title page were written the words: 'If you will it, it is no dream' – words that became the motto and inspiration of the Zionist movement. In *Altneuland* there is a passage about Africa which I used to quote sometimes to African friends and which I should like to quote now:

... 'There is still one other question arising out of the disaster of the nations which remains unsolved to this day, and whose profound tragedy only a Jew can comprehend. This is the African question. Just call to mind all those terrible episodes of the slave trade, of human beings who, merely because they were black, were stolen like cattle, taken prisoner, captured and sold. Their children grew up in strange lands, the objects of contempt and hostility because their complexions were different. I am not ashamed to say, though I may expose myself to ridicule in saying so, that once I have witnessed the redemption of the Jews, my people, I wish also to assist in the redemption of the Africans.

Also, although I think, and hope, that I was responsible for much of the initial scope and intensity of the nearly 200 development programmes that Israel has carried out to date in over eighty countries of Africa, Asia, Latin America and, more recently, the Mediterranean basin – drawing upon the sheer enthusiasm, perseverance and talent of some 5,000 Israeli advisers – I cannot claim to have invented the idea. The first Israeli to have explored the possibility of this form of international cooperation was my good friend Reuven Barkatt, who, as head of the *Histadrut*'s Political Department, brought several Africans and Asians to Israel to see for themselves how we had gone about solving various problems. And by the time I became foreign minister in 1956 – on the eve of the independence of Ghana – a young Israeli diplomat appointed by Sharett, Chanan Yavor, was already packing his bags and getting ready to represent Israel there. When Ghana became independent in 1957, Ehud Avriel was appointed Israel's ambassador to that state, and to Liberia, and he suggested that I attend the first anniversary of Ghana's independence in 1958 and that I also visit Liberia, Senegal, the Ivory Coast and Nigeria. So I started to plan the journey, on which, we decided, Ehud and our then ambassador to France, Jacob Tzur, would accompany me.

I had met Africans before, of course, chiefly at various international socialist meetings, but I had never been to Africa and I couldn't really imagine it at all. I remember packing for the trip (one of my great drawbacks as a traveller, incidentally, is that I unfailingly take much more than I ever need) and losing myself in a daydream for hours about Africa and the role that we might be able to play in the waking of that great continent. I didn't have any illusions whatsoever about the fact that this role would inevitably be small, but I was fired by the prospect of going to a part of the world to which we were so new and which was so new to us. I was as excited as a child about what lay ahead.

My first stop was Monrovia, the capital of Liberia, where I was the guest of President Tubman. Liberia's social and economic elite lived in incredibly luxurious conditions – bordering very often on the fantastic – while the rest of the population was destitute. But I hadn't come to Africa to preach, to interfere or to convert. I had come to meet the Africans, and I was well aware of the fact that President Tubman was a devoted friend of the Jews, chiefly, as I recall, because in the long history of his complicated relationship with the United States he had been befriended by a Jewish congressman, that wonderful man Emanuel Celler, who – alone of all Tubman's contacts in Washington – had understood the loneliness of a black leader at a time when it was neither fashionable nor necessary to consider the feelings of any black. Liberia was the world's first black state, born of an impulse not entirely dissimilar to the Zionist impulse, and I couldn't help but respond both to Tubman's evident affection for Israel and to his strong feeling that we had much in common. But what most charmed and interested me was not the Liberia of Monrovia but the Africa I saw in the interior of the country.

We travelled for miles in Liberia. I talked to hundreds of people and answered thousands of questions about Israel, many of them about Israel as the land of the Bible. A very nice young woman from the Liberian Foreign Office accompanied us, and I remember that on the last day of my visit she said very bashfully to me: 'I have an old mother to whom I explained that I would be busy all week with a visitor from Jerusalem. My mother just stared at me. "Don't you know," she said, "that there is no such place as Jerusalem. Jerusalem is in Heaven." Do you think, Mrs Meir, that you could possibly see her for a minute and tell her about Jerusalem?' Of course, I went to meet her mother that day and took with me a little bottle of water from the Jordan River. The old woman just walked around and around me, though she never actually touched me. 'You come from Jerusalem,' she kept on saying. 'You mean, there's a *real* city, with streets and houses where *real* people live?' 'Yes, I live there,' I answered, but I don't think she believed me for a moment. It was a question that I was asked all over Africa, and I used to tell the Africans that the only thing that was heavenly about Jerusalem was that it still existed!

The highlight of that visit to Liberia, for me, was the ceremony in which I was made a paramount chief – an honour rarely bestowed on women – of the tribe of Gola (when I told the story later it was regarded in Israel as a remarkable coincidence that the Hebrew word for the Diaspora is also *gola*) in northern Liberia. It was certainly one of the most extraordinary things that ever happened to me, and I confess that as I stood there in the blazing sun, with the tribesmen singing and dancing all around me, I could hardly believe that it was I, Golda Meir, from Pinsk, Milwaukee and Tel Aviv, to whom this great tribute was being paid. Two thoughts were uppermost in my mind: 'I must behave as though an initiation ceremony in the middle of Africa is something to which I have been accustomed all my life' and 'I wish that the grandchildren could see me now.' When the dancing was finished, I was led by about 200 women of the tribe into a tiny, airless, straw hut where I was dressed in the bright robes of a paramount chief and underwent a secret initiation – the details of which I have no intention of disclosing. But I shall never forget the looks in the eyes of my Israeli escorts (including Ehud and my security officers) when I vanished into the darkness of that hut to the sound of African drums and the chant of the women – or the relief on their faces when I walked out of it intact and very pleased with myself. What I can say about that ceremony is that I was immensely impressed and delighted by the colourfulness, the naturalness and the wholeheartedness of the proceedings. They had the kind of warmth and joy about them that made me feel immediately at home wherever I went in Africa and that I never found to quite the same degree anywhere else, certainly not in Asia.

From Liberia, we moved on to Ghana, Africa's first decolonized independent state, where I met with Dr Kwame Nkrumah, the charming demi-god of African nationalism in those days. It was impossible not to like or admire Nkrumah, but the long talk I had with him as soon as I arrived in Accra nonetheless left me with reservations about his reliability and candour. There was something very unrealistic and even unattractive about his rhetoric and his quite evident eagerness to remain *the* symbol of African liberation. He talked about the problems of Africa as though all that mattered was formal independence, and he seemed far less interested in discussing the development of Africa's resources or even how he could raise the standard of life for his people. He talked on one level and I talked on another. He talked about the glories of freedom, and I talked about education, public health and the need for Africa to produce its own teachers, technicians and doctors. We spoke for hours but I think that neither of us convinced the other.

I couldn't help being pragmatic and trying to stress technique and know-how, while Nkrumah, I imagine, couldn't help his rather high-flown oratory. At one point, for instance, he explained to me why he had had an enormous statue of himself put up in front of the parliament building in Accra and why the new coins in Ghana were decorated with a bust of himself: 'Independence doesn't signify anything to the people in the bush. They don't understand what the word means. But when they pick up a coin and see Nkrumah's portrait on it instead of that of the Queen of England, *then* they will know the meaning of independence.' It was a fundamental difference of approach, but it didn't get in the way of the eventual establishment of a very close relationship indeed between Ghana and Israel, which was to express itself in the dozens of training programmes we launched both in Israel and in Ghana and in the construction work and engineering services that were carried out by Israeli personnel there. We also helped to create and run Ghana's Black Star shipping line. In fact, today there are hundreds of Israelis for whom Ghana was a second home and to whom Ghana's future mattered almost as much as Israel's.

Later, I met other African leaders, for example, President Houphouët-Boigny, of the Ivory Coast, whose personal order of priorities was much closer to mine. Houphouët-Boigny (who, by the way, belonged to the same tribe as Nkrumah and could converse with him only in their tribal language, because Nkrumah knew no French while Houphouët-Boigny knew no English) was convinced, in 1958, that development was as important as independence. He saw much more clearly than Nkrumah ever did the dangers that would certainly face the Africans if they continued to press for independence without adequate preparation: Moslem extremism; the even more lethal combination of Communism – Russian or Chinese – with Islam; the return – in a slightly altered guise – of the former masters of Africa and the weakening of moderate progressive elements throughout the continent; and he was able to resist Nasser's blandishments and threats for many years. In November 1973, however, even Houphouët-Boigny gave in and broke relations with us, explaining sadly that he had to choose between his Arab 'brothers' and his Israeli 'friends'. But, of course, in 1958, all that lay in the future, and it was just as well that it did.

Although I was rather dejected about my first meeting with Nkrumah, my visit to Ghana turned out to be not only fascinating but also crucial to our entire African enterprise. As part of the anniversary celebrations, Ghana was playing host to the First All-African Peoples' Conference, a gathering of the representatives of all of the African liberation movements, including the Algerian FLN. I had already met Dr George Padmore, a brilliant West Indian ex-communist, then the most important ideologist of the forces of 'progressive' Pan-Africanism who had fathered a concept of African development that rested, among other things, on massive financial support from the US Negro community – along the lines, as he put it, of the United Jewish Appeal. He was extremely interested in Israel and insisted that I meet with the other African leaders who were assembled in Accra. It was a God-sent opportunity, he said, for me and for them. The conference was due to start at 4 p.m. at the Ambassador Hotel, Ghana's one brand-new modern hotel, but a special meeting was called for three o'clock, and when I entered the conference room with Padmore, some sixty men were already sitting around an enormous table waiting for me.

It was a curious and dramatic confrontation. Here we were, in the first African country to achieve independence (excluding, of course, Liberia and Ethiopia). I, the foreign minister of a Jewish state that was all of ten years old, and sixty men whose countries would achieve their freedom within only two or three years. We had all lived through so much, all struggled so hard for our liberty – they, representing still uncounted millions upon millions of people spread over the vastness of

Africa, and we, in our one tiny country that had been battered and besieged for so long. It seemed to me that afternoon that this was a truly historic meeting of the kind that perhaps Herzl himself had envisaged. I couldn't identify most of the Africans by name, but Padmore told me who they were: the leaders of fighting Algeria, of all the other French colonies, of Tanganyika, of Northern and Southern Rhodesia. The atmosphere in the room was very charged. I could feel the tension and the suspicion, neither of which were much allayed by Padmore's opening words. 'I have called this meeting,' he said, 'so that you can meet the foreign minister of a young country that has just achieved its independence and that has taken remarkable strides forward in every field of human endeavour.'

For a few seconds, there was an uncomfortable silence, then the representative of Algeria rose. In an ice-cold voice, he asked the most provocative – and relevant – of all possible questions. 'Mrs Meir,' he said, 'your country is being armed by France, the arch-enemy of all those who sit around this table, a government that is fighting a ruthless and brutal war against my people and that uses terror against my black brethren. How do you justify your intimacy with a power that is the primary foe of the self-determination of the African people?' And he sat down. I was not at all surprised by the question, only by the fact that it opened the meeting. Somehow I had expected more phraseology and more time. But I was glad that we were not going to indulge in any amenities or shadow boxing, and I didn't need time for preparation.

I lit a cigarette and looked around the table again. Then I answered the question. 'Our neighbours,' I said to the sixty African leaders staring at me with such coldness and hostility, 'are out to destroy us with arms that they receive free of charge from the Soviet Union and for very little money from other sources. The one and only country in the world that is ready – for hard currency, and a lot of it – to sell us some of the arms we need in order to protect ourselves is France. I do not share your hatred for de Gaulle, but let me tell you the truth – whether or not you like it. If de Gaulle were the devil himself, I would regard it as the duty of my government to buy arms from the only source available to us. And now let me ask you a question. If you were in that position, what would you do?'

I could almost hear the sigh of relief that swept the room. The tension was over. The Africans knew that I had told them the truth and that I was not trying to put anything over on them, and they relaxed at once. Now there was no stopping the barrage of their questions about

Israel. They were hungry for information – about the kibbutzim, the *Histadrut*, the army – and they bombarded me with queries. They were also quite frank in return. One young man from Northern Nigeria (which is almost entirely Moslem) even stood up and said: 'We have no Jews in Northern Nigeria, but we know that we are supposed to hate them!'

That dialogue with the African revolutionaries went on for the duration of my stay in Ghana, and it laid the foundation for our International Cooperation Programme. I won the respect and the friendship of the African leaders, and they were anxious to meet and work with other Israelis. They were not used to white men who laboured with their own hands or to foreign experts who were willing to leave their offices and work at the site of a project, and the fact that we were what they termed 'colour blind' was tremendously important. Things that came quite naturally to me filled the Africans with amazement – whether it was my not very graceful but very sincere attempts to learn African dances or my enthusiasm for teaching the stiff young officials of Ghana's Foreign Office how to dance Israel's *hora*. Most of all, they couldn't help but feel how much I liked them. I remember sitting under an enormous mango tree in Ghana and combing my hair one morning when, as if from nowhere, ten or eleven little girls appeared who had apparently never seen long hair before. One little girl, braver than the rest, came up to me. I could see that she wanted to touch my hair, so for the next half hour I let them take turns combing it and didn't even notice the crowd of awe-struck Africans who had gathered behind me.

By not behaving as they had learned to expect foreigners to behave, I think we helped to build much more than farms, industrial plants, hotels, police forces or youth centres for so many of the African countries; we helped to build the self-confidence of the Africans. We proved to them, by working with them, that they could become surgeons, pilots, citrus growers, community workers and foresters and that technical ability was not – as they had been made to believe for so many decades – the permanent prerogative of the white race.

Of course, the Arabs did their best, even then, to convince the Africans that we were fundamentally no different from other 'colonialists', but the Africans, for the most part, knew better. They knew that when Israeli experts were engaged by Zambia, it didn't turn Zambian chickens into 'colonialist' chickens, and that the fish-processing programme that Israelis developed in Mali didn't result in 'imperialist' fish. They also knew that the hundreds of African trainees who studied agriculture in Israel were not being trained in exploitation. In fact, we set up three basic criteria for our programme, and I think that it is not immodest to claim that even these criteria were a new departure. We asked ourselves, and the Africans, three questions about each proposed project: is it desired, is it really needed, and is Israel in a position to help in this particular sphere? And we only initiated projects when the answer to all three questions was 'yes', so the Africans knew that we didn't regard ourselves as being able, automatically, to solve all their problems.

I returned to Africa over and over again, and got used to being told before each trip that it was 'too much' for me. I learned to accustom myself to the heat, to the frequent lack of cleanliness, to washing my teeth with boiled water (and, when I couldn't get that, with coffee) and to spending hours doing things that I had never in my wildest dreams expected to do, such as presiding over the election of a beauty-queen during the Independence Day festivities of Cameroon, or going out to dinner in Abijan, on the Ivory Coast, with a group of African leaders and hearing an African band strike up a stirring rendition of '*Die Yiddishe Mama*' as soon as I walked in. The more I travelled in Africa, the more I liked it and, fortunately, the more the Africans liked me. To this day, I correspond with some of the many African parents who named a daughter after me. Recently I received a letter from a man in Rivers State, Nigeria. 'I acknowledge with grateful thanks,' he wrote, 'the receipt of your kind letter in which you enclosed a necklace for little Golda. Please find enclosed here little Golda's picture given you as a token of our appreciation for your good work in helping mankind.' And I was deeply flattered by the many other ways in which the Africans showered me with affection.

In December 1959 I visited Cameroon, returned to Ghana, went for the first time to Togo (where, apart from other projects, we helped to set up a national youth movement and organize a cooperative village), visited President Tubman in Monrovia again and toured Sierra Leone and Gambia. I also travelled to Guinea and had my first encounter with Sekou Touré. It was not, however, an unqualified success. He was one of the few African leaders with whom I didn't manage to develop a personal relationship, although I was greatly impressed by his intellectual abilities. Like Nkrumah and, to a lesser extent, Tanzania's Nyerere, Sekou Touré was more concerned with his country's international standing than with its well-being. Although he was a radical left-winger, he seemed to have no real social concepts, and there was very little, therefore, that we could offer him – though we did extend aid to Guinea, and there is a beautiful vocational high school in Conakry which we helped to bring into existence. But Guinea was never really friendly to Israel, and when, after the Six Day War, she broke relations with us – the only African state to do so then – I wasn't particularly surprised. Not that I think the attitude of a given state towards Israel is inevitably a conclusive test of the calibre of that state's leadership, but it was certainly a fact that the more an African leader concerned himself with his nation's progress, rather than with playing games with one power bloc or another, the more that state wanted our assistance, and the better we got along together.

I put some of my feelings about this – and about other aspects of my African experiences – into a speech that I made before the General Assembly towards the end of 1960, by which time sixteen independent African states were already represented there. As I spoke, I saw before me the men, women and children I had met all over Africa, with many of whom I couldn't even speak without an interpreter, but with all of whom I had always felt a genuine bond, the bond of real brotherhood and of shared aspirations, and I also saw in my mind's eye the deprived, under-privileged, ill-educated masses of Jews that had come to Israel – in their hundreds of thousands – expecting a paradise on earth. What I was really talking about was the pitfall of unrealistic expectations and of political fantasies either about the past or about the future – things to which we ourselves were not immune, so it was natural for me to talk in terms of 'us' and not 'them'.

There are two dangers that face those of us who have emerged as newly independent states: first, lingering in the past and, secondly, the illusion that political independence will provide instant solutions for all our problems.

What do I mean by lingering in the past? It is natural that many new peoples should have unhappy and, in some cases, bitter memories. It is understandable that many of them should feel a sense of grievance against their former rulers and should view their present plight as the legacy of the past. It is to them a painful paradox that while some countries have problems of surpluses and overproduction, they should have been left behind in poverty. As they look about them at their lands, rich with minerals and vegetation – gold and diamonds, bauxite, iron and copper, cocoa and cotton, sugar and rubber – they must come to the conclusion that it was not God's will that they should be hungry.

How can we expect Africans to be impressed by the feats of the space age, when so many of their own people still are illiterate? You cannot expect a mother in an African village to be elated over the advance of medicine in the world when she sees her children suffering from trachoma, tuberculosis and malaria. All this must be understood. It is natural that their former suffering and degradation should be remembered by these new free peoples. No people can build its future if it does not remember its past. But a people cannot live only by brooding over the past; it must invest all its energy and ability in the future.

And then I spoke about the challenge of the future.

We, the new countries, have gained our independence in an era of man's greatest achievements. In some parts of the world, the standard of living and development has reached fantastic heights. We should not be told to go slow in our development; we should not be told that the advances of the developed countries have taken generations and centuries to attain. We cannot wait. We must develop quickly. As a friend from Kenya who visited Israel said: 'Must I walk in an age of jet planes just because those that now have jets were walking generations ago?'

This challenge is one not only for the new nations, but for the entire world. Much has been said and done about what I would call 'first aid': the sharing of food, the transfer of surplus to the hungry. But I wish to say that we will never be really free as long as our children need to be fed by others. Our freedom will be complete only when we have learned to bring forth the food that we need from our own soil. The cry that goes out from the African and Asian continents today is: share with us not only food, but also your knowledge of how to produce it. The most frightening inequality in the world today lies in the gap between those that literally reach for the moon and those who do not know how to reach efficiently into their own soil to produce their daily necessities.

To satisfy the hunger of the mind is no less urgent than to satisfy the hunger for bread. The real question is how can the world organize itself to span the time lag of generations and share this knowledge with those who need it. The science and technology of our century that have been available to the industrially advanced states must be made available freely and fully to the new nations towards the solution of their acute economic, social, and health problems.

In addition to Israel's International Cooperation Programme, the Afro-Asian Institute established by the *Histadrut* with the aid of the AFL, and our participation in the various specialized UN agencies that concern themselves with the developing countries, there were – and still are – two Israeli activities that hold a particular appeal for me and that to some extent at least answered the question I had asked at the United Nations. In the summer of 1960, under the guidance of Abba Eban – who had just returned from his spectacularly successful years of

service as Israel's ambassador to Washington and representative to the
United Nations and who, in 1966, became my successor as Israel's
foreign minister – the first International Conference on Science in the
Advancement of New States was held in Rehovot on the beautiful
campus of the Weizmann Institute of Science. Its purpose was to try
and build a real bridge between the developed and the developing
nations of the world by exploring the ways in which science and technology could most effectively be harnessed on behalf of states and
peoples that had just achieved independence. Half of the participants
were Africans and Asians, the other half were leading European and
US scientists. For almost all of the participants, as well as for me, it
was an intensely moving and extremely stimulating gathering, the first
of its kind to take place anywhere.

Some of the speeches were too long, some of the scientific papers were
too abstruse, some of the questions, and answers, were out of place;
but it was a giant step in the direction of true international cooperation, the kind of step that meant more in a way even than the formal
equality bestowed by membership in the United Nations. In Rehovot,
representatives of two cultures met to chart together the specific path-
ways by which one part of mankind could most usefully assist the other,
and I never tired of watching African statesmen (many of them in their
native robes) whom I had last met in Africa – new ministers of education,
of health and of technology – deep in conversation with Nobel Prize-
winners and other world-famous members of the international scientific community, with whom they were slowly developing a common
language. That first Rehovot Conference was to turn into a tradition.
Every two years since 1960, a similar meeting has taken place on the
campus of the Weizmann Institute, dealing, in turn, with topics such
as public health, economics, education and agriculture, and each one
of those conferences has given to its participants something that money
alone can certainly never buy: the feeling that, when all is said and
done, this is indeed one world.

The other project that remains as exciting and as interesting to me
as it was when we began it in 1960 is the Mount Carmel Centre (known
more formally, as the International Training Centre for Community
Services), which concentrates on training women from the developing
countries of Asia, Africa and Latin America in social services. Over the
past fifteen years, I have seen the centre make it possible for hundreds
of women – whether a kindergarten teacher from Nepal, a nutritionist
from Lesotho, a social welfare worker from Kenya for a teacher of

reading from Malawi – to play a vital role in the development of their own countries. For all of these women, Israel itself served as a living laboratory, because, as a student from Kenya once said to me: 'If I had gone to study in the United States, I might have learned the history of development, but here in Israel I have seen development as it takes place.'

The centre has always held a very special place in my heart, not only because I helped to found it, together with Sweden's Inga Thorsson and Israel's Mina Ben-Zvi, but also because I so greatly admire these women from developing countries who leave their towns and villages, and their families, and travel so far to a strange country in order to learn the skills that will eventually make the life of their people easier and richer. There is something heroic, I think – and this is not a word I use easily or often – in the effort made by such women to ensure a better and fuller existence for themselves, for their children and for their children's children through the long, difficult process of self-education. Among the women I met at the centre, I remember most clearly a striking woman judge from Ghana, a shy young midwife from Swaziland, an impressive elderly woman doctor who had led the family-planning activities of Nigeria and an articulate, committed Ethiopian dietician. All of them were wives and mothers who had become pioneers in their respective fields and whose greatest hope was that the women of Africa would one day take their rightful place in African society as full contributors to Africa's future, much as they had seen the women of Israel do in the Jewish state. I don't think I have ever encountered a more hard-working, enthusiastic or attractive group of women than those I used to talk to for hours in Haifa. On the surface, our life experiences had been entirely different, but in reality we were struggling for much the same things.

Our involvement in the training of Africans was not restricted to activities held in Israel, though, and my visit to the training school for social workers that was established with the support and help of the Mount Carmel Centre – originally as a joint Kenya–Israel enterprise – at Machakos, Kenya, was one of the highlights of my first tour of East Africa in 1963, when I flew thousands of miles, mostly in very small planes, across Kenya, Tanganyika, Uganda and Madagascar. Every now and then, we would touch down at some tiny village where an Israeli adviser was hard at work, and I would spend an hour or two with him and his family and see for myself the trust and fondness with which they were treated by the Africans, marvelling at the determination and personal involvement that kept those young Israelis, living under such unfamiliar and primitive conditions, at their self-imposed jobs.

Not that there weren't Israelis who failed, or that everything was always sweetness and light. It often took an Israeli family months to adjust to the climate, to the food, to the slower, traditional African way of doing things, to understanding what underlay African sensitivity and superstition and to curb the sort of impatience and even arrogance that might have undone all the good work. There were quarrels, projects that came unstuck and hurt feelings on both sides. But for the most part, because both the Africans and Israelis so deeply understood the value of what they were trying to do, the cooperation worked. And nothing delighted me more than meeting Africans who had trained in Israel and who showed me around their African clinics, farms or schools, cheerfully explaining everything to me in fluent Hebrew – to say nothing of the African *sabras* I met everywhere, the black children who had been born in Israel and whose first language had been Hebrew. Those African children – however 'radicalized' they may become – will never, I know, think of the friends they made in Beersheba, Haifa or Jerusalem or, for that matter, of me as their 'enemy', regardless of what they may say in public.

One of the most instructive though not most important things I learned on that 'grand tour' of East Africa was that we ourselves had to alter the way in which we entertained official guests to Israel. Like the Israelis, the Africans insisted on sightseeing that often lasted for twelve hours or more a day and that was mercilessly followed by a full-scale banquet, complete with speeches in which everyone endlessly congratulated everyone else. I used to sit through those banquets in a state of total exhaustion, knowing that in a few hours we would be off on another sun-scorched tour that was doomed to end with another banquet and more speeches. So I took an oath that, when I got back to Israel, I would see to it that we cut down on our own overly zealous hospitality, though I can't honestly say that my efforts in this direction were very successful.

At all events, in the end I fell ill and had to cut short that particular trip, though it meant cancelling a reception for me given by Milton Obote, the level-headed, intelligent president of Uganda who was later so ruthlessly removed by Idi Amin. In a certain sense, it occurs to me now, Obote and Idi Amin perhaps represent the two extremes of the current African dilemma. Obote was everything that Amin is not –

rational, serious, hardworking and effective – and I am afraid that Uganda's progress has been set back many years by the rise to power of someone like Idi Amin, who has been so hopelessly injured by having been placed in a position of virtually unlimited control over a country that is still so new to independence. I hadn't known Idi Amin when he was training as a paratrooper in Israel (Israeli 'wings' are still worn proudly not only by him but by a number of other African leaders, including Zaire's President Mobutu), but I had heard even then, when he thought that the sun rose and set on Israel, that he was very eccentric – to put it politely. And my last meeting with him, in Jerusalem when I was prime minister, convinced me that he was really quite mad. In fact, our discussion might have been staged by Charlie Chaplin.

'I have come to see you,' he said to me very seriously, 'because I want a few Phantoms from you.' 'Phantoms! We don't manufacture Phantoms,' I answered. 'We buy them from the United States, when we can – which is not always or often enough. They aren't things that you buy and sell. Anyhow, why do you need Phantoms?' 'Oh,' he said blandly, 'to use against Tanzania.' Then he sent me a message, 'I need ten million pounds sterling at once.' I couldn't give him that either, so he left Israel in a tremendous huff, went off to Colonel Kaddafi of Libya – and Uganda broke diplomatic relations with us in 1972, a year and a half before the Yom Kippur War. But Idi Amin is not Uganda and even he can't remain a dictator forever, which is some consolation.

Thinking back on the African leaders I met – Kenya's splendid old man, Jomo Kenyatta, and the late Tom Mboya, Zambia's Kenneth Kaunda, Senegal's poet-president Senghor, and General Mobutu Sese Seko of Zaire, to name just a few – I must say that, the tragedy of their break with us apart, they were and are a credit to their peoples and to the African liberation movement. One of the reasons, I think, that I got along so well with them – even though we did not always see eye-to-eye on everything – was that I practised what I preached, and they saw me do it. In 1964, for instance, I attended the Independence Day ceremonies of Zambia (formerly Northern Rhodesia) including a visit for all the guest VIPs to the Victoria Falls, which are partly in Zambia and partly on the territory of what was then still called Southern Rhodesia. We were taken to the falls in buses, and when we reached the border between the two countries, the police of Southern Rhodesia had the effrontery to refuse to let the blacks on my bus get out, although they were all African dignitaries and President Kaunda's personal guests. I couldn't believe my ears when I heard a police officer say, 'whites only.' 'In that case,' I said, 'I'm sorry, but I won't be able to enter Southern Rhodesia either.' There was great consternation, and the Rhodesians tried very hard to get me to leave the bus, but I wouldn't hear of it. 'I have no intention of being separated from my friends,' I repeated. The whole busload of us then happily travelled back to Lusaka, where Kaunda received me as though I were Joan of Arc rather than just a woman who couldn't and wouldn't tolerate racial discrimination in any form.

On that trip I was also involved in another incident that helped to clarify further to the Africans that we really meant what we said – a characteristic which they had previously had little reason to attribute to Europeans. I was scheduled to visit Nigeria on my way home from Zambia. En route, I stopped over in Nairobi, where a special plane had been rented to fly me to Lagos, since there was no other way I could get there from East Africa unless I overflew or touched down in an Arab state. In Nairobi I got a phone call from our ambassador in Lagos. He told me that I would be greeted by anti-Israel demonstrations in Lagos. The wives of all the ambassadors of Arab countries had gotten together to organize protests against my visit. It might be wise if I cancelled my trip. Nigeria was on the eve of elections and many of the ministers were away from Lagos in any case; it was not the best time to go. What if something happened to me? I was very tired at that point and didn't at all relish being the object of violence on the streets of a major African city. On the other hand, I was certainly not going to be bullied, I answered, by Arab ambassadors hiding behind their wives' skirts. 'I won't impose myself on the Nigerian government,' I said, 'but if the government doesn't recall its invitation to me, I intend to go.'

As we reached the airport at Lagos I saw masses of people waiting on the ground, hundreds and hundreds of Africans. 'This is it,' I thought, 'and it's going to be very unpleasant.' But instead of hysterical demonstrators, I was being met by a huge crowd of men and women who either had trained in Israel or had been trained by Israelis in Nigeria. All of them were singing *'Hevenu Shalom Aleichem'* ('We bring peace unto you', the 'theme song' of Israel's International Cooperation Programme), which I have heard literally thousands of times but have never been as touched by as I was on that night. The next morning I was received by President Azikiwe: 'We respect and greet you as an ambassador of true goodwill,' he said, and that trip to Nigeria turned out to be a great success, after all.

I spent less time in Asia, though there, too, I always felt welcome. Still, I missed the vividness and the drama that I associate with Africa. Maybe it was because I never quite understood the elaborate codes of behaviour in the Far East, or maybe it was because Jews, the Jewish heritage and the Jewish ethic are all less known in Asia than they are in Africa, where Christianity brought with it a real familiarity with the Bible. Even the place names of Israel – Galilee, Nazareth, Bethlehem – have meaning for educated Africans, and I met almost as many 'Moseses', 'Samuels' and 'Sauls' in Africa as I do at home. But Asia was something else. It lay outside the traditions of the Old Testament, and there was more need to explain and interpret who we were and where we came from. Even a man as cultured as the former Burmese prime minister, U Nu, once told our ambassador to Rangoon, David Hacohen, that he had known nothing at all about us until one day 'by accident, I came across a book', and it was only then, when he read the Bible as an adult, that he discovered the existence of the Jews. As a matter of fact, what may well have made U Nu's relationship with Ben-Gurion so warm was that Ben-Gurion also only learned about Buddhism relatively late in life.

But before I write anything about my own travels in the Far East, I want to say again that the one Asian nation with which we have, alas, made no headway whatsoever is China, a fact to which I referred briefly before. There are Israelis, David Hacohen among them, who believe that we simply didn't try hard enough to make friends with the Chinese, but I am not at all sure that we could have done more than we did. In 1955, we sent a trade mission, headed by Hacohen, to China, and, of course, we invited the Chinese to send a mission to us. They never as much as answered the invitation, and at the Bandung Conference later that year the Chinese–Egyptian rapprochment began. It resulted in a violent Chinese response to the Sinai Campaign and eventually in open Chinese identification with Arab anti-Israel terror. The Chinese government, in fact, is totally committed to the Arab war against Israel, and Mr Arafat and his comrades are constantly given arms, money and moral support by Peking, though I, for one, have never really understood why, and for years lived under the illusion that if we could only talk to the Chinese, we might get through to them.

Two pictures come to my mind when I mention China. The first is the horror with which I once picked up a mine manufactured in China – so far away and remote from us – which had put an end to the life of a six-year old girl in a border settlement in Israel. I stood there near that small coffin, surrounded by weeping enraged relatives. 'What on earth can the Chinese have against us?' I kept thinking. 'They don't even know us.' Then I remember, at the celebration of Kenya's independence, sitting with Ehud Avriel at a table near that of the Chinese delegation. It was a very relaxed festive occasion, and I thought to myself, 'Perhaps if I go over and sit down with them, we can talk a bit.' So I asked Ehud to introduce himself to the Chinese. He walked over, held out his hand to the head of the delegation and said, 'My foreign minister is here and would like to meet you.' The Chinese just averted their gaze. They didn't even bother to say, 'No, thank you, we don't want to meet her.'

But Israelis don't easily take no for an answer, least of all I. Not long ago, my dear friend and fellow-socialist the Italian statesman Pietro Nenni was invited to China. Before he went, he visited me in Jerusalem. We sat on the porch of my house there, drank coffee and talked, as old socialists always do, about the future. Inevitably, in this connection, we also talked about China. 'Look,' I said to him, 'the Chinese will listen to you. Please try to discuss Israel with them.' So he did; he tried to explain to various important Chinese statesmen what sort of country Israel is, how it is run, what it stands for – but they weren't interested. They didn't tell Nenni, as they usually do, that Israel is only 'a puppet of the United States'; someone just said that if every group of 3 million people tried to set up their own state, what would the world come to.

I tried several times to persuade each of my children to accompany me on my travels, but Sarah wouldn't be dislodged from Revivim and Menachem was just as reluctant to be parted from Aya and the boys (they had three sons, Amnon, Daniel and Gideon by then) or from his cello. Each time I went to Africa, I came back with basketfuls of masks, carvings, handwoven cloth and more anecdotes about what I had seen, but, of course, it wasn't the same as actually sharing these experiences with them. I longed for the children to take at least one trip with me – not because they hadn't travelled enough (we had all done more than our share of that), but I wanted them to see some of the things that I was seeing and meet some of the people whom I was meeting. I often wondered in those years, and even more later on when I was prime minister, how they felt – or how my grandchildren really felt – about the way I lived. It wasn't something we ever talked about much, but I don't think that any of them especially enjoyed being 'related to Golda Meir'. We always talked a great deal together, and very freely, about politics, both domestic and international; and my grandchildren were never excluded from these conversations, even when they were very small. But other than the fact that I was a potential source of valuable autographs for classmates, or that they grew up knowing that what they heard around my table was not to be repeated, I don't think they were in any way different from other children. They certainly treated me like a very ordinary grandmother. Visitors were always amazed that Menachem's boys ran in and out of my house with such freedom and amused by the fact that they were clearly so much more interested in the contents of my refrigerator than in the world-famous guests I entertained so often. As for me, like all grandmothers, I fussed over them more than was necessary, and I still do. But then my five grandchildren are my greatest joy in life and nothing is too good for them, as far as I am concerned. I only wish that I could be sure they will not have to go through any more wars – but, of course, that is the one thing that I cannot promise them.

At any rate, it was a great deprivation for me to be away from all of them so frequently, and I kept on at Menachem and Sarah until each of them, in turn, agreed to make one journey with me. In 1962 Sarah travelled with me to Kenya and to Ethiopia, where I introduced her to Haile Selassie and we visited the large community of Israelis working in that country in agriculture, fishing, transport, helping to train the police and the army and teaching at the University of Addis Ababa. Even Ethiopia, with which we had had such a very special relationship for so many years, broke with us in 1973, but at the time of which I write the ties were still very strong – though never publicized by the Ethiopians and therefore also not by us. For me, Haile Selassie was almost a storybook character, a man from a far-off, exotic land who dared to stand up in 1936 and call the attention of an indifferent world to the Italian invasion of Ethiopia. He and his family had spent a year in Jerusalem as refugees during the Italian occupation, and I used to see him sometimes – a dark, bearded little man with huge sad eyes – walking with his empress in the street while his adored little dogs ran after them. He was not just another refugee from Fascism; he is descended from that line of Ethiopian kings who claim that their ancestor was the son born to King Solomon and the Queen of Sheba and that they are therefore our distant kin. The Lion of Judah has always been the symbol of the Ethiopian monarchy, and the links between the Jews and Ethiopia have always been unique.

But although Ethiopia is a Christian country, it is part of Africa and, as such, was subjected for years to strong anti-Israeli pressure by the Arabs. For a long time, however, Haile Selassie warily trod a tight-rope; many of his dealings with Israel were kept secret, and we sent an ambassador only in 1961. The Sinai Campaign – because it opened up the Straits of Tiran – became the start of an even closer relationship, and Israeli ships and planes helped to develop a steady flow of trade between the Ethiopians and ourselves. At the same time, we did a great deal to develop the educational facilities of Ethiopia, and several Israeli professors settled in Addis Ababa for a few years. Sarah was too young, I expect, to feel about Haile Selassie as I did. For her he was only the ruler of a fascinating country; for me he was always much more. I can't say that we became fast friends, but when I saw him in his own palace and remembered the lonely exiled figure I used to see in Jerusalem in the 1930s, I felt that justice had – for a change – been done, and I was immensely disappointed when even Haile Selassie – for all of his own experience with appeasement – did not stand by us. It proved to me once again – though I didn't need very much more proof by then – that one can never count on anyone but oneself.

Anyhow, that same year, to my delight, Menachem also agreed to make a journey with me, and we went to the Far East together. It was really very noble of both Aya and him because Gidi had just been born. We spent over a week in Japan, where I was received by the emperor, the prime minister and the foreign minister. I don't know what I ex-pected Hirohito to be like, but I was certainly not prepared for the modest, very pleasant gentleman with whom I exchanged courtesies – never quite sure, I suspect, that we were getting through to each other. I found the Japanese very courteous but very non-committal. I knew that they were extremely cautious about their relationship with us and handled it as though the Middle East were a flower arrangement in which all the elements had to be balanced in one particular way.

One rather funny thing that happened in connection with my Japa-nese trip was the excessive worry of the Japanese officials regarding my visiting a geisha house. On the plane going to Japan, Ya'akov Shimoni (then the head of our Far Eastern desk), who accompanied us, told Menachem that 'since Golda is both a woman and a foreign minister, the Japanese have not suggested giving her the traditional geisha party, which they usually throw for distinguished foreign guests. They don't think it would be proper in her case.' When we got to Tokyo, I told Menachem to make it clear to the Japanese that I certainly did want to go to a geisha party and that I had nothing at all against geishas. In the end a lovely geisha party was laid on for me in Kyoto by the governor and his wife, and everyone was satisfied, though I think Shimoni never got over the sight of me sitting on cushions while the geishas fluttered around me like butterflies.

Like most people, I was tremendously impressed by the beauty of Japan and even more by the ability of the Japanese to create beauty in their everyday surroundings. And, of course, we met Jews there, too, in particular some of the many Japanese who have become converts to Judaism, including – to my astonishment – a member of the imperial family who chatted away with me in Hebrew. In recent years, by the way, there have been regular visits to Israel of large ardently pro-Israel groups from Japan, and I am no longer so taken aback as I used to be by the sight and sound of dozens of Japanese singing 'Jerusalem the Golden', in perfect Hebrew, near the Western Wall.

From Japan we flew to the Philippines, where I received an honorary degree from the Catholic University of Manila and found myself marching in solemn procession down a hall filled with lavishly robed church notables, with priests holding crosses on either side of me. I knew that it was a very great honour that this Catholic institution was bestowing on a Jewish woman, from a Jewish state, and as I walked I thought to myself that Jews were not always welcome in all universities and that there were still institutions of higher learning, even in the free world, that could only tolerate a small number of us in their midst. And as I spoke I recalled – not for the first time – the letter that Sheyna, who always worried lest my head be turned, had once written to me: 'Never forget who you are,' she had warned me. But she needn't have worried. I have never forgotten that I came from a poor family, or ever fooled myself into thinking that I was honoured anywhere – Manila included – for my beauty, wisdom or erudition.

Manila, Hong Kong, Thailand, Cambodia – I could write pages about my impressions of the people we met and the sights we saw in those countries, but the heart of that trip to the Far East was our visit to Burma, a country with which we had had close ties ever since 1952, when a delegation of Burmese socialists had first visited Israel. Sharett had gone to Rangoon a year later to attend the first Asian Socialist Congress, and by 1955 there were full diplomatic relations between Burma and Israel. David Hacohen opened the Israeli embassy in Rangoon, and Burma's prime minister, U Nu, came to Israel as Ben-Gurion's guest.

I think there was no developing country in the world – not even Ghana or Kenya – with which we conducted such an ardent love affair. For years there seemed to be nothing about Israel that the Burmese did not admire or want to emulate, and as Asia's only socialist state, it was natural for them to be profoundly interested in our special brand of socialism, in the *Histadrut*, the kibbutz movement and the way in which we had created a citizen army and turned it into one of our most effective educational institutions, with an Education Corps that was teaching thousands of culturally deprived children from immigrant families (and in many cases their mothers too) to read and write. The Burmese were fascinated also by the methods we had used to combine military service with pioneering on the land, and they took over from us, almost intact, the idea that people could work as farmers and at the same time be trained in self-defence. For the Burmese, whose border with China was a constant source of harassment and who couldn't maintain a large standing army, Israel's *Nahal* (the initials of the Hebrew words for 'Fighting Pioneer Youth') was the perfect answer. It gave idealistic young people the opportunity to get agricultural and military training simultaneously within the framework of existing kibbutzim so that they could go on to establish their own collective settlements. I had suggested to the Burmese that they create border settlements of their own in this way, and I invited them to send a large group of demobilized Burmese soldiers and their families to Israel for a year or so to work on our kibbutzim and more often *moshavim* (cooperative villages) and accustom themselves to the communal or cooperative way of life, while we would send Israelis to Burma to help plan Burmese-style *moshavim* there. And that was just what happened. The *moshav* seemed to suit the Burmese temperament more.

There were many other joint Burmese–Israeli enterprises, including the establishment of a major pharmaceutical industry in Burma, the training of dozens of Burmese doctors and nurses and the creation of vast irrigation schemes, but for me personally, the Burmese *moshavim* of the Namsang region in the north of Burma were more exciting than anything else. I had, of course, followed their progress with enormous interest, but I still could hardly believe that I was not dreaming when we landed at a northern airport and all the Burmese wives and children who had once been in Israel greeted me with Hebrew songs and Israeli flags. I don't think I will ever forget walking up to one of the little houses in Namsang and saying in Hebrew to a young Burmese who stood in the doorway: *'Shalom, ma nish mah?'* (Shalom, how are things?) and hearing him answer, like a real Israeli, *'Beseder, aval ein maspeek mayim.'* ('Fine, but there isn't enough water.') I might have been in Revivim.

I travelled all over Burma with Ne Win, then Burma's chief-of-staff. Within a few weeks he had taken over in Burma with a new policy that was pro-Russian, anti-American and emphasized non-involvement with any non-Burmese interests. It didn't end trade relations between Burma and Israel, but it did end the love affair.

I was very much taken by the Burmese, and I felt comfortable with them, though I can't say that Burmese delicacies are *my* idea of good food. There was very little I wouldn't have done in 1963 for Burma, but I just couldn't eat the fish paste on which the Burmese live, or even taste the roasted leopard offered to me in Namsang, let alone drink the soup made of birds' nests that we served at the dinner I gave in Rangoon in honour of U Nu. Menachem explained all about the sublety of oriental food to me, but I didn't think it would seriously impair Israel's relationship with Burma if I left a thousand-year-old egg – which it would have killed me to swallow – untouched on my plate. Of course, there were also things about us that it took the Burmese a long time to understand. I remember, on U Nu's first visit to Israel, when Ben-Gurion was driving with him through the young forests that line part of the road from Tel Aviv to Jerusalem – of which we are so proud because such a tremendous effort went into afforesting the rocky land there – U Nu looked very worried indeed. 'You must be extremely careful,' he said to Ben-Gurion. 'Take it from me that those trees will *grow.*' His problem, of course, was keeping jungles at bay, and he couldn't imagine that for us each tree was a gem to be treasured.

By the time we returned to Israel, I had seen enough rice paddies and rickshaws to last me for several years – if not for a lifetime – and I wanted and badly needed a rest, but in 1964, 1965 and 1966 I was in orbit again. I travelled back to Europe, Africa and to Latin America and I was frequently ill. I had begun to feel the strain of perpetual travel; I seemed always to be either en route to somewhere or from somewhere or sick. Besides, I was no longer as young as I had been. In 1963, I had celebrated my sixty-fifth birthday. I didn't feel at all old or depleted of energy, but I was beginning to think how nice it would be to have a day to myself or to visit old friends again without having a

bodyguard follow me around, and the children, and my doctor, kept
telling me that the time had come for me to take it easy. I tried but I
never succeeded in learning how to do so. There was always a pressing
commitment either abroad or in Israel, and however early I began
my work day, it never ended until the early hours of the next morning.
Sometimes I did treat myself to doing what I wanted to do, but very
rarely.

One such occasion was the party I gave in July 1961 to the friends
with whom I had come to Palestine aboard the *Pocahontas* forty years
earlier. I can't remember now how or when I got the idea of an anniversary celebration, but I was very curious to meet the group again, to
find out who had settled in Israel and who had gone back to the States,
and I wanted to see their children. One of the topics of conversation
and debate between myself and my colleagues in *Mapai* in those days
was why there was such a relatively small immigration of Jews from
the West. 'They have it too good,' was one explanation. 'They will only
come to us when they face real anti-Semitism elsewhere.' But I felt
this to be a very unjust oversimplification, and I used to have long
arguments with Ben-Gurion about the unimpressive rate of immigration
from such countries as the United States, Canada and Britain. 'They
will come, one day, if we are patient,' I used to tell him. 'It is not as
simple to transplant oneself and one's family as it used to be. Also
people are not as idealistic, as romantic or as dedicated any more. It
takes a tremendous amount of determination for a Zionist from Pitts-
burgh, Toronto, or Leeds to decide one day to settle permanently in
Israel. It means much more than merely moving to another country. It
involves learning a new language, accepting a different standard and
way of life, and getting used to the sort of tensions and insecurities
that we take for granted.' I was no less anxious than Ben-Gurion for
Western Jews to join us in their hundreds of thousands, millions even,
but I was not as intolerant of their hesitation, and I was certainly not
prepared – at this point in Israel's history – to demand of Jews who
supported the State of Israel without actually living there that they
should no longer consider themselves Zionists but rather 'friends of
Zion', a very diluted formula angrily suggested by Ben-Gurion.

But the nineteen men and women who had taken that trip on the
Pocahontas with Morris and me in 1921 had made that great decision,
and I had a sudden urge to see them again. I didn't have all their
addresses, so I put an advertisement in the paper: 'The foreign minister
invites all the members of the *Pocahontas* contingent to an evening at

her home; not only the original group but husbands, wives, children and grandchildren.'

Most of the people who had made that dreadful journey with me in 1921 did not come. They were either dead or too infirm and one had gone back to the United States for good. But seven or eight of the original group loyally turned up and, what's more, brought their children and grandchildren with them. We had a wonderful party, reminiscing, singing and eating cake and fruit in my garden. There weren't any formal speeches, and I refused to let the press attend – although the journalists implored me to let them come 'only for a few minutes'. But it was a personal marking of a very personal anniversary, and I wanted it to be a private gathering.

I suppose that some of the songs we sang (which were the same songs with which we had tried to boost our morale on that miserable ship) must have sounded very sentimental and naïve, maybe even banal, to our children. They were all about building the land and pioneering. But they reminded us of the days when we believed we could do anything and everything, and we sang for hours. Afterwards, when the party was over and all the guests had gone home, I sat on for a while in the dark garden, thinking about those forty years and wishing that Morris could have been with us. Of one thing I was quite sure that night: none of us had ever regretted, for one moment, having remained on the *Pocahontas* until she finally sailed from Boston, taking us most of the way to Palestine.

By the end of 1965, even I began to realize that I needed a change. The election campaign in the summer of that year had exhausted me. I have never felt really well in the heat, and now the migraine headaches from which I had suffered off and on for years were getting worse. I couldn't avoid coming to the conclusion that the responsibilities I had shouldered for more than thirty years were starting to weigh on me too heavily. I didn't want to live forever, but also I didn't want to turn into a semi-invalid. However, it wasn't only my health that bothered me; it was also the need to recharge my emotional batteries that seemed to be running down slightly because I was tired. And the internal situation in Israel was not good. There was a severe economic depression, emigration – which we call '*yerida*' (descent) as opposed to the 'ascent' of immigration – and the aftermath of the Lavon Affair, which was demoralizing the public and wreaking havoc in the ranks of the Labour movement. My own battles with Ben-Gurion were, of course, not the least of my headaches. Nothing catastrophic would happen if I left public life: the party would heal its own wounds and I couldn't do much to solve Israel's economic plight, which was largely caused by the fact that German reparations were coming to an end while neither our defence budget (nor the Arab boycott) were reduced at all.

To add to my dispiritedness, Sheyna was not at all well. She, too, was growing old and, like our mother before her, was aging in both body and mind. Eshkol, who became prime minister in 1963, and Pinchas Sapir, who was minister of finance, tried valiantly to keep me from resigning, but I knew that Abba Eban was waiting in the wings to become foreign minister and I could see no reason, under the circumstances, for my clinging to the ministry. Eshkol offered me the deputy prime ministership, but it held no appeal for me at all. Better, I thought, to be a full-time grandmother than a part-time minister, and I told Eshkol that I really wanted to retire. 'I won't go into a political nunnery,' I assured him, 'but I do want to be able to read a book without feeling guilty or to go to a concert on the spur of the moment, and I don't want to see another airport for several years.'

We are alone

Iт тоок ме some time, several months in fact, to 'organize' my retirement. To begin with, there was the move from Jerusalem to the small, semi-detached house on a quiet, tree-lined street of a Tel Aviv suburb, right next door to Menachem and Aya. It wasn't just a matter of moving from one city to another; it involved hours and hours of sorting things out, deciding what was mine and what belonged to the government, what I wanted to take with me and what I was going to give away. I had travelled so extensively for the past twenty-five years and accumulated so many mementoes of my trips that going through them was almost a full-time job – and not one that I particularly relished. But Clara came from the States to visit me, and she, Lou and I finally disposed of everything. Luckily, by nature I am not a collector, and living in a private museum is certainly not my idea of comfort, so it wasn't difficult for me to shed most of the possessions and presents and keep only those books, paintings, scrolls and keys to cities that had some special meaning for me. Of course, I was quite sure at that point that I would never have to go through the ordeal of selecting, packing and unpacking again – and the feeling of blessed finality also helped.

My new home – which is where I still live – was probably a quarter of the size of the foreign minister's residence that I had occupied for nine years, but it was exactly what I wanted and needed, and I felt comfortable in it from the very first day. I had planned it to suit my own requirements – a combined living-room–dining-room lined with bookshelves, that opens on to the garden I share with Menachem's family; a kitchen that is big enough for me to work in efficiently; and an upstairs with one bedroom and a study that serves also as a guest room. This year I hope, at last, to add one more room to the house, but even without that extra room, it has always been big enough for me, and it was wonderful in 1965 to feel that I was settling in somewhere for good.

Even my immediate family, I suspect, didn't really believe that I would enjoy the transition to life as an ordinary citizen, but I was as happy as I had known I would be. For the first time in years I was free – to do my own shopping, to use public transport instead of being driven everywhere and being concerned about the fact that a driver was forever waiting for me outside, and, most of all, to call my time my own. I really felt like a prisoner released from jail. I made long lists of the books I wanted to read, called up old friends whom I hadn't seen for years and planned a series of visits to Revivim. What's more, I cooked, ironed and cleaned house with enormous pleasure. I had stepped out of office at exactly the right time, of my own accord and before anyone could say 'For God's sake, when is that old woman going to realize that it's time for her to quit,' and I felt as though I had taken on a new lease on life.

The public got used to my new role almost as quickly as I did, though every now and then, I must confess, I was accorded special treatment. Shopkeepers in the neighbourhood often volunteered to deliver my orders to the house because they didn't think it was right for the former foreign minister to be carrying bags of groceries, and bus drivers were equally kind about making unscheduled stops so I could get off nearer home sometimes – and once or twice I was even driven in state right up to my door. But I didn't care at all what I carried or how far I had to walk; my liberation from obligatory appointments and official receptions was like a daily miracle. Nor did I for a moment feel isolated or out of touch with what was happening in the country. I had remained a member of the Knesset and of the *Mapai* executive and in both places did as much work as I felt like doing – but no more than that. All in all, I was very satisfied with my lot.

I should have guessed, I suppose, that this new-found tranquillity with which I was so pleased wouldn't last long. There was a succession of interruptions, of which by far the most pressing was the appeal made by my colleagues in the party that I return on a full-time basis – at least for a while – to help bring about the unification of all or most of the various sectors of the Labour movement, which had recently been so seriously shaken by the Lavon Affair. If ever there was a time for unification, this was certainly it. The economic situation in Israel, and the national mood, were such that for the first time it was possible to imagine an end to the Labour leadership of the country unless a united Labour front could be brought into effective existence, very soon. *Mapai* itself had been critically weakened by the secession of *Rafi* (the splinter party headed by Ben-Gurion and Dayan) and, to tell the truth, had never quite recovered from the much earlier split (in 1944), of *Achdut Ha-Avodah* or from the formation four years later of the anti-Western, Marxist *Mapam*, whose chief support lay in the membership of the more radical kibbutzim and a number of young intellectuals who still cherished the idea that an Israel–Soviet rapprochement was possible and could be achieved simply if Israel wanted it enough!

The ideological differences between *Mapai*, *Rafi* and *Achdut Ha-Avodah* were not, however, so great that a united Labour party was out of the question. But someone would have to undertake the actual job of bridge-building, of reconciling the various points of view and personalities, of healing old wounds without making fresh ones and of creating a new and viable structure. Whoever that person was, it would have to be someone utterly committed to the vision of a single Labour party able to contain within itself political factions that had been at odds with each other for years and believing implicitly in the urgent need for a Labour coalition. There was, said my colleagues (who took to coming to talk to me in relays), only one person who had all the necessary qualifications – and time. If I were unwilling to take the job, for purely selfish reasons, it would never be done. All that they were asking of me was that I become secretary-general of *Mapai* until the unification was achieved – and assured. Then I could go back into retirement.

It was the one appeal that I couldn't turn down. Not because I was so sure that I would succeed or because I so yearned to be in the middle of a crucial struggle all over again, and not because I was bored, as many people probably thought, but for a much simpler and much more important reason: I truly believed that the future of the Labour movement was at stake. And although I could hardly bear the idea of giving up the peace and quiet I had finally attained – even if for only a few months – I couldn't turn my back at this stage of my life either on my principles or my colleagues. So I said yes and went back to work, to travelling, to incessant meetings and to the bondage of an appointment book, but I promised myself – and my children – that this was the last job I would ever do.

In the meantime a number of events had occurred in the Middle East which were to place Israel's future in far greater jeopardy than Labour disunity at home could ever have done. In 1966 preparations were already being made by the Arabs for another round of war. The symptoms were all familiar. As a matter of fact, in a way the prelude to the Six Day War of 1967 was identical with the prelude to the Sinai Campaign. Terrorist gangs – as actively encouraged and supported by President Nasser as the *fedayeen* had been in the 1950s – were operating against Israel both from the Gaza Strip and Jordan. They included a new organization, founded in 1965, known as Al Fatah which, under Yassir Arafat's leadership, subsequently became the most powerful and well-publicized element in the Palestine Liberation Organization. Also, a united Egyptian–Syrian high command had been established and vast sums of money were allocated at an Arab summit conference for the express purpose of stockpiling weapons to be used against Israel – and, of course, the Soviet Union was still pumping both arms and money into the Arab states. The Syrians seemed bent on an escalation of the conflict; they kept up an endless bombardment of the Israeli settlements below the Golan Heights, and Israeli fishermen and farmers faced what was sometimes virtually daily attack by snipers. I used to visit those settlements occasionally and watch the settlers go about their work as though there was nothing at all unusual in ploughing with a military escort or putting children to sleep – every single night – in underground air-raid shelters. But I never believed them when they said that they had got quite used to living under perpetual fire. I don't think parents ever get 'used' to the idea that their children's lives are in danger.

Then, in the autumn of 1966, the Soviet Union suddenly began to accuse Israel of readying her forces for a full-scale attack against Syria. It was an absurd charge, but it was duly investigated by the United Nations and, naturally, found to be without any basis. The Russians, however, kept on making the same accusations and talking about the Israeli 'aggression' that was bound to cause a third round of the Arab–Israel war, while the Syrians, receiving arms and financial aid from the Soviet Union, kept up their raids on our border settlements. Whenever the Syrian terror reached an intolerable point, Israel's air force would go into action against the terrorists, and for a few weeks the border settlements could relax. But by the early spring of 1967 these periods of relative relaxation were becoming fewer and shorter. In April 1967, the air force was sent up in an action that turned into an air battle and resulted in the downing by Israeli planes of six Syrian MIGs. When this happened, the Syrians, egged on as always by the Soviet Union, once again screamed that Israel was making preparations for a major offensive against Syria, and an official complaint to this effect was even made on Syria's behalf to Prime Minister Eshkol by the Soviet ambassador to Israel, Mr Chuvakhin. Not only was this one of the most grotesque incidents of the period, but it actually helped to trigger off the war that broke out in June.

'We understand,' Chuvakhin said very unpleasantly to Eshkol, 'that in spite of all your official statements, there are, in fact, extremely heavy concentrations of Israeli troops all along the Syrian borders.' This time, Eshkol did more than merely deny the allegation. He asked Chuvakhin to go up north and look at the situation along the border for himself, and he even offered to accompany Chuvakhin on the trip. But the ambassador promptly said he had other things to do and refused the invitation, although all that was involved was only a few hours' drive. Of course, had he gone he would have been forced to report to the Kremlin – and to the Syrians – that no Israeli soldiers were massed on the border and that the supposed Syrian alarm was absolutely unjustified. But this was exactly what he didn't want to do. By refusing to take that trip, he successfully breathed new life into the lie that helped set in motion Nasser's entry into the picture, and therefore the Six Day War.

At the beginning of May, responding to what he termed the 'desperate plight' of the Syrians, Nasser ordered Egyptian troops and armour to mass in Sinai, and just in case anyone misunderstood his intentions, Cairo Radio shrilly announced that 'Egypt, with all its resources ... is ready to plunge into a total war that will be the end of Israel.'

On 16 May, Nasser moved again – only now he gave orders not to his own army but to the United Nations. He demanded that the UN Emergency Force that had been stationed both at Sharm el-Sheikh and in the Gaza Strip since 1956 get out at once. Legally, he had a right to evict the UNEF because it was only with Egypt's consent that the international police force had been stationed on Egyptian soil; but I don't for a minute believe that Nasser actually expected the United Nations to do his bidding meekly. It was against all rhyme or reason

for a force that had come into existence for the sole purpose of supervising the ceasefire between Egypt and Israel to be removed at the
request of one of the combatants the very first moment that the ceasefire was seriously threatened, and I am sure that Nasser anticipated a
long round of discussions, arguments and haggling. If nothing else, he
almost certainly reckoned that the United Nations would insist on
some kind of phasing-out operation. However, for reasons which have
never been understood by anyone – least of all by me – the UN secretary-general, U Thant, gave in to Nasser at once. He didn't refer the
matter to anyone else. He didn't ask the Security Council for an
opinion. He didn't even suggest a delay of a few days. Entirely of his
own accord, U Thant instantly agreed to the immediate withdrawal of
the UNEF. It started to move out of Sharm and the Gaza Strip the
very next day, and by 19 May, to the tune of wild Egyptian applause,
the last unit of the UNEF had pulled out, leaving the Egyptians in full
control of their border with Israel.

I don't think that anyone could have felt more bitter than I did
about U Thant's ludicrous surrender to Nasser. Not, God forbid,
because I was the only person to understand what was happening. Far
from it. But because it brought back to me, in an almost intolerable
rush of pain and anxiety, the memory of those frightful months in New
York after the Sinai Campaign, when the entire world seemed bent on
forcing us to withdraw our troops from Sinai and the Gaza Strip, regardless of what we knew, and said, would inevitably happen as a
result. I went over and over those months in my mind: the hours of
difficult fruitless conversation with Mr Dulles, the equally difficult
and fruitless behind-the-scenes negotiations we had held with the delegates of other powerful states, the incessant efforts we had made – without the slightest success – to explain that there was only one way to
ensure peace in the Middle East: not by continuing to appease the
Arabs at our expense but by insisting on a non-aggression pact between
the Arab states and Israel, on regional disarmament and on direct
negotiations. Why had it seemed so simple and so obvious to us but so
impossible of attainment to everyone else? Hadn't we explained the
realities of life in our part of the world properly? Had I made some
dreadful mistake or left something crucial unsaid? The more I thought
about those months in 1956 and 1957, the more apparent it became to
me now that nothing at all had changed since then and that the Arabs
were once again being permitted to delude themselves that they could
wipe us off the face of the earth.

That delusion was further strengthened on 22 May when Nasser, intoxicated by the success of his dismissal of the UNEF, made another test of the world's reaction to his stated intention of entering an all-out war with Israel. He announced that Egypt was reimposing her blockade of the Straits of Tiran, despite the fact that a score of nations (including the United States, Britain, Canada and France) had guaranteed Israel's right of navigation through the Gulf of Aqaba. It was without any question another deliberate challenge, and Nasser waited to see how it would be met. He didn't have to wait very long. No one was going to do much about that either. Of course, there were protests and angry reactions. President Johnson described the blockade as 'illegal' and 'potentially disastrous to the cause of peace', and suggested that an international convoy, including an Israeli vessel, sail through the straits to call Nasser's bluff; but he couldn't persuade the French or British to join him. The Security Council met in an emergency session, but the Russians saw to it that no conclusions were reached. The British prime minister, my good friend Harold Wilson, flew to the States and to Canada to suggest that an international naval task force be organized to police the Straits of Tiran, but he also got nowhere with his suggestion. Even U Thant – realizing at last what a terrible mistake he had made – finally bestirred himself sufficiently to go to Cairo and try to reason with Nasser, but it was too late.

Nasser had drawn his own conclusions: if the so-called guarantees that had been given to Israel after the Sinai Campaign by the maritime powers were as worthless as they now appeared to be, then what and who was to stop the Egyptians from winning that final, glorious and total victory over the Jewish state that would make Nasser the supreme figure of the Arab world? To the extent that he had any remaining doubts regarding the adventure into which he was about to plunge himself and his nation, they were swept away by the Russians. The Soviet minister of defence brought Nasser a last-minute message of encouragement from Kosygin: the Soviet Union would stand by Egypt in the battle that lay ahead. So the stage was set. As for war aims, to the extent that Nasser felt obliged to explain anything to the Egyptian people – who were already in the first throes of war hysteria – it was enough to go on repeating the phrase 'We aim at the destruction of the State of Israel' and to tell the Egyptian National Assembly, as he did in the last week of May, 'The issue is *not* the question of Aqaba, the Straits of Tiran or the UNEF . . . The issue is the aggression against Palestine that took place in 1948.' In other words, the war that was now in the making was to be the ultimate Arab war against us, and on the face of it, Nasser had every reason for thinking that he would win it.

By 1 June, there were 100,000 Egyptian soldiers and over 900 Egyptian tanks in Sinai, plus six Syrian brigades and nearly 300 Syrian tanks straining at the leash in the north. Also – after having hesitated for a few weeks – Jordan's King Hussein had finally decided to take the risk of joining Nasser in the great exploit. Although we had sent him constant messages promising that if he kept out of the war nothing would happen to him (the last of these messages was sent to Hussein by Eshkol through the good offices of the UN Truce Supervision Organization on the very morning that the war broke out), the temptation of participating in the victory – as well as his fear of defying Nasser – finally got the better of Hussein, and he, too, threw his lot in with the Egyptians, which provided the Arab war effort with seven more brigades, about 270 more tanks and a small but competent air force. The last to join in the coalition against Israel was Iraq, which signed a mutual defence pact with Egypt a day before the war began. It was certainly a most formidable array of military might, and since the West seemed to be either paralysed or totally indifferent, while the Russians were backing the Arabs to the hilt, one can't really blame Nasser very much for having assumed that at last he was in a position to deal a death blow to Israel.

Well, so much for the Arab mood and the Arab dream. What was happening to us? I neither want – nor do I think that it is necessary – to retell in detail the story of the Six Day War, about which so much has already been written. But no one who lived in Israel during the weeks that preceded it will ever, I believe, forget the way in which we faced the terrible danger that confronted us. And no one can possibly understand Israel's reaction to her current situation without first understanding what we learned about ourselves, about the Arab states and about the rest of the world in the course of those three weeks in the spring of 1967 that came to be known in Hebrew as the period of *konnenut* (preparedness). Of course, I was not a member of the cabinet any longer, but it was only natural that in the developing crisis I should be called upon to help arrive at some of the life-or-death decisions that faced the cabinet, and it was taken for granted, I think, by everyone that I had to make myself available.

From the beginning, there was no question in anyone's mind that war had to be averted – at almost any cost. There was no question that if we had to fight, we would do so – and win – but first every possible avenue had to be explored. Eshkol, his face grey with weariness and tension, set in motion a search for some kind of diplomatic intervention. That was the sum total of his requests; needless to say, we never asked for military personnel. Eban was sent on a round of missions to Paris, London and Washington, and at the same time Eshkol quietly gave the signal for the nation to ready itself for the third time in nineteen years to defend its right to exist. Eban came back with nothing except the worst possible news. Our gravest fears had been confirmed. London and Washington were sympathetic and worried, but still not prepared to take any action. It was too bad, but maybe the Arab frenzy would wear itself out. At all events, they recommended patience and self-control. There was no alternative other than for Israel to wait and see. De Gaulle had been more direct: whatever happened, he told Eban, Israel must not make the first move until and unless the Arab attack actually began. When that happened, France would step in to save the situation. To Eban's question: 'But what if we are no longer there to be saved?' de Gaulle chose not to reply, but he made clear to Eban that France's continued friendship with us depended entirely on whether or not we obeyed him.

Within a matter of a few days, our survival was suddenly at stake. In the most literal sense of these dreadful words, we were alone. The Western world, of which we had always considered ourselves to be a part, had heard what we had to say, had listened to our assessment of the extreme danger confronting us, and had turned us down – though in the streets and assembly halls everywhere, the people were with us. So we began to get ready for the inevitable war. The army turned to its contingency plans, Eshkol ordered a general mobilization. And the over-age men and women and children of Israel buckled down to clean out basements and cellars for use as makeshift air-raid shelters, to fill thousands of sandbags with which to line the pathetic home-made trenches that fathers and grandfathers dug in every garden and school yard throughout the country and to take over the essential chores of civilian life, while the troops waited, under camouflage nets in the sands of the Negev – waited, trained and went on waiting. It was as though some gigantic clock were ticking away for all of us, though no one except Nasser knew when the zero hour would be.

By the end of May, ordinary life – as we had known it in the previous months – came to an end. Each day seemed to contain double the normal number of hours, and each hour seemed endless. In the heat of the early summer, I did what everyone else was doing: I packed a little overnight bag with a few essential belongings that might be needed in the shelter and put it where it could most easily be grabbed as soon as the sirens started to wail. I helped Aya make identification discs out of oilcloth for the children to wear and blacked out one room in each house so that we could put on the light somewhere in the evenings. I went to Revivim one day to see Sarah and the children. I watched the kibbutz that I had known from its first day calmly prepare itself for the Arab onslaught that might turn it into rubble, and I met with some of Sarah's friends – at their request – to talk about what might happen. But what they really wanted to know was when the waiting would end, and that was a question I couldn't answer. So the clock ticked on, and we waited and waited.

There were also the grim preparations that had to be kept secret: the parks in each city that had been consecrated for possible use as mass cemeteries; the hotels cleared of guests so that they could be turned into huge emergency first-aid stations; the iron rations stockpiled against the time when the population might have to be fed from some central source; the bandages, drugs, and stretchers obtained and distributed. And, of course, above all, there were the military preparations, because even though we had by now absorbed the fact that we were entirely on our own, there wasn't a single person in Israel, as far as I know, who had any illusions about the fact that there was no alternative whatsoever to winning the war that was being thrust upon us. When I think back on those days, what stands out in my mind is the miraculous sense of unity and purpose that transformed us within only a week or two from a small, rather claustrophobic community, coping – and not always well – with all sorts of economic, political and social discontents into 2½ million Jews, each and every one of whom felt personally responsible for the survival of the State of Israel and each and every one of whom knew that the enemy we faced was committed to our annihilation.

So the issue was not, as it is perhaps for other countries, how best to remain intact and least damaged by an inevitable war, but rather how to survive as a people. The answer to that question was never in doubt. We could survive only by being victorious, and everything else – all the complaints, pettinesses and dissensions – fell away from us; we became, to put it very simply, one family, determined not to budge. Not one Jew left Israel during those awful weeks of waiting. Not one of the mothers in the settlements below the Golan Heights or in the Negev took her children and ran. Not one survivor of the Nazi death camps, many of whom had lost their children in the gas chambers, said, 'I cannot bear to suffer again.' And hundreds upon hundreds of Israelis who had gone abroad returned, though no one had called them back. They returned because they just could not stay away.

More than that, world Jewry looked on, saw our extreme peril and our isolation and asked itself, for the first time I think: what if the State of Israel ceases to exist? And to this question there was also only one possible and short answer: no Jew anywhere in the world would ever feel free again if the Jewish state were to be eradicated. After the war – on its last day, to be accurate – I flew to the United States for a few days and I spoke at a huge rally that was organized at Madison Square Garden by the United Jewish Appeal. My schedule was very crowded, and I was in a great hurry to get home again, but I very much wanted to meet some of the thousands of young American Jews who had besieged Israeli consulates throughout the United States in their clamour to be with us in the war. I wanted to know what had impelled them – and others, like the young British Jews who rioted at London Airport because El Al (the only airline flying to Israel during the war) couldn't possibly take all the volunteers who wanted to come – to put their heads in the noose that was already being so tightly bound around our throats. After all, it wasn't a romantic skirmish that awaited them in Israel. A tremendous apparatus for killing, mutilating and destroying us had been assembled on our frontiers, and every day that apparatus was moving in, closer and closer. Like us, they too had been treated to the revolting nightly spectacle of televised mobs throughout the Arab world clamouring hysterically for the bloodbath that was to spell the end of Israel. So they had certainly known the score. In the end, most of them had not managed to come to Israel. The State Department had stopped them, and anyhow the fighting was over in six days. But I felt an overwhelming need to ascertain for myself what Israel really meant to them, and I asked my friends in New York to arrange a meeting for me with at least some of the 2,500 young Jews from that city who had volunteered to go to Israel during the war.

It wasn't easy to arrange the meeting within twenty-four hours, but it was done, and over 1,000 of those youngsters came to talk to me. 'Tell me,' I asked them, 'why did you want to come? Was it because of the way you were brought up? Or because you thought it would be exciting? Or because you are Zionists? What did you think about when you stood in line last month and asked to be allowed to go to Israel?' There wasn't a uniform answer to my question, of course, but it seemed to me that one young man spoke for all of them when he got up and said: 'I don't know how to explain it to you, Mrs Meir, but I do know one thing. My life will never be the same again. The Six Day War, and the fact that Israel came so close to being destroyed, has changed everything for me – my feelings about myself, my family, even my neighbours. Nothing will ever be quite the same for me as it was before.' It wasn't a very coherent reply but it came from his heart, and I knew what he was talking about. It was about his identity as a Jew and about the larger family to which he suddenly knew he belonged, for all of the differences between us. The threat we were experiencing, to be very blunt, was the threat of extinction, and to that Jews respond in the same way, whether they go to synagogue or not, whether they live in New York, Buenos Aires, Paris, Moscow or Petach Tikvah. It is a deeply familiar threat, and when Nasser and his associates made it, they doomed their war to failure because we had decided – all of us – that there was to be no repetition of Hitler's 'Final Solution', no second Holocaust.

In a certain respect, that great coming-together of a nation to meet a collective threat was responsible also for the demand that arose in Israel for a 'wall-to-wall' coalition of all our political parties (except the communists), and for the assumption of the defence portfolio by someone with more practical experience than Levi Eshkol. I must say that I was not in favour of either development. National coalitions – with which I was subsequently to have some experience myself – may all be very well under normal circumstances, when there is time for lengthy discussions that represent contrasting points of view, but they are positively counterproductive, in my opinion, at moments when truly fateful decisions must be taken and when only shared ideologies, attitudes and backgrounds make it possible for a cabinet to do its job in the most efficient and harmonious way. If it were necessary to strengthen Eshkol's government in those last few days before the war – which I doubted – I thought that this could and should be done without making major alterations and without major changes of personnel. I knew – though many people in Israel did not know this then – that Eshkol in his dual role as prime minister and minister of defence had seen to it, without fanfare or drawing attention to himself in any way, that the Israeli Defence Forces were ready for the task that lay ahead of them. His relationship with the army, his understanding of its needs and his ability to secure for it what it needed were never in doubt.

I was no blinder than anyone else to Eshkol's somewhat tentative manner. He addressed the nation during the worst days of the *konnenut*, and he said all that anyone else could or should have said, but he said it hesitantly and without any flair, when what the country wanted was more dynamic leadership. Personally, I didn't think – and don't think even in retrospect – that any of this mattered. He was a very wise and dedicated man who found himself shouldering about as staggering a responsibility as any statesman has ever shouldered and who felt weighed down by it. Only a fool would have felt differently, and if he stuttered a little when he spoke about sending his people to war, it was only to his eternal credit.

I myself have learned since then how it feels, and I thought about Eshkol more than once during the Yom Kippur War, when I had to appear on television and did so feeling and looking as grim as death because what I had to say – and what no one else could say for me – was so serious that I couldn't worry much about my choice of words or how I delivered my speech. But, like other things, if you have never been there yourself, it is hard to imagine, and many Israelis – their nerves stretched close to the breaking point – felt let down by Eshkol's broadcast and by his continued desperate attempts to find some way other than war that would break the impasse. What was the point of sending Eban to knock on yet another door? How much longer could the uncertainty last? Were we going to remain like this for ever – mobilized, and waiting? Eshkol seemed to be too uncertain, too reluctant to take action. These were heroic times, but where was the hero?

In all this storm of criticism, there was no real demand that Eshkol resign; there was only a growing, though unreasonable, dissatisfaction with him, which turned into growing pressure for the appointment of a new minister of defence, someone bolder and much more charismatic. And by the end of May, it was clear that thousands of Israelis were looking to Moshe Dayan to express the national determination to endure and to prevail. It was as though the Israelis (not all of them, but a great many) were counting on Dayan to provide something which Eshkol couldn't offer. Even now, I can't define exactly what it was they sought. Maybe it was the assurance of being led, in a time of such stress, by a fighter; or maybe it had to do with that quality of fearlessness that is so strong a part of Dayan's personality. Whatever it was, there was no withstanding the pressure. In the end, Eshkol, hurt to the core, but realizing that it was essential to maintain maximum unity, gave in, and I stopped asking myself how come, if Dayan was such an obvious candidate to head the Ministry of Defence, even Ben-Gurion had never given him this portfolio.

Dayan remained Israel's minister of defence until 1974; he was the only minister of defence to serve in my cabinet, and we worked together extremely well. Nevertheless, I hope he will forgive me for saying that I still don't believe that his appointment in 1967 changed the course of the Six Day War in any basic way or that he was the main architect of our victory. The Israel Defence Forces had not waited until 1 June either to plan their strategy or to train for it, and the real heroes of that victory were, of course, the people of Israel. It is hard for me to imagine that the war would have ended differently had Dayan not entered the government. Having said this, however, I must in all fairness admit that although I felt a great injustice was being done to Eshkol, the Israeli public had at last acquired the dynamic and dramatic military leadership it so badly wanted, and perhaps even needed, and I was grateful that the issue was settled.

There are two other general comments I must make about the Six Day War. The first should go without saying, but I have learned not to take anything for granted, and there may still be people who do not understand that we fought that war so successfully not only because we were made to fight it, but also because we most profoundly hoped that we would achieve a victory so complete that we would never have to fight again. If the defeat of the Arab armies massed against us could be made total, then perhaps our neighbours would finally give up their 'holy war' against us and realize that peace was as necessary for them as for us and that the lives of their sons were as precious as the lives of our sons. We were wrong about that. The defeat was total, and the Arab losses were devastating, but the Arabs still couldn't, and didn't, come to grips with the fact that Israel was not going to accommodate them by disappearing from the map. The second point of which I would like to remind my readers is that in June 1967 Sinai, the Gaza Strip, the West Bank, the Golan Heights and East Jerusalem were all in Arab possession, so that it is ludicrous to argue today that Israel's presence in those territories since 1967 is the cause of tension in the Middle East or was the cause of the Yom Kippur War. When Arab statesmen insist that Israel withdraw to the pre-June 1967 lines, one can only ask: if those lines are so sacred to the Arabs, why was the Six Day War launched to destroy them?

The war began early on the morning of Monday, 5 June. As soon as we heard the whine of the air-raid sirens, we knew that the waiting was over, though it was not until very late that night that the dimensions of Israel's strike were revealed to the nation. All day, while wave after wave of our planes flew over the Mediterranean to blast the Egyptian airfields and demolish the aircraft poised to attack us, we waited for news, ears glued to the transistor radios that we all carried around with us but on which there was nothing to hear except music, Hebrew songs and the passwords that were used to call up reservists who had still not been mobilized. It was only after midnight that the official and almost incredible story of the first of those six days was unfolded to the civilian population by the chief of the air force and that, sitting in their blacked-out rooms, the people of Israel learned that they had been delivered from destruction within the six hours that it had taken the air force to put over 400 enemy planes out of action, including those parked on Syrian and Jordanian airfields, and to gain full command of the air from Sinai to the Syrian border. I had been kept informed all day of the general situation, but even I had not quite grasped the implications of what had happened until after the broadcast. I stood alone for a few minutes at the door of my house, looked up at the cloudless and undisturbed sky and realized that we had been rescued from the terrible fear of air raids that had haunted us all for so many days. True, the war had only started; there would still be death and mourning and misery. But the planes that had been readied to bomb us were all mortally crippled, and the airfields from which they had been about to take off were now in ruins. I stood there and breathed in the night air as though I had not drawn a really deep breath for weeks.

It was not only in the air that we had won a conclusive victory, however. That same day, racing along the three routes they had taken in 1956, our ground forces, backed by the air force, had pushed their way deep into Sinai, were already gaining the upper hand in tank battles that involved even more armour than had clashed in the Western Desert in the Second World War, and were already well on their way to the Suez Canal. Israel's hand, held out in peace for so long, turned into a fist, and there was no stopping the forward advance of our troops. But Nasser was not the only Arab ruler whose plans were shattered on 5 June.

There was also Hussein, who had measured Eshkol's promise that nothing would happen to Jordan if he kept out of the war against the message he had received from Nasser that very morning informing him that Tel Aviv was being bombed by the Egyptians – never mind that

Nasser didn't have a single bomber to his name by then. Like his grandfather before him, Hussein had carefully weighed the odds and made a mistake. On 5 June he ordered his troops to start shelling Jerusalem and the Jewish settlements on the Jordan–Israel border. His army was to serve as the eastern arm of the pincer movement that was to do us in, but it failed in its mission. As soon as the Jordanian shelling began, the IDF struck at Hussein also, and although the fighting on the Jerusalem front cost the lives of very many young Israelis – who fought hand to hand and street by narrow street, rather than resort to the mortars and tanks that might have damaged the city and the Christian and Moslem holy places – it was already clear that night that Hussein's greed was going to lose him his hold on eastern Jerusalem, at the very least. At the risk of repeating myself, I must emphasize, at this point, that just as in 1948 the Arabs had hammered at Jerusalem without the slightest regard for the safety of its churches and holy places, so in 1967 Jordanian troops didn't hesitate to use churches and even the minarets of their own mosques for emplacements. This may explain why we resent the fears that are sometimes expressed for the sanctity of Jerusalem under Israeli administration, to say nothing of what we discovered when we finally entered East Jerusalem; Jewish cemeteries had been desecrated, the ancient synagogues of the Jewish Quarter of the Old City had been razed to the ground and Jewish tombstones from the Mount of Olives had been used to pave Jordanian roads and Jordanian army latrines. So let no one ever try to convince me that Jerusalem is better off in Arab hands or that we cannot be trusted to take care of it.

It took all of three days for the Egyptians to be beaten and two days for Hussein to pay for his error of judgement. By Thursday, 8 June, the governor of the Gaza Strip had surrendered, Israeli forces were settled in on the east bank of the Suez Canal, the Straits of Tiran were back under Israel's control and 80 per cent, if not more, of Egypt's military equipment had been destroyed. Even Nasser, not the most accurate of men, admitted that 10,000 Egyptian soldiers and 1,500 Egyptian officers had been lost, and we had nearly 6,000 Egyptian prisoners. The whole of Sinai and the Gaza Strip had fallen to Israel again. So had East Jerusalem, the Old City and virtually half of the Kingdom of Jordan. But we had still not learned how many of our boys had died in the fighting, and there was still one more aggressor to deal with. On Friday, 9 June, the IDF turned its attention to Syria and to rectifying the Syrian mistake in believing that the guns on top of the Golan Heights that had been pounding away relentlessly at the Jewish villages in the valley below were really invincible. I must confess that there was some justification for the Syrian self-confidence. After the war, when I visited the Golan Heights and saw for myself the miles upon miles of reinforced concrete bunkers bristling with barbed wire and filled with anti-tank guns and artillery, I understood why the Syrians had been so sure of themselves and why it took two bloody days and one terrible night for the IDF to scale the Golan Heights, inch by inch, and then force its way into those bunkers. But it was done – by the army, the air force, the paratroopers and brave engineers in bulldozers – and by 10 June, the Syrians were begging the United Nations to arrange a ceasefire. General David Elazar (our chief-of-staff during the Yom Kippur War) was then the commander of the northern front. When the fighting was over, he sent a message to those Israeli settlements in the valley: 'Only from these heights can I see how really great you are.'

It was all over. The Arab states and their Soviet patrons had lost their war. But this time, the price for our withdrawal was going to be very high, higher than it had been in 1956. This time the price would be peace, permanent peace, peace by treaty based on agreed and secure borders. It had been a lightning war, but it had also been a cruel one. All over Israel there were military funerals again, many of them the funerals of boys whose fathers or older brothers had fallen in the War of Independence or the fighting that had plagued us ever since. We were not going to go through that anguish again if we could possibly help it. We were not going to be told what a wonderful people the Israelis are – they win wars every ten years, and they have done it again. Fantastic! Now that they have won this round, they can go back where they came from, so that Syrian gunners on the Golan Heights can again shoot into the kibbutzim, so that Jordanian Legionnaires on the towers of the Old City can again shell at will, so that the Gaza Strip can again be a nest for terrorists and the Sinai Desert can again become the staging ground for Nasser's divisions.

'Is there anybody,' I asked at that rally in New York, 'who is bold enough to say to us: "Go home! Start preparing your nine- and ten-year-olds for the next war." I am sure that every decent person in the world will say "no", and – forgive me for being so blunt – most important of all, we ourselves say "no".'

We had fought alone for our existence and our security and paid for them, and it seemed to most of us that a new day was really about to dawn, that the Arabs – trounced on the battlefield – might agree at last to sit down and thrash out the differences between us, none of which ever were, or are, insoluble.

There was no sense of triumph, only an enormous surge of hopefulness. And in the sheer relief of the victory, in the delight of finding ourselves alive and relatively unscathed, and dazed momentarily by the prospect of peace, the whole of Israel went on a sort of holiday that lasted most of the summer. I don't think that there was a single family, including my own, that didn't take off a few days right after the Six Day War to indulge in what looked to strangers like mass sightseeing but was really a kind of pilgrimage to those parts of the Holy Land from which we had been excluded for nearly twenty years. In the first place, of course, the Jews streamed to Jerusalem; thousands and thousands of people daily crowded the Old City, praying in front of the Western Wall and picking their way through the ruins of what had been the Jewish Quarter. But also we went to Bethlehem, Jericho, Hebron and to Gaza and Sharm el-Sheikh. Offices, factories, kibbutzim and schools all participated in the endless excursions, and hundreds of cars, buses, trucks and even taxis, packed to the brim, criss-crossed the country for months *en route* to Mount Hermon in the north or Mount Sinai in the south. Everywhere we went during that elated, almost carefree summer, we met the Arabs of the territories that we now administered, smiled at them, bought their produce and talked to them, sharing with them – even if not always in words – the vision of peace that suddenly seemed about to become a reality, and trying to convey to them our joy that now we would all be able to live together normally.

Everyone was on wheels in those days because the Arabs in the administered territories were travelling around almost as much as we were: they flocked to Tel Aviv, to the seashore and to the zoo, stared at the shop windows in West Jerusalem and sat in the cafés of all the main streets. Most of them were as excited and as curious as we were and, like us, were absorbed in looking at landscapes which the adults had forgotten and the children had never seen. All this may sound too good to be true, and I certainly don't want to convey the impression that the Arabs turned to Mecca five times a day to thank Allah for their good fortune in having been defeated, or that there were not Jews who preferred to stay at home rather than participate in what they felt to be an indecent celebration of peace before the scars of war had had time to heal. But anyone who visited Israel in the summer of 1967 will testify to the extraordinary euphoria that gripped the Jews and appeared also to affect the Arabs. It was, in short, as though a death sentence had been lifted – which was, after all, literally true.

If I have to choose one particular aspect of that immediate post-war period as an illustration of the general atmosphere, I would certainly point to the tearing down of the concrete barricade and barbed wire fences that had separated the two halves of the city of Jerusalem ever since 1948. More than anything else, those hideous barricades had signified the abnormality of our life, and when they were bulldozed away and Jerusalem overnight became one city, it was like a sign and symbol of a new era. As someone who came to Jerusalem then for the very first time said to me: 'There is light from within the city,' and I understood exactly what he meant. 'Very soon,' I told my grandchildren, 'the soldiers will come home; there will be peace; we will be able to travel to Jordan and to Egypt and all will be well.' I honestly believed it, but it wasn't to be.

In August 1967, at a summit conference in Khartoum, the Arab leaders reviewed the situation and came to an altogether different conclusion. They issued their notorious three noes: there would be no peace with Israel, no recognition of the Jewish state and no negotiations. No, no, no! Israel must withdraw, totally and unconditionally, from the territories taken in the Six Day War, and the Arab terrorists who were invited to the conference added a fourth helpful statement of their own: Israel must be destroyed, even within the pre-1967 boundaries. This was their answer to the Israeli government's appeal: 'Let us meet not as conqueror and conquered but as equals to negotiate peace – with no pre-conditions.' Never mind who started the war and never mind who won it. As far as the Arabs were concerned, nothing had changed. So the so-called 'fruits of the victory' turned into ashes before they could ripen, and the lovely dream of immediate peace faded away. But if the Arabs had learned nothing, we had learned something. We were not prepared to repeat the exercise of 1956. Discuss, negotiate, compromise, concede – all of these, yes! But not go back to where we had been on 4 June 1967. That accommodating we couldn't afford to be, even to save Nasser's face or to make the Syrians feel better about not having destroyed us! It was a great pity that the Arab states felt so humiliated by losing the war which they had started that they just couldn't bring themselves to talk to us, but on the other hand, we couldn't be expected to reward them for having tried to throw us into the sea. We were bitterly disappointed, but there was only one possible reply: Israel would not withdraw from any of the territories until the Arab states, once and for all, put an end to the conflict. We decided – and, believe me, it was not a painless decision – that whatever it cost us in terms of public opinion, money or energy, and regardless of the pressures that might be brought to bear on us, we would stand fast on the ceasefire lines. We waited for the Arabs to accept the fact that the only alternative to war was peace and that the only road to peace was negotiation.

In the meantime, the close to 1 million Arabs living in the territories on our side of the ceasefire lines – about 600,000 on the West Bank of the Jordan and some 365,000 in the Gaza Strip and Sinai, plus the Druze villagers who had opted to stay on the Golan Heights after the Syrian army had gone – would live pretty much as they had lived before the Six Day War. It is never a great pleasure to be accountable to a military government, and none of the Arabs in the territories enjoyed having Israeli patrols move around in their midst. But the army kept a very low profile indeed, and the military government – thanks largely to Dayan's concept of its role – interfered with daily life as little as possible. Local laws were retained and so were local leaders. The bridges over the Jordan were open, and the Arabs on the West Bank went on trading with the Arab states, studying in the Arab states and visiting their relatives there, while their relatives were free to visit them – which they did by the thousands. It was only going to be an interim arrangement anyhow; no sane Israeli ever assumed that all the territories were going to remain under Israeli rule. Jerusalem, of course, would stay united, but an arrangement could be made regarding Moslem control over the Moslem holy places. New borders would have to be drawn up between Jordan and Israel; it was unlikely that the Golan Heights would be handed back lock, stock and barrel to the Syrians or that all of Sinai would be returned at once to the Egyptians; and the Gaza Strip was certainly a problem. But there was no point whatsoever in drawing maps of what the Middle East would look like or even arguing among ourselves what territory would be returned to whom until these matters could be taken up with the only other people to whom they were of real concern – our neighbours. After all, you can't return territory by parcel post. So we went on waiting for a response to our repeated call for talks.

In the meantime, the Security Council passed a resolution – the celebrated Resolution 242, sponsored by the British – which outlined a framework for the peaceful settlement of 'the Arab–Israel dispute' and appointed a special representative, Dr Gunnar V. Jarring, who was charged with supervising a 'peaceful and accepted settlement'. So much has been written and said about Resolution 242, and it has been so thoroughly distorted by the Arabs and the Russians, that I think it might be useful for me to quote it, particularly since it isn't very long:

The Security Council,

Expressing its continuing concern with the grave situation in the Middle East.

Emphasizing the inadmissibility of the acquisition of territory by war and the need to work for a just and lasting peace in which every state in the area can live in security.

Emphasizing further that all Member States in their acceptance of the Charter of the United Nations have undertaken a commitment to act in accordance with Article 2 of the Charter.

1. Affirms that the fulfilment of Charter principles requires the establishment of a just and lasting peace in the Middle East, which should include the application of both the following principles:
   (i) Withdrawal of Israeli armed forces from territories occupied in the recent conflict;
   (ii) Termination of all claims or states of belligerency and respect for and acknowledgement of the sovereignty, territorial integrity and political independence of every state in the area and their right to live in peace within secure and recognized boundaries free from threats or acts of force; and
2. Affirms further the necessity
   (i) For guaranteeing freedom of navigation through international water-ways in the area;
   (ii) For achieving a just settlement of the refugee problem;
   (iii) For guaranteeing the territorial inviolability and political independence of every state in the area, through measures including the establishment of demilitarized zones.

It will be noted that it does *not* say that Israel must withdraw from all territories, nor does it say that Israel must withdraw from *the* terri-tories, but it *does* say that every state in the area has a right to live in peace within 'secure and recognized boundaries' and it *does* specify the 'termination of belligerency'. Furthermore, it does *not* speak of a Palestinian state, while it *does* speak of a refugee problem. But it wasn't only Resolution 242 that was misinterpreted; it was also our attitude that was being misinterpreted. After the Six Day War, Israel's leading satirical writer, Ephraim Kishon, together with the Israeli cartoonist Dosh, published a book called *So Sorry We Won*. It was a bitter title, but not in the least ambiguous to its Israeli readers. In fact, it summed up rather succinctly the way we were beginning to feel, by 1968, which was that the only recipe for improving Israel's rapidly deteriorating image was to forget all about peace. Our crime appeared to be that we kept saying to the Arabs 'Let's negotiate.' Not, as we were entitled to do, 'This is the new map; sign on the dotted line,' but 'Let's negotiate.'

In some mysterious way, this made us the villains. I couldn't for the life of me ever grasp, for instance, why Willy Brandt got (and richly deserved) the Nobel Prize and was hailed as a great statesman and a man of peace when he recognized the Oder–Neisse border because the time had come to put right the wrong that Germany had done to Poland in the Second World War, while Eshkol, and later I, were branded as expansionists for wanting exactly the same kind of border adjustments between Israel and her neighbours. And not only were we called expansionists by our critics, we were constantly being asked by our friends whether we weren't worried about Israel's turning into a militaristic nation ('a little Sparta' was the phrase most often used) that had to rely on its 'brutal' occupation forces to preserve law and order in the administered territories. And, of course, 'intransigent' was to become my middle name. But neither Eshkol nor I, nor the overwhelming majority of other Israelis, could make a secret of the fact that we weren't at all interested in a fine, liberal, anti-militaristic, dead Jewish state or in a 'settlement' that would win us compliments about being reasonable and intelligent but that would endanger our lives. Dr Weizmann used to say that he had become the president of a country where everybody is a president; Israeli democracy is so lively that there were, and are, almost as many 'doves' as 'hawks', but I have yet to come across any Israeli who thinks that we should turn ourselves, permanently, into clay pigeons – not even for the sake of a better image.

At all events, I still had an assignment to complete: the unification of the Labour movement, which kept me busy through the winter of 1967 and the beginning of 1968. I was also, of course, at Eshkol's disposal whenever a new crisis broke out, either in connection with the stepped-up activities, in the administered territories, of the Fatah and the other smaller Arab terrorist groups that now declared themselves to be the only true representatives of the Arab people, or in connection with the incessant attempts that were being made to use Resolution 242 as a device for forcing upon Israel withdrawal from all the territories in a way and at a time that was not acceptable to us. In January 1968, the Israel Labour Party was formed – a union of *Mapai, Achdut Ha-*

Avodah and *Rafi* – and in February I was elected its secretary-general. It was really only a partial unification at this stage, a federation of three parties, and it wasn't until the next year that the larger alignment – *Ma'arach*, as it is called in Hebrew – which also involved an alliance with *Mapam*, was created. But despite the looseness of the ties that bound the three parties, at last they were now under one political roof, which was what I had undertaken to accomplish. So I thought that I could allow myself at last to go back into retirement, and in July I did so.

Now I was seventy. It is not a sin to be seventy, but it is also no joke. I had been ill again in 1967, and neither the Six Day War nor the creation of the *Ma'arach* were exactly what the doctor had ordered. I felt that I owed myself some peace and quiet, and this time nothing and no one would change my mind. I went to the States for an Israel Bond drive and visited Menachem, Aya and the children in Connecticut, where, at that point, Aya was working on a university research grant and Menachem was teaching cello. I even spent a few weeks in Switzerland on what I think was the first complete holiday I had ever taken – and I came back home feeling as fit as a fiddle.

The situation at home, however, hadn't progressed much. Despite the ceasefire, there was still a war of sorts going on at the Suez Canal. The Egyptians, secure in the knowledge that the Russians had already replaced all the guns, tanks and planes that they had lost in the Six Day War, were keeping up a constant barrage of bombardments which underlined their desire to open up full-scale hostilities again just as soon as they dared. 'When the time comes, we will strike,' Nasser roared, and he repeated what he called 'the principles of Egyptian policy': no negotiations with Israel, no peace with Israel, no recognition of Israel. And in the spring of 1969, he launched what was to become known as his 'war of attrition'.

I suppose that, from a distance, that continuous shelling of the IDF positions on the Canal might have seemed merely like another one of the protracted 'incidents' that had been going on in the Middle East since anyone could remember, another demonstration of the supposed inability of Jews and Arabs to get along together; and I imagine that at first no one abroad took the reports about the endless Egyptian violations of the ceasefire very seriously. But we did, because we knew what those violations foretold, and we began to build a fortified defence line – the Bar-Lev line – to protect our troops on the banks of the Canal.

At the same time, when the Arab terrorist organizations found that they were unable to persuade or provoke the population of the administered territories into taking any major action against the Israelis – other than an occasional, though certainly deeply felt, protest march in Hebron or strike in Jenin – they decided to go in for terrorism thousands of miles away from Israel. It was obviously much safer for them and a great deal more effective, and there was a wide choice of potential targets, including civilian aircraft and innocent passengers in foreign air terminals. Besides, the terrorists would then not have to restrict their terror to Jews. The Saudi Arabians saw to it that the Fatah didn't lack money; Nasser again bestowed his official blessings on them ('The Fatah,' he proclaimed, 'fulfils a vital task in drawing the enemy's blood'), and King Hussein took another stroll on his tightrope. Although the terrorists were soon to fight him tooth and nail for control of Jordan and to endanger him more than they had ever endangered us, Hussein – with the same lack of foresight that he had shown in the Six Day War – gave them his enthusiastic support. In 1970, when he found himself in such trouble with the so-called Palestinian terrorist organizations and began looking around everywhere for aid, I couldn't help thinking that he was like a man who murders his mother and father and then begs for mercy on the grounds that he is an orphan!

In the north, there was also no peace. Southern Lebanon was gradually being turned into a playground for the terrorists; Israeli towns, villages and farms – even school buses filled with children – were regularly being shelled and fired upon from what was now nicknamed 'Fatahland', while the Lebanese government wept crocodile tears and said it could do 'nothing' about the activity of the terrorists or even the fact that they were trained in and operating from Lebanese territory.

But we had decided that we were going to defend the ceasefire lines regardless of Nasser or the Fatah and, what's more, press on with our search for peace, however disheartening that search had become. Somehow we managed to cope with everything, without losing hope, mostly because our young men, for the sake of Israel's future, were willing to sit for weeks on Mount Hermon, or in Sinai, or in the Jordan Valley holding those ceasefire lines, which was a very small joy. Let there be no misunderstanding of the extent of the sacrifice involved. This was an army made up of the reserves – farmers, waiters, students, owners of dry cleaning establishments, doctors, truckdrivers and so forth – none of whom were professional soldiers drawing decent pay for their military service. They were men who had answered the call to arms, done their duty magnificently and badly wanted to go home.

They had other things to do and other obligations, and I don't think that there was ever a sadder victorious army in history, because the war it had fought never came to a real end. The reservists went home for a few weeks or months and then were called up again. They grumbled and muttered, but no one questioned the need to stay on those lines until a permanent peace was attained.

Then, on 26 February 1969, my dear friend Levi Eshkol, with whom I had worked for so many years and whom I had loved and admired so much, had a heart attack and died. I was at home alone when the news reached me and I sat by the phone for several minutes in a state of shock, unable even to pull myself together enough to find someone to drive me to Jerusalem. It seemed impossible that Eshkol was gone. I had talked to him only the night before and we were to meet the next day. I couldn't imagine what would happen now or who would take his place as prime minister. In Jerusalem, I went immediately to Eshkol's home. While the cabinet met in an emergency session, I sat in someone's office and waited for it to end so that I would know what had been decided about the funeral arrangements. As I sat there, an Israeli newspaperman came in.

'I know how you must feel,' he said to me. 'But I have just come from the Knesset. Everyone says there is only one solution. Golda must come back.'

'I don't know what you are talking about,' I answered furiously. 'Please don't bother me now. This is no time to talk politics. Please, please, go away.'

'Well,' he said, 'my editor wants to know where you'll be tonight. *He* wants to talk to you.'

'Look,' I said, 'I don't want to see anyone now. I don't know anything and I don't want to know anything. I just want you to leave me alone.'

The cabinet meeting ended. Yigal Allon, who was deputy prime minister, took over as acting prime minister. I went with a group of cabinet ministers to see Miriam Eshkol again. Then, towards evening, I returned to Tel Aviv. At about 10 p.m., the editor rang my doorbell. 'I come to tell you,' he said, 'that everybody has decided that you must take Eshkol's place. You are the only person with enough authority, experience and credit within the party to be acceptable to almost everyone.'

If I had been in a different mood, I might have reminded him then and there that in a recent poll, when the public was asked about its choice of the next prime minister, I had won exactly 3 per cent of the votes, which was alright by me but not what one would call a landslide! The greatest number of votes had been received by Moshe Dayan, and Yigal Allon had not done so badly either. But I was in no frame of mind to discuss the matter. 'Eshkol isn't even buried yet,' I said to the editor. 'How can you talk to me about these things,' and I sent him away.

But within a few days, the party began to press me. 'National elections are scheduled to take place in October; an interim prime minister will have to be appointed; it is only a question of a few months! And there is no one else.' Even Allon himself beseeched me, for the sake of the party, so recently unified, and for the sake of the country, which was still in such peril, to perform this last service. Not that the entire Labour Party was so keen on me. The ex-*Rafi* faction, headed by Dayan and Peres, was less than anxious to have me as prime minister and I could certainly understand the reservations of those other people in the country who thought that a seventy-year-old grandmother was hardly the perfect candidate to head a twenty-year-old state.

As for me, I couldn't make up my mind. On the one hand, I realized that, unless I agreed, there would inevitably be a tremendous tug-of-war between Dayan and Allon, which was one thing that Israel didn't need then. It was enough that we had a war with the Arabs on our hands; we could wait for that to end before we embarked on a war of the Jews. On the other hand, I honestly didn't want the responsibility, the stress and strain of being prime minister. I wanted to talk to the family, so I telephoned Menachem and Aya in Connecticut and then I called up Sarah and Zechariah in Revivim and told them that I had to see them but was much too tired to go to the Negev. Could they possibly come to me? They managed to get in by truck at midnight, and we sat up all through the night, talking, smoking and drinking coffee. In the morning, Sarah told me that Zechariah and she had made up their minds. They agreed with Menachem and Aya; I had no choice. '*Ima*, we know it will be terribly hard for you, harder than anyone will ever guess. But there is simply no way out – you must say yes.'

So I did. On 7 March the Central Committee of the Labour Party voted to nominate me as prime minister; there were seventy votes in favour, none against, and the *Rafi* faction abstained. I have often been asked how I felt at that moment, and I wish that I had a poetic answer to the question. I know that tears rolled down my cheeks and that I held my head in my hands when the voting was over, but all that I recall about my feelings is that I was dazed. I had never planned to be prime minister; I had never planned any position, in fact. I had planned to come to Palestine, to go to Merhavia, to be active in the Labour movement. But the position I was now to occupy? That never. I only knew that now I would have to make decisions every day that would affect the lives of millions of people, and I think perhaps that is why I cried. But there wasn't much time for reflection, and any thoughts I had about the path that had begun in Kiev and led me to the prime minister's office in Jerusalem had to wait. Today, when I can take time for those reflections, I find I have no appetite for them. I became prime minister because that was how it was, in the same way that my milkman became an officer in command of an outpost on Mount Hermon. Neither of us had any particular relish for the job, but we both did it as well as we could.

13   The prime minister

So I moved again, this time to the large, not especially attractive prime minister's residence in Jerusalem – in which Ben-Gurion, Sharett and Eshkol had lived before me – and began to accustom myself to the permanent presence of police and bodyguards, to a work day of at least sixteen hours and to the minimum of privacy. Obviously some days were easier, shorter and less tense than others, and I have no intention of pretending that I spent the five years that I was prime minister of Israel in a state of martyrdom or that I never enjoyed myself at all. But my term of office began with one war and ended with another, and I can't help thinking how symbolic it was that the very first instruction I gave to anyone in my capacity as prime minister was to tell my military secretary, Yisrael Lior, that I was to be informed as soon as the reports from any military action came in – even if it was in the middle of the night.

'I want to know the moment that the boys get back,' I told him, 'and I want to know how they are.' I didn't use the word 'casualties', but Lior understood and was horrified by the request. 'You don't really want me to phone you at 3 a.m.,' he said. 'After all, there is nothing you can do about it if there are any casualties. I promise to call you first thing in the morning.' But I knew that I wouldn't be able to bear the idea of sleeping soundly through the night not even knowing if soldiers had been killed or wounded, and I forced poor Lior to obey me. When the news was bad, of course, I couldn't fall asleep again, and I spent more nights than I care to remember padding around that big, empty house waiting for morning and for more detailed information. Sometimes the bodyguards outside the house would see that the kitchen light was on at 4 a.m., and one of them would look in to make sure that I was alright. I'd make us both a cup of tea and we'd talk about what was happening at the Canal or in the north until I felt that I could go back to bed again.

The Egyptian War of Attrition had started at the beginning of March 1968 and went on, with increasing ferocity, till the summer of 1970. Not only did the Soviet Union refrain from pressuring Nasser to end the violence and the killing; it rushed to Egypt thousands of Soviet instructors, to help retrain the battered Egyptian army and lend it a helping hand in combat against us, and a flood of military equipment, conservatively valued at some 3½ billion dollars. Egypt was not the sole beneficiary of this Soviet largesse; it went to Syria and Iraq also. But Nasser was certainly the main beneficiary. Two-thirds of all of the hundreds of tanks and fighter aircraft that Russia poured into the area immediately following the Six Day War were earmarked for Egyptian use in the hope that, in the face of the incessant fire and our own mounting losses, we would be unable to maintain our position along the Canal and that, broken in spirit as well as in body, we would finally agree to withdraw from the Canal zone without achieving peace or any kind of end to the conflict.

In theory, I suppose, it looked simple to Nasser and to the Russians: if they could keep up their hammering of our fortifications on the Canal – making life a hell on earth for Israeli troops there – sooner or later (but probably sooner) we would have to cry 'quits'. After all, it was no secret either to the Egyptians or to the Soviet Union that each Israeli casualty, each of the many Israeli military funerals that went on all through that period, each bereaved Israeli family was like a knife being turned in the heart of the entire nation; and I can understand all too well why Nasser and his patrons were sure that we would eventually give up. But we didn't – because we couldn't afford to. We weren't very eager to go on fighting anyone – not the Egyptians and even less the Russians – but we had absolutely no alternative. The only way we could possibly prevent that total war which Nasser himself proclaimed day and night to be the ultimate goal of his War of Attrition was by striking back, and striking hard, at the Egyptian military installations; by bombing Egyptian military targets, not only at the ceasefire line but inside Egypt itself; and, if and when necessary, even bring our message to the very doorstep of the Egyptians by raiding deep into Egyptian territory. It wasn't an easy decision to make, particularly since we knew that the Soviets might extend their involvement in Egypt even further. (Incidentally, this was the first actual Soviet intervention anywhere outside the accepted Soviet sphere of influence since the Second World War.) But one can't always choose one's opponents. So we reluctantly began our strategic 'in-depth' retaliatory bombardments, using our planes as flying artillery and trusting that the Egyptian people, hearing those planes over the military airfield near Cairo, would understand that they couldn't have it both ways: war for us and peace for themselves.

So much has happened since then that reading about the War of Attrition today may not be very vivid for most people. Even the terrible story of the Soviet ships that sailed secretly to Egypt laden with the SA-3 ground-to-air missiles that were to be installed, manned and operated by Soviet specialists throughout the Canal Zone is probably not of any great interest now, though we all know how those missiles were used against Israel in the autumn of 1973. But for us, the War of Attrition was a real war, and it took all of the determination, courage, strength and skill of our soldiers and pilots to hold the ceasefire lines and to try, regardless of the cost, to stop the forward movement of the missile pads that the Egyptians and the Russians were so busy setting up adjacent to the ceasefire lines. Still, there was a limit to our ability to go it alone. We had to have support and help, aircraft and arms, and we had to have them soon.

There was only one world power to whom we could turn: the United States, our traditional and great friend, which was selling us planes but did not, at that point, seem fully to understand our situation and might, we feared, cut that aid at any moment. President Nixon was more than just friendly. But neither he nor his secretary of state, William Rogers, were sympathetic to our refusal to accept any solution for the Middle East that would be imposed upon us by others or to my strong opposition to Mr Rogers' idea that the Russians, the Americans, the French and the British should sit down comfortably somewhere to work out a 'feasible' compromise for the Arabs and for us. Such a compromise, I had repeatedly explained to Mr Rogers, might satisfy the demands of the US-Soviet détente, but it would almost certainly not result in any binding guarantees for Israel's safety. How could it? The Russians were feeding and manipulating the entire Egyptian war effort; the French were almost as pro-Arab as the Russians; the British were not far behind the French; only the Americans were at all concerned with Israel's survival. At best, it would be three against one and I couldn't envisage a workable solution ever being achieved under such conditions. On the other hand, if we went on incurring both President Nixon's and Mr Rogers's displeasure, we might get no arms at all. Something had to be done at once to break the impasse.

Let me say at the outset that personally I always liked William Rogers. He is a very nice, very courteous and extremely patient man, and in the end it was he who proposed and brought about the ceasefire in August 1970. But (and I hope he will forgive me for writing this) I suspect that he never really understood the background to the Arab wars against Israel or ever realized that the verbal reliability of the Arab leaders was not, in any way, similar to his own. I remember how enthusiastically he told me about his first visits to the Arab states and how immensely impressed he was by Feisal's 'thirst for peace'. As is true of many other gentlemen I have known, Rogers assumed – wrongly, unfortunately – that the whole world was made up solely of other gentlemen.

All my own attempts to establish direct contact with the Arab leaders had failed miserably – including the appeal I made on the first day I assumed office, when I had declared that 'we are prepared to discuss peace with our neighbours, any day and on all matters', only to read, within seventy-two hours, Nasser's reply that 'there is no voice transcending the sounds of war . . . and no call holier than the call to war'. Nor were the responses from Damascus, Amman or Beirut any more encouraging. To quote just one example of the reaction of the Arab world to my plea that we enter into negotiations at once, here is an excerpt from an article published in a leading Jordanian newspaper in June 1969:

. . . Mrs Meir is prepared to go Cairo to hold discussions with President Nasser but, to her sorrow, has not been invited. She believes that one fine day a world without guns will emerge in the Middle East. Golda Meir is behaving like a grandmother telling bedtime stories to her grandchildren . . .

I felt as if we were caught in a vice. All the time the war was going on, people abroad were asking whether our real intention was not to bring Nasser down – as though we had set him up and were now preoccupied with plans to replace him. What enraged me, though, was that we were also being questioned whether our bombing in depth was 'really' necessary and a matter of self-defence, as though one must wait till a murderer actually reaches one's home before it is morally permissible to stop him from trying to kill one particularly when – as in

Nasser's case – we were being left in no doubt whatsoever as to his intentions.

It was, in short, a difficult period, and one not made any easier for me by having inherited from Eshkol the National Unity Government, which included the anti-socialist bloc known as *Gahal* (made up of the extreme right-wing *Herut* Party and the far more moderate but smaller Liberal Party, and led by Menachem Begin). Quite apart from the deep-seated and very basic differences in ideology that had obviously always existed between the left and the right wings of Israel's political spectrum, there was a serious immediate difference in our approaches to the situation in which Israel now found itself. In June, Secretary of State Rogers proposed that Israel hold discussions with Egypt and Jordan, under the auspices of Dr Jarring, with the aim of arriving at a just and lasting peace. These discussions were to be based upon 'mutual acknowledgement of each other's sovereignty, territorial integrity and political independence' and on 'Israeli withdrawal from territories occupied in the 1967 conflict', in accordance with Resolution 242. He also proposed that the ceasefire with Egypt, which had been shattered by the War of Attrition, be renewed for at least ninety days. *Gahal*, however, stood firm on the fact that the policy of the government of Israel since 1967 had been – and still was, as far as *Gahal* was concerned – that the IDF would remain on the ceasefire lines until peace was attained. Formally, of course, *Gahal* had a point. I knew that I would have to go to the Knesset to get its consent for this change in policy. But it didn't matter how hard I argued that the situation had changed. Though it accepted the ceasefire proposal, *Gahal* refused to agree to any negotiations on the subject of withdrawal from the territories until there was peace.

'But we won't have any ceasefire unless we also accept some of the less favourable conditions,' I tried to explain repeatedly to Mr Begin. 'And what's more, we won't get any arms from America.' 'What do you mean, we won't get arms?' he used to say. 'We'll *demand* them from the Americans.' I couldn't get it through to him that although the American commitment to Israel's survival was certainly great, we needed Mr Nixon and Mr Rogers much more than they needed us, and Israel's policies couldn't be based entirely on the assumption that American Jewry either would or could force Mr Nixon to adopt a position against his will or better judgement. But *Gahal*, intoxicated by its own rhetoric, had convinced itself that all we had to do was to go on telling the United States that we wouldn't give in to any pressure whatsoever, and if we did this long enough and loud enough, one day that pressure would just vanish. I can only describe this belief as mystical, because it certainly wasn't based on reality as I knew it, and today I shudder to think what would have happened in October 1973 if we had behaved in 1969 and 1970 as defiantly and self-destructively as *Gahal* wanted us to. There might well have been no US military aid at all from 1970 on, and the Yom Kippur War would then have ended very differently.

And in August 1970, when the four *Gahal* ministers resigned from the cabinet on the absurd grounds that the Israeli government's acceptance of the ceasefire was the beginning of a major unconditional retreat from the ceasefire lines, I wasn't particularly taken aback. For the sake of avoiding additional problems, we asked them to stay. But they were adamant, and left.

The other (though minor) bane of my life during all the time that I was prime minister – and one that it took me months to accustom myself to, even partially – was the freedom with which various ministers confided in the press, to put it very politely. The constant leaks from cabinet meetings infuriated me, and although I had my own suspicions all along as to the source of the sensational revelations by so-called diplomatic correspondents which greeted me so often in the morning papers, I could never prove them – which meant that I couldn't do much about them. But my staff very quickly got used to seeing me turn up at the office on the day after a cabinet meeting looking as black as thunder because over breakfast I had read something garbled in the paper that shouldn't have been there at all, garbled or otherwise. But these, need I say, were not my major anxieties. The real problems, as they had been for so long, were survival and peace, in that order.

Then, a number of months after I had taken office, I made a decision. I would go to Washington myself – if it could be arranged – to speak with President Nixon, to talk to congressmen and senators and to find out just what the American people thought and felt about us and what they were willing to do to help us. It wasn't that I deluded myself for a moment that I had any magical powers of persuasion. After all, I hadn't succeeded in changing Mr Rogers's mind about the need for the Russians to participate in the Middle Eastern settlement – though I had certainly tried my best to do so. Nor did I expect to accomplish more than gifted men like our foreign minister, Abba Eban, or our new ambassador to Washington, General Yitzhak Rabin, had been able to accomplish. But I felt a deep need to establish, for and by myself, just where we stood as far as our relationship with the United States was concerned, and the cabinet thought it was a very good idea for me to go. As soon as the official invitation arrived from the White House, I began to prepare for the trip.

I certainly had doubts about its prospects for success. I had never met Richard Nixon, and I didn't even know most of the men around him. I had no idea what the president was being told about me; for all I knew, he might regard me (understandably enough) as a stop-gap premier who didn't carry much weight in her own country and would probably not be re-elected. But I was sure of one thing: whatever impression I might make on him, I had to lay before the president all of our problems and difficulties, quite candidly, and try to convince him, beyond a shadow of doubt, that there was a great deal that could be asked of us by way of compromise and concessions, but that we could not be expected to give up our dream of peace or to withdraw a single soldier from one inch of land until an agreement could be reached between the Arabs and ourselves. And that was not all. We desperately needed arms, and I felt that I should ask him for them myself. On the face of it, they weren't very complicated messages, but I think that I would have been less than human and a fool if I hadn't been extremely nervous about delivering them.

My personal preparations were very simple. I bought two evening dresses (including the beige lace and velvet one that I wore to the White House dinner), a knitted suit, a couple of hats (that I never wore at all) and some gloves (to hold in my hand). With the consideration that was to typify his entire relationship with me, President Nixon saw to it that Clara and Menachem and his family were also invited to the White House dinner that was to be held on my first evening in Washington, and we arranged to meet on 24 September in Philadelphia (which, for some reason – perhaps because of its historic importance – is a customary first stop for presidential guests from abroad). From Philadelphia, we were flown by helicopter to the lawn of the White House. With all the arrangements made, I was free to spend the weeks before my departure working overtime with my advisers, in particular with Dayan and the chief-of-staff, Chaim Bar-Lev, on the 'shopping list' that I was going to take to Washington with me. In addition to a specific request for twenty-five Phantoms and eighty Skyhawk jets, I planned also to ask the president for low interest loans of 200 million dollars a year for five years to help us pay for the planes we hoped to be able to buy.

I must explain here that the first US president to authorize the sale of Phantoms and Skyhawks to Israel was President Johnson, whom Eshkol had visited in Texas and who had promised to give 'sympathetic consideration' to the request. But it had taken some time before those first Skyhawks had actually been delivered to us, and I was sure that even if President Nixon agreed to sell us Phantoms, we would not be able to get them quickly unless I was able to convey to him the urgency of our situation and of the imbalance in the flow of arms to the Middle East. As for the money, I thought we would probably get that (though money is also something one can never be sure about) if for no other reason than that our credit was excellent. As a matter of fact, Israel has never fallen down on a single payment due to anyone. I even cheered myself up on this score by remembering how in 1956–7, after the Sinai Campaign, when we were paying off a big loan we had received from the US Import-Export Bank (and this at a time when the official US attitude towards Israel was very cool indeed), we had been greatly tempted to ask for a postponement of the large repayment that had become due. A recession was going on in Israel then, and it was really very hard for us to scrape up the money we owed. But we weighed the pros and cons and finally decided that, no matter how difficult it was, we were not going to be in default, even by a day. And I shall never forget Eban's description of the surprise on the usually guarded faces of the people at the Import-Export Bank in Washington when he walked in – at exactly the specified time and date – and presented our cheque.

Anyhow, on the plane going to the States, I was immersed in my thoughts, trying to guess what my visit to Nixon would be like and whether we would get along together. I wasn't even sure any more of the reception I would get in the United States as a whole. After the Six Day War I had been greeted with warmth, love and pride by American Jewry; but more than two years had passed since then, and it seemed possible that the enthusiasm for Israel's cause might have waned somewhat. But I needn't have worried so much, on either score.

At the Philadelphia airport, a crowd of thousands was waiting for me; hundreds and hundreds of schoolchildren singing '*Hevenu Shalom Aleichem*' were waving and carrying banners. I remember one of those banners read 'We dig you, Golda', and I thought it was the most charming expression of support for Israel – and perhaps for me – that I had ever seen. But I had no idea, other than smiling and waving at them, how to make clear to those youngsters that I certainly 'dug' them too. So I just smiled and waved and was delighted when I spotted my own family. At Independence Square, an even larger crowd greeted me – 30,000 American Jews, many of whom had been standing there for several hours to see me. I couldn't get over the sight of all those people pressing against the police barricades and applauding. I spoke to them only very briefly, but as someone said to me, 'You could have read a page from the telephone book, and that crowd would still have cheered.'

We stayed overnight in Philadelphia and then flew on to Washington in the morning. It had rained all night, and the sky was still cloudy and grey, as if it was going to go on raining. But (as though that, too, had been arranged by the White House) the sun came out just after my two-minute ride in a limousine from the helicopter to the bright green White House lawn. President Nixon put me at ease at once. He helped me out of the car, and Mrs Nixon handed me a huge bunch of red roses. There was something about the way the Nixons received me that made me feel at home with them from the start, and I was very grateful to both of them.

The formal ceremony was very formal indeed, full of spit and polish. The president and I stood on a raised platform covered by a red carpet, while a Marine band played the two national anthems. I listened to 'Hatikvah' and although I made an effort to look perfectly calm, my eyes filled with tears. There I was, the prime minister of the Jewish state, which had come into existence and survived against such odds, standing to attention with the president of the United States while my country was accorded full military honours. I remember thinking: 'If only the boys at the Canal could see this', but I knew, at least, that in Israel thousands of people would be watching the ceremony on television that evening and be as profoundly moved and heartened by it as I was. Perhaps other nations take these ceremonies for granted, but we don't yet. In fact, it was all a little like a dream, the kind of dream I used to dream with my friends years ago when we sometimes talked about what it would be like when we actually had not only a state of our own but also the trappings of statehood.

Mr Nixon's speech was short and to the point. He talked about the US stake in peace in the Middle East and paid me some nice compliments. Nothing, he said, could be solved in one meeting or even in several, but the struggle to attain peace was of the highest priority. I spoke very briefly too. I had written down a few words – also about peace and friendship – and I read them out. But I hadn't come to the

White House either to hear or to make little speeches, or even to inspect troops – though I think I did that fairly well, all things considered.

My meetings with the president were as warm as his initial welcome. We were together for a couple of hours and we talked about everything as bluntly and frankly as I had hoped we would. We were in complete agreement that Israel should stay put until some kind of acceptable agreement with the Arabs was reached and that a Big Power which promises assistance to a small country when it is in trouble must keep its word. We also talked about the Palestinians and I spoke my mind as openly on that topic as I did on others. 'Between the Mediterranean and the borders of Iraq,' I said, 'in what was once Palestine, there are now two countries, one Jewish and one Arab, and there is no room for a third. The Palestinians must find the solution to their problem together with that Arab country, Jordan, because a "Palestinian state" between us and Jordan can only become a base from which it will be even more convenient to attack and destroy Israel.' Mr Nixon listened very closely to everything I had to say about the Middle East, as though he had nothing to do except to sit and talk to Golda Meir about Israel's problems, but he was still very anxious for the Big Two and the Big Four talks to go on, despite the fact that he seemed to accept my argument that Russia was most unlikely to agree to anything to which her Arab clients objected. I must say that I took some pleasure in the knowledge that at the same time as President Nixon and I were talking together, the Soviet foreign minister, Andrei Gromyko, and Mr Rogers were meeting in New York, and I couldn't help but think how annoyed Mr Gromyko must have been by the timing of his sessions with the US secretary of state.

As to the more substantive matters that I discussed with Mr Nixon, I can only say that I would not quote him at the time and I will not quote him now. The press badgered me almost to death, but all that I would say was that my impression, my own personal assessment, of the result of our talks was that 'the American administration intends to continue its policy of maintaining the balance of military power in the region'. Because no official communiqué was issued after my conversations with the president, some journalists assumed that I had come away with empty hands. But the truth was that I couldn't see any point to communiqués (which very rarely communicate anything), and President Nixon felt much the same way, so we decided together that no formal statement would be released. As for my shopping list, well, it eventually changed hands, as it was meant to.

That night, President and Mrs Nixon gave a state dinner in my honour. People in Washington said later that it was one of the finest White House parties of the Nixon administration – though no one could explain just what made it such a success. For me it was, from start to finish, one of the most wonderful evenings of my life, partly, I expect, because I had met with such understanding from President Nixon, and partly because I now felt sure that the United States would stand by us and I really relaxed for the first time in months. Also everything had been superbly planned to give me pleasure – from the presence of my family to the 'Charlotte Revivim' dessert that so tactfully indicated that Sarah and Zechariah were also included in the celebration. Of the 120 guests, many were old friends of mine from both political parties, among them the former US ambassador to the United Nations, Arthur Goldberg, and Senator Jacob Javits. And, of course, Mr Rogers, Dr Kissinger, Eban and Rabin, as well as various high-ranking members of the administration were there. Throughout the dinner itself, Israeli music was played, and then – as a special treat – both Leonard Bernstein and Isaac Stern performed, giving us one encore after another. I could see and hear how tremendously moved they both were, and I was so enraptured by their music and their presence that when they stopped playing I forgot where I was and I jumped up to hug them both.

Before the dinner, the Nixons and I had exchanged gifts: they gave me a covered Grecian urn, reproduced in gold and beautifully inscribed, and a lovely floral centrepiece made of blue and gold opaline, while I had brought them Israeli antiques: a necklace of carnelian beads shaped like lotuses and dating back to the eleventh century BC for Mrs Nixon, an ancient Jewish oil lamp for the president, silver candlesticks for Julie and David Eisenhower and a silver Yemenite necklace and earrings for Tricia Nixon. After the dinner there were toasts. Again, the president was very kind to Israel, and to me.

'The people of Israel,' he said, 'have earned peace – not the fragile peace that comes with the kind of document that neither party has an interest in keeping, but the kind of peace that will last. We hope that as a result of our meeting we will have taken a significant step forward towards that peace which can mean so much to the people of Israel, to the people of the Middle East and also to the people of the world.'

I felt that he spoke from his heart, and I know that I did when I replied:

'Mr President, thank you, not only for your hospitality, not only for this great day and for every moment that I have had this day, but thank you most of all for enabling me to go home and tell my people that we have a friend, a great friend, in the White House. It will help. It will help us overcome many difficulties.'

At about 11 p.m., the president, Mrs Nixon and I left the party, and at my car Mrs Nixon and I kissed each other goodnight, as though we had been friends for years. But the rest of the guests went on dancing until long after midnight.

In all, I spent four days in Washington. Walking in step with the bemedalled adjutant general of the United States army (not the easiest thing I have ever done), I placed a wreath of blue and white flowers on the Tomb of the Unknown Soldier at Arlington National Cemetery, preceded by a nineteen-gun salute and colour bearers carrying Israeli flags. I visited Mr Rogers at the State Department and was entertained to lunch by him, saw Mr Melvin Laird at the Defence Department, met with members of the House Foreign Affairs Committee and 'appeared' at the National Press Club, where I met the toughest and most experienced journalists in the United States and felt at first as if I was in a boxing ring with them. But they were very nice to me, too, and seemed to like the fact that I answered their questions as briefly and as simply as I could – though I can't say that they asked me anything that I hadn't been asked a dozen times before.

There were only two queries that were at all new. One newspaperman asked: 'Would Israel employ nuclear weapons if her survival were in jeopardy?' to which I could only reply, truthfully, that I thought we hadn't done so badly with conventional weapons – an answer that was greeted by laughter and applause. The second was a request from the president of the Press Club that made me laugh. 'Your grandson Gideon says that you make the best *gefilte* fish [stuffed fish] in Israel,' he said 'Would you reveal your recipe to us?' 'I'll do better than that,' I answered. 'When I come here again, I promise to arrive three days in advance and make *gefilte* fish for lunch for all of you.' (Months later, incidentally, I was once interviewed in Los Angeles and asked if I made good chicken soup. 'Of course I do,' I replied. Would I send the recipe? 'Gladly,' I said, never imagining that within a week the interviewer would get 40,000 requests for it. I only hope it resulted in 40,000 pots of good Jewish soup! Anyhow, it wasn't my skill as a cook that mattered in Washington; it was the bond of friendship between the United States and Israel and the US attitude towards our counter-attrition policy. Before I left, Mr Nixon made a statement to the press on his behalf and mine which I thought summed up the results of my visit, even though it lacked any details.

'I think,' he said, 'that we have a very good understanding of the positions we both take, and that from this meeting there could come some progress, some solution of the terribly difficult problems confronting us in the Middle East. We do not expect them to be susceptible to instant diplomacy. On the other hand, we must try, and I was glad to find a willingness on the part of the prime minister and her colleagues to try and find a way to peace. We have no new initiatives to announce, but we do think that we have a better understanding of how we should move from here on out.'

From Washington I went to New York, where one function followed another so rapidly that I didn't even have time to feel tired. I got a marvellous welcome at City Hall, lunched with U Thant, held a series of meetings at my suite in the Waldorf Astoria, attended a reception for diplomats hosted by Eban and went to a huge banquet sponsored by the United Jewish Appeal, Israel Bonds and fifty other Jewish organizations – all on the first day I was there. Then on to Los Angeles, Milwaukee and finally back to the east coast. I had intended to return home by 5 October, but there was one invitation I couldn't refuse, and I stayed on an extra day to address the AFL-CIO biennial convention in Atlantic City. For many years, the AFL-CIO had been very close to Israel, particularly to the *Histadrut*, and its president, George Meany, a dear old friend of mine, was the honorary chairman of the American Trade Union Council for the *Histadrut*. Talking to that immense audience of trade unionists, I felt for the first time since I had left Israel that I was really on home territory. I talked about exactly the same things that I had talked about in Philadelphia, Washington, Milwaukee, Los Angeles and New York, the things that I still talk about – peace between us and the Arabs. 'It will be a great day,' I told my friends, the workers and the trade union leaders of America, 'when Arab farmers will cross the Jordan not with planes or tanks, but with tractors and with their hands outstretched in friendship, as between farmer and farmer, as between human beings. A dream it may be, but I am sure that one day it will come true.'

When I got back to Israel, although I could not yet make any announcement about the Phantoms, I knew we were going to get them and my heart was much lighter than it had been when I took off. But the War of Attrition was still being waged, the terrorists were still active, the number of Soviet military personnel in Egypt was increasing by leaps and bounds, including combat pilots and the crews of the ground-to-air missiles. In a word, peace was as remote as ever. In fact, nothing at all had changed substantially since I had assumed office. Whatever reasons existed then for my becoming prime minister were, unfortunately, still valid on the eve of our national elections – the seventh since the state was established. In the months that had passed, however, my so-called 'rating' had improved, and although I wasn't out to win any popularity contests, it certainly feels a lot better to have a rating of seventy-five or eighty than of three! At all events, the election results weren't exactly unpredictable. The *Ma'arach* won fifty-six of the 120 Knesset seats, and I presented the Knesset with that 'wall to wall' cabinet, from which *Gahal* was to walk out in the summer.

Now that I was prime minister in my own right, so to speak, I very much hoped that I would be able to do something to help solve those of Israel's growing social and economic problems that were beginning to cause a real rift between various sections of the population. For years, both in the *Histadrut* and in the party, I had pleaded that since we unfortunately couldn't do anything about having to maintain our enormous defence budget, we should at least pull together and try to do away with the widening gap between the people who had everything they needed – if not everything they wanted – and those tens of thousands who were still ill-housed, ill-clothed, under-educated and sometimes even ill-fed. For the most part, this segment of our population belonged to what was bitterly called 'the second Israel', Jews who had come to us in 1948, 1950 and 1951 from the Yemen, the Middle East and North Africa, and whose standard of living in the late 1960s and early 1970s still left a great deal to be desired. Of course, we could go on congratulating ourselves on the fact that between 1949 and 1970 we had built over 400,000 units of public housing, and that there wasn't a single place in the country – however isolated – that didn't have a school, a kindergarten and, in most cases, also a nursery school. But no amount of justified pride in what we had managed to achieve could possibly eliminate the other less pleasant facts. There was poverty in Israel, and there was also wealth. Neither the poverty nor the wealth was great, but they both existed.

There were, and still are, Israelis who live ten to a two-room house, whose children are dropouts (even though they would probably be totally exempt from paying secondary school fees) and delinquents (largely because of their disadvantaged background) and who, because they believe that they are in danger of turning into permanently under-privileged second-class citizens, regard all other newer immigrants as inevitably making their own situation worse. There are also Israelis, though not many, who live in relative luxury, who drive large cars, entertain lavishly, dress in the height of fashion and have adopted a life-style that is imported from abroad and has nothing whatsoever to do either with our real national economic capacity or with the real circumstances of our national life. In between these two groups are the masses of skilled labourers and white-collar workers who have a hard time making ends meet, who can't maintain their standard of living (which is in no way immodest) on one salary, who for decades have proven themselves capable of the most remarkable self-discipline, patriotism and sacrifice, but who were nonetheless responsible, I believe, for the strikes that plagued us and guilty of insisting that each time the low-wage earners got an increase, everyone – right up the ladder – also had to get a pay rise.

It was with this strata that I tried, though not very successfully, to reason. Something was happening to the rank-and-file of the *Histadrut*, to the good sense of the Israeli worker, that frightened me, and I couldn't and didn't keep quiet about it. No one believed more strongly than I did that a trade union was not only entitled but obliged to safeguard the rights of workers and to call for strikes when negotiations dragged on for too long or when agreements weren't being met. But agreements that were signed had to be honoured without new claims being submitted at once; and those who were not at the bottom of the nation's economic scale had to understand and accept the fact that whatever increases could be given had to be given to those whose need was greatest. There is nothing sacred about the principle of differentials. I had fought it in the *Histadrut* years ago, and I was prepared to fight it again. The line had to be held somewhere. God knows that Israel's doctors, nurses and teachers didn't have an easy time economically, but they could keep going, while lower paid groups were becoming submerged in the rising inflation and high cost of living had to be given salary increases or they couldn't have survived. It was just that simple.

I was also extremely unsympathetic to the idea of strikes in essential services, especially in a country in a state of war. I don't think that I need to explain to anyone what it meant to me personally to have to decide on issuing restraining orders when the staffs of hospitals went on strike. But there was no other way to ensure that there wouldn't be a resultant loss of life, so I grit my teeth and did it.

'The government,' I told the nation, 'cannot do everything all at once. It can't wave a magic wand and meet everyone's demands simultaneously: eradicate poverty without imposing taxes, win wars, go on absorbing immigration, develop the economy and still give everyone their due. No government can do all this at one and the same time.' But it wasn't only a question of money. Social equality isn't attained merely with material resources. To wipe out poverty and its aftermath you need two partners who are equally willing to make an effort, and I didn't mince any words about this either.

'In the first place,' I said, 'those among us who are poor mustn't permit themselves to be turned into the passive objects of other people's concern. They must be active on their own behalf. And the more settled, more affluent sections of the population will have to join in a great volunteer movement aimed at achieving social integration. The gap between those who have education and training and those who don't is at least as great and as tragic as the gap between those who can cope economically and those who can't.'

Some progress was made, but nowhere near enough. I formed a prime minister's committee for tackling the problems of underprivileged youngsters. It included distinguished educators, psychologists, doctors, probation officers and so forth, all of whom worked voluntarily. Although it took two years, instead of what I hoped would be just a few months, for it to come up with recommendations, we implemented many of its recommendations even before they were published. When we had to raise the price of staple foods, we gave tax benefits to lower-income groups, and we went on building as much low-income housing as we possibly could, while I waged a ceaseless war of my own for the building of rental housing that would be subsidized if necessary. And, of course, whatever we tried to do had to be done either in the midst of actual warfare or during periods of terrorism, and there was never enough time or money to concentrate even on our most urgent domestic problems – for which, apart from everything else, I found it impossible to forgive our neighbours. Given peace, I knew that although we might never be able to build an ideal society, we could certainly build a much better one. But where was that peace?

Then in August 1970 Mr Rogers's ceasefire materialized. Nasser said that as far as he was concerned, it would only last for three months, but – as though the timing were symbolic – he died in September and Anwar Sadat became the president of Egypt. Not only did Sadat seem, at first glance, to be a more reasonable man who might soberly consider

the benefits of an end to the war to his own people, but there were also
indications that he wasn't getting along too well with the Russians.
And in Jordan, King Hussein, having happily sheltered the Palestinian
terrorists for months, suddenly found himself so threatened by them
that in September he turned on them and crushed them. So though it
may have been a Black September for the Fatah, to me it looked, at
long last, as if the US peace initiative and Dr Jarring might have some
slim chance of success. The Arab leaders didn't modify their statements
about Israel in any way or alter their demands for a total withdrawal
of our troops, but there was talk about re-opening the Suez Canal and
rebuilding the ruined Egyptian towns along its banks, so that normal
life could be restored in them – all of which gave rise to some optimism
in Israel. Well, the ceasefire held; we stayed where we were; the Arabs
continued to refuse to meet us or deal with us in any way, and the
optimism in Israel slowly died down – but it didn't vanish altogether
and war didn't break out in 1971 or 1972! But neither did peace, and
Arab terrorism mounted both in its ferocity and its inhumanity.

Certainly no one in the civilized world approved of the gunning down,
at Lydda airport, of Catholic pilgrims from Puerto Rico and one of
Israel's most distinguished scientists, of the horrifying public kidnapping
and murder of Israeli athletes at the Munich Olympic Games or of the
slaughter of Israeli children trapped in the school building in the
development town of Ma'alot. No one approved, and each outrage
brought me its flood of official condolences and expressions of shock and
sympathy. But nonetheless we were expected (and still are expected by
many) to come to terms with the murderers in the way that other
governments had, as if these suicidal fanatics should have been allowed
to blackmail us and bring us to our knees. It has certainly been proven
time and again that giving in to terror only leads to more terror. No one
will ever know, however, what it cost the government of Israel to say
no to the demands of the terrorists or what it was like to feel that no
Israeli official working abroad was entirely safe from death by letter
bomb, to say nothing of the fact that any quiet border town in Israel
could be turned (as several were) into the scene of massacres caused
by a few demented men who had been reared on hatred and the belief
that they could drain Israel of its ability to stand firm in the face of
grief and pain.

But we learned to hold out against the terror, to protect our aircraft
and passengers, to turn our embassies into small fortresses and to patrol
our schoolyards and city streets. I walked behind the coffins and visited

the bereaved families of the victims of Arab terrorism and I was filled
with pride that I belonged to a nation which was able to take these
blows – these cowardly and evil blows – without saying 'Enough. We
have had enough. Give the terrorists whatever they want because we
have taken all that we can take.' Other governments surrendered to the
demands of the terrorists, put planes at their disposal and released them
from gaol, while the foreign press and the New Left called them
'guerrillas' and 'freedom fighters'. For us, however, they remained
criminals, not heroes, and though each funeral was a torment for me,
I remained unimpressed by the 'glory' of hiding mines in supermarkets
and buses or the 'glamour' of a holy war that required killing seven old
Jews in a home for the aged in Munich. And I was literally physically
sickened when the Arabs who had murdered the eleven Israeli athletes
at the Olympic Games in 1972 were set free in a blaze of publicity and
flown to Libya only six weeks later. The Arab states went on giving the
terrorists money, arms and backing and then screaming to high heaven
whenever we made clear, by raiding the terrorist bases in Syria and
Lebanon, that we held the governments of those states responsible for
what was happening.

The only solution, the only possible solution, was peace – not only
peace with honour, but a lasting peace. And the only way of achieving
it was to go on trying to convince our friends that our stand was right –
since our enemies wouldn't even talk to us – and to examine every single
possibility that might lead to negotiations.

Many of the trips I took and talks I held must still remain secret,
but I think that today I can write about one of them. At the beginning
of 1972, the deputy foreign minister of Rumania came to Israel on a
visit, ostensibly just to meet with people in our Foreign Office. But he
made one special request: he asked to see me, and he stressed that he
wanted to see me alone; no one else should be present at our conversation. We had very good relations with Rumania. It was the only East
European country that hadn't severed diplomatic relations with us after
the Six Day War and that consistently refused to take part in the Soviet
Union's vicious anti-Israel propaganda campaign or join in the Soviet
bloc's denunciations of our 'aggression'. We had entered into mutually
profitable trade agreements with the Rumanians, exchanged art exhibi-
tions, musicians, choirs and theatrical groups, and there was some
immigration from Rumania. I had met (and liked) the attractive and
energetic president of Rumania, Nicolai Ceauşescu, in 1970 and I
admired him for not giving way to Arab pressure and for managing to

retain diplomatic links with us as well as with the Arab states. I knew that Ceauşescu was anxious to promote a Middle Eastern peace settlement, and I wasn't really surprised when his deputy foreign minister announced to me as soon as we were alone that actually he had come to Israel only in order to tell me the following:

'I have been sent by my president,' he said, 'to inform you that when he visited Egypt recently, he saw President Sadat and that, as a result of their meeting, my president has a most important message for you. He would like to bring it to you himself, but since he can't [he was going to China], he suggests that you come to Bucharest. You can come either *incognito* or, if you prefer, we will gladly issue you a formal invitation.' I didn't accept that going to China automatically ruled out a visit to Israel, but I said that, of course, I would come to Bucharest as soon as possible. Not *incognito* – that didn't appeal to me as a way for the prime minister of Israel to travel (unless it was absolutely essential) – but just as soon as I got an official invitation. Ceauşescu's invitation arrived shortly afterwards, and I flew to Rumania.

I spent fourteen hours (in two long sessions) with Ceauşescu, who told me that he understood from Sadat himself that the Egyptian leader was ready to meet with an Israeli – maybe with me, maybe not; maybe the meeting would be on a slightly lower level than the heads of state, but a meeting of some sort could take place. I said, 'Mr President, this is the best news I have heard for many years' – as indeed it was. We talked for hours about it, and Ceauşescu was almost as excited as I was. There was no question in his mind that he was delivering an historic and absolutely genuine message. He even talked to me about details. 'We won't work through ambassadors or Foreign Offices,' he said, 'not mine and not yours.' He suggested that his deputy foreign minister maintain personal contact with me through Simcha Dinitz, then my political secretary, who had come with me to Bucharest.

After so many years, it really looked as though the ice was about to break. But it didn't. When I came back to Israel, we waited and waited – in vain. There was no follow-up at all. Whatever Sadat had told Ceauşescu – and he had certainly told him something – was totally meaningless, and I suspect that the reason I never heard anything more from Ceauşescu about the meeting with Sadat was that he couldn't bring himself to confess, even to me, that Sadat had fooled him.

As far as the public and press – both in Israel and Rumania – were concerned, this had just been a standard visit; Ceauşescu gave me a luncheon, the prime minister gave me a dinner and I gave him a dinner.

But the only meaningful result of my visit to Bucharest – on which I had pinned such high hopes – was that I was able to attend the Friday night services at the Chorale Synagogue in Bucharest and meet many hundreds of Rumanian Jews – infinitely freer than the Jews of Moscow had been, or are, but almost as overwhelmed by my presence among them. They greeted me with such a torrent of love for Israel that I felt bodily buffeted by it, and I don't think I have ever heard Hebrew songs sung more beautifully or with greater tenderness than on that Friday night. As I walked to my car, I saw a vast crowd waiting for me in complete silence; 10,000 Jews had come from all over Rumania to see me. I turned, crossed over to them and said *'Shabbat shalom'*, and I heard 10,000 voices call back *'Shabbat shalom'*. That encounter in itself was more than worth the trip for me. And the only tangible thing I brought back with me (though I didn't know it then) was the huge black bearskin given to me by the prime minister of Rumania (a cele-brated huntsman) which I later 'lent' to the children of Revivim. They adored it, and for them it did not hold the bitter memories that it did for me.

There were also other journeys to other places and once even an adventure abroad which taught me that nothing I did was ever going to go unnoticed again. In the spring of 1971, I made a ten-day trip to Denmark, Finland, Sweden and Norway. Between my visit to Helsinki and to Stockholm, there was a weekend and a rare chance, if I planned it properly, to be out of reach of the telephone, the telex, cables and reporters. But it isn't so simple to find a secluded place for a rest and still conform to the security regulations that increasingly governed where and how I travelled. My office in Jerusalem asked the Israeli ambassador in Stockholm to look around for some suitable spot not too far from the Swedish capital and to let us know in good time. Just before I left Israel, there was a phone call: one of the ministers wanted to say how sorry he was that he wouldn't be able to see me off, but there *was* something interesting he wanted to tell me. We chatted for a couple of minutes, and then I left for the airport.

In Helsinki, I got word from our embassy in Stockholm that nothing had been found and that the best thing for me to do with those two free days was to go to Stockholm and take it easy in my hotel there until my official visit began. All of a sudden, I remembered that last-minute phone call I had received just before my departure, and I asked Lou Kaddar – to her amazement – whether she fancied a weekend in Lapland. 'Lapland?' She couldn't believe that I was serious. 'Well,' I explained, 'I forgot all about it till just now, but we have been invited to stay at a marvellous lodge in the wilds of Finnish Lapland that belongs to a devoted friend of Israel. He has promised to give us a very good time there, and I, for one, would like to go.' There were all kinds of objections: my bodyguards said it was much too isolated and much too far away; Lou said that we didn't have the right clothes and that we'd freeze to death; the Finnish and Swedish security people were appalled at the idea of my taking off for a place that was only about 100 miles from the Soviet border; and everyone decided that it was mad to travel a total of 1,200 miles for a two-day vacation. But I wanted to go – and go we did.

Our trip was veiled in the utmost secrecy, of course. We went to Stockholm and flew on to Lapland in a small plane, arriving at Rovaniemi, the capital of Finnish Lapland, in the brilliant sunshine of the early afternoon. At the airport, which was the size of a small tennis court, there were some taxis waiting for us and the mayor of Rovaniemi with his wife. He had only been told that some important guests were coming, but he hadn't even been told who they were. There was also, it turned out, one newspaperman who just happened to be there and just happened to notice that the mayor's wife was holding a rose. Who sees roses in Lapland? He took another look at the people who were getting off the plane, stared at the short woman in a heavy coat who was obviously the VIP traveller for whom that precious rose was intended, told himself it was impossible and then, when we were already on our way through the snow to the lodge, suddenly realized that it was really me and immediately sent a cable off to his editor.

I had a wonderful time in Rovaniemi, rested and came back to Stockholm in great shape only to discover that the whole world wanted to know about my clandestine meeting with the Russians. Why else would Golda Meir have gone to Finnish Lapland? What had we talked about? With whom had I met? No one in Scandinavia or anywhere else, for that matter, believed the truth until Mr Tsarapkin, the Soviet deputy foreign minister, arrived in Oslo the day before I left it – without seeing me. The press then finally resigned itself to the undramatic fact that all I had done in Lapland for forty-eight hours was eat, sleep, buy souvenirs made of reindeer fur for my grandchildren and drive around the lovely, silent, frozen lakes.

There were times during those five years when I would have gladly run away from it all if I had felt free to do so, not because my strength was giving out or because the pace was too much for me, but primarily because I was so tired of repeating myself so often, saying the same things over and over again and getting nowhere. I was also tired of hearing about my supposed complexes from people who thought we should act in a way that would result in handing Israel over either to President Sadat or, better yet, to Mr Arafat. This meant, I gathered, that I should stop remembering the lessons of the past and try to persuade the population of Israel that because our national home had been broken into once, twice, three times, we should now move out and go elsewhere, instead of putting up iron bars on the windows and extra strong locks on the doors. Yes, I had complexes. They had started, if not in Kiev, then at the Évian Conference in 1938, and nothing that had happened to us since was conducive to lessening them. Even in Israel itself, there were people who thought – and said loudly – that the government wasn't doing 'enough' to find common ground with the Arabs, though they never managed to suggest anything that we hadn't tried ourselves.

There was also a constant uproar from a numerically small but exceedingly vocal segment of the population about such things as the government's decision, after the Six Day War, to allow a number of Jews to settle in Hebron, a town on the West Bank of the Jordan River (some 35 kilometres south of Jerusalem) in which, according to Jewish tradition, the biblical Patriarchs are buried and which was King David's capital before he moved it to Jerusalem. The Crusaders had expelled the Jews from Hebron, but during Ottoman rule in Palestine some Jews had returned there, and the town had had a Jewish community right up to the time when a terrible Arab massacre finally drove the surviving Jews out of the town in 1929. After 1948 the Jordanians wouldn't even let the Jews visit the holy Cave of Machpelah to pray at the Tomb of the Patriarchs. But Hebron remained holy to the Jews, and on Passover eve 1968, after it had come under Israeli administration, a group of young and militant orthodox Jews, defying the military ban on settlement in the West Bank, moved into the Hebron police compound and remained there without permission. There was no question but that they were behaving most improperly and in a manner that was very damaging to Israel's 'image'. The Arabs at once set up a great hue and cry about the 'Jewish annexation' of Hebron, and Israeli public opinion was very divided on the subject. On the one hand, the would-be settlers were obviously trying to create a *fait accompli* and force the Israeli government to make up its mind prematurely about the future of the West Bank and Jewish settlement there. On the other hand, though I

deplored the way in which they had taken the law into their own hands,
as though they were in the Wild West, I thought that the real issue
was not really what they had done or even how they had done it, but
something far more serious.

Was it logical, I asked myself and my colleagues, for the world
(including our own super-pious 'doves') to demand of a Jewish government that it pass legislation expressly forbidding Jews to settle anywhere
on earth? I didn't know any more than anyone else did exactly what
would happen to Hebron eventually. But let's suppose, I said, that one
day, please God, we will sign a peace treaty with Jordan and 'return'
Hebron. Would that mean that we would agree that no Jews would
ever be allowed to live there again? Obviously, no Israeli government
could ever obligate itself to a permanent banning of Jews from any
part of the Holy Land. And Hebron was not an ordinary market town;
it meant a lot to believing Jews.

We debated and argued and examined the pros and cons for months
and then, in 1970, we permitted the building of a limited number of
housing units for Jews in an area on the outskirts of Hebron that the
settlers named Kiryat Arba ('The Town of the Four', Hebron's other
Hebrew name) – and that particular storm died down. But other subsequent attempts at illegal settlements were more firmly dealt with –
however painful it was for the government to have to order Israeli
soldiers to drag Jews away from places in the West Bank in which they
wanted to settle. We did allow Jews to settle in certain spots in the administered territories, but only when such settlement was fully in
accordance with our political and military interests.

Another constant focus of international attention was the Christian
holy places both in the West Bank and in Jerusalem. So, needless to
say, I was very glad to be able to go to the Vatican in January 1973 when
I was received by Pope Paul VI in an eighty-minute audience. It was the
first time that a prime minister of Israel had been given an audience by
the pope, though, on his one-day visit to Israel in 1964 when he came to
the Holy Land as a pilgrim, the pontiff had met President Shazar, Eshkol
and virtually the entire Israeli cabinet. It had not been the happiest of
meetings. The pope had made it quite clear that his visit in no way
constituted full recognition by the Vatican of the State of Israel; he
had made Jordan rather than Israel his headquarters for three days,
and the parting message he had sent us from his plane was carefully
addressed to Tel Aviv, not Jerusalem.

The relations between the Vatican and the Zionist movement had always been delicate, ever since Theodor Herzl, who had been granted an audience by Pius x in 1904, had been told by the pope: 'We cannot prevent Jews from going to Jerusalem, but we could never sanction it . . . the Jews have not recognized our Lord; we cannot recognize the Jews.' Other popes had been friendlier. Sharett was received twice (once as Israel's foreign minister) by Pius xII. Pope John xxIII had been sympathetic and even warm to Israel, and we were invited to send a representative both to his funeral and to Paul vI's coronation. In 1969 Paul had received Abba Eban in an official audience, and our ambassadors to Rome always had good and fairly close contacts with various high-ranking Vatican personalities. Although the Vatican has recognized all the Arab states, recognition is still withheld from Israel; and the exact stand of the Vatican on the question of Jerusalem has still to be clarified. But it seems to me that the Vatican has indeed reconciled itself after all to the reality of the Jewish state.

The story of my audience with the Pope began not in Rome but in Paris. For years I have attended the annual meetings of the Socialist International (of which I am a vice-president) wherever they are held. In 1973 a socialist leadership meeting was to take place in Paris – about a month and a half before the French national elections – and, of course, I planned to go, as did the socialist heads of other governments, including Austria, Denmark, Finland and Sweden, as well as heads of parties that were in opposition. To everybody's amazement, Georges Pompidou promptly charged me with coming to Paris chiefly in order to sway 'the Jewish vote' (which is non-existent in France) in favour of the socialists. As a result of the subsequent uproar in France, the Socialist International – to which no one, unfortunately, pays much attention as a rule – got an enormous amount of publicity, and so did the French government's apparently uncontrollable hostility towards Israel. In any case, since I was going to France, our ambassador to Rome, Amiel Najjar, suggested that perhaps it would be a good time to take up the recommendation made on several occasions by friends of his at the Vatican that I meet with the pope. I said that I would be delighted to do so, and after a while we were told to request an audience for me. Within a few days, a letter addressed to me arrived at the embassy in Rome. It was from the *prefettura* of the Vatican and it read: 'Your Excellency. I have the honour of informing you that the Holy Father will receive you in audience on Monday, 16 January 1973.'

I was immensely impressed – it is impossible not to be – not only (or even mostly) by the Vatican, but by the pope himself, by the simplicity and graciousness of his manner and the penetrating gaze of his deep-set dark eyes. I think I would have been much more nervous about our talk if he hadn't started it by telling me that he found it hard to accept the fact that the Jews – who, of all people, should have been capable of mercy towards others because they had suffered so terribly themselves – had behaved so harshly in their own country. Well, that is the kind of talk that I can't bear, and particularly since it is simply not true that we have mistreated the Arabs in the administered terri-tories. There is still no death penalty in Israel, and the most we have ever done is jail terrorists, blown up the houses of Arabs who have gone on sheltering terrorists, despite repeated warnings, and sometimes, when we have had no alternative, even expelled Arabs who have openly incited and encouraged the terrorists. But I challenge anyone to cite chapter and verse about brutality or repression. I was very tempted to ask the pope what his sources of information were, since they were obviously so different from mine, but I didn't. Instead I said, and I could hear my own voice trembling a little with anger: 'Your Holiness, do you know what my own very earliest memory is? It is waiting for a pogrom in Kiev. Let me assure you that my people know all about real "harshness" and also that we learned all about real mercy when we were being led to the gas chambers of the Nazis.'

It may not have been a conventional way of talking to the pope, but I felt that I was speaking for all Jews everywhere, for those who were alive and for those who had perished while the Vatican maintained its neutrality in the Second World War. I had a sense of participating in a truly historic confrontation, and the pope and I stared at each other for a second. I think he was quite surprised by my words, but he didn't say anything. He just looked at me, right into my eyes, and I looked back at him in the same way. Then I went on to tell him, very respect-fully but very firmly and at some length, that now that we had a state of our own, we were through forever with being 'at the mercy' of others. 'This is truly an historic moment,' he said, as though he had read my mind.

Then we went on to talk about other matters, the status of Jerusalem and the Middle East in general. There would have to be special pro-visions for the holy places, and that, I gathered, could be taken up in 'the continuing dialogue' between the Church and ourselves, to which he enthusiastically referred. He also went out of his way to express his deep appreciation for the care that Israel had taken of the Christian holy places. For my part, I assured the pope that we would make whatever arrangements would be required of us for the administration not only of the Christian but also of the Moslem holy places in Israel, but that Jerusalem itself would remain the capital of Israel. I also asked the pope to use his influence to try to bring about a settlement in the Middle East and to do whatever he could to secure the return to Israel of the Israeli prisoners who had been in Egyptian and Syrian jails ever since the War of Attrition and whom the Arab states had refused to release.

After the first difficult minute or two, the atmosphere was very relaxed and cordial. We sat in the pope's private library on the second floor of the Apostolic Palace and conversed without any strain – all of which made the unpleasant episode that immediately followed my visit very hard to understand. Along with the customary statement that had been initially agreed upon, the pope's spokesman, Professor Alessandrini, issued an unusual 'verbal note' to the press. It was an obvious attempt to appease the Arab states about the implications of my meeting with the pope. Announcing that 'it was not a gesture of preference or exclusive treatment', Professor Alessandrini went on to say: 'The pope accepted the request of Mrs Meir because he considers it his duty not to let slip any opportunity to act in favour of peace, in defence of all religious interests, particularly of the weakest and most defenceless, and most of all of the Palestinian refugees.'

Najjar telephoned the Vatican at once and protested most strongly about the utterly misleading statement. And I didn't mince words either. I hadn't broken into the Vatican, and I told that to the journalists at the press conference I held that afternoon at the Israeli embassy in Rome. Regardless of whether or not the Vatican tried to play down the importance of my audience with Paul vi, 'it was greatly appreciated', I said, 'by me and by my people . . . In the quest for peace and good-will all over the world, there is a complete identity of views between the pope and the Jews.'

The next day, I got lovely gifts from the Vatican: a magnificent silver dove of peace with an inscription to the prime minister of Israel from the pope, a beautiful Bible and – as a gesture, I suspect, to make up for Professor Alessandrini's inaccurate 'note' – a catalogue of all the Hebrew publications in the Vatican Library. Lou and Simcha were also presented with a gift of a medallion. All in all, it was an intensely interesting and intensely meaningful experience for me, and I hope that, in a small way, it brought the Vatican closer to understanding Israel, Zionism and the feeling of Jews like me about themselves.

When I think back on the spring and summer of 1973, I must say
that I do so with very little pleasure. There were days when I fell into
bed at 2 in the morning and lay there, telling myself that I was crazy.
At seventy-five, I was working longer hours than I had ever worked
before and travelling more, both inside Israel and abroad, than was
good for anyone. Although I really did my very best to cut down on
appointments and delegate more work, it was much too late for me to
turn myself into another person. Regardless of all the good advice I was
given by the people closest to me – the children, Clara (who was now
coming fairly regularly from Bridgeport to stay with me for a few weeks
at a time), Simcha and Lou, there was only one way I could be
prime minister, if that was what I had to be, and that was by talking
to the people who wanted to talk to me and listening to the people
who had something to tell me.

I couldn't just go to the opening of a symposium being held by the
Teachers' Union, for instance, without preparing myself for it ahead of
time, and reading memos wasn't my idea of doing my homework
properly. Memos always left unanswered questions in my mind that
often turned out to be the most crucial questions. I was very worried
about the rate of dropouts from schools in the development towns and
thought that might be a topic for the speech that the teachers had
asked me to give. But I couldn't get the *exact* number of dropouts from
anyone – not from the chairman of the Teachers' Union, not from the
Ministry of Education – and that bothered me. How come no one
knew exactly how many children had dropped out of school in each
town? If teachers reported non-attendance to principals and principals
reported to the Ministry of Education, then why were the specific
figures unavailable? The more questions I asked, the more I understood about the dropout situation, about the way that schools and the
ministry operated, and, most of all, about life in the new towns and
the standards of teaching in them. And when I went to that symposium,
I had something to say, more questions to ask and a chance of getting
more answers that would eventually help me to suggest ways of doing
something about a problem that vitally concerned Israel's future.

I also wasn't about to make myself unavailable to anyone. When I
invited Jews who had just immigrated from the Soviet Union after
months, often years, of persecution and suffering and who wanted and
deserved to talk to the prime minister, I tried to spend as much time as
possible with them. And when party leaders came to talk to me in the
evening about urgent local political matters, I also didn't want to cut

these sessions short. Either I was the head of the Labour Party or I was not, but if I was, then I wasn't going to be a figurehead. Nor was I going to limit the amount of time I spent with delegations of oriental Jews or students or landlords or anyone else who wanted to tell me how badly (or sometimes even how well) I was conducting the affairs of the nation. There were also the constant visitors from abroad who felt themselves entitled – and rightly so – to spend half an hour with me. Some were American Jews who had given Israel the staunchest moral and financial support for years; some were European would-be investors whom we needed like lifeblood; others were people sent to me by other people whom I had met and who had helped us in the States, or in Africa, or in Latin America.

I liked seeing people and I felt that it was my duty to do so. But the more people I saw in my office or at home, the more papers and mail I had to plough through at night. I tried to get home for lunch whenever I could; sometimes there were official lunches, but sometimes I would just drive back home with Lou around two o'clock, eat quickly and be back at the office by three for another round of meetings and phone calls. If I was lucky, and no evening functions were planned, I would leave the office by seven or eight, go home, shower, change and have some supper. I had a maid, of course. She left as soon as she had done the lunch dishes (unless there was an official luncheon, in which case we got outside help), but she usually left something in the refrigerator for my evening meal. Occasionally I could stay home in the evenings and someone from the office would come over with piles of correspondence that had to be attended to. And sometimes, but very rarely indeed, I could just sit in an armchair and look at an old movie on television or fiddle around with little things, like tidying up my shelves, which always relaxed me.

Now and then, different members of the cabinet dropped in so that we could talk about specific problems in a relaxed and informal way. These were not official meetings, and no decisions were ever taken at them, of course. But I am convinced that they helped to make the process of government more efficient just because we could talk things out over a cup of coffee or a bite to eat around my kitchen table. Every two or three weeks, Pinchas Sapir, my minister of finance (and now chairman of the Jewish Agency) came over so that we could discuss in depth suggestions that he wanted to bring before the cabinet. Sapir is a man with an immense capacity for work and he is also Israel's most successful fund-raiser. When Sapir meets a Jew abroad, he says, 'How much money have you got?' And the funny thing is, the man tells him! One of his great preoccupations is the bettering of life – and in particular of education – in the development towns, for which he has done a great deal more than most people know. We always worked very well together, despite the fact that we were poles apart on a number of policy questions, and I personally couldn't have imagined heading a cabinet without him.

Another indispensable member of my cabinet was Yisrael Galili, a minister without portfolio, upon whom I relied very heavily for advice. Galili is not only a wise and unusually modest man, but he is also someone with a unique talent for getting to the heart of complicated issues and formulating things in the most lucid way possible. I suspect I shall go on asking Galili for his opinions on important matters for a long time.

Generally speaking, I was very fortunate in having good people around me: the director-general of my ministry, the late Yaacov Herzog, was among the most intellectually sophisticated men I have met. And no one could have asked for more devoted aides than Mordechai Gazit, Yisrael Lior, Eli Mizrachi and, of course, Simcha Dinitz and Lou.

One nice thing that happened in 1973 was that Sarah decided to take a year's leave of absence from the kibbutz and study English literature at the Hebrew University, which meant that I wasn't alone at night any more. But the penalty for that was that she and I would sit up until all hours talking, mostly about whether I should head the party list again and run for office (to the extent that one can 'run' for anything at 75!) in the elections that were scheduled to take place that autumn. I thought a great deal about retiring, but wherever I turned, I heard the same arguments that I had heard in 1969: the problem of my so-called succession was no less acute than the problem of Eshkol's succession had been; the three elements that made up the Labour Party were still very uneasy partners; the military situation – though it was fairly quiescent since the War of Attrition – was certainly liable to worsen at any time; my relationship with President Nixon was one of great rapport and not likely to be established quickly by anyone else; and so on and so forth. I loathed being the subject of endless speculation – will she or won't she? – but I couldn't honestly counter any of those arguments with effective arguments of my own, other than the fact that I felt I owed it to myself to retire. All through the spring the conversations went on with my colleagues in the party, followed avidly by the press, as though Israel had no other worries. In the end, I said: 'Alright. There is no point to dragging the decision out any longer, and there are other things to think about.' Later I often thought to myself bitterly that even if I had then refused to head the party list again, I would still have been prime minister in October 1973, because the elections were only due to take place in November.

In March, I visited Washington again. There had just been a most unfortunate incident that might have cast something of a cloud over my visit: the Israeli air force had shot down a Libyan Boeing 727 that had strayed over the Sinai Peninsula, and the lives of 106 people had been lost. It was one of those tragedies that can't be avoided when a nation has to stay on the alert, night and day, against terrorism. We had been warned that a possible suicide attack was being readied against us somewhere in Israel by terrorists who would try to land a plane loaded with explosives, and we were in no mood to take chances – though we would have done so if we had had even the slightest inkling that there were any passengers aboard that plane. But the pilot had ignored all our attempts to identify him, as was proven later when the 'black box' was found. Both President Nixon and the House Foreign Affairs Committee listened sympathetically to my explanation of what had happened and why, and in the ninety minutes that I spent with the president, he again assured me warmly that US aid to Israel would continue and that we would go on getting US backing for our demand for negotiations with our neighbours. But I was no less eager to explain our position to the nations of Europe, and when the president of the Council of Europe invited me to attend the meeting of the Council's Consultative Assembly in Strasbourg, I said I would be glad to come. This time, however, I would not go to Paris. I asked our ambassador only to notify the French Foreign Office that I would be visiting France and not in any way, directly or indirectly, to give the French the impression that I wanted to be invited to Paris. So I went directly to Strasbourg.

But just before I left Israel, I got some devastating news. Arab terrorists had succeeded in 'convincing' the Austrian government to shut down the Jewish Agency transit camp at Schonau Castle, near Vienna, which had served for a number of years as the indispensable half-way station for Jews leaving the Soviet Union en route to Israel. Before I go into the story of this surrender to blackmail and what I tried to do about it, let me say something about the function of Schonau. As most people probably know by now, those courageous Soviet Jews

who have dared to apply for an exit permit in order to immigrate to
Israel are usually forced to wait for it for years. And when it is granted,
there is no prior notice whatsoever – only the curt stipulation that its
recipient must leave the USSR within a week or, at most, ten days.
There have been exceptions, of course; some Jews have even been told
that if they want to go, they must clear out within a matter of hours.
But most of the time prospective emigrants are given a few days to put
all their personal affairs in order: arrange for those possessions that
they are allowed to send to Israel to be packed, cleared by customs and
dispatched, organize their own passage, give up their Soviet citizenship
and go through a whole host of other formalities while finding time to
say their goodbyes to people whom they will probably never see again
as long as they live. It is not the way that most emigrants leave their
countries; it is neither human nor decent; but it is the only way that
Jews can leave the Soviet Union, as though they are criminals who are
being deported.

The first stop for the trains that bring them into freedom, generally
via Prague, is a little railway crossing on the Czechoslovak–Austrian
frontier, where the Austrian authorities stamp the vital transit visas
that make it possible for the immigrants to enter the free world and
for the Jewish Agency officials in Austria, who welcome them into it,
to learn the number and names of the Jews aboard a particular train.
From the frontier, the trains – with their special compartment for the
Jewish immigrants – continue on to Vienna, where buses stand ready
to take the immigrants to the transit camp. Schonau, a large white
stucco *Schloss* rented to the Jewish Agency by an Austrian countess, was
much more, however, than just a place for the immigrants to rest and
realize that they were at last on their way to the Jewish state. It was a
place where the immigrants – confused and exhausted – could be given
information about Israel, be classified according to their professions and
prepared, if only very minimally, for the new life they were going to
lead in a new land.

No one stayed long in Schonau. The average immigrant family spent
only two or three days there before being bussed to the airport and to the
El Al planes that brought them, still weary but ecstatic, to us. I had
visited Schonau two years before and seen for myself the state of mind
and body in which those people had come from the Soviet Union,
and I knew the importance of that gateway to freedom. I also knew
that there was virtually no other way for the Jews to leave the Soviet
Union except through Austria, and I knew that for millions of

Russian Jews who were still there, Schonau was a symbol of liberty and hope.

But the Arab terrorists knew all this, too, and at the end of September 1973, two gunmen broke into one of those trains just as it crossed into Austria, kidnapped seven Russian Jews (including a seventy-one-year-old man, an ailing woman and a three-year-old child) and brazenly informed the Austrian government that unless it instantly put an end to the assistance it had given the Soviet Jewish immigrants and closed down Schonau, not only would the hostages be killed but there would be violent retaliation against Austria. To our astonishment and horror, the Austrian cabinet, led by Chancellor Bruno Kreisky, gave in at once, to the tune of loud rejoicing both from the gunmen (who were immediately whisked away to Libya) and from the entire Arab press, which could hardly contain its glee at what it called 'the successful commando blow to the movement of Russian Jews emigrating to Israel'.

I had known Kreisky for quite a long time and fairly well. He served for several years as the foreign minister of Austria, and we used to meet at the United Nations. He was also a socialist, and I had, in fact, seen him last at the Socialist International that had taken place in Vienna two years before. I remember that once I invited him to come to Israel and he began to hem and haw and generally look rather unhappy. 'I know exactly what you want to say,' I told him. 'You want to say that if you come to Israel, you'll have to go to Egypt and to the other Arab countries first. So go ahead. We don't mind in the least who goes where first, but do come and visit us.' I could see that he was very relieved that I had said it for him. 'Yes, I will come,' he said, and he did. As a Jew, Mr Kreisky had not displayed any interest in Israel, though in 1974 he was to visit us as the head of a delegation of European socialist leaders. There were many socialists in Austria, some Jews, some not, with whom we had a much closer relationship, but I wanted to talk to Kreisky himself and explain to him the full implications of closing Schonau and what it would do not only to Austria, but to the Jews of Russia. I told our ambassador in Vienna to ask Kreisky whether he would see me on my way to Strasbourg.

To be quite fair, I must note that although I don't believe there is ever a good enough excuse for knuckling under to terrorism, the Austrian decision was not altogether unreasonable. To begin with, Schonau had become far too well known, although we had all tried very hard to discourage visitors from going there and the press from writing about it too often, and there were rumours all the time that the terrorists would attack it. The Austrian security was very good indeed; the trains were met, the immigrants were escorted to Schonau; the castle itself was well guarded. The Austrians were extremely helpful in this regard and very efficient. But if Schonau were closed, then whatever other place was made available would also be held to ransom. I felt that if I could discuss it all with Kreisky, I might get him to change his mind. I waited very tensely for a reply; when it came, I learned that Kreisky couldn't see me on my way to Strasbourg, but would see me on my way back.

I had prepared an address for presentation at the Council of Europe meeting, in which I thanked the council and individual European parliaments and political parties for having raised their voices in the demand that Soviet Jewry be permitted to emigrate and touched upon a variety of other subjects, including the refusal of the Arab states to deal with us and the prospects, as we saw them, of Arab-Jewish co-existence. I had ended that address by appealing to the council to help enable the Middle East to 'emulate the model that the council itself has established', and my last words were to be a quotation from that great European statesman Jean Monnet, who once said: 'Peace depends not only on treaties and promises. It depends essentially on the creation of conditions which, if they do not change the nature of men, at least guide their behaviour towards each other in a peaceful direction.' I thought those words summed up better than any words of mine could have what it was that the State of Israel really wanted from the Arabs – and from the rest of the world.

But by the time I arrived in Strasbourg, it seemed idiotic to read out that speech. There were other more urgent things I had to say to the Council now.

'I have written a speech,' I said. 'I think you have it before you. But I have decided, at the last minute, not to place between you and me the paper on which my speech is written, especially in the context of what has happened in the course of the past two or three days.' And I went on to talk about the Austrian decision:

Having failed in Israel itself, the Arab organizations, aided by Arab governments, have taken their terror into Europe . . . I fully understand the feelings of a prime minister and other members of the government of a country who say 'We have nothing to do with this conflict. Why has our territory been chosen for these activities?' I also understand that such a government may reach the conclusion that the only way to free itself from this headache is to make its country out of bounds, either for the Jews (and then certainly for Israelis) or for the terrorists. It is a choice that every government must make these days . . . *But there can be no deals with terrorism.* What has happened in Vienna is that, for the first time, a government has come to an understanding, an agreement, with the terrorists. A basic principle of the freedom of movement of peoples has been put under question, at any rate for Jews, and this in itself is a great victory for terrorism and for terrorists.

Believe me, we are most grateful to the Austrian government for all that it has done for the tens of thousands of Jews who have gone through Austria from Poland, Rumania and the Soviet Union. But if it has decided that rather than do away with terrorism it will set terrorists free and give them whatever they ask for, then it will have raised the question of whether any country can permit itself to be involved in allowing Jews to use its soil for transit . . .

I stayed in Strasbourg for two days and attended the necessary luncheons and dinners, but my mind was fixed on Schonau all the time, and when I got to Vienna, I went straight to Kreisky's office. The prime minister listed for me all the reasons for his government's capitulation to the Arabs and asked why Austria should be the only country to have the problem of the Russian Jews? Why not the Dutch? They could let immigrants through also. I told him that I thought the Dutch were surely prepared to share this burden with him. But it didn't depend on them; it depended on the Russians. And the Russians had agreed to let the Jews out via Austria. Then Kreisky said something I really couldn't accept: 'You and I belong to two different worlds,' he told me. Under normal circumstances, there wouldn't have been any more for me to say, but I wasn't there for my own sake and I had to continue the conversation.

Kreisky was adamant about closing Schonau. 'I will never be responsible for any bloodshed on the soil of Austria,' he repeated. 'Other arrangements must be made.' 'But if you close Schonau,' I pleaded, 'you will be handing the Russians the perfect excuse for not letting the Jews go, because they will certainly say that if there is no possibility of transit, then they won't allow any emigrants to leave Russia.' 'Well,' Kreisky said, 'there isn't anything I can do about that. Let the Jews be picked up by your people just as soon as the trains arrive.' 'That is impossible,' I said, 'since we never know how many Jews are on each train. Anyhow, I don't think it is safe to have dozens of people waiting at the airport for an El Al plane to collect them.' But I could see that it was no use. Nothing I said would make any difference. Above all, Kreisky wanted to avoid more trouble with the Arabs. I thanked him for having received me and I left.

A press conference had been called so that both Kreisky and I could answer questions, but when we passed the room in which the press was waiting for us and Kreisky held the door open for me, I shook my head. 'No,' I said, 'I have nothing to say to the press. I don't want to come in.' I don't know to this day whether he spoke to the press alone or cancelled the conference; I only know that I felt as though my mouth were filled with ashes. *We* belonged to different worlds? The things that Kreisky had said to me just went round and round in my head. Of course, I had no idea what awaited me in Israel.

14   The Yom Kippur War

Of ALL THE EVENTS upon which I have touched in this book, none is so hard for me to write about as the war of October 1973, the Yom Kippur War. But it happened, and so it belongs here – not as a military account, because that I leave to others, but as a near disaster, a nightmare that I myself experienced and which will always be with me. I found myself in a position of ultimate responsibility at a time when the state faced the greatest threat it had known. Even as a personal story, there is still a great deal that cannot be told, and what I write is far from being definitive. But it is the truth as I felt and knew it in the course of that war, which was the fifth to be forced on Israel in the twenty-seven years that have passed since the state was founded.

There are two points I should like to make at once. The first is that we won the Yom Kippur War, and I am convinced that in their heart of hearts the political and military leaders of both Syria and Egypt know that they were defeated again, despite their initial gains. The other is that the world in general and Israel's enemies in particular should know that the circumstances which took the lives of the over 2,500 Israelis who were killed in the Yom Kippur War will never ever recur.

The war began on 6 October, but when I think about it now my mind goes back to May, when we received information about the reinforcement of Syrian and Egyptian troops on the borders. Our intelligence people thought that it was most unlikely that war would break out, but nonetheless we decided to treat the matter seriously. At that time, I went to GHQ myself. Both the minister of defence and the chief-of-staff, David Elazar, who is known throughout the country by his nickname, 'Dado', briefed me thoroughly on the armed forces' state of preparedness, and I was convinced that the army was ready for any contingency – even for full-scale war. Also my mind was put at rest about the question of a sufficiently early warning. Then, for whatever reason, the tension relaxed.

In September we started to receive information about a build-up of Syrian troops on the Golan Heights, and on the 13th of that month an air battle took place with the Syrians, which ended in the downing of thirteen Syrian MIGs. Despite this, 'our intelligence people were very reassuring: it was most unlikely, they said, that there would be any major Syrian reaction. But this time, the tension remained, and what's more, it had spread to the Egyptians. Still our intelligence assessment remained the same. The continued Syrian reinforcement of troops was caused, they explained, by the Syrians' fear that we would attack, and throughout the month, including on the eve of my departure to Europe, this explanation for the Syrian move was repeated again and again.

On Monday, 1 October, Yisrael Galili called me in Strasbourg. Among other things, he told me that he had talked to Dayan and that they both felt that as soon as I got back we should have a serious discussion about the situation in the Golan Heights. I told him that I would definitely return the next day and that we should meet the day after.

Late on Wednesday morning I met with Dayan, Allon, Galili, the commander of the air force, the chief-of-staff and, because the head of intelligence was sick that day, with the head of military intelligence research. Dayan opened the meeting, and the chief-of-staff and the head of intelligence research described the situation on both fronts in great detail. There were things that disturbed them, but the military evaluation was still that we were in no danger of facing a joint Syrian–Egyptian attack, and what's more that it was very unlikely that Syria would attack us alone. The build-up and movement of Egyptian forces in the south was probably due to the manoeuvres that were always held around this time of the year; and in the north, the bolstering and new deployment of forces was still explained as it had been before. The fact that several Syrian army units had been transferred only a week before from the Syrian–Jordanian border was interpreted as part of a recent détente between the two countries and as a Syrian gesture of goodwill towards Jordan. Nobody at the meeting thought that it was necessary to call up the reserves, and nobody thought that war was imminent. But it was decided to put a further discussion of the situation on the agenda for Sunday's cabinet meeting.

On Thursday, as usual, I went to Tel Aviv. For years, I had been spending Thursdays and Fridays in my Tel Aviv office, Saturdays at my house in Ramat Aviv and returning to Jerusalem either late Saturday evening or early Sunday morning and there seemed to be no reason for changing the pattern that week. In fact, it was a short week in any case, because *Yom Kippur* (the Day of Atonement) was to begin on Friday evening, and most people in Israel were taking a long weekend.

I suppose that by now, thanks in part to the war, even non-Jews who had never heard of *Yom Kippur* before know that this is the most solemn and the most sacred of all the days in the Jewish calender. It is the one day in the year that Jews throughout the world – even if they are not very pious – unite in some sort of observance. Believing Jews, totally abstaining from food, drink and work, spend *Yom Kippur* (which, like all Jewish holidays and the Sabbath itself, begins in the evening of one day and ends in the evening of the next) in the synagogue, praying and atoning for sins that they may have committed in the course of the past year. Other Jews, including those who do not actually fast, usually find their own individual way of marking *Yom Kippur*, by not going to work, by not eating in public and by going to synagogue, even if for only an hour or two, to hear the great opening prayer, *Kol Nidrei*, on the eve of *Yom Kippur* or listen to the ritual blowing of the *shofar*, the ram's horn, that closes the fast. But for most Jews everywhere, regardless of how they observe it, *Yom Kippur* is a day unlike any other.

In Israel, it is a day on which the country comes to a virtual standstill. For Jews, there are no newspapers, no television or radio broadcasts, no public transport, and all schools, shops, restaurants, cafés, and offices are closed for twenty-four hours. Since nothing, however, not even *Yom Kippur*, is as important to Jews as life itself, danger to life overrides everything, and all essential public services function, though many make do for those twenty-four hours with skeleton staffs. The most essential public service of all in Israel, unfortunately, is the army, but as many soldiers as possible are always given leave so that they can be at home with their families on this day.

On Friday, 5 October, we received a report that worried me. The families of the Russian advisers in Syria were packing up and leaving in a hurry. It reminded me of what had happened prior to the Six Day War, and I didn't like it at all. Why the haste? What did those Russian families know that we didn't know? Was it possible that they were being evacuated? In all the welter of information pouring into my office, that one little detail had taken root in my mind, and I couldn't shake myself free of it. But since no one around me seemed very perturbed about it, I tried not to become obsessive. Besides, intuition is a very tricky thing; sometimes it must be acted upon at once, but sometimes it is merely a symptom of anxiety and then it can be very misleading indeed.

I asked the minister of defence, the chief-of-staff and the head of intelligence whether they thought this piece of information was very important. No, it hadn't in any way changed their assessment of the situation. I was assured that we would get adequate warning of any real trouble, and anyway, sufficient reinforcements were being sent to the fronts to carry out any holding operation that might be required. Everything that was necessary had been done, and the army was placed on high alert, particularly the air force and the armoured corps. When he left me, the head of intelligence met Lou Kaddar in the corridor. Later, she told me that he had patted her shoulder, smiled and said: 'Don't worry. There won't be a war.' But I was worried, and further-more I couldn't understand his certainty that all was well. What if he were wrong? If there were even the slightest chance of war, we should at least call up the reserves. At any rate, I wanted a meeting at least of those cabinet ministers who would be spending the *Yom Kippur* weekend in Tel Aviv. It turned out that very few of them were around. I was reluctant to ask the two National Religious Party minis-ters who lived in Jerusalem to come to a meeting in Tel Aviv on the eve of *Yom Kippur*, and several other ministers had already left for their kibbutzim, which were all fairly far away. Still, nine ministers were in town, and I told my military secretary to schedule an emergency meet-ing for Friday noon.

We gathered in my Tel Aviv office. In addition to the cabinet mem-bers, the meeting was attended by the chief-of-staff and the head of intelligence. We heard all the reports again, including the one that concerned the rushed – and to me still inexplicable – departure of the Russian families from Syria, but again, no one seemed very alarmed. Nevertheless, I decided to speak my mind. 'Look,' I said, 'I have a terrible feeling that this has all happened before. It reminds me of 1967, when we were accused of massing troops against Syria, which is exactly what the Arab press is saying now. And I think that it all means something.' As a result, although as a rule a cabinet decision is required for a full-scale call-up, that Friday we passed a resolution, suggested by Galili, that if necessary, the minister of defence and I could do so by ourselves. I also said that we should get in touch with the Americans so that they could contact the Russians and tell them in no uncertain terms that the US was not in the mood for trouble. The meeting broke up, but I stayed on at the office for a while, thinking.

How could it be that I was still so terrified of war breaking out when the present chief-of-staff, two former chiefs-of-staff (Dayan and Chaim Bar-Lev, who was my minister of commerce and industry) and the head of intelligence were far from sure that it would? After all, they weren't just ordinary soldiers. They were all highly experienced generals, men who had fought and led other men in spectacularly victorious battles. Each one of them had an outstanding military record, and as for our intelligence services, they were known to be among the best in the world. Not only that, but foreign sources with whom we were in constant touch agreed absolutely with the assessment of our experts. So why was it that I was still so ill at ease? Was I perhaps talking myself into something? I couldn't answer my own questions.

Today I know what I should have done. I should have overcome my hesitations. I knew as well as anyone else what full-scale mobilization meant and how much money it would cost, and I also knew that only a few months before, in May, we had had an alert and the reserves had been called up, but nothing had happened. But I also understood that perhaps there had been no war in May exactly because the reserves had been called up. That Friday morning I should have listened to the warnings of my own heart and ordered a call-up. For me, that fact cannot and never will be erased, and there can be no consolation in anything that anyone else has to say or in all of the common-sense rationalizations with which my colleagues have tried to comfort me.

It doesn't matter what logic dictated. It matters only that I, who was so accustomed to making decisions – and who did make them throughout the war – failed to make that one decision. It isn't a question of feeling guilty. I, too, can rationalize and tell myself that in the face of such total certainty on the part of our military intelligence – and the almost equally total acceptance of its evaluations on the part of our foremost military men – it would have been unreasonable of me to have insisted on a call-up. But I know that I should have done so, and I shall live with that terrible knowledge for the rest of my life. I will never again be the person I was before the Yom Kippur War.

Then, however, I sat in the office, thinking and agonizing until I just couldn't sit there any more and I went home. Menachem and Aya had invited a few friends to drop in after dinner. Jews eat dinner early on the eve of *Yom Kippur* because traditionally it is their last meal for twenty-four hours, and by the time the stars are out the fast has begun. We sat down to eat, but I was very restless and had no appetite at all; and though they wanted me to stay on with their friends, I excused myself and went to bed. But I couldn't sleep.

It was a still, hot night and through the open window I could hear the voices of Menachem and Aya's friends talking quietly in the garden below. Once or twice the children's dog barked, but otherwise it was a typically silent *Yom Kippur* night. I lay awake for hours, unable to sleep. Eventually I must have dozed off. Then, at about 4 a.m., the phone next to my bed rang. It was my military secretary. Information had been received that the Egyptians and the Syrians would launch a joint attack on Israel 'late in the afternoon'. There was no doubt any more. The intelligence source was authoritative. I told Lior to ask Dayan, 'Dado', Allon and Galili to be in my office before 7 a.m. On the way there, I caught sight of an old man going to synagogue, his prayer shawl over his shoulders, holding the hand of a small child. They looked like symbols of Judaism itself, and I remember thinking sorrowfully that all over Israel young men were fasting in synagogues today and that it was from their prayers that they would soon be called to arms.

By eight o'clock the meeting began. Dayan and 'Dado' differed as to the scale of the call-up. The chief-of-staff recommended the mobilization of the entire air force and four divisions and said that if they were called up at once they could go into action the next day, that is, Sunday. Dayan, on the other hand, was in favour of calling up the air force and only two divisions (one for the north and one for the south), and he argued that if we had a full mobilization before a single shot was fired, the world would have an excuse for calling us the 'aggressors'. Besides, he thought that the air force plus two divisions could handle the situation, and if towards evening the situation worsened, we could always call up more within a few hours. 'That's my suggestion,' he said, 'but I won't resign if you decide against me.' 'My God,' I thought, '*I* have to decide which of them is right?' But what I said was that I had only one criterion: if there really was a war, then we had to be in the very best position possible. The call-up should be as Dado suggested. But, of course, it was the one day of the year that even our legendary ability to mobilize rapidly partly failed us.

'Dado' was in favour of a pre-emptive strike since it was clear that war was inevitable in any case. 'I want you to know,' he said, 'that our air force can be ready to strike at noon, but you must give me the green light now. If we can make that first strike, it will be greatly to our advantage.' But I had already made up my mind. 'Dado', I said, 'I know all the arguments in favour of a pre-emptive strike, but I am against it. We don't know now, any of us, what the future will hold, but there is always the possibility that we will need help, and if we strike first, we will get nothing from anyone. I would like to say yes because I know what it would mean, but with a heavy heart I am going to say no.' Then Dayan and 'Dado' went to their offices, and I told Simcha Dinitz (now our ambassador to Washington, who happened to be in Israel that week) to fly back to the States immediately and I called in Menachem Begin to tell him what was happening. I also asked for a cabinet meeting for noon and called the then US ambassador Kenneth Keating, and asked him to come and see me. I told him two things: that according to our intelligence, the attacks would start late in the afternoon and that we would not strike first. Maybe something could still be done to avert the war by US intervention with the Russians or maybe even directly with the Syrians and the Egyptians. At all events, we would not make a pre-emptive strike. I wanted him to know that and to relay that information as soon as possible to Washington. Ambassador Keating had been a very good friend to Israel for many years, both in the US Senate and in Israel itself. He was a man I liked and trusted, and on that dreadful morning I was grateful to him for his assistance and understanding.

When the cabinet met at noon, it heard a full description of the situation, including the decision to mobilize the reserves and also my decision regarding a pre-emptive strike. Nobody raised any objections whatsoever. Then, while we were meeting, my military secretary burst into the room with the news that the shooting had started, and almost at once we heard the wailing of the first air-raid sirens in Tel Aviv. The war had begun.

Not only had we not been warned in time, we were fighting on two fronts simultaneously and fighting enemies who had been preparing themselves for years to attack us. We were overwhelmingly outnumbered –

in guns, tanks, planes and men – and were at a severe psychological disadvantage. The shock wasn't only over the way in which the war had started, but also the fact that a number of our basic assumptions were proven wrong; the low probability of an attack in October, the certainty that we would get sufficient warning before any attack took place and the belief that we would be able to prevent the Egyptians from crossing the Suez Canal. The circumstances could not possibly have been worse. In the first two or three days of the war, only a thin line of brave young men stood between us and disaster. And no words of mine can ever express the indebtedness of the people of Israel to those boys on the Canal and on the Golan Heights. They fought, and fell, like lions, but at the start they had no chance.

What those days were like for me I shall not even try to describe. It is enough, I think, to say that I couldn't even cry when I was alone. But I was very rarely alone. I stayed in the office most of the time, though now and then I went to the War Room and sometimes Lou made me go home and lie down until the phone summoned me back. There were meetings all through the day and all through the night, incessantly interrupted by phone calls from Washington and bad news from the front. Plans were presented, analysed and debated. I couldn't bear to be away from the office for more than an hour at a time because Dayan, 'Dado', Foreign Office people and various ministers were constantly coming in either to report to me on the most recent developments or to ask my advice on various matters.

But even on the worst of those early days, when we already knew what losses we were sustaining, I had complete faith in our soldiers and officers, in the spirit of the Israel Defence Forces and their ability to face any challenge, and I never lost faith in our ultimate victory. I knew we would win sooner or later, but each report of the price we were paying in human lives was like a knife being turned in my heart, and I shall never forget the day when I listened to the most pessimistic prediction I had yet heard.

On the afternoon of 7 October, Dayan returned from one of his tours of the front and asked to see me at once. He told me that in his opinion the situation in the south was so bad that we should pull back substantially and establish a new defensive line. I listened to him in horror. Allon, Galili and my military secretary were in the room. Then I asked 'Dado' to come in too. He had another suggestion – that we should go on with the offensive in the south. He asked if he could go to the southern front to supervise things himself and for permission to make whatever decisions might have to be made on the spot. Dayan agreed and 'Dado' left. That night I called a cabinet meeting and got the ministers' approval for us to launch a counter-attack against the Egyptians on 8 October. When I was alone in the room, I closed my eyes and sat perfectly still for a minute. I think that if I hadn't learned, during all those years, how to be strong, I would have gone to pieces then. But I didn't.

The Canal had been crossed by the Egyptians and our forces in Sinai had been battered. The Syrians had penetrated in depth on the Golan Heights. On both fronts, the casualties were already very high. One burning question was whether at this point we should tell the nation how bad the situation really was, and I felt very strongly that we should wait for a while. The very least we could do for our soldiers, and for their families, was to keep the truth to ourselves for a few more days. Nonetheless, some kind of statement had to be made at once, so on that first day of the war I addressed the citizens of Israel. It was one of the most difficult assignments of my life because I knew that, for everyone's sake, I could not tell all the facts. Talking to a nation that had no idea yet of the terrible toll being taken in the north and in the south or of the peril that Israel faced until the reserves were fully mobilized and in action, I said:

We are in no doubt that we shall prevail. But we are also convinced that this renewal of Egyptian and Syrian aggression is an act of madness. We did our best to prevent the outbreak. We appealed to quarters with political influence to use it in order to frustrate this infamous move of the Egyptian and Syrian leaders. While there was still time we informed friendly countries of the confirmed information that we had of the plans for an offensive against Israel. We called on them to do their utmost to prevent war, but the Egyptian and Syrian attack had started.

On Sunday, Dayan came in to my office. He closed the door and stood in front of me. 'Do you want me to resign?' he asked. 'I am prepared to do so if you think I should. Unless I have your confidence, I can't go on.' I told him – and I have never regretted this – that he had to stay on as minister of defence. We decided to send Bar-Lev to the north for a personal assessment of the situation. Then we began our negotiations to get military aid from the US. Decisions had to be taken very quickly – and they had to be the right ones. There was no time nor any margin for mistakes.

By Wednesday, the fifth day of the war, we had pushed the Syrians back across the 1967 ceasefire line and begun our attack into Syria, while in Sinai the situation was sufficiently static for the cabinet to consider our crossing of the Canal. But what if our troops crossed and then were trapped? I also had to consider the possibilty that the war would not be a short one and that we might find ourselves without the planes, tanks and ammunition we needed. We needed those arms really desperately, and, in the beginning, they were slow in coming.

I talked to Dinitz in Washington at all hours of the day and the night. Where was the airlift? Why wasn't it under way yet? I remember calling him once at 3 a.m., Washington time, and he said, 'I can't speak to anyone now, Golda. It's much too early.' But I couldn't listen to reason. I knew that President Nixon had promised to help us, and I knew from my past experience with him that he would not let us down. Let me, at this point, repeat something that I have said often before (usually to the extreme annoyance of many of my American friends). However history judges Richard Nixon – and it is probable that the verdict will be very harsh – it must also be put on the record forever that he did not break a single one of the promises he made to us. So why was there a delay? 'I don't care what time it is,' I raged at Dinitz. 'Call Kissinger now. In the middle of the night. We need the help today because tomorrow it may be too late.'

The story has already been published of that delay, of the US Defence Department's initial reluctance to send military supplies to us in US planes and of the problems that arose when we feverishly shopped around for other planes – when all the time huge transports of Soviet aid were being brought by sea and air to Egypt and Syria and we were losing aircraft at a disturbing rate (not in air battles but to the Soviet missiles on both fronts). Each hour of waiting that passed was like a century for me, but there was no alternative other than to hold on tight and hope that the next hour would bring better news. I phoned Dinitz and told him that I was ready to fly to Washington incognito to meet with Nixon if he thought it could be arranged. 'Find out immediately,' I said, 'I want to go as soon as possible.' But it wasn't necessary. At last, Nixon himself ordered the giant C-5 Galaxies to be sent, and the first flight arrived on the ninth day of the war, on 14 October. The airlift was invaluable. It not only lifted our spirits, it also served to make the American position clear to the Soviet Union and it undoubtedly served to make our victory possible. When I heard that the planes had touched down in Lydda, I cried for the first time since the war had begun, though not for the last. That was also the day on which we published the first casualty list: 656 Israelis had already died in battle.

But even the Galaxies that brought us tanks, ammunition, clothing, medical supplies and air-to-air rockets couldn't bring all that was required. What about the planes? The Phantoms and Skyhawks had to be refuelled en route, so they were refuelled in the air. But they came – and so did the Galaxies that landed in Lydda, sometimes at the rate of one every fifteen minutes.

When it was all over, in the spring, the US colonel who had been in charge of the airlift came back to visit Israel with his wife, and they came to see me. They were lovely young people, filled with enthusiasm for the country and with admiration for our ground crews, who had learned, almost overnight, to use the special equipment for unloading those giants. I remember going out to Lydda once to watch the Galaxies come in. They looked like some kind of immense prehistoric flying monsters and I thought to myself: 'Thank God I was right to reject the idea of a pre-emptive strike! It might have saved lives in the beginning, but I am sure that we would not have had that airlift, which is now saving so many lives.'

In the meantime, 'Dado' shuttled from one front to the other. Bar-Lev returned from the north and we sent him to the south to straighten out the confusion that had arisen there because the generals on the spot had such critical differences of opinion about the tactics to be employed, and he was asked to stay there as long as necessary. On Wednesday he phoned me from Sinai. It was right after a colossal tank battle in which our forces had smashed the Egyptian armoured advance. He has a slow, very deliberate way of speaking and when I heard him say 'G-o-l-d-a, it will be all right. We are back to being ourselves and they are back to being themselves,' I knew that the tide had turned, though there were still bloody battles ahead in which hundreds of young men, and older ones too, lost their lives. It was not for nothing that people bitterly suggested later that this war should be known not as the Yom Kippur War but as the War of the Fathers and Sons, for all too often they fought side by side on both fronts.

For days I was tormented by the fear that a third front would be opened and that Jordan would join in the attack upon us. But apparently King Hussein had learned his lesson in the Six Day War and luckily his contribution to the Yom Kippur War was only one Jordanian armoured brigade sent to help the Syrians. But, by then, we were already attacking strategic targets deep inside Syria, and our artillery had come well within range of the suburbs of Damascus, so Hussein's tanks were not much use, after all.

On 15 October, the tenth day of the war, the Israel Defence Forces began their crossing of the Canal in order to establish a bridgehead on the other side. I spent that night in my office and thought that it would never end. The time for the actual crossing had been set, originally, for 7 p.m., and I decided to call a meeting of the cabinet an hour earlier so that I could inform the ministers of what was happening. Then I was told that the crossing had been delayed until nine o'clock, and we rescheduled the cabinet meeting for 8 p.m. But the crossing was postponed again, this time till ten o'clock, and then delayed once more because there was trouble with the bridge. In the meantime, however, the ministers had already come to my office, and they stayed there with me all that night, waiting for news about the operation. Every ten or fifteen minutes, someone would come in and say: 'It will be very soon now. Only another quarter of an hour.' That was how the night passed, in an agony of suspense. The paratroops had crossed on time, but the crossing by the infantry, artillery and tanks was held up by fierce fighting. I couldn't go home until I knew that the crossing had taken place.

The next day I addressed the Knesset. I was very tired but I spoke for forty minutes because I had a lot to say, though most of it didn't make pleasant hearing. But at least I could tell the Knesset that, as I was speaking a task force was already operating on the west bank of the Canal. I wanted also to make public our gratitude to the president and the people of America, and, equally clear, our rage at those governments, notably the French and British, that had chosen to impose an embargo on the shipment of arms to us when we were fighting for our very lives. And most of all, I wanted the world to know what would have happened to us had we withdrawn before the war to the pre-Six Day War lines of 1967 – the very same lines, incidentally, that had not prevented the Six Day War itself from breaking out, though no one seems to remember that.

I have never doubted for an instant that the true aim of the Arab states has always been, and still is, the total destruction of the State of Israel or that even if we had gone back far beyond the 1967 lines to some miniature enclave, they would not still have tried to eradicate it and us. Nor am I so naïve as to believe that speeches inevitably persuade everyone of everything. But on 16 October 1973, when Israel was still in such peril, I felt that it was my duty to remind the member-states of the United Nations and the Arabs just why it was that we had held on, so stubbornly – pending peace talks – to the territories we took in 1967. As I said to the Knesset that day,

> One needn't have a fertile imagination to realize what the situation of the State of Israel would have been if we had been on 4 June 1967 lines. Anyone who finds it difficult to visualize this nightmarish picture should direct his mind and attention to what happened on the northern front – on the Golan Heights – during the first days of the war. Syria's aspirations are not limited to a piece of land but to deploying their artillery batteries once again on the Golan Heights against the Galilee settlements, to setting up missile batteries against our aircraft, so as to provide cover for the break-through of their armies into the heart of Israel.
>
> Nor is a fertile imagination required to imagine the fate of the State of Israel had the Egyptian armies managed to overcome the Israel Defence Forces in the expanses of Sinai and to move in full force towards Israel's borders . . . War has been launched once more against our very existence as a state and a nation. The Arab rulers pretend that their objective is limited to reaching the lines of 4 June 1967, but we know their true objective: the total subjugation of the State of Israel. It is our duty to realize the truth; it is our duty to make it clear to all men of goodwill who tend to ignore it. We need to realize this truth in all its gravity, so that we may continue to mobilize from among ourselves and from the Jewish people all the resources necessary to overcome our enemies, to fight back until we have defeated our attackers.

Also, I wanted to put on record the culpability of the Soviet Union and to stress the evil role Russia was once again playing in the Middle East.

> The hand of the Soviet Union is obvious in the equipment, the tactics and the military doctrines that the Arab armies are trying to imitate and adopt. Above everything else, the Soviet Union's all-out support for Israel's enemies in the course of the war has been manifested in the airlift reaching our ene-mies' airfields and the ships calling at their ports. The Soviet planes and ships carry military equipment, including missiles of various types, and it may be assumed that the planes are also bringing in advisers and experts on opera-tional matters, as well as on equipment and armament.
>
> The Soviet airlift up to October 15 included: to Syria, 125 Antonov-12 planes; to Egypt, 42 Antonov-12 planes and 16 Antonov-22 planes; to Iraq, 17 Antonov-12 planes.
>
> Intelligence reports indicate that the Soviet Union has succeeded in involv-ing other countries of the Soviet bloc in the supply of aid to Egypt and Syria. Such conduct on the part of the USSR goes beyond the limits of unfriendly policy. It is a policy of irresponsibility not only towards Israel, but towards the Middle East and towards the world.

Then I returned to my office for what was perhaps my grimmest
duty, another of the many meetings I held with the distraught parents
of boys who were missing in battle. One of the most terrible aspects of
the Yom Kippur War was that for days we could not determine the
fate of soldiers who had failed to communicate in any way with their
families since the attacks began. Israel is a very small country, and its
army, as everyone knows, is a citizens' army, made up of a limited
standing force and of reserves. We have never fought far from our
own borders, and contact between our soldiers and their homes is
always closely maintained. But this war was already lasting longer than
any other war we had ever had to fight – with the exception of the
War of Independence – and we had been taken by surprise.

Reservists throughout the country had been called away from synagogue and their homes. In the rush, some had not even taken time to
look for dog-tags or been able to find their units. Reservists in the
armoured corps had joined improvised tank crews, jumped from one
burning tank to another and then from that, when it exploded, into a
third. And, of course, the war against us had been waged with terrifying weapons, the anti-tank missiles supplied to the Egyptians and
Syrians by the Russians which left tanks in flames and their crews so
badly burned that often identification was almost impossible. One of
the proudest traditions of the Israel Defence Forces is that our dead
and wounded are never left to the enemy; but in the first days of the
Yom Kippur War, there was often no alternative, and hundreds of
parents were now beside themselves with worry. 'Is he dead? If so,
where is his body? Is he a prisoner of war? If so, why doesn't anyone
know?'

I had been through this torment with the parents of boys taken prisoner in the War of Attrition, and there were days in the winter of 1973
when I could hardly bring myself to face yet another group of parents,
knowing that I had nothing to tell them and that the Egyptians and
Syrians had not only refused to give the Red Cross lists of captured
Israelis months after the ceasefire, but even to let our army chaplains
search the battlefields for our dead.

But how could I say no to parents and wives who thought that if they
reached *me*, I would, magically, have some sort of answer for them,
though I knew that in their hearts some of them blamed me for the war
and for our lack of preparedness. So I saw them all, and for the most
part they were very brave indeed. All they wanted from me was some
scrap of information; a fact or two, however bitter, that they could

cling to; something concrete to ease their pain. But for weeks, there was nothing I could say. After one such meeting with the parents, I thought of *their* parents in 1948, when 6,000 had fallen – 1 per cent of the entire *yishuv* killed in the course of eighteen months.

I spent dozens of hours with those poor parents, though all that I could tell them in the beginning was that we were doing whatever we could to find their boys and that we would not agree to any arrangement that did not include the return of prisoners. But how many prisoners were there? I don't think I ever wanted anything as desperately as I wanted those POW lists that were dangled in front of us so long and so cruelly. There is much for which I personally shall never forgive the Egyptians or the Syrians, but above all I shall never forgive them for withholding that information for so many days, out of sheer malice, and for trying to use the anguish of Israeli parents as a political trump card against us.

After the ceasefire and after the months of negotiations that led at last to the disengagement of troops on both fronts, when our prisoners finally returned from Syria and Egypt, the world at last learned for itself what we had already known for years: that amenities such as the Geneva Convention go by the board when Jews fall into the hands of Arabs – particularly into the hands of the Syrians – and perhaps our anxiety about our POWs was better understood. Often when I sat with those frantic parents, wives and sisters, listening to their plans for yet another petition or demonstration, and when all that I could tell them for weeks on end was that we were doing everything possible to get the lists, I thought to myself that torture by our enemies is worse than death.

By 19 October, the thirteenth day of the war, although the fighting had certainly not ended, Mr Kosygin had already made a rushed visit to Cairo. His 'clients' were obviously losing the war they had begun with his assistance, and it was therefore not only Egyptian 'face' that needed saving but also that of the Soviet Union itself. It was bad enough that the Egyptians hadn't managed to destroy the Israeli bridgehead on the west bank of the Canal, but worse that they now had to admit to their patron that the Israeli Defence Forces were entrenched west of the Canal, some 60 miles away from Cairo, in an area that soon became known in Israel as 'Africa'. As for the situation of the Soviet Union's other protégé, Syria, it was even graver. That being the case, the Russians did what they have always done: they began a full-scale campaign for a quick ceasefire. Never mind who started the war and never mind who lost it. The important thing was to get the Arabs out of the mess that they had got themselves into and to rescue the Egyptian and Syrian forces from total defeat.

But although we had neither wanted nor started the Yom Kippur War, we had fought and won it, and we had a war aim of our own – peace. For once, we were not going to bury our dead quietly, looking on while the Arabs and their supporters were solacing themselves at the United Nations for their humiliation. This time, the Arabs were going to have to meet us, not only on battlefields but at the negotiating table, and together with us find a solution to a problem that had taken thousands of young lives – theirs and ours – over the past three decades. For years we had been shouting 'peace' and hearing the echo 'war' come back from the other side. For years we not only saw our sons killed but we had tolerated a situation so grotesque that it is almost unbelievable: the only time that Arab states were prepared to recognize the existence of the State of Israel was when they attacked it in order to wipe it out.

I remember driving back from the office through Tel Aviv's blacked-out streets on one of those nights when the Brezhnev–Kissinger talks about a ceasefire were going on in Moscow and taking a silent oath that, to the extent that it depended in any way at all on me, this war would end in a peace treaty obliterating, for all time, the famous three 'noes' of the Arabs, declared in Khartoum after the Six Day War, when their response to our plea that we sit down with them and negotiate was no recognition, no negotiation, no peace! I looked at the dark windows of the houses I passed and wondered behind which of them families were sitting *shiva* (the traditional first week of mourning) and behind which other families were trying to carry on as usual, though there was still no answer to the question: where is he? Dead somewhere in Sinai, dead on the Golan Heights or a prisoner of war? That night I swore that I would do whatever lay in my power to bring about the peace which the Arab people needed no less than we did and which could be secured only in one way – by negotiation.

I had held a press conference a few days before, on 13 October, and a journalist had asked me then if Israel would agree to a ceasefire on the basis of the lines that had existed on 5 October, one day before the Arab attack.

'There is no sense whatsoever,' I had answered, 'in speculating on what Israel will or will not agree to as long as our neighbours to the south and our neighbours to the north have still not indicated any desire to stop the fighting. When we come to a proposition for a cease-fire, we will consider it very seriously and decide, because we wish to end this war as quickly as possible.'

'But,' I had added, 'although we are a very small people and there is no comparison between the numbers in our army and those in any of the countries fighting us, and although we do not have the wealth of arms and ammunition they have, we do have two things that give us an advantage over them – our hatred for war and for death.'

Now that we were about to be placed under extreme pressure regarding a ceasefire, I felt more strongly than ever that we must make no substantive concession of any sort that did not include direct negotiations – at any time or in any place that the Arabs chose. Not that I made light of the oil embargo with which Saudi Arabia, Libya, Kuwait and other enlightened Arab states were holding the West, including the United States, to ransom; but a limit had to be set as to how accommodating we were going to be.

In the final analysis, to put it bluntly, the fate of small countries always rests with the super powers, and they always have their own interests to guard. We would have liked the call for a ceasefire to have been postponed for a few more days so that the defeat of the Egyptian and Syrian armies would be even more conclusive than it was, and on 21 October there was every reason to believe that, given just a little more time, this would have happened. North of Ismalia, we were pressing hard on the Egyptian Second Army. South of Suez, we were completing the encirclement of the Egyptian Third Army. On the Golan Heights, the Syrian positions on Mount Hermon had fallen to our forces. We had complete supremacy on both fronts and thousands of prisoners. But Sadat, of course, was in a far stronger position than we were diplomatically, and the bait he held out to the United States was very tempting; its re-entry into the Middle East plus the removal of the oil embargo. Nor was the Soviet Union without its own means of persuasion. The stakes in Moscow were very high indeed. So I was not at all surprised when, early on the morning of 22 October, the Security Council, meeting in an emergency session, predictably enough passed a resolution calling for a ceasefire to go into effect within twelve hours.

There was no question but that Resolution 338, passed with such indecent speed, was intended to avert the total destruction of the Egyptian and Syrian forces by us, though the pill was sugar coated, to some extent. The resolution called for 'negotiations to start between the parties concerned under appropriate auspices aimed at establishing a just and durable peace in the Middle East,' but it did not spell out how this would be done. The US secretary of state flew from Moscow to Jerusalem to convince me that we ought to accept the ceasefire, and we announced that we would do so. But the Syrians did not accept it at all, and although the Egyptians declared their acceptance, they did not stop shooting on 22 October. The fighting went on, and we completed the encirclement of the Third Army and gained control of parts of the city of Suez.

On 23 October I made a statement in the Knesset about the cease-fire. I wanted the people of Israel to know that we had not accepted it out of military weakness, nor had we asked for it. If the Egyptians did not conform to it, I said, we would certainly not remain silent. Our position on both fronts was better than it had been when the war broke out. True, Egypt held a narrow strip on the east bank of the Suez Canal, but the Israel Defence Forces sat firmly on a large section of the Canal's west bank, and in the north, on the Golan Heights, we had occupied all of the territory that had been under our control before the war and moved into a salient in Syria. Nonetheless, I said, and I meant every word with all my heart, 'Israel wants peace negotiations to start immediately and concurrently with the ceasefire. It can display the inner strength necessary to bring about an honourable peace within secure borders.' But unless and until the Egyptians and Syrians felt the same way and acted accordingly, these would, of course, remain just words.

The war entered its nineteenth day with a new crisis. Knowing that the request had no chance of being accepted by us, Sadat asked that a Soviet–US force be entrusted with supervising the ceasefire, and the Russians themselves made active preparations to step into that area. The story of the subsequent US alert is not for me to tell. There is only one thing that I wish to say about it. I know that in the United States at that time many people assumed that the alert was 'invented' by President Nixon in order to divert attention from the Watergate problem, but I didn't believe that then and I do not believe it now. I have never claimed to be unusually perceptive about people, but I think that at this stage of my life I can probably tell when someone speaks with true conviction.

One of my most vivid recollections of President Nixon is a conversation we had in Washington at the time that two US diplomats were murdered by terrorists in Khartoum. The evening before they were killed, I was dining at the White House. Before we went into dinner, President Nixon, Mrs Nixon, Yitzhak Rabin (then our ambassador to the United States) and I stood talking about what was happening in Khartoum, and President Nixon said to me very quietly, 'You must know, Mrs Meir, that I will never give in to blackmail. Never. If I compromise with the terrorists now, I shall be risking the lives of many more men in the future.' He was as good as his word. Then, on his visit to Israel in 1974 – when we ourselves had just been through the unspeakable outrage of the slaughter of children by terrorists at Ma'alot – Nixon returned to the subject. 'I was brought up,' he told me when he visited me at my home in Jerusalem, 'to abhor capital punishment. I come from a Quaker background. But terrorists cannot be dealt with in any other way. You must never give in to blackmail.'

I was absolutely sure, on both occasions, that the man speaking to me – without the benefit of press or TV cameras – spoke with complete sincerity, and I am still sure that President Nixon ordered the US alert on 24 October 1973 because, détente or no détente, he was not about to give in to Soviet blackmail. It was, I think, a dangerous decision, a courageous decision and a correct decision.

But it brought about an escalation of the crisis, and someone had to pay to bring about a relaxation of tension. The price demanded, needless to say from Israel, included our agreeing to permit supplies to reach the encircled Egyptian Third Army and to accept a second ceasefire that was to go into effect under the supervision of a UN force. The demand that we feed the Third Army, give it water and generally help its 20,000 soldiers to recover from their defeat was not, in any way, a matter of humanitarianism. We would gladly have given them all this had the Egyptians been willing to lay down their arms and go home. But this was exactly what President Sadat wanted to avoid. He was desperately anxious not to make public within Egypt the fact that Israel had prevailed in yet another attack upon her – the more so since for a few days in October the Egyptians were intoxicated by their apparent victory over us. So once again there was the standard concern for the tender feelings of the Arab aggressor, rather than for those of the victims of Arab aggression, and we were urged to compromise in the name of 'world peace'.

'At least,' I told the cabinet that week, 'let's call things by their right name. Black is black and white is white. There is only one country to which we can turn and sometimes we have to give in to it – even when we know we shouldn't. But it is the only real friend we have, and a very powerful one. We don't have to say yes to everything, but let's call things by their proper name. There is nothing to be ashamed of when a small country like Israel, in this situation, has to give in sometimes to the United States. And when we do say yes, let's, for God's sake, not pretend that it is otherwise and that black is white.'

But we didn't agree to everything. We had minimum demands of our own, which I had listed in the Knesset on 23 October as follows:

It is our intention to clarify and ensure, *inter alia*, that the ceasefire shall be binding upon all the regular forces stationed in the territory of a state accepting the ceasefire, including the forces of foreign states, such as the armies of Iraq and Jordan in Syria and also forces sent by other Arab states which took part in the hostilities.

The ceasefire shall also be binding upon irregular forces acting against Israel from the area of the states accepting the ceasefire.

The ceasefire shall assure the prevention of a blockade or interference with free navigation, including oil tankers in the Bab El Mandeb Straits on their way to Eilat.

It shall ensure that the interpretation of the term referring to 'negotiations between the parties' is direct negotiations and, naturally, it must be assured that the procedures, the drawing up of maps and the subject of ceasefire supervision shall be determined by agreement.

A subject of great importance . . . is the release of prisoners. The government of Israel has decided to demand an immediate exchange of prisoners. We have discussed this with the government of the United States, which was one of the initiators of the ceasefire.

There was nothing new in the list, nothing untoward and nothing that was not – by any criteria – our due.

At this point, the outstanding personality in the Middle East became not President Sadat, or President Assad, or King Feisal or even Mrs Meir. It was the US secretary of state, Dr Henry Kissinger, whose efforts on behalf of peace in the area can only be termed super-human. My own relationship with Henry Kissinger had its ups and downs. At times it became very complicated, and at times I know I annoyed and perhaps even angered him – and vice versa. But I admired his intellectual gifts, his patience and his perseverance were always limitless, and in the end we became good friends. I met and spent time in Israel with his wife, too, and liked and admired her immensely. I think that possibly one of the most impressive of Kissinger's many impressive qualities is his fantastic capacity for dealing with the minutest details of whatever problems he undertakes to solve. He told me once that two years ago he had never heard of a place called Kuneitra. But when he became involved in negotiating the disengagement of the Syrian and Israeli forces on the Golan Heights, there wasn't a road, a house or even a tree there about which he didn't know everything there was to know. As I said to him then, 'With the exception of the former generals who are now members of the Israeli cabinet, I don't think we have a single minister who knows as much about Kuneitra as you do.'

When he first started on the long and rocky road that was to lead to the disengagement of forces on the Golan Heights, and we said that we could not give up certain positions on the hills near Kuneitra because to do so would mean endangering the Israeli settlement below, he was very sceptical. 'You talk about those hills as though they were the Alps or the Himalayas,' he said to me. 'I've been to the Golan Heights and I couldn't see any Alps there.' But, as he always did, he listened very attentively, learned every detail of the topography for himself and when he was quite satisfied that we were making sense, he was prepared to spend days upon days persuading Assad that on such and such a point the Syrians must give way. And in the end, they did. But all the time, Kissinger went back and forth as though he had never heard of the word 'fatigue'.

Several times, the negotiations with the Syrians were almost broken off and Kissinger was already writing out drafts of statements for them and for us so that at least it could be said that the negotiations would only be postponed, not terminated altogether. Then, on the last day, he came to us with yet another new demand from Assad and we said, 'No. Not this. *This* is unacceptable.' So Kissinger said, 'Alright. Then this is the end. Sisco will go to Damascus today with instructions to say that there will be "no more negotiations" and that we suggest a joint communiqué be issued.' That afternoon, Kissinger came in to see me – he was supposed to leave at night – and said again, 'Well, this is the end.' Then he looked at me and said, 'Do you think perhaps I should go to Damascus instead of Sisco?' 'I didn't dare ask it of you,' I said. 'You told me that you would never meet with Gromyko in Damascus, and that is exactly where Gromyko is right now.' Kissinger thought for a minute and then said, 'Yes, I must see him, even if it's just a brief courtesy call. What do you think? I'll do what you suggest.' So I said, 'Look, I know one thing. If you yourself go, there is some chance that you will make it this time. Otherwise, there is no chance at all.' Joseph Sisco, who was in the room with us, nodded his head and said 'I agree absolutely.' 'O.K.,' said Kissinger, 'I'll go. Maybe I can do something after all.' And he went at once.

He came back to Israel at about 1.30 a.m. and sent a message from his plane to say that he wanted us to meet that night, at 2.30 in the morning. He turned up, as fresh as though he had spent the past month in a summer resort, though everyone else around him was wilting. He bounced in and said, 'It's alright. That's it. We've done it.' Of course, even with that really brilliant mind and with that astounding capacity for hard work, if Kissinger had been the foreign minister of Gabon, he wouldn't have gotten far with the Syrians, but he had everything: intelligence, diligence, stamina *and* the fact that he represented the greatest power in the world, which made for a very effective combination indeed.

As to his being Jewish, I don't think it either aided or hindered him in all those months of negotiation. But if he was emotionally involved with us, such an involvement never reflected itself, for one moment, in anything he said to us or did on our behalf. The first time he went to Saudi Arabia, he was treated to a long lecture by Feisal on 'Communists, Israelis and Jews.' Feisal's theory – which he didn't hesitate to explain in detail to Kissinger – was that the Jews had created the communist movement in order to conquer the world. Part of the world was already theirs, but in that part which the Jews couldn't conquer, they placed Jews in important governmental positions. Then he continued, 'Did you know that Golda Meir was born in Kiev?' 'Yes,' Kissinger replied. 'Doesn't that mean anything to you?' 'No,' said Kissinger, 'not necessarily.' 'Kiev, Russia, Communism, that's the formula,' declared Feisal. Afterwards, Feisal had tried to give him the *Protocols of the Elders of Zion*, that notorious czarist Russian forgery, as a present, but, of course, he didn't accept it.

I had one or two very difficult conversations with Kissinger regarding the Soviet and Egyptian allegations that we had violated the cease-fire. Kissinger apparently was inclined to believe this, and at one point Dinitz called from Washington to implore me to give Kissinger my personal assurance that we had done no such thing. All that week there had been an exchange of messages between us in which President Nixon and Kissinger had asked us to yield – first on one thing, then another, then on a third – and while I understood the US position in regard to the Soviet Union only too well, I found this stream of requests very disturbing. I wrote a letter to Kissinger asking him to tell us everything he wanted all at once, so that we could meet and make some decisions ourselves, rather than get a new request every few hours. So when Dinitz called in such a state, I decided to pick up the phone and talk to Kissinger, rather than send yet another letter. I said 'You can say anything you want about us and do anything you want, but we are *not* liars. The allegations are *not* true.'

On 31 October, I flew to Washington to try to straighten out the rather strained relationship that had come into being with Washington and to explain, in person, exactly why some of the demands being made of us were not only unfair but unacceptable. The day before, I had gone to 'Africa' myself with Dayan and 'Dado' to visit the commanders there, get their explanations about the terrain and spend some time with the troops. We made three stops at the front, and I must say that the soldiers were all rather surprised to see me in the middle of the desert, and I myself had certainly never expected to be answering questions showered at me by Israeli boys on Egyptian territory. I spoke to large gatherings of soldiers once deep underground, once in the sand outside a tent, and once in a battered Egyptian customs house at Suez. Most of the boys' questions had to do, naturally, with the ceasefire. Why had we allowed supplies to be brought to the Third Army? Why had we agreed to a premature ceasefire? Where were our prisoners of war? I did my best to explain the facts of political life to them, and later I flew to the Golan Heights, and had the same conversations there.

I also had questions that weren't answered to my satisfaction. I was still enraged over the refusal of my socialist comrades in Europe to let the Phantoms and Skyhawks land for refuelling as part of the airlift operation. One day, weeks after the war, I phoned Willy Brandt, who is much respected in the Socialist International, and said: 'I have no demands to make of anyone, but I want to talk to my friends. For my own good, I need to know what possible meaning socialism can have when not a single socialist country in all of Europe was prepared to come to the aid of the only democratic nation in the Middle East. Is it possible that democracy and fraternity do not apply in our case? Anyhow, I want to hear for myself, with my own ears, what it was that kept the heads of these socialist governments from helping us.'

The leadership meeting of the Socialist International was called in London and everyone came. Such meetings consist of the heads of socialist parties, those in government and those that are in parliamentary opposition. On that occasion, since I had asked that the meeting be called, I opened it. I told my fellow-socialists exactly what the situation had been, how we were taken by surprise, fooled by our own wishful thinking into believing the interpretation we were given of our intelligence reports, and how we had won the war. But it had been touch and go for days. Then I said: 'I just want to understand, in the light of this, what socialism is really about today. Here you are, all of you. Not one inch of your territory was put at our disposal for refuelling the planes that saved us from destruction. Now, suppose Richard Nixon had said: 'I am sorry but since we have nowhere to refuel in Europe, we just can't do anything for you, after all.' What would all of you have done then? You know us and who we are. We are all old comrades, long-standing friends. What did you think? On what grounds did you make your decisions not to let those planes refuel? Believe me, I am the last person to belittle the fact that we are only one tiny Jewish state and that there are over twenty Arab states with vast territories, endless oil and billions of dollars. But what I want to know from you today is whether these things are decisive factors in socialist thinking too?'

When I got through, the chairman asked if anybody wanted to speak. But nobody did. Then someone behind me – I didn't want to turn my head and look at him because I didn't want to embarrass him – said, very clearly: 'Of course they can't talk. Their throats are choked with oil.' And although there was a discussion, there wasn't really any more to say. It had all been said by that man whose face I never saw.

In Washington, I spent an hour and a half with President Nixon. Afterwards, the press wanted to know whether Israel was being pressured to make further concessions to the Arabs. I assured them that there had been no pressure. 'If so, Madam Prime Minister,' said one of the reporters, 'then why did you come to Washington?' 'Just to find out that there is no pressure,' I said. 'That in itself was worthwhile!'

The focal point of my talks with Kissinger had to do with the cease-fire lines in the south and they were not easy or pleasant talks, but then we were not discussing easy matters. I had brought a six-point proposal, and I remember that Kissinger and I sat up practically all of one night at Blair House, where I was staying. At one stage I said to him, 'You know, all we have, really, is our spirit. What you are asking me to do is to go home and help destroy that spirit, and then no aid will be necessary at all.'

The text of the agreement between Israel and Egypt was signed

on 11 November 1973 at Kilometre 101 of the Cairo–Suez road by
Israel's General Aharon Yariv and Egypt's General Abdel Gamasy. It
read:

1. Egypt and Israel agree to observe scrupulously the ceasefire called for by
   the UN Security Council.
2. Both sides agree that discussions between them will begin immediately to
   settle the question of the return to the 22 October positions in the framework of agreement on the disengagement and separation of forces under
   the auspices of the United Nations.
3. The town of Suez will receive daily supplies of food, water and medicine.
   All wounded civilians in the town of Suez will be evacuated.
4. There shall be no impediment to the movement of non-military supplies
   to the east bank.
5. The Israeli checkpoints on the Cairo–Suez road will be replaced by UN
   checkpoints. At the Suez end of the road, Israeli officers can participate
   with the UN to supervise the non-military nature of the cargo at the bank
   of the Canal.
6. As soon as the UN checkpoints are established on the Cairo–Suez road,
   there will be an exchange of all POWs, including wounded.

For the first time in a quarter of a century, there was direct, simple,
personal contact between Israelis and Egyptians. They sat in tents
together, hammered out details of the disengagement and shook hands.
And our prisoners of war came back from Egypt, those who had been captured in the War of Attrition and those taken in the Yom Kippur War.
Miraculously, they returned without a scratch on their spirits, despite
everything they had gone through, though some of them wept like
babies when we met. They even brought presents with them, things
they made in jail, including a blue-and-white Star of David which
they had knitted themselves and which had served as their flag during
the long imprisonment. 'Now that our "unit" has been disbanded,' a
group of young officers told me, 'we would like you to have it.' So I
framed it and it now hangs on my living-room wall.

But we still knew nothing about our POWs in Syria, and almost every
day there were military funerals for boys killed in Sinai whose charred
bodies had only now been found in the sand, identified and brought to
burial. Worst of all, despite the growing feeling that perhaps this time
the disengagement would grow into a real peace, the general mood in
Israel was very black. From all sections of the population there came
demands that the government resign, accusations that the army's poor
state of preparedness was the result of faulty leadership, of complacency

and of a total lack of communication between the government and the people.

A number of protest movements arose. They were different in emphasis and they had different programmes, but they shared a demand for change. And they included reservists who often expressed themselves hastily and sometimes even in a way that was painful for me. I disagreed with much of what they had to say about the past, but some of their criticism was justified. At all events I had to hear what they had to say, and I met with many of the young people from these movements. I tried to make it easy for them to talk to me, and I came away with the feeling that they were often surprised by the difference between the woman who listened to them so attentively and the image they had of me. In that atmosphere charged by suspicion and accusation, I think they were often equally surprised by what I had to say to them.

Much of the outcry was genuine. Most of it, in fact, was a natural expression of outrage over the fatal series of mishaps that had taken place. It was not just my resignation or Dayan's that was being called for in that storm of protest: it was a call to eliminate from the scene everyone who could possibly be held responsible for what had happened and to start all over again with new people, younger people, people who were not tainted by the charge of having led the nation astray. It was an extreme reaction to the extreme situation we were in, and therefore, though it was very painful, it was understandable. But part of the outburst was vicious, and some of it was demagoguery, pure and simple, and the making of political capital by the opposition over a national tragedy.

At the first political debate in the Knesset after the war, I listened to speeches by the opposition, including Menachem Begin and Shmuel Tamir, which tore me apart. They were so full of rhetoric and theatricality that I couldn't stand it, and when I got up to close the debate, I told them that the nature of their addresses was such that I was not going to reply. 'I just want to say one thing,' I said. 'I want to quote a very dear friend of mine, an American Labour-Zionist, who once attended a debate on some very serious matter – though it wasn't nearly as serious as what we are talking about here and now – and a man got up to speak. He spoke so effortlessly and so easily that all that my friend could say was "If only he had stammered or hesitated occasionally"' That is exactly how I felt about the flowing rhetoric in the Knesset. Begin and Tamir were talking about a near catastrophe, about men who had been killed or crippled, about terrible things, but they spoke smoothly, without as much as a pause, and I was disgusted.

The centre of the storm was Moshe Dayan. The first open request for his resignation, as far as I can remember, was made by another minister in my cabinet, Ya'akov Shimshon Shapiro, the minister of justice. I shall never get over my anger with him for having chosen to make this demand at the height of the crisis that preceded the second ceasefire and for having made it at a meeting, where he knew it would be picked up by the press. As if that weren't enough, I was told that he had walked around the Knesset restaurant going from one group to another to report on what he had done. So I asked him to come and see me. He came to my office and said, 'Since I know you will not ask Dayan to go, I have come to offer my resignation.' I said that I had only two questions. I wouldn't ask him to stay, because I thought that he had made it impossible for me to do so. But I wanted to know, first of all, why he had picked that particular day, and he replied: 'Well, because today is the day of the ceasefire.' 'Is that so?' I said. 'I have news for you. There is still fighting going on today. Some of our men have been killed, others have been wounded. It is no day at all, in fact, for you to have made this kind of demand of another minister. And, secondly, why don't you ask *me* to resign? I am prime minister.' To this, Shapiro only said, 'You are not responsible. You are not the minister of defence.'

Afterwards Dayan came to my office and once again asked: 'Do you want me to resign? I am prepared to do so.' Once again I said no. I knew that an official commission of enquiry would have to be formed soon – as it was under the chairmanship of Supreme Court President Shimon Agranat on 18 November – and certainly until it completed its work and submitted its findings, the principle of collective cabinet responsibility still held and was at least as important as that of ministerial responsibility. The one thing that Israel did not need at that point was a cabinet crisis. Anyhow, we had rescheduled the elections from their original 31 October date to 31 December, and the nation would be able to give adequate and effective vent to its feelings then. So although I myself was tremendously tempted to resign, I thought I ought to hold on for a little longer – and so should Dayan.

Of all the members of the cabinet, Dayan was, of course, the most controversial and probably the most complicated. He is, and always has been, a man who elicits very strong responses from the public. Naturally, he has his faults and, like his virtues, they are not small ones. One of the things of which I am most proud, to be quite frank, is that

for over five years I kept together a cabinet that included not only
Dayan but also a number of men who greatly disliked and resented him.
But from the start, I had a good idea of the problems I was likely to
face in this respect. I had known Dayan for years, and I knew that he
had opposed my becoming prime minister when Eshkol died. The only
way in which I could operate, therefore, was to take whatever stands
I would have to take on the essence of each and every issue, and to
prove to the cabinet – and to Dayan himself – that I was not in the
habit of evaluating propositions according to who fathered them.

To his credit, I must say that when I did not support Dayan in
something, he always took it very well, although he doesn't work
easily with people and is used to getting his own way. In the end, we
became good friends, and there was not a single occasion when I could
complain of any disloyalty on his part. Not once. Even on military
matters, he would always come – with the chief-of-staff – to talk to me
first. Sometimes I said to him, 'I won't vote in favour of this, but you
are free to take your proposal to the cabinet.' But if I didn't go along
with one of his ideas, he never took it any further. Considering Dayan's
reputation for not being able to function as part of a team – and mine
for not being able to compromise easily – I think that on the whole
we did very well.

It is also not true that he is a hard man. I saw him come back shattered from those agonizing funerals following the war, when children
were pushed at him by mothers who shrieked 'You killed their father'
and mourners shook their fists at him and called him a murderer. I
know how I felt – and I know how Dayan felt. In the first days of the
Yom Kippur War, he was very pessimistic and wanted to prepare the
nation for the worst. He called a meeting of newspaper editors to
describe to them the situation as he saw it – which was certainly not
easy for him.

I kept him from resigning during the war but I think perhaps he
should have done so immediately after the Agranat Commission of
Enquiry published its first preliminary report on 2 April 1974. That
report cleared Dayan (and myself) of any 'direct responsibility' for
Israel's unpreparedness on *Yom Kippur*, but it dealt so harshly with
the chief-of-staff and the head of military intelligence that 'Dado'
resigned at once. I have always suspected that Dayan might have
retained his 'charismatic' image – or at least some of it – had he then,
publicly, stuck by his comrades-in-arms. He read that preliminary
(and only partial) report in my office and, for the third time, asked me

whether he should resign. 'This time,' I said, 'it must be the decision of the party.' But he was following a logic of his own, and I didn't feel that on such a weighty matter I should give him advice.

As for me, the commission said that on *Yom Kippur* morning 'she decided wisely, with common sense and speedily, in favour of the full mobilization of the reserves, as recommended by the chief-of-staff, despite weighty political considerations, thereby performing a most important service for the defence of the state'.

To many outsiders, the situation in Israel appeared brighter in the winter of 1973–4 than it did to the Israelis themselves. One of my visitors around that time was the late Richard Crossman, who had been so involved in the birth of the state and couldn't understand the current gloom and despondency. 'You people have gone crazy,' he said to me. 'What's happening to all of you?' 'Tell me,' I asked him, 'what would have been the reaction in England if something similar had happened to the British?' He was so astonished at my question that he almost dropped his coffee cup. 'Do you think things like that haven't happened to us?' he said. 'That Churchill never made a mistake during the war? That we had no Dunkirk and a great many other setbacks as well? We just didn't take things in such an intense way.' But we are different, I suppose, and the word 'trauma' that was on everyone's lips all that winter most accurately describes that national sense of loss and injury that Crossman thought was so excessive.

15

The end of
the road

THE WEEKS PASSED. The reserves were still mobilized in the south and in the now-icy north. Even the shooting hadn't come to an end, and the mood in Israel remained black, restive and very anxious. Kissinger continued his efforts to secure a separation of forces between Syria and Israel, to produce a list of the Israeli prisoners of war in Syria and to bring about the Geneva talks between the Egyptians, the Jordanians and ourselves – the Syrians having announced in December that they would not participate. Although, on the surface, we seemed to be closer to peace than we had ever been before, the truth is that neither I nor most other Israelis really believed, in our heart of hearts, that we would leave Geneva with peace treaties in our hands, and we didn't go there with many illusions or in a state of euphoria. Still, the Egyptians and Jordanians had agreed to sit in the same room with us, and that, in itself, was something that they had never consented to do before.

The Geneva talks opened on 21 December and, as I had feared, led almost nowhere. There was no real dialogue between the Egyptians and us. On the contrary, from the very first moment it was all too clear that nothing much had changed. The Egyptian delegation literally refused to permit its table to be placed next to ours, and the atmosphere was far from friendly. A military agreement was obviously a necessity for the Egyptians, but peace, we realized once again, was not what they were driving at. Still, even though no political solution came of that meeting, within a few days, at Kilometre 101, the disengagement treaty was signed, and we went on hoping that somehow or other a political solution could be found. Surely the Messiah had not come all the way to Kilometre 101 and then been too lazy to go on.

On 31 December we held our elections. The ballots showed that the country was not keen on changing horses in midstream, and although we lost some votes – as did the National Religious Party – the *Ma'arach* still came out as the leading bloc. But the opposition to the *Ma'arach* had become more forceful because the entire right wing had now combined into a bloc of its own. A coalition would have to be formed again, and it would clearly be a back-breaking job to form it, since the religious bloc, which was a traditional coalition partner of ours, was itself deeply divided on the question of who should lead it and what its policy should be at this tremendously difficult time.

I was beginning to feel the physical and psychological effects of the past few months. I was dead tired and not at all sure that, in this kind of situation, I could ever succeed in forming a government – or even whether I should go on trying to do so. Not only were there problems from without, but there were also difficulties within the party. At the beginning of March, I felt I couldn't go on, and I told the party that I had had enough. But I was bombarded by delegations imploring me to change my mind. It was still quite likely that war would break out again, since there was still no disengagement of forces with Syria and the Syrians were continually violating the ceasefire. And again I was told that the *Ma'arach* would disintegrate unless I stayed on.

Sometimes it seemed to me that everything that had happened since the afternoon of 6 October had happened on one endless day – and I wanted that day to end. I was deeply distressed by the breaking down of solidarity within the inner circle of the party. People who had been ministers in my government, colleagues with whom I had worked closely throughout my years in office and who had been full partners in the formation of government policy now appeared unwilling to stand up to the barrage of unjust criticism, even slander, that was being hurled against Dayan, Galili and myself on the grounds that the three of us – without consulting others – had presumed to make crucial decisions that had allegedly led to the war. I also resented the irresponsible talk of my so-called 'kitchen cabinet' that had supposedly replaced the government to some extent by acting as a decision-making body. This accusation was utterly without foundation. It was only natural on my part to seek the advice of people whose judgement I valued. At no time and in no way, however, did these informal consultations ever take the place of government decisions.

Nonetheless, throughout March I went on with the struggle to form a government, though, increasingly, it began to look like an impossible task, particularly in the face of growing demands for a 'wall-to-wall' coalition, something to which both I and most of the party were more opposed than ever. This was certainly not the time for political experimentation, and I had no more faith than I ever had in the ability of the opposition to apply good judgement, common sense or flexibility to Israel's attempts to arrive, at last, at some sort of understanding with our neighbours. I didn't want the cabinet to be burdened by an element that would refuse to negotiate – if and when the time came – because of its totally negative attitude towards any territorial compromise, especially as far as the West Bank was concerned. I knew that – for historical reasons – there was a difference in the attitude of the population regarding territorial compromise on Sinai, for instance, and on the West Bank – though I myself felt that most Israelis would be prepared for a reasonable compromise on the West Bank too. However, I also thought it necessary to include in the government's policy statement a clause to the effect that although the cabinet was authorized to negotiate and decide on territorial compromise with Jordan, before any actual treaty were signed the issue would be taken to the people in the form of new elections.

Then two things happened: first, Dayan resigned, and although I persuaded him to return to the cabinet, the continuing uproar about him within the party brought the danger of a split in its ranks perilously near. There seemed to be no way of finding a formula that would satisfy the growing insistence inside the party that Dayan relinquish the Ministry of Defence and at the same time keep the *Rafi* faction he headed from walking out of the *Ma'arach*. There were also other problems: the religious bloc, which had been pressuring us for weeks and weeks to form a National Unity Government, suddenly decided, as the result of internal difficulties of its own, that it was not going to become a partner in a narrower coalition and that it would not join my cabinet. This meant forming a minority government, but I didn't think that would be too serious a problem because we would have the support of various small parties in the Knesset. The really crucial issue, as I saw it, remained the possible disintegration of the *Ma'arach*. I managed to form a cabinet with Dayan as minister of defence, but the storm about him raged on and on. It now focused on the Interim Agranat

Report, which, as I said earlier, had exonerated him from any direct responsibility for the errors of judgement that had been made by the military authorities on the eve of the Yom Kippur War.

The report, however, had not gone into the question of parliamentary or ministerial responsibility, and it was precisely over *that* issue that public opinion – within the party and outside it – now expressed itself most vehemently. Many people in the country felt that the chief-of-staff had been dealt with unfairly and that Dayan, as minister of defence, was at least as much to blame for what had happened as 'Dado'. (Without commenting in any way on the Agranat Report, I do want, however, to say in this connection that Dado's conduct of the war itself was brilliant and beyond reproach.) There was tremendous discontent with the report's treatment of Dayan, and feelings were running very high indeed.

The more I talked with my colleagues about the on-going conflict in the party and the more I analysed it for myself, the more I began to feel that I couldn't go on any longer. I had reached a point where I felt that without the support of the entire party (the majority was with me all the time) I couldn't function as its head any more. And the moment came when I said to myself: 'This is it. I am going to resign and other people will have to see what they can do about forming a coalition. There is a limit to what I can take, and I have now reached that limit.'

During all those weeks of interminable talk, argument and bitterness, I had been getting the most moving letters of encouragement and support from people all over Israel whom I had never met but who seemed to understand what I was going through. Some of these were wounded soldiers, still in hospital; others were parents of boys who had fallen. 'Be well. Be strong. Everything will be alright,' they wrote to me. I truly didn't want to fail them, but on 10 April I told the party leadership that I had had enough.

'Five years are sufficient,' I said. 'It is beyond my strength to continue carrying this burden. I don't belong to any circle or faction within the party. I have only a circle of one to consult – myself. And this time my decision is final, irrevocable. I beg of you not to try to persuade me to change my mind for any reason at all. It will not help.' Of course, attempts were made all the same to talk me out of my decision, but they were to no avail. I was about to conclude fifty years of public service, and I knew with absolute certainty that I was doing the right thing. I had wanted to do it much earlier, but now *nothing* was going to stop me, and nothing did. My political career was over.

Still, I had to stay on as head of a caretaker government until a new cabinet could be formed. Before I left office on 4 June, I was able, thank God, to tell the Knesset that a disengagement agreement with Syria had been concluded through the good offices of Dr Kissinger. On 5 June, that agreement was signed in Geneva and our POWs returned. It meant more to me than I can ever say to have been able to welcome them back – though fewer returned from their imprisonment than we had hoped.

And then I myself went home, this time for good. The new prime minister of Israel is a *sabra* – Yitzhak Rabin – born in Jerusalem the year that Morris and I had come to Merhavia. There are many differences between his generation and mine – differences of style, of approach and of experience. And that is how it should be, because Israel is a country of growth in which everything moves forward. But these differences are not as significant as the similarities.

Like my generation, this generation of *sabras* will strive, struggle, make mistakes and achieve. Like us, they are totally committed to the development and security of the State of Israel and to the dream of a just society here. Like us, they know that for the Jewish people to remain a people, it is essential that there be a Jewish state where Jews can live as Jews, not on sufferance and not as a minority. I am certain that they will bring at least as much credit to the Jewish people everywhere as we tried to bring. And at this point I would like to add something about being Jewish. It is not only a matter, I believe, of religious obser-vance and practice. To me, being Jewish means and has always meant being proud to be part of a people that has maintained its distinct identity for over 2,000 years, with all the pain and torment that have been inflicted upon it. Those who have been unable to endure and who have tried to opt out of their Jewishness have done so, I believe, at the expense of their own basic identity. They have pitifully impoverished themselves.

I don't know what forms the practice of Judaism will assume in the future or how Jews, in Israel and elsewhere, will express their Jewish-ness a thousand years hence. But I do know that Israel is not just some small beleaguered country in which three million people are trying hard to survive; Israel is a Jewish state that has come into existence as the result of the longing, the faith and the determination of an ancient people. We in Israel are only part of the Jewish nation, and not even its largest part, but because Israel exists Jewish history has been changed forever, and it is my deepest conviction that there are few Israelis today who do not understand and fully accept the responsibility that history has placed on their shoulders as Jews.

As for me, my life has been greatly blessed. Not only have I lived to see the State of Israel born, but I have also seen it take in and success-fully absorb masses of Jews from all parts of the world. When I came to this country in 1921, its Jewish population amounted to 80,000 and the entry of each Jew depended on permission granted by the manda-tory government. We are now a population of over three million, of whom over one million are Jews who have arrived since the establishment of the state under Israel's Law of Return, a law that guarantees the right of every Jew to settle here. I am also grateful that I live in a country whose people have learned how to go on living in a sea of hatred without hating those who want to destroy them and without abandoning their own vision of peace. To have learned this is a great art, the prescription for which is not written down anywhere. It is part of our way of life in Israel.

Finally, I wish to say that from the time I came to Palestine as a young woman, we have been forced to choose between what is more dangerous and what is less dangerous for us. At times we have all been tempted to give in to various pressures and to accept proposals that might guarantee us a little quiet for a few months, or maybe even for a few years, but that could only lead us, eventually, into even greater peril. We have always been faced by the question: 'Which is the greater danger?' And we are still in that situation, or perhaps in an even graver one. The world is harsh, selfish and materialistic. It is insensitive to the sufferings of small nations. Even the most enlightened of governments, democracies that are led by decent leaders who represent fine decent people, are not much inclined today to concern themselves with problems of justice in international relations. At a time when great nations are capable of knuckling under to blackmail and decisions are being made on the basis of Big Power politics, we cannot always be expected to take their advice, and therefore we must have the capacity and the courage to go on seeing things as they really are and to act upon our own most fundamental instincts for self-preserva-tion. So to those who ask: 'What of the future?' I still have only one answer: I believe that we will have peace with our neighbours, but I am sure that no one will make peace with a weak Israel. If Israel is not strong, there will be no peace.

My vision of our future? A Jewish state in which masses of Jews from all over the world will continue to settle and to build; an Israel bound in a collaborative effort with its neighbours on behalf of all the people of this region; an Israel that remains a flourishing democracy and a society resting firmly on social justice and equality.

And now I have only this desire left: never to lose the feeling that it is I who am indebted for what has been given to me from the time that I first learned about Zionism in a small room in Russia all the way through to my half century here, where I have seen my five grand-children grow up as free Jews in a country that is their own. Let no one anywhere have any doubts about this: our children and our children's children will never settle for anything less.

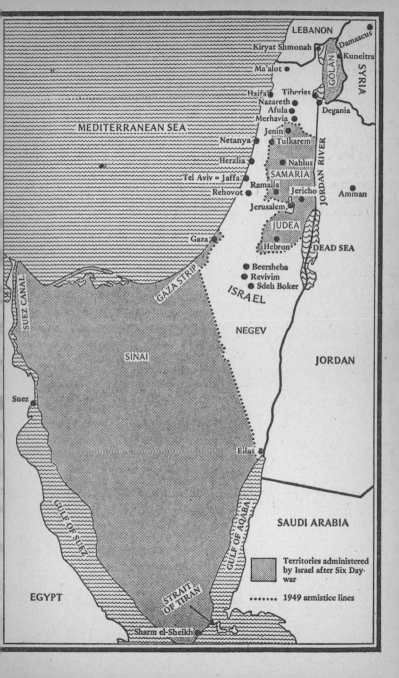

INDEX